CompTIA® Security+™
Study Guide
Sixth Edition

Emmett Dulaney

Chuck Easttom

SYBEX®
A Wiley Brand

Senior Acquisitions Editor: Jeff Kellum
Development Editor: Gary Schwartz
Technical Editors: George Murphy and Josh More
Production Editor: Rebecca Anderson
Copy Editor: Elizabeth Welch
Editorial Manager: Pete Gaughan
Production Manager: Tim Tate
Vice President and Executive Group Publisher: Richard Swadley
Associate Publisher: Chris Webb
Media Project Manager 1: Laura Moss-Hollister
Media Associate Producer: Josh Frank
Media Quality Assurance: Doug Kuhn
Book Designers: Judy Fung and Bill Gibson
Proofreader: Kim Wimpsett
Indexer: Johnna VanHoose Dinse
Project Coordinator, Cover: Todd Klemme
Cover Design: Wiley
Cover Image: ©Getty Images Inc./Jeremy Woodhouse

Dear Reader,

Thank you for choosing *CompTIA Security+ Study Guide, Sixth Edition*. This book is part of a family of premium-quality Sybex books, all of which are written by outstanding authors who combine practical experience with a gift for teaching.

Sybex was founded in 1976. More than 30 years later, we're still committed to producing consistently exceptional books. With each of our titles, we're working hard to set a new standard for the industry. From the paper we print on to the authors we work with, our goal is to bring you the best books available.

I hope you see all that reflected in these pages. I'd be very interested to hear your comments and get your feedback on how we're doing. Feel free to let me know what you think about this or any other Sybex book by sending me an email at contactus@wiley.com. If you think you've found a technical error in this book, please visit http://sybex.custhelp.com. Customer feedback is critical to our efforts at Sybex.

Best regards,

Chris Webb
Associate Publisher
Sybex

For Karen, Kristin, Evan, and Spencer
—Emmett

About the Authors

Emmett Dulaney is a professor at Anderson University and the former director of training for Mercury Technical Solutions. He is a columnist for both Certification Magazine and Campus Technology as well as the author of more than 30 books on certification, operating systems, and cross-platform integration. Emmett can be reached at eadulaney@comcast.net.

Chuck Easttom is a teacher, consultant, and expert witness in the field of computer security. He has expertise in software engineering, operating systems, databases, web development, and computer networking. His website is http://chuckeasttom.com/index.htm.

Acknowledgments

This book would not exist were it not for Mike Pastore, the author of the first edition. He took a set of convoluted objectives for a broad exam and wrote the foundation of the study guide that you now hold in your hands. All subsequent editions are indebted to his hard work and brilliance so early on.

Thanks are also due to Jeff Kellum, one of the best acquisitions editors in the business; Gary Schwartz; and all of those at Wiley who worked on this title.

Contents at a Glance

Foreword   *xxv*

Introduction   *xxvii*

Chapter 1   Measuring and Weighing Risk   1

Chapter 2   Monitoring and Diagnosing Networks   45

Chapter 3   Understanding Devices and Infrastructure   71

Chapter 4   Access Control, Authentication,
                   and Authorization   129

Chapter 5   Protecting Wireless Networks   167

Chapter 6   Securing the Cloud   195

Chapter 7   Host, Data, and Application Security   213

Chapter 8   Cryptography   243

Chapter 9   Malware, Vulnerabilities, and Threats   297

Chapter 10   Social Engineering and Other Foes   353

Chapter 11   Security Administration   395

Chapter 12   Disaster Recovery and Incident Response   429

Appendix   A   Answers to Review Questions   467

Appendix   B   About the Additional Study Tools   483

Index   *487*

Contents

Foreword   *xxi*

Introduction   *xxiii*

Chapter   1   Measuring and Weighing Risk   1

Risk Assessment   3
   Computing Risk Assessment   4
   Acting on Your Risk Assessment   9
   Risks Associated with Cloud Computing   17
   Risks Associated with Virtualization   19
Developing Policies, Standards, and Guidelines   19
   Implementing Policies   20
   Understanding Control Types and
      False Positives/Negatives   26
   Risk Management Best Practices   28
   Disaster Recovery   36
   Tabletop Exercise   39
Summary   39
Exam Essentials   39
Review Questions   41

Chapter   2   Monitoring and Diagnosing Networks   45

Monitoring Networks   46
   Network Monitors   46
Understanding Hardening   52
   Working with Services   52
   Patches   56
   User Account Control   57
   Filesystems   58
Securing the Network   60
Security Posture   61
   Continuous Security Monitoring   61
   Setting a Remediation Policy   62
Reporting Security Issues   63
   Alarms   63
   Alerts   63
   Trends   63
Differentiating between Detection Controls and
   Prevention Controls   64
Summary   65
Exam Essentials   66
Review Questions   67

Chapter	**3**	**Understanding Devices and Infrastructure**	**71**
		Mastering TCP/IP	73
		OSI Relevance	74
		Working with the TCP/IP Suite	74
		IPv4 and IPv6	78
		Understanding Encapsulation	79
		Working with Protocols and Services	80
		Designing a Secure Network	87
		Demilitarized Zones	87
		Subnetting	89
		Virtual Local Area Networks	89
		Remote Access	92
		Network Address Translation	93
		Telephony	94
		Network Access Control	95
		Understanding the Various Network Infrastructure Devices	95
		Firewalls	96
		Routers	100
		Switches	102
		Load Balancers	103
		Proxies	103
		Web Security Gateway	103
		VPNs and VPN Concentrators	103
		Intrusion Detection Systems	105
		Understanding Intrusion Detection Systems	106
		IDS vs. IPS	110
		Working with a Network-Based IDS	111
		Working with a Host-Based IDS	116
		Working with NIPSs	117
		Protocol Analyzers	118
		Spam Filters	118
		UTM Security Appliances	119
		Summary	122
		Exam Essentials	123
		Review Questions	124
Chapter	**4**	**Access Control, Authentication,**	
		and Authorization	**129**
		Understanding Access Control Basics	131
		Identification vs. Authentication	131
		Authentication (Single Factor) and Authorization	132
		Multifactor Authentication	133

Layered Security and Defense in Depth   133
Network Access Control   134
Tokens   135
Federations   135
Potential Authentication and Access Problems   136
Authentication Issues to Consider   137
Authentication Protocols   139
Account Policy Enforcement   139
Users with Multiple Accounts/Roles   141
Generic Account Prohibition   142
Group-based and User-assigned Privileges   142
Understanding Remote Access Connectivity   142
Using the Point-to-Point Protocol   143
Working with Tunneling Protocols   144
Working with RADIUS   145
TACACS/TACACS+/XTACACS   146
VLAN Management   146
SAML   147
Understanding Authentication Services   147
LDAP   147
Kerberos   148
Single Sign-On Initiatives   149
Understanding Access Control   150
Mandatory Access Control   151
Discretionary Access Control   151
Role-Based Access Control   152
Rule-Based Access Control   152
Implementing Access Controlling Best Practices   152
Least Privileges   153
Separation of Duties   153
Time of Day Restrictions   153
User Access Review   154
Smart Cards   154
Access Control Lists   156
Port Security   157
Working with 802.1X   158
Flood Guards and Loop Protection   158
Preventing Network Bridging   158
Log Analysis   159
Trusted OS   159
Secure Router Configuration   160
Summary   161
Exam Essentials   161
Review Questions   163

Chapter	5	**Protecting Wireless Networks**	**167**
		Working with Wireless Systems	169
		IEEE 802.11x Wireless Protocols	169
		WEP/WAP/WPA/WPA2	171
		Wireless Transport Layer Security	173
		Understanding Wireless Devices	174
		Wireless Access Points	175
		Extensible Authentication Protocol	181
		Lightweight Extensible Authentication Protocol	182
		Protected Extensible Authentication Protocol	182
		Wireless Vulnerabilities to Know	183
		Wireless Attack Analogy	187
		Summary	188
		Exam Essentials	189
		Review Questions	190

Chapter	6	**Securing the Cloud**	**195**
		Working with Cloud Computing	196
		Software as a Service (SaaS)	197
		Platform as a Service (PaaS)	198
		Infrastructure as a Service (IaaS)	199
		Private Cloud	200
		Public Cloud	200
		Community Cloud	200
		Hybrid Cloud	201
		Working with Virtualization	201
		Snapshots	203
		Patch Compatibility	203
		Host Availability/Elasticity	204
		Security Control Testing	204
		Sandboxing	204
		Security and the Cloud	205
		Cloud Storage	206
		Summary	207
		Exam Essentials	207
		Review Questions	208

Chapter	7	**Host, Data, and Application Security**	**213**
		Application Hardening	215
		Databases and Technologies	215
		Fuzzing	218
		Secure Coding	218
		Application Configuration Baselining	219

Operating System Patch Management	220
Application Patch Management	220
Host Security	220
Permissions	220
Access Control Lists	221
Antimalware	221
Host Software Baselining	226
Hardening Web Servers	227
Hardening Email Servers	228
Hardening FTP Servers	229
Hardening DNS Servers	230
Hardening DHCP Services	231
Protecting Data Through Fault Tolerance	233
Backups	233
RAID	234
Clustering and Load Balancing	235
Application Security	235
Best Practices for Security	236
Data Loss Prevention	236
Hardware-Based Encryption Devices	237
Summary	238
Exam Essentials	238
Review Questions	239
Chapter 8 Cryptography	**243**
An Overview of Cryptography	245
Historical Cryptography	245
Modern Cryptography	249
Working with Symmetric Algorithms	249
Working with Asymmetric Algorithms	251
What Cryptography Should You Use?	254
Hashing Algorithms	255
Rainbow Tables and Salt	256
Key Stretching	256
Understanding Quantum Cryptography	257
Cryptanalysis Methods	257
Wi-Fi Encryption	258
Using Cryptographic Systems	258
Confidentiality and Strength	259
Integrity	259
Digital Signatures	261
Authentication	261
Nonrepudiation	262
Key Features	262

Understanding Cryptography Standards and Protocols 263
   The Origins of Encryption Standards 263
   Public-Key Infrastructure X.509
     /Public-Key Cryptography Standards 266
   X.509 267
   SSL and TLS 268
   Certificate Management Protocols 270
   Secure Multipurpose Internet Mail Extensions 270
   Secure Electronic Transaction 270
   Secure Shell 271
   Pretty Good Privacy 272
   HTTP Secure 274
   Secure HTTP 274
   IP Security 274
   Tunneling Protocols 277
   Federal Information Processing Standard 278
Using Public-Key Infrastructure 278
   Using a Certificate Authority 279
   Working with Registration Authorities and
     Local Registration Authorities 280
   Implementing Certificates 281
   Understanding Certificate Revocation 285
   Implementing Trust Models 285
   Hardware-Based Encryption Devices 290
   Data Encryption 290
Summary 291
Exam Essentials 291
Review Questions 293

Chapter 9   Malware, Vulnerabilities, and Threats   297

Understanding Malware 300
Surviving Viruses 310
   Symptoms of a Virus Infection 311
   How Viruses Work 311
   Types of Viruses 312
   Managing Spam to Avoid Viruses 316
   Antivirus Software 317
Understanding Various Types of Attacks 318
   Identifying Denial-of-Service and
     Distributed Denial-of-Service Attacks 319
   Spoofing Attacks 321
   Pharming Attacks 322
   Phishing, Spear Phishing, and Vishing 323
   Xmas Attack 324

Man-in-the-Middle Attacks	324
Replay Attacks	325
Smurf Attacks	326
Password Attacks	326
Privilege Escalation	328
Malicious Insider Threats	332
Transitive Access	332
Client-Side Attacks	333
Typo Squatting and URL Hijacking	333
Watering Hole Attack	334
Identifying Types of Application Attacks	334
Cross-Site Scripting and Forgery	334
SQL Injection	335
LDAP Injection	336
XML Injection	337
Directory Traversal/Command Injection	337
Buffer Overflow	338
Integer Overflow	338
Zero-Day Exploits	338
Cookies and Attachments	338
Locally Shared Objects and Flash Cookies	339
Malicious Add-Ons	339
Session Hijacking	340
Header Manipulation	340
Arbitrary Code and Remote Code Execution	341
Tools for Finding Threats	341
Interpreting Assessment Results	341
Tools to Know	342
Risk Calculations and Assessment Types	344
Summary	346
Exam Essentials	346
Review Questions	348
Chapter 10 Social Engineering and Other Foes	**353**
Understanding Social Engineering	355
Types of Social Engineering Attacks	356
What Motivates an Attack?	361
The Principles Behind Social Engineering	362
Social Engineering Attack Examples	363
Understanding Physical Security	366
Hardware Locks and Security	369
Mantraps	371
Video Surveillance	371
Fencing	372

Access List	373
Proper Lighting	374
Signs	374
Guards	374
Barricades	375
Biometrics	375
Protected Distribution	376
Alarms	376
Motion Detection	376
Environmental Controls	377
HVAC	378
Fire Suppression	378
EMI Shielding	380
Hot and Cold Aisles	382
Environmental Monitoring	383
Temperature and Humidity Controls	383
Control Types	384
A Control Type Analogy	385
Data Policies	385
Destroying a Flash Drive	386
Some Considerations	387
Optical Discs	388
Summary	389
Exam Essentials	389
Review Questions	391

Chapter 11	**Security Administration**	**395**
	Third-Party Integration	397
	Transitioning	397
	Ongoing Operations	398
	Understanding Security Awareness and Training	399
	Communicating with Users to Raise Awareness	399
	Providing Education and Training	399
	Safety Topics	401
	Training Topics	402
	Classifying Information	409
	Public Information	410
	Private Information	411
	Information Access Controls	413
	Security Concepts	413
	Complying with Privacy and Security Regulations	414
	The Health Insurance Portability and Accountability Act	415
	The Gramm-Leach-Bliley Act	415

The Computer Fraud and Abuse Act   416
The Family Educational Rights and Privacy Act   416
The Computer Security Act of 1987   416
The Cyberspace Electronic Security Act   417
The Cyber Security Enhancement Act   417
The Patriot Act   417
Familiarizing Yourself with International Efforts   418
Mobile Devices   418
BYOD Issues   419
Alternative Methods to Mitigate Security Risks   420
Summary   422
Exam Essentials   422
Review Questions   424

Chapter   12   Disaster Recovery and Incident Response   429

Issues Associated with Business Continuity   431
Types of Storage Mechanisms   432
Crafting a Disaster-Recovery Plan   433
Incident Response Policies   445
Understanding Incident Response   446
Succession Planning   454
Tabletop Exercises   454
Reinforcing Vendor Support   455
Service-Level Agreements   455
Code Escrow Agreements   457
Penetration Testing   458
What Should You Test?   458
Vulnerability Scanning   459
Summary   460
Exam Essentials   461
Review Questions   462

Appendix   A   Answers to Review Questions   467

Chapter 1: Measuring and Weighing Risk   468
Chapter 2: Monitoring and Diagnosing Networks   469
Chapter 3: Understanding Devices and Infrastructure   470
Chapter 4: Access Control, Authentication, and
    Authorization   471
Chapter 5: Protecting Wireless Networks   473
Chapter 6: Securing the Cloud   474
Chapter 7: Host, Data, and Application Security   475
Chapter 8: Cryptography   476
Chapter 9: Malware, Vulnerabilities, and Threats   477
Chapter 10: Social Engineering and Other Foes   478

Chapter 11: Security Administration   480

Chapter 12: Disaster Recovery and Incident Response   481

Appendix   B   About the Additional Study Tools   483

Additional Study Tools   484

Sybex Test Engine   484

Electronic Flashcards   484

PDF of Glossary of Terms   484

Adobe Reader   484

System Requirements   485

Using the Study Tools   485

Troubleshooting   485

Customer Care   486

Index   *487*

Table of Exercises

Exercise 1.1 Risk-Assessment Computations 6

Exercise 2.1 Viewing the Event Logs 48

Exercise 3.1 Viewing the Active TCP and UDP Ports 83

Exercise 3.2 Installing Snort in Linux. 118

Exercise 3.3 Configuring Web Filtering 120

Exercise 4.1 Validating a Trust Relationship 137

Exercise 5.1 Changing the Order of Preferred Networks. 179

Exercise 5.2 Configuring a Wireless Connection Not Broadcasting 183

Exercise 7.1 Configuring a Pop-up Blocker 222

Exercise 7.2 Configuring Windows Firewall 223

Exercise 7.3 Verifying the Presence of a TPM Chip in Windows 7 237

Exercise 8.1 Encrypting a Filesystem in Linux 249

Exercise 8.2 SSL Settings in Windows Server 2012. 269

Exercise 8.3 Looking for Errors in IPSec Performance Statistics 275

Exercise 8.4 Viewing a Certificate 282

Exercise 9.1 Viewing Running Processes on a Windows-Based Machine 302

Exercise 9.2 Viewing Running Processes on a Linux-Based Machine. 304

Exercise 9.3 Scanning with Microsoft Baseline Security Analyzer 329

Exercise 9.4 Validating a Trust Relationship 333

Exercise 10.1 Test Social Engineering 364

Exercise 10.2 Security Zones in the Physical Environment. 377

Exercise 12.1 Creating a Backup in SUSE Linux 437

Exercise 12.2 Using Automated System Recovery in Windows Server 2012 442

CompTIA.

It Pays to Get Certified

In a digital world, digital literacy is an essential survival skill. Certification proves that you have the knowledge and skill to solve business problems in virtually any business environment.

Certification makes you more competitive and employable. Research has shown that people who study technology get hired. In the competition for entry-level jobs, applicants with high school diplomas or college degrees who included IT coursework in their academic load fared consistently better in job interviews, and were hired in significantly higher numbers. If considered a compulsory part of a technology education, testing for certification can be an invaluable competitive distinction for IT professionals.

LEARN		CERTIFY		WORK
IT is Everywhere	**IT Knowledge and Skills Get Jobs**	**Job Retention**	**New Opportunities**	**High Pay-High Growth Jobs**
IT is mission critical to almost all organizations and its importance is increasing.	Certifications verify your knowledge and skills that qualifies you for:	Competence is noticed and valued in organizations.	Certifications qualify you for new opportunities in your current job or when you want to change careers.	Hiring managers demand the strongest skill set.
• 79% of U.S. businesses report IT is either important or very important to the success of their company	• Jobs in the high growth IT career field • Increased compensation • Challenging assignments and promotions • 60% report that being certified is an employer or job requirement	• Increased knowledge of new or complex technologies • Enhanced productivity • More insightful problem solving • Better project management and communication skills • 47% report being certified helped improve their problem solving skills	• 31% report certification improved their career advancement opportunities	• There is a widening IT skills gap with over 300,000 jobs open • 88% report being certified enhanced their resume

How Certification Helps Your Career

- **Security is one of the highest demand job categories,** which has grown in importance as the frequency and severity of security threats continue to be a major concern for organizations around the world.

- **Jobs for security administrators are expected to increase by 18%**—the skill set required for these types of jobs maps to the CompTIA Security+ certification.

- **Network Security Administrators** can earn as much as $106,000 per year.

- **CompTIA Security+ is the first step** in starting your career as a Network Security Administrator or Systems Security Administrator.

- **More than** 250,000 individuals worldwide are CompTIA Security+ certified.

- **CompTIA Security+ is regularly used in organizations** such as Hitachi Systems, Fuji Xerox, HP, Dell, and a variety of major U.S. government contractors.

- **CompTIA Security+ is approved by the U.S. Department of Defense (DoD)** as one of the required certification options in the DoD 8570.01-M directive, for Information Assurance Technical Level II and Management Level I job roles.

Steps to Getting Certified and Staying Certified	
• Review Exam Objectives	Review the Certification objectives to make sure that you know what is covered in the exam: http://certification.comptia.org/examobjectives.aspx
• Practice for the Exam	After you have studied for the certification, review and answer the sample questions to get an idea what types of questions might be on the exam. http://certification.comptia.org/samplequestions.aspx
• Purchase an Exam Voucher	Purchase exam vouchers on the CompTIA Marketplace: www.comptiastore.com
• Take the Test!	Go to the Pearson VUE website and schedule a time to take your exam: www.pearsonvue.com/comptia/locate/
• Stay Certified! Continuing Education	New CompTIA Security+ certifications are valid for three years from the date of certification. There are a number of ways the certification can be renewed. For more information, go to: http://certification.comptia.org/ce

How to obtain more information

- **Visit CompTIA online** - http://certification.comptia.org/home.aspx to learn more about getting CompTIA certified.
- **Contact CompTIA** - call 866-835-8020 and choose Option 2—or email questions@comptia.org.
- Connect with us on LinkedIn, Facebook, Twitter, Flicker, and YouTube

Introduction

If you're preparing to take the Security+ exam, you'll undoubtedly want to find as much information as you can about computer and physical security. The more information you have at your disposal and the more hands-on experience you gain, the better off you'll be when attempting the exam. This study guide was written with that in mind. The goal was to provide enough information to prepare you for the test, but not so much that you'll be overloaded with information that's outside the scope of the exam.

This book presents the material at an intermediate technical level. Experience with and knowledge of security concepts, operating systems, and application systems will help you get a full understanding of the challenges you face as a security professional.

We've included review questions at the end of each chapter to give you a taste of what it's like to take the exam. If you're already working in the security field, we recommend that you check out these questions first to gauge your level of expertise. You can then use the book mainly to fill in the gaps in your current knowledge. This study guide will help you round out your knowledge base before tackling the exam.

If you can answer 90 percent or more of the review questions correctly for a given chapter, you can feel safe moving on to the next chapter. If you're unable to answer that many correctly, reread the chapter and try the questions again. Your score should improve.

> Don't just study the questions and answers! The questions on the actual exam will be different from the practice questions included in this book. The exam is designed to test your knowledge of a concept or objective, so use this book to learn the objectives behind the questions.

Before You Begin the CompTIA Security+ Certification Exam

Before you begin studying for the exam, it's imperative that you understand a few things about the Security+ certification. Security+ is a certification from CompTIA (an industry association responsible for many entry-level certifications) granted to those who obtain a passing score on a single entry-level exam. In addition to adding Security+ to your resume as a standalone certification, you can use it as an elective in many vendor-certification tracks.

> The CompTIA Advance Security Practitioner (CASP) certification is designed for those with up to 10 years of security experience. It builds on Security+ and authenticates knowledge at a higher level.

When you're studying for any exam, the first step in preparation should always be to find out as much as possible about the test; the more you know up front, the better you can plan your course of study. The current exam, and the one addressed by this book, is the 2014 update. Although all variables are subject to change, as this book is being written, the exam consists of 100 questions. You have 90 minutes to take the exam, and the passing score is based on a scale from 100 to 900. Both Pearson VUE and Prometric testing centers administer the exam throughout the United States and several other countries.

The exam is predominantly multiple choice with short, terse questions usually followed by four possible answers. Don't expect lengthy scenarios and complex solutions. This is an entry-level exam of knowledge-level topics; you're expected to know a great deal about security topics from an overview perspective rather than implementation. In many books, the glossary is filler added to the back of the text; this book's glossary (located on the book's companion website, www.sybex.com/go/securityplus6e) should be considered necessary reading. You're likely to see a question on the exam about what a Trojan horse is, not how to identify it at the code level. Spend your study time learning the different security solutions and identifying potential security vulnerabilities and where they would be applicable. Don't get bogged down in step-by-step details; those are saved for certification exams beyond the scope of Security+.

You should also know that CompTIA is notorious for including vague questions on all of its exams. You might see a question for which two of the possible four answers are correct—but you can choose only one. Use your knowledge, logic, and intuition to choose the best answer and then move on. Sometimes, the questions are worded in ways that would make English majors cringe—a typo here, an incorrect verb there. Don't let this frustrate you; answer the question, and go to the next. Although we haven't intentionally added typos or other grammatical errors, the questions throughout this book make every attempt to re-create the structure and appearance of the real exam questions.

CompTIA frequently does what is called *item seeding*, which is the practice of including unscored questions on exams. It does that to gather psychometric data, which is then used when developing new versions of the exam. Before you take it, you are told that your exam may include unscored questions. So if you come across a question that does not appear to map to any of the exam objectives—or for that matter, does not appear to belong in the exam—it is likely a seeded question. You never really know whether or not a question is seeded, however, so always make your best effort to answer every question.

As you study, you need to know that the exam you'll take was created at a certain point in time. You won't see a question about the new virus that hit your systems last week, but you'll see questions about concepts that existed when this exam was created. Updating the exam is a difficult process and results in an increment in the exam number.

Why Become Security+ Certified?

There are a number of reasons for obtaining a Security+ certification. These include the following:

It provides proof of professional achievement.   Specialized certifications are the best way to stand out from the crowd. In this age of technology certifications, you'll find hundreds of thousands of administrators who have successfully completed the Microsoft and Cisco certification tracks. To set yourself apart from the crowd, you need a little bit more. The Security+ exam is part of the CompTIA certification track that includes A+, Network+, and other vendor-neutral certifications such as Linux+, Project+, and more. This exam will help you prepare for more advanced certifications because it provides a solid grounding in security concepts and will give you the recognition you deserve.

It increases your marketability.   Almost anyone can bluff their way through an interview. Once you're Security+ certified, you'll have the credentials to prove your competency. Moreover, certifications can't be taken from you when you change jobs—you can take that certification with you to any position you accept.

It provides opportunity for advancement.   Individuals who prove themselves to be competent and dedicated are the ones who will most likely be promoted. Becoming certified is a great way to prove your skill level and show your employer that you're committed to improving your skill set. Look around you at those who are certified: They are probably the people who receive good pay raises and promotions.

It fulfills training requirements.   Many companies have set training requirements for their staff so that they stay up-to-date on the latest technologies. Having a certification program in security provides administrators with another certification path to follow when they have exhausted some of the other industry-standard certifications.

It raises customer confidence.   As companies discover the advantages of CompTIA, they will undoubtedly require qualified staff to achieve these certifications. Many companies outsource their work to consulting firms with experience working with security. Firms that have certified staff have a definite advantage over firms that don't.

How to Become a Security+ Certified Professional

The first place to start to get your certification is to register for the exam at any Pearson VUE testing center. Exam pricing might vary by country or by CompTIA membership. You can contact Pearson at:

Pearson VUE   www.vue.com/comptia   U.S. and Canada: 877-551-PLUS (7587)

When you schedule the exam, you'll receive instructions regarding appointment and cancellation procedures, ID requirements, and information about the testing center location. In addition, you'll receive a registration and payment confirmation letter. Exams can be scheduled up to six weeks out or as late as the next day (or, in some cases, even on the same day).

 Exam prices and codes may vary based on the country in which the exam is administered. For detailed pricing and exam registration procedures, refer to CompTIA's website at http://certification.comptia.org.

After you've successfully passed your Security+ exam, CompTIA will award you a certification. Within four to six weeks of passing the exam, you'll receive your official CompTIA Security+ certificate and ID card. (If you don't receive these within eight weeks of taking the test, contact CompTIA directly using the information found in your registration packet.)

Who Should Read This Book?

If you want to acquire a solid foundation in computer security and your goal is to prepare for the exam by learning how to develop and improve security, this book is for you. You'll find clear explanations of the concepts you need to grasp and plenty of help to achieve the high level of professional competency you need in order to succeed in your chosen field.

If you want to become certified as a certification holder, this book is definitely what you need. However, if you just want to attempt to pass the exam without really understanding security, this study guide isn't for you. It's written for people who want to acquire hands-on skills and in-depth knowledge of computer security.

 In addition to reading this book, you might consider downloading and reading the white papers on security that are scattered throughout the Internet.

What Does This Book Cover?

This book covers everything you need to know to pass the Security+ exam.

Chapter 1: Measuring and Weighing Risk

Chapter 2: Monitoring and Diagnosing Networks

Chapter 3: Understanding Devices and Infrastructure

Chapter 4: Access Control, Authentication, and Authorization

Chapter 5: Protecting Wireless Networks

Chapter 6: Securing the Cloud

Chapter 7: Host, Data, and Application Security

Chapter 8: Cryptography

Chapter 9: Malware, Vulnerabilities, and Threats

Chapter 10: Social Engineering and Other Foes

Chapter 11: Security Administration

Chapter 12: Disaster Recovery and Incident Response

Tips for Taking the Security+ Exam

Here are some general tips for taking your exam successfully:

- Bring two forms of ID with you. One must be a photo ID, such as a driver's license. The other can be a major credit card or a passport. Both forms must include a signature.

- Arrive early at the exam center so that you can relax and review your study materials, particularly tables and lists of exam-related information. After you are ready to enter the testing room, you will need to leave everything outside; you won't be able to bring any materials into the testing area.

- Read the questions carefully. Don't be tempted to jump to an early conclusion. Make sure that you know exactly what each question is asking.

- Don't leave any unanswered questions. Unanswered questions are scored against you.

- There will be questions with multiple correct responses. When there is more than one correct answer, a message at the bottom of the screen will prompt you to either "Choose two" or "Choose all that apply." Be sure to read the messages displayed to know how many correct answers you must choose.

- When answering multiple-choice questions about which you're unsure, use a process of elimination to get rid of the obviously incorrect answers first. Doing so will improve your odds if you need to make an educated guess.

- On form-based tests (nonadaptive), because the hard questions will take the most time, save them for last. You can move forward and backward through the exam.

- For the latest pricing on the exams and updates to the registration procedures, visit CompTIA's website at http://certification.comptia.org.

What's Included in the Book

We've included several testing features in this book and on the companion website. These tools will help you retain vital exam content as well as prepare you to sit for the actual exam:

Assessment Test   At the end of this introduction is an assessment test that you can use to check your readiness for the exam. Take this test before you start reading the book; it will help you determine the areas on which you might need to brush up. The answers to the assessment test questions appear on a separate page after the last question of the test. Each answer includes an explanation and a note telling you the chapter in which the material appears.

Objective Map and Opening List of Objectives   After this book's introduction, we have included a detailed exam objective map showing you where each of the exam objectives is covered in this book. In addition, each chapter opens with a list of the exam objectives it covers. Use these to see exactly where each of the exam topics is covered.

Exam Essentials   Each chapter, just before the summary, includes a number of exam essentials. These are the key topics you should take from the chapter in terms of areas to focus on when preparing for the exam.

Review Questions   To test your knowledge as you progress through the book, there are review questions at the end of each chapter. As you finish each chapter, answer the review questions and then check your answers. The correct answers and explanations are in Appendix A. You can go back to reread the section that deals with each question you got wrong to ensure that you answer correctly the next time you're tested on the material.

Additional Study Tools

We've included a number of additional study tools that can be found on the book's companion website, www.sybex.com/go/securityplus6e. All of the following should be loaded to your computer when you're ready to start studying for the test:

Sybex Test Engine   On the book's companion website, you'll get access to the Sybex test engine. In addition to taking the assessment test and the chapter review questions via the electronic test engine, you'll find practice exams. Take these practice exams just as if you were taking the actual exam (without any reference material). When you've finished the first exam, move on to the next one to solidify your test-taking skills. If you get more than 90 percent of the answers correct, you're ready to take the certification exam.

Electronic Flashcards   You'll find flashcard questions on the website for on-the-go review. These are short questions and answers. You use them for quick and convenient reviewing. There are 100 flashcards that you can find on the website.

PDF of Glossary of Terms   The glossary of terms is on the website in PDF format.

Bonus Labs   Also online, you will find additional bonus labs. These include activities such as labs you can do on a system as well as mental exercises (crossword puzzles, word searches, etc.) to help you memorize key concepts.

 You can get the additional study tools by visiting the website at www.sybex .com/go/securityplus6e. Here, you'll get instructions on how to download the files to your hard drive and how to access the tools.

How to Use This Book and Additional Study Tools

If you want a solid foundation for preparing for the Security+ exam, this is the book for you. We've spent countless hours putting together this book with the sole intention of helping you prepare for the exam.

This book is loaded with valuable information, and you will get the most out of your study time if you understand how we put the book together. Here's a list that describes how to approach studying:

1. Take the assessment test immediately following this introduction. It's okay if you don't know any of the answers—that's what this book is for. Carefully read over the explanations for any question you get wrong, and make a note of the chapters where that material is covered.

2. Study each chapter carefully, making sure that you fully understand the information and the exam objectives listed at the beginning of each one. Again, pay extra-close attention to any chapter that includes material covered in the questions that you missed on the assessment test.

3. Read over the summary and exam essentials. These will highlight the sections from the chapter with which you need to be familiar before sitting for the exam.

4. Answer all of the review questions at the end of each chapter. Specifically note any questions that confuse you, and study those sections of the book again. Don't just skim these questions—make sure you understand each answer completely.

5. Go over the electronic flashcards. These help you prepare for the latest Security+ exam, and they're really great study tools.

6. Take the practice exams.

Performance-Based Questions

CompTIA recently introduced performance-based questions in their certification exams, including Security+. These are not the traditional multiple-choice questions with which you're probably familiar. These questions require the candidate to know how to perform a specific task or series of tasks. Although the new Security+ exam was not live by the time this book was published, we have a pretty good idea of how these questions will be laid out. In some cases, the candidate might be asked to fill in the blank with the best answer. Alternatively, they may be asked to match certain items from one list into another. Some of the more involved performance-based questions might present the candidate with a scenario and then ask them to complete a task. They will be taken to a simulated environment where they will have to perform a series of steps, and they will be graded on how well they complete the task.

The Sybex test engine does not have the ability to include performance-based questions. However, we have included numerous hands-on exercises throughout the book, and we have also included some bonus labs that can be found in the additional learning tools. These labs are designed to measure how well you understood the chapter topics. Some simply ask you to complete a task where there is only one correct response. Others are more subjective, with multiple ways to complete them. We will provide the most logical or practical solution to the labs in a companion answer sheet. Note that these may cover topic areas not covered in the actual Security+ performance-based questions. However, we feel that being able to think logically is a great way to learn.

Exam SY0-401 Exam Objectives

CompTIA goes to great lengths to ensure that its certification programs accurately reflect the IT industry's best practices. They do this by establishing committees for each of its exam programs. Each committee comprises a small group of IT professionals, training providers, and publishers who are responsible for establishing the exam's baseline competency level and who determine the appropriate target-audience level.

Once these factors are determined, CompTIA shares this information with a group of hand-selected Subject Matter Experts (SMEs). These folks are the true brainpower behind the certification program. In the case of this exam, they are IT-seasoned pros from the likes of Microsoft, Oracle, VeriSign, and RSA Security, to name just a few. The SMEs review the committee's findings, refine them, and shape them into the objectives that follow this section. CompTIA calls this process a job task analysis (JTA).

Finally, CompTIA conducts a survey to ensure that the objectives and weightings truly reflect job requirements. Only then can the SMEs go to work writing the hundreds of questions needed for the exam. Even so, they have to go back to the drawing board for further refinements in many cases before the exam is ready to go live in its final state. Rest assured that the content you're about to learn will serve you long after you take the exam.

Exam objectives are subject to change at any time without prior notice and at CompTIA's sole discretion. Visit the certification page of CompTIA's web-site at www.comptia.org for the most current listing of exam objectives.

CompTIA also publishes relative weightings for each of the exam's objectives. The following table lists the six Security+ objective domains and the extent to which they are represented on the exam. As you use this study guide, you'll find that we have administered just the right dosage of objective knowledge by tailoring coverage to mirror the percentages that CompTIA uses.

Domain	% of Exam
1.0 Network Security	20%
2.0 Compliance and Operational Security	18%
3.0 Threats and Vulnerabilities	20%
4.0 Application, Data and Host Security	15%
5.0 Access Control and Identity Management	15%
6.0 Cryptography	12%
Total	100%

Objectives

Objective	Chapter

1.0 Network Security

1.1 Implement security configuration parameters on network devices and other technologies — Chapter 3

Firewalls; Routers; Switches; Load Balancers; Proxies; Web security gateways; VPN concentrators; NIDS and NIPS (Behavior based; Signature based; Anomaly based; Heuristic); Protocol analyzers; Spam filter, UTM security appliances (URL filter; Content inspection; Malware inspection); Web application firewall vs. network firewall; Application aware devices (Firewalls; IPS; IDS; Proxies)

(continued)

Objective	Chapter
1.2 Given a scenario, use secure network administration policies	Chapter 4
Rule-based management; Firewall rules; VLAN management; Secure router configuration; Access control lists; Port Security; 802.1x; Flood guards; Loop protection; Implicit deny; Network separation; Log analysis; Unified Threat Management	
1.3 Explain network design elements and components	Chapters 3, 4, and 6
DMZ; Subnetting; VLAN; NAT; Remote Access; Telephony; NAC; Virtualization; Cloud Computing (Platform as a Service; Software as a Service; Infrastructure as a Service, Private, Public, Hybrid, Community); Layered security/Defense in depth	
1.4 Given a scenario, implement common protocols and services	Chapter 3
Protocols (IPSec; SNMP; SSH; DNS; TLS; SSL; TCP/IP; FTPS; HTTPS; SCP; ICMP; IPv4; IPv6; iSCSI; Fibre Channel; FCoE; FTP; SFTP; TFTP; TELNET; HTTP; NetBIOS); Ports (21; 22; 25; 53; 80; 110; 139; 143; 443; 3389): OSI relevance	
1.5 Given a scenario, troubleshoot security issues related to wireless networking	Chapter 5
WPA; WPA2; WEP; EAP; PEAP; LEAP; MAC filter; Disable SSID broadcast; TKIP; CCMP; Antenna Placement; Power level controls; Captive portals; Antenna types; Site surveys; VPN (over open wireless)	
2.0 Compliance and Operational Security	
2.1 Explain the importance of risk related concepts	Chapter 1
Control types (Technical; Management; Operational); False positives; False negatives; Importance of policies in reducing risk (Privacy policy; Acceptable use; Security policy; Mandatory vacations; Job rotation; Separation of duties; Least privilege); Risk calculation (Likelihood; ALE; Impact; SLE; ARO; MTTR; MTTF; MTBF); Quantitative vs qualitative; Vulnerabilities; Threat vectors; Probability/threat likelihood; Risk-avoidance, transference, acceptance, mitigation, deterrence; Risks associated with Cloud Computing and Virtualization; Recovery time objective and recovery point objective	

Objective	Chapter
2.2 Summarize the security implications of integrating systems and data with third parties	Chapter 11

On-boarding/off-boarding business partners; Social media networks and/
or applications; Interoperability agreements (SLA; BPA; MOU; ISA); Privacy
considerations; Risk awareness; Unauthorized data sharing; Data ownership;
Data backups; Follow security policy and procedures; Review agreement
requirements to verify compliance and performance standards

Objective	Chapter
2.3 Given a scenario, implement appropriate risk mitigation strategies	Chapter 1

Change management; Incident management; User rights and permissions
reviews; Perform routine audits; Enforce policies and procedures to prevent
data loss or theft; Enforce technology controls (Data Loss Prevention (DLP))

Objective	Chapter
2.4 Given a scenario, implement basic forensic procedures	Chapter 12

Order of volatility; Capture system image; Network traffic and logs; Capture
video; Record time offset; Take hashes; Screenshots; Witnesses; Track man
hours and expense; Chain of custody; Big Data analysis

Objective	Chapter
2.5 Summarize common incident response procedures	Chapter 12

Preparation; Incident identification; Escalation and notification; Mitigation
steps; Lessons learned; Reporting; Recover/reconstitution procedures; First
responder; Incident isolation (Quarantine; Device removal); Data breach;
Damage and loss control

Objective	Chapter
2.6 Explain the importance of security related awareness and training	Chapter 11

Security policy training and procedures; role-based training; Personally
identifiable information; Information classification (High; Medium; Low;
Confidential; Private; Public); Data labeling, handling and disposal; Compliance
with laws, best practices and standards; User habits (Password behaviors; Data
handling; Clean desk policies; Prevent tailgating; Personally owned devices);
New threats and security trends/alerts (New viruses; Phishing attacks; Zero
days exploits); Use of social networking and P2P; Follow up and gather training
metrics to validate compliance and security posture

Objective	Chapter
2.7 Compare and contrast physical security and environmental controls	Chapter 10

Environmental controls (HVAC; Fire suppression; EMI shielding; Hot and cold
aisles; Environmental monitoring; Temperature and humidity controls); Physical
security (Hardware locks; Mantraps; Video surveillance; Fencing; Proximity
readers; Access list; Proper lighting; Signs; Guards; Barricades; Biometrics;
Protected distribution (cabling); Alarms; Motion detection); Control types
(Deterrent; Preventive; Detective; Compensating; Technical; Administrative)

(continued)

Objective	Chapter
2.8 Summarize risk management best practices	Chapters 1, 7, and 12

Business continuity concepts (Business impact analysis; Identification of critical systems and components; Removing single points of failure; Business continuity planning and testing; Risk assessment; Continuity of operations; Disaster recovery; IT contingency planning; Succession planning; High availability; Redundancy; Tabletop exercises); Fault tolerance (Hardware; RAID; Clustering; Load balancing; Servers); Disaster recovery concepts (Backup plans/policies; Backup execution/frequency; Cold site; Hot site: Warm site)

2.9 Given a scenario, select the appropriate control to meet the goals of security	Chapter 11

Confidentiality (Encryption; Access controls; Steganography); Integrity (Hashing; Digital signatures; Certificates; Non-repudiation); Availability (Redundancy; Fault tolerance; Patching); Safety (Fencing; Lighting; Locks; CCTV; Escape plans; Drills; Escape routes; Testing Controls)

3.0 Threats and Vulnerabilities

3.1 Explain types of malware	Chapter 9

Adware; Virus; Spyware; Trojan; Rootkits; Backdoors; Logic bomb; Botnets; Ransomware; Polymorphic malware; Armored virus

3.2 Summarize various types of attacks	Chapter 9

Man-in-the-middle; DDoS; DoS; Replay; Smurf attack; Spoofing; Spam; Phishing; Spim; Vishing; Spear phishing; Xmas attack; Pharming; Privilege escalation; Malicious insider threat; DNS poisoning and ARP poisoning; Transitive access; Client-side attacks; Password attacks (Brute force; Dictionary attacks; Hybrid; Birthday attacks; Rainbow tables); Typo squatting/ URL hijacking; Watering hole attack

3.3 Summarize social engineering attacks and the associate effectiveness with each attack	Chapter 10

Shoulder surfing; Dumpster diving; Tailgating; Impersonation; Hoaxes; Whaling; Vishing; Principles (reasons for effectiveness) (Authority; Intimidation; Consensus/Social proof; Scarcity; Urgency; Familiarity/liking; Trust)

Objective	Chapter
3.4 Explain types of wireless attacks	Chapter 5

Rogue access points; Jamming/Interference; Evil twin; War driving; Bluejacking; Bluesnarfing; War chalking; IV attack; Packet sniffing; Near field communication; Replay attacks/ WEP/WPA attacks; WPS attacks

Objective	Chapter
3.5 Explain types of application attacks	Chapter 9

Cross-site scripting; SQL injection; LDAP injection; XML injection; Directory traversal/command injection; Buffer overflow; Integer overflow; Zero-day; Cookies and attachments; LSO (Locally Shared Objects); Flash Cookies; Malicious add-ons; Session hijacking; Header manipulation; Arbitrary code execution/remote code execution

Objective	Chapter
3.6 Analyze a scenario and select the appropriate type of mitigation and deterrent techniques	Chapters 2, 3, and 10

Monitoring system logs (Event logs; Audit logs; Security logs; Access logs); Hardening (Disabling unnecessary services; Protecting management interfaces and applications; Password protection; Disabling unnecessary accounts); Network security (MAC limiting and filtering; 802.1x; Disabling unused interfaces and unused application service ports; rogue machine detection); Security posture (Initial baseline configuration; Continuous security monitoring; Remediation); Reporting (Alarms; Alerts; Trends); Detection controls vs. prevention controls (IDS vs. IPS; Camera vs. guard)

Objective	Chapter
3.7 Given a scenario, use appropriate tools and techniques to discover security threats and vulnerabilities	Chapter 9

Interpret results of security assessment tools; Tools (Protocol analyzer; Vulnerability scanner; Honeypots; Honeynets; Port scanner; Passive vs. active tools; Banner grabbing); Risk calculations (Threat vs. likelihood); Assessment types (Risk; Threat; Vulnerability); Assessment technique (Baseline reporting; Code review; Determine attack surface; Review architecture; Review designs)

Objective	Chapter
3.8 Explain the proper use of penetration testing versus vulnerability scanning	Chapter 12

Penetration testing (Verify a threat exists; Bypass security controls; Actively test security controls; Exploiting vulnerabilities); Vulnerability scanning (Passively testing security controls; Identify vulnerability; Identify lack of security controls; Identify common misconfigurations; Intrusive vs. non-intrusive; Credentialed vs. non-credentialed; False positive); Black box; White box; Gray box

(continued)

Objective	Chapter
4.0 Application, Data and Host Security	
4.1 Explain the importance of application security controls and techniques	Chapters 7 and 9
Fuzzing; Secure coding concepts (Error and exception handling; Input validation); Cross-site scripting prevention; Cross-site Request Forgery (XSRF) prevention; Application configuration baseline (proper settings); Application hardening; Application patch management; NoSQL databases vs. SQL databases; Server-side vs. Client-side validation	
4.2 Summarize mobile security concepts and technologies	Chapter 11
Device security (Full device encryption; Remote wiping; Lockout; Screen-locks; GPS; Application control; Storage segmentation; Asset tracking; Inventory control; Mobile device management; Device access control; Removable storage; Disabling unused features); Application security (Key management; Credential management; Authentication; Geo-tagging; Encryption; Application white-listing; Transitive trust/authentication); BYOD concerns (Data ownership; Support ownership; Patch management; Antivirus management; Forensics; Privacy; On-boarding/off-boarding; Adherence to corporate policies; User acceptance; Architecture/infrastructure considerations; legal concerns; Acceptable use policy; On-board camera/video)	
4.3 Given a scenario, select the appropriate solution to establish host security	Chapters 6, 7, and 10
Operating system security and settings; OS hardening; Anti-malware (Anti-virus; Anti-spam; Anti-spyware; Pop-up blockers); Patch management; White listing vs. black listing applications; Trusted OS; Host-based firewalls; Host-based intrusion detection; Hardware security (Cable locks; Safe; Locking cabinets); Host software baselining; Virtualization (Snapshots; Patch compatibility; host availability/elasticity; Security control testing; Sandboxing)	
4.4 Implement the appropriate controls to ensure data security	Chapters 6, 7, 8, and 10
Cloud storage; SAN; Handling Big Data; Data encryption (Full disk; Database; Individual files; Removable media; Mobile devices); Hardware based encryption devices (TPM; HSM; USB encryption; Hard drive); Data in-transit, Data-at-rest, Data-in-use; Permissions/ACL; Data policies (Wiping; Disposing; Retention; Storage)	

Objective	**Chapter**
4.5 Compare and contrast alternative methods to mitigate security risks in static environments	Chapter 11

Environments (SCADA; Embedded (Printer, Smart TV, AVC control); Android, iOS, Mainframe; Game consoles; In-vehicle computing systems); Methods (Network segmentation; Security layers; Application firewalls; Manual updates; Firmware version control; Wrappers; Control redundancy and diversity)

5.0 Access Control and Identity Management

5.1 Compare and contrast the function and purpose of authentication services	Chapter 4

RADIUS; TACACS; TACACS+; Kerberos; LDAP; XTACACS; SAML; Secure LDAP

5.2 Given a scenario, select the appropriate authentication, authorization or access control	Chapter 4

Identification vs. authentication vs. authorization; Authorization (Least privilege; Separation of duties; ACLs; Mandatory access control; Discretionary access; Rule-based access control; Role-based access control; Time of day restrictions); Authentication (Tokens; Common access card; Multifactor authentication; TOTP; HOTP; CHAP; PAP; Single sign on; Access control; Implicit deny; Trusted OS); Authentication factors (Something you are; Something you have; Something you know; Somewhere you are; Something you do); Identification (Biometrics; Personal identification verification card; Username); Federation; Transitive trust/authentication

5.3 Install and configure security controls when performing account management based on best practices	Chapter 4

Mitigate issues associated with users with multiple account/roles and/or shared accounts; Account policy enforcement (Credential management; Group policy; Password complexity; Expiration; Recovery; Disablement; Lockout; Password history; Password reuse; Password length; Generic account prohibition); Group based privileges; User assigned privileges; User access reviews; Continuous monitoring

(continued)

Objective	Chapter

6.0 Cryptography

6.1 Given a scenario, utilize general cryptography concepts	Chapter 8

Symmetric vs. asymmetric; Session keys; In-band vs. out-of-band key exchange; Fundamental differences and encryption methods (Block vs. stream); Transport encryption; Non-repudiation; Hashing; Key escrow; Steganography; Digital signatures; Use of proven technologies; Elliptic curve and quantum cryptography; Ephemeral key; perfect forward secrecy

6.2 Given a scenario, use appropriate cryptographic methods	Chapters 4 and 8

WEP vs. WPA/WPA2 and preshared key; MD5; SHA; RIPEMD; AES; DES; 3DES; HMAC; RSA; Diffie-Hellman; RC4; One-time-pads; NTLM; NTLMv2; Blowfish; PGP/GPG; TwoFish; DHE; ECDHE; CHAP; PAP; Comparative strengths and performance of algorithms; Use of algorithms/protocols with transport encryption (SSL; TLS; IPSec; SSH; HTTPS); Cipher suites (Strong vs. weak ciphers); Key stretching (PBKDF2; Bcrypt)

6.3 Given a scenario, use appropriate PKI, certificate management and associated components	Chapter 8

Certificate authorities and digital certificates (CA; CRLs; OCSP; CSR); PKI; Recovery agent; Public key; Private key; Registration; Key escrow; Trust models

Exam objectives are subject to change at any time without prior notice and at CompTIA's discretion. Please visit CompTIA's website (www.comptia.org) for the most current listing of exam objectives.

Assessment Test

1. Which type of audit can be used to determine whether accounts have been established properly and verify that privilege creep isn't occurring?

    A. Privilege audit

    B. Usage audit

    C. Escalation audit

    D. Report audit

2. What kind of physical access device restricts access to a small number of individuals at one time?

    A. Checkpoint

    B. Perimeter security

    C. Security zones

    D. Mantrap

3. Which of the following is a set of voluntary standards governing encryption?

    A. PKI

    B. PKCS

    C. ISA

    D. SSL

4. Which protocol is used to create a secure environment in a wireless network?

    A. WAP

    B. WEP

    C. WTLS

    D. WML

5. What type of exercise involves discussing possible security risks in a low-stress environment?

    A. White box

    B. Tabletop

    C. Black hat

    D. DHE

6. You want to establish a network connection between two LANs using the Internet. Which technology would best accomplish that for you?

    A. IPSec

    B. L2TP

    C. PPP

    D. SLIP

7. Which design concept limits access to systems from outside users while protecting users and systems inside the LAN?

   A. DMZ

   B. VLAN

   C. I&A

   D. Router

8. In the key recovery process, which key must be recoverable?

   A. Rollover key

   B. Secret key

   C. Previous key

   D. Escrow key

9. Which kind of attack is designed to overload a particular protocol or service?

   A. Spoofing

   B. Back door

   C. Man in the middle

   D. Flood

10. Which component of an IDS collects data?

    A. Data source

    B. Sensor

    C. Event

    D. Analyzer

11. What is the process of making an operating system secure from attack called (choose the best answer)?

    A. Hardening

    B. Tuning

    C. Sealing

    D. Locking down

12. The integrity objective addresses which characteristic of information security?

    A. Verification that information is accurate

    B. Verification that ethics are properly maintained

    C. Establishment of clear access control of data

    D. Verification that data is kept private and secure

13. Which mechanism is used by PKI to allow immediate verification of a certificate's validity?

   A. CRL

   B. MD5

   C. SSHA

   D. OCSP

14. Which of the following is the equivalent of a VLAN from a physical security perspective?

   A. Perimeter security

   B. Partitioning

   C. Security zones

   D. Physical barrier

15. A user has just reported that he downloaded a file from a prospective client using IM. The user indicates that the file was called `account.doc`. The system has been behaving unusually since he downloaded the file. What is the most likely event that occurred?

   A. Your user inadvertently downloaded a virus using IM.

   B. Your user may have a defective hard drive.

   C. Your user is imagining what cannot be and is therefore mistaken.

   D. The system is suffering from power surges.

16. Which mechanism or process is used to enable or disable access to a network resource based on an IP address?

   A. NDS

   B. ACL

   C. Hardening

   D. Port blocking

17. Which of the following would provide additional security to an Internet web server?

   A. Changing the port address to 80.

   B. Changing the port address to 1019.

   C. Adding a firewall to block port 80.

   D. Web servers can't be secured.

18. What type of program exists primarily to propagate and spread itself to other systems?

   A. Virus

   B. Trojan horse

   C. Logic bomb

   D. Worm

19. An individual presents herself at your office claiming to be a service technician. She wants to discuss your current server configuration. This may be an example of what type of attack?

    A. Social engineering

    B. Access control

    C. Perimeter screening

    D. Behavioral engineering

20. Which of the following is a major security problem with FTP servers?

    A. Password files are stored in an unsecure area on disk.

    B. Memory traces can corrupt file access.

    C. User IDs and passwords are unencrypted.

    D. FTP sites are unregistered.

21. Which system would you install to provide active protection and notification of security problems in a network connected to the Internet?

    A. IDS

    B. Network monitoring

    C. Router

    D. VPN

22. The process of verifying the steps taken to maintain the integrity of evidence is called what?

    A. Security investigation

    B. Chain of custody

    C. Three As of investigation

    D. Security policy

23. What encryption process uses one message to hide another?

    A. Steganography

    B. Hashing

    C. MDA

    D. Cryptointelligence

24. Which policy dictates how computers are used in an organization?

    A. Security policy

    B. User policy

    C. Use policy

    D. Enforcement policy

25. Which algorithm is used to create a temporary secure session for the exchange of key information?

   A. KDC

   B. KEA

   C. SSL

   D. RSA

26. You've been hired as a security consultant for a company that's beginning to implement handheld devices, such as smartphones. You're told that the company must use an asymmetric system. Which security standard would you recommend it implement?

   A. ECC

   B. PKI

   C. SHA

   D. MD

27. Which of the following backup methods will generally provide the fastest backup times?

   A. Full backup

   B. Incremental backup

   C. Differential backup

   D. Archival backup

28. You want to grant access to network resources based on authenticating an individual's retina during a scan. Which security method uses a physical characteristic as a method of determining identity?

   A. Smart card

   B. I&A

   C. Biometrics

   D. CHAP

29. Which access control method is primarily concerned with the role that individuals have in the organization?

   A. MAC

   B. DAC

   C. RBAC

   D. STAC

30. The process of investigating a computer system for clues about an event is called what?

   A. Computer forensics

   B. Virus scanning

   C. Security policy

   D. Evidence gathering

Answers to Assessment Test

1. A. A privilege audit is used to determine that all groups, users, and other accounts have the appropriate privileges assigned according to the policies of an organization. For more information, see Chapter 1.

2. D. A mantrap limits access to a small number of individuals. It could be, for example, a small room. Mantraps typically use electronic locks and other methods to control access. For more information, see Chapter 10.

3. B. Public-Key Cryptography Standards is a set of voluntary standards for public-key cryptography. This set of standards is coordinated by RSA. For more information, see Chapter 8.

4. B. Wired Equivalent Privacy (WEP) is designed to provide security equivalent to that of a wired network. WEP has vulnerabilities and isn't considered highly secure. For additional information, see Chapter 5.

5. B. A tabletop exercise involves sitting around the table and discussing (with the help of a facilitator) possible security risks in a low-stress format. For more information, see Chapter 1.

6. B. L2TP (Layer 2 Tunneling Protocol) is a tunneling protocol that can be used between LANs. L2TP isn't secure, and you should use IPSec with it to provide data security. For more information, see Chapter 3.

7. A. A DMZ (demilitarized zone) is an area in a network that allows restrictive access to untrusted users and isolates the internal network from access by external users and systems. It does so by using routers and firewalls to limit access to sensitive network resources. For more information, see Chapter 3.

8. C. A key recovery process must be able to recover a previous key. If the previous key can't be recovered, then all of the information for which the key was used will be irrecoverably lost. For more information, see Chapter 8.

9. D. A flood attack is designed to overload a protocol or service by repeatedly initiating a request for service. This type of attack usually results in a DoS (denial of service) situation occurring because the protocol freezes or since excessive bandwidth is used in the network as a result of the requests. For more information, see Chapter 9.

10. B. A sensor collects data from the data source and passes it on to the analyzer. If the analyzer determines that unusual activity has occurred, an alert may be generated. For additional information, see Chapter 3.

11. A. Hardening is the term used to describe the process of securing a system. This is accomplished in many ways, including disabling unneeded protocols. For additional information on hardening, see Chapter 11.

12. A. To meet the goal of integrity, you must verify that the information being used is accurate and hasn't been tampered with. Integrity is coupled with accountability to ensure that data is accurate and that a final authority exists to verify this, if needed. For more information, see Chapter 8.

13. D. Online Certificate Status Protocol (OCSP) is the mechanism used to verify immediately whether a certificate is valid. The Certificate Revocation List (CRL) is published on a regular basis, but it isn't current once it's published. For additional information, see Chapter 8.

14. B. Partitioning is the process of breaking a network into smaller components that can each be individually protected. The concept is the same as building walls in an office building. For additional information, see Chapter 11.

15. A. IM and other systems allow unsuspecting users to download files that may contain viruses. Due to a weakness in the file extension naming conventions, a file that appears to have one extension may actually have another extension. For example, the file account.doc.vbs would appear in many applications as account.doc, but it's actually a Visual Basic script and could contain malicious code. For additional information, see Chapter 4.

16. B. Access control lists (ACLs) are used to allow or deny an IP address access to a network. ACL mechanisms are implemented in many routers, firewalls, and other network devices. For additional information, see Chapter 5.

17. B. The default port for a web server is port 80. By changing the port to 1019, you force users to specify this port when they are using a browser. This action provides a little additional security for your website. Adding a firewall to block port 80 would secure your website so much that no one would be able to access it. For more information, see Chapter 3.

18. D. A worm is designed to multiply and propagate. Worms may carry viruses that cause system destruction, but that isn't their primary mission. For more information, see Chapter 4.

19. A. Social engineering is using human intelligence methods to gain access or information about your organization. For additional information, see Chapter 10.

20. C. In most environments, FTP sends account and password information unencrypted. This makes these accounts vulnerable to network sniffing. For additional information, see Chapter 3.

21. A. An intrusion detection system (IDS) provides active monitoring and rule-based responses to unusual activities on a network. A firewall provides passive security by preventing access from unauthorized traffic. If the firewall were compromised, the IDS would notify you based on rules that it's designed to implement. For more information, see Chapter 7.

22. B. The chain of custody ensures that each step taken with evidence is documented and accounted for from the point of collection. Chain of custody is the Who, What, When, Where, and Why of evidence storage. For additional information, see Chapter 12.

23. A. Steganography is the process of hiding one message in another. Steganography may also be referred to as electronic watermarking. For additional information, see Chapter 8.

24. C. The use policy is also referred to as the usage policy. It should state acceptable uses of computer and organizational resources by employees. This policy should outline consequences of noncompliance. For additional information, see Chapter 11.

25. B. The Key Exchange Algorithm (KEA) is used to create a temporary session to exchange key information. This session creates a secret key. When the key has been exchanged, the regular session begins. For more information, see Chapter 8.

26. A. Elliptic Curve Cryptography (ECC) would probably be your best choice. ECC is designed to work with smaller processors. The other systems may be options, but they require more computing power than ECC. For additional information, see Chapter 8.

27. B. An incremental backup will generally be the fastest of the backup methods because it backs up only the files that have changed since the last incremental or full backup. See Chapter 12 for more information.

28. C. Biometrics is the authentication process that uses physical characteristics, such as a palm print or retinal pattern, to establish identification. For more information, see Chapter 4.

29. C. Role-based access control (RBAC) is primarily concerned with providing access to systems that a user needs based on the user's role in the organization. For more information, see Chapter 4.

30. A. Computer forensics is the process of investigating a computer system to determine the cause of an incident. Part of this process would be gathering evidence. For additional information, see Chapter 12.

Chapter

1

Measuring and Weighing Risk

✓ **2.8 Summarize risk management best practices.**

■ Business continuity concepts: business impact analysis; identification of critical systems and components; removing single points of failure; business continuity planning and testing; risk assessment; continuity of operations; disaster recovery; IT contingency planning; succession planning; high availability; redundancy; tabletop exercises

As an administrator, you know the risks involved in working with data. You know that data can be corrupted, it can be accessed by those who shouldn't see it, values can be changed, and so on. If you think that being armed with this knowledge is enough to drive you into taking the steps necessary to keep any harm from happening, however, you'll be sadly mistaken. One of the actions that administrators can be instructed to take by upper management regarding potential threats is to accept that they exist. If the cost of preventing a particular risk from becoming a reality exceeds the value of the harm that could occur, then a cost–benefit risk calculation dictates that the risk should stand.

Risk calculations weigh a potential *threat* against the *likelihood* or *probability* of it occurring. As frustrating as it may seem, you should accept the fact that some risks, often called *residual risk*, will and must remain. This chapter focuses on risk and the various ways of dealing with it, all of which you will need to understand fully to succeed on the Security+ exam.

Risk Assessment

Risk assessment is also known as *risk analysis* or *risk calculation*. For purposes of uniformity, we will use *risk assessment* as the term of choice for this discussion. *Risk assessment* deals with the threats, vulnerabilities, and impacts of a loss of information-processing capabilities or a loss of information itself. A *vulnerability* is a weakness that could be exploited by a threat. Each risk that can be identified should be outlined, described, and evaluated for the likelihood of it occurring. The key here is to think outside the box. Conventional threats and risks are often too limited when considering risk assessment.

The key components of a risk-assessment process are outlined here:

Risks to Which the Organization Is Exposed This component allows you to develop scenarios that can help you evaluate how to deal with these risks if they occur. An operating system, server, or application may have known risks in certain environments. You should create a plan for how your organization will best deal with these risks and the best way to respond.

Risks That Need Addressing   The risk-assessment component also allows an organization to provide a reality check on which risks are real and which are unlikely. This process helps an organization focus on its resources as well as on the risks that are most likely to occur. For example, industrial espionage and theft are likely, but the risk of a hurricane damaging the server room in Indiana is very low. Therefore, more resources should be allocated to prevent espionage or theft as opposed to the latter possibility.

Coordination with BIA   The risk-assessment component, in conjunction with the business impact analysis (BIA), provides an organization with an accurate picture of the situation facing it. It allows an organization to make intelligent decisions about how to respond to various scenarios.

 Real World Scenario

Conducting a Risk Assessment

You've been asked to do a quick assessment of the risks your company faces from a security perspective. What steps might you take to develop an overview of your company's problems?

1. Interview the department heads and the data owners to determine what information they feel requires additional security and to identify the existing vulnerabilities from their perspective.

2. Evaluate the network infrastructure to determine known vulnerabilities and how you might counter them.

3. Perform a physical assessment of the facility to evaluate what physical risks must be countered.

Armed with this information, you have a place to start, and you can determine which countermeasures may be appropriate for the company to mitigate risk.

Computing Risk Assessment

When you're doing a risk assessment, one of the most important things to do is to prioritize. Not everything should be weighed evenly because some events have a greater likelihood of happening. In addition, a company can accept some risks, whereas others would be catastrophic for the company.

One document you should read is the National Institute of Standards and Technology (NIST) Guide for Conducting Risk Assessments, publication number 800-30. Revision 1 of this document can be found at the following address:

http://csrc.nist.gov/publications/nistpubs/800-30-rev1 /sp800_30_r1.pdf

It is worth noting that the revision to the original document refocuses it from being primarily just about risk management to one that strongly emphasizes risk assessment.

Risk Calculations

For purposes of risk assessment, both in the real world and for the exam, you should familiarize yourself with a number of terms to determine the *impact* an event could have:

- *ALE* is the *annual loss expectancy* value. This is a monetary measure of how much loss you could expect in a year.

- *SLE* is another monetary value, and it represents how much you expect to lose at any one time: the *single loss expectancy*. SLE can be divided into two components:

  - AV (asset value)

  - EF (exposure factor)

- *ARO* is the likelihood, often drawn from historical data, of an event occurring within a year: the *annualized rate of occurrence*.

When you compute risk assessment, remember this formula:

SLE × ARO = ALE

As an example, if you can reasonably expect that every SLE, which is equal to asset value (AV) times exposure factor (EF), will be the equivalent of $1,000 and that there will be seven such occurrences a year (ARO), then the ALE is $7,000. Conversely, if there is only a 10 percent chance of an event occurring within a year time period (ARO = 0.1), then the ALE drops to $100.

In Exercise 1.1, we'll walk through some risk-assessment computations.

EXERCISE 1.1

Risk-Assessment Computations

As a security professional, you should know how to compute SLE, ALE, and ARO. Given any two of the numbers, it's possible to calculate the third. Here are three scenarios detailing a hypothetical risk-assessment situation followed by the details for figuring out the ALE. They are intended to give you experience working with scenarios similar to those that you may find on the Security+ exam. For this exercise, compute the missing values:

1. You're the administrator of a web server that generates $25,000 per hour in revenue. The probability of the web server failing during the year is estimated to be 25 percent. A failure would lead to three hours of downtime and cost $5,000 in components to correct. What is the ALE?

   The SLE is $80,000 ($25,000 × 3 hours + $5,000), and the ARO is 0.25. Therefore the ALE is $20,000 ($80,000 × 0.25).

2. You're the administrator for a research firm that works on only one project at a time and collects data through the Web to a single server. The value of each research project is approximately $100,000. At any given time, an intruder could commandeer no more than 90 percent of the data. The industry average for ARO is 0.33. What is the ALE?

   The SLE equals $90,000 ($100,000 × 0.9), and the ARO is 0.33. Therefore, the ALE is $29,700 ($90,000 × 0.33).

3. You work at the help desk for a small company. One of the most common requests to which you must respond is to help retrieve a file that has been accidentally deleted by a user. On average, this happens once a week. If the user creates the file and then deletes it on the server (about 60 percent of the incidents), then it can be restored in moments from the shadow copy and there is rarely any data lost. If the user creates the file on their workstation and then deletes it (about 40 percent of the incidents), and if it can't be recovered and it takes the user an average of two hours to re-create it at $12 an hour, what is the ALE?

   The SLE is $24 ($12 × 2), and the ARO is 20.8 (52 weeks × 0.4). Therefore, the ALE equals $499.20 ($24 × 20.8).

Key to any risk assessment is identifying both assets and threats. You first have to identify what it is that you want to protect and then what possible harm could come to those assets. You then analyze the risks in terms of either cost or severity.

Quantitative vs. Qualitative Risk Assessment

Risk assessment can be either *qualitative* (opinion-based and subjective) or *quantitative* (cost-based and objective), depending on whether you are focusing on dollar amounts. The formulas for single loss expectancy (SLE), annual loss expectancy (ALE), and annualized rate of occurrence (ARO) are all based on doing assessments that lead to dollar amounts and are thus quantitative.

To understand the difference between quantitative and qualitative, it helps to use a simple example. Imagine that you get an emergency call to help a small company that you have never heard from before. It turns out that their one and only server has crashed and that their backups are useless. One of the lost files was the only copy of the company's history. This file detailed the company from the day it began to the present day and had the various iterations of the mission statement as it changed over time. As painful a loss as this file represents to the company's culture, it has nothing to do with filling orders and keeping customers happy, and thus its loss is qualitative in nature.

Another loss was the customer database. This held customer contact information as well as the history of all past orders, charge numbers, and so on. The company cannot function without this file, and it needs to be re-created by pulling all of the hard copy invoices from storage and re-entering them into the system. This loss can be calculated by the amount of business lost and the amount of time it takes to find/re-enter all the data, and thus it is a quantitative loss.

Anytime you see the word *quantitative*, think of the goal as determining a dollar amount. Anytime you see the word *qualitative*, think of a best guess or opinion of the loss, including reputation, goodwill, and irreplaceable information, pictures, or data that get you to a subjective loss amount.

Additional Risk Terminology

Make sure that you understand the scope and terms of hardware and service-level agreement (SLA)–related terms. Doing so can help avoid frustration and prevent unanticipated disruptions from crippling your organization. The following are key measures with which you should be familiar:

Likelihood   The meaning of the word *likelihood* is usually self-explanatory; however, there are actual values that can be assigned to likelihood. The National Institute of Standards and Technology (NIST) recommends viewing likelihood as a score representing the possibility of threat initiation. In this way, it can be expressed either in qualitative or quantitative terms. Table 1.1 shows an assessment scale for the likelihood of threat event initiation adapted from Appendix G of NIST Publication 800-30.

TABLE 1.1   Likelihood assessment scale

Qualitative values	Semi- quantitative values	Description
Very High	10	Adversary is almost certain to initiate threat event.
High	8	Adversary is highly likely to initiate threat event.
Moderate	5	Adversary is somewhat likely to initiate threat event.
Low	2	Adversary is unlikely to initiate threat event.
Very Low	0	Adversary is highly unlikely to initiate threat event.

Guide for Conducting Risk Assessments, National Institute of Standards and Technology, Publication: 800-30.

Threat Vectors   The term *threat vector* is the way in which an attacker poses a threat. This can be a particular tool that they can use against you (a vulnerability scanner, for example) or the path(s) of attack that they follow. Under that broad definition, a threat vector can be anything from a fake email that lures you into clicking a link (phishing) or an unsecured hotspot (rouge access point) and everything in between.

Mean Time Between Failures   The *mean time between failures (MTBF)* is the measure of the anticipated incidence of failure for a system or component. This measurement determines the component's anticipated lifetime. If the MTBF of a cooling system is one year, you can anticipate that the system will last for a one-year period; this means that you should be prepared to replace or rebuild the system once a year. If the system lasts longer than the MTBF, it's a bonus for your organization. MTBF is helpful in evaluating a system's reliability and life expectancy.

Mean Time to Failure   Similar to MTBF, the *mean time to failure (MTTF)* is the average time to failure for a nonrepairable system. If the system can be repaired, the MTBF is the measurement to focus on, but if it cannot, then MTTF is the number to look at. Sometimes, MTTF is improperly used in place of MTBF, but as an administrator you should know the difference between them and when to use one measurement or the other.

Mean Time to Restore   The *mean time to restore (MTTR)* is the measurement of how long it takes to repair a system or component once a failure occurs. (This is often also referenced as *mean time to repair*.) In the case of a computer system, if the MTTR is 24 hours, this tells you that it will typically take 24 hours to repair it when it breaks.

Although MTTR is considered a common measure of maintainability, be careful when evaluating it because it doesn't typically include the time needed to acquire a component and have it shipped to your location. This author (Emmett) once worked with a national vendor who thought MTTR meant mean time to respond—that is, a technician would show up on site within the time the contract called for but would only then begin to look at the problem and make a list of any needed supplies. Make sure the contract or service-level agreement spells out exactly what you want.

Recovery Time Objective   The *recovery time objective (RTO)* is the maximum amount of time that a process or service is allowed to be down and the consequences still be considered acceptable. Beyond this time, the break in business continuity is considered to affect the business negatively. The RTO is agreed on during BIA creation.

Recovery Point Objective   The *recovery point objective (RPO)* is similar to RTO, but it defines the point at which the system needs to be restored. This could be where the system was two days before it crashed (whip out the old backup tapes) or five minutes before it crashed (requiring complete redundancy). As a general rule, the closer the RPO matches the item of the crash, the more expensive it is to obtain.

Most SLAs that relate to risk management stipulate the definitions of these terms and how they apply to the agreement. You should understand how these terms are used and what they mean to the vendor and to your organization to ensure there is concurrence.

Acting on Your Risk Assessment

Once you've identified and assessed the risks that exist, for the purpose of the exam you have five possible actions that you can choose to follow:

Risk Avoidance   *Risk avoidance* involves identifying a risk and making the decision not to engage any longer in the actions associated with that risk. For example, a company may decide that many risks are associated with email attachments and choose to forbid any email attachments from entering the network.

Risk Transference   *Risk transference*, contrary to what the name may imply, does not mean that you shift the risk completely to another entity. What you do instead is share some of the burden of the risk with someone else, such as an insurance company. A typical policy would pay you a cash amount if all of the steps were in place to reduce risk and your system was still harmed.

Risk Mitigation   *Risk mitigation* is accomplished any time you take steps to reduce risk. This category includes installing antivirus software, educating users about possible threats, monitoring network traffic, adding a firewall, and so on. In Microsoft's Security

Intelligence Report, Volume 13, the following suggestions for mitigating risk through user awareness training are listed:

- Keep security messages fresh and in circulation.
- Target new employees and current staff members.
- Set goals to ensure that a high percentage of the staff is trained on security best practices.
- Repeat the information to raise awareness.

CompTIA is fond of risk mitigation and confronting it through the use of routine *audits* that address *user rights* and *permission reviews, change management*—the structured approach that is followed to secure a company's assets—and *incident management*—the steps followed when events occur (making sure controls are in place to prevent unauthorized access to, and changes of, all IT assets). Policies addressing data loss or theft need to be in place, and technology controls should be enforced.

Data loss prevention (DLP) systems monitor the contents of systems (workstations, servers, and networks) to make sure that key content is not deleted or removed. They also monitor who is using the data (looking for unauthorized access) and transmitting the data. DLP systems share commonality with network intrusion prevention systems. One of the best-known DLP systems is MyDLP, an open source solution that runs on most Windows platforms and can be found at www.mydlp.org. Also, a large number of commercial programs are available for purchase, including Microsoft Forefront: www.microsoft.com/forefront.

Risk Deterrence   *Risk deterrence* involves understanding something about the enemy and letting them know the harm that can come their way if they cause harm to you. This can be as simple as posting prosecution policies on your login pages and convincing them that you have steps in place to identify intrusions and to act on them.

Risk Acceptance   *Risk acceptance* is often the choice you must make when the cost of implementing any of the other four choices exceeds the value of the harm that would occur if the risk came to fruition. To truly qualify as acceptance, it cannot be a risk where the administrator or manager is unaware of its existence; it has to be an identified risk for which those involved understand the potential cost or damage and agree to accept it.

It can often be helpful to create interesting or memorable examples to help in understanding or memorizing various lists. This works well for the five possible risk actions.

🌐 Real World Scenario

A Visual Guide to Risk Management Strategies

Assume that the area in which you live has a mailbox vandalism problem. A group of troublemakers regularly drives around smashing mailboxes with a baseball bat. The following discussion shows the risk strategies that apply to dealing with this situation and ways that they can be manifested in the workplace and on your systems.

Risk acceptance is nothing more than acknowledging that a risk exists and choosing to do nothing about it. It does not necessarily mean that you will be affected by the risk, but only that you realize that such a possibility exists. Quite often, this is the choice that you make when the cost of implementing any of the other options exceeds the value of any harm that could occur if the risk is realized. In the case of the mailbox destruction, you simply ignore the problem and hope that the mischief-makers don't come down your street and stop at your mailbox. Considering all of the mailboxes in your area, this may be a reasonable approach. However, if your house is two blocks away from the high school, the odds may be against you.

To truly qualify as acceptance, it cannot be a risk where the administrator or manager is wholly unaware of its existence. That is, they must be fully aware of the risk, understand the potential cost or damage, and make an informed decision to accept it. Every firm has a different level of *risk tolerance* (sometimes called a *risk appetite*) that they are willing to accept.

Contrary to acceptance, *risk avoidance* involves identifying a risk and making the decision not to engage any longer in the actions associated with that risk. For example, a company may decide that many risks are associated with email attachments and simply ban all such attachments from entering the network. As a part of risk avoidance, the company takes steps to remove the risk, chooses to engage in some other activity, or puts a stop to their exposure to the risk. Avoidance should be based on an informed decision that the best course of action is to deviate from what could lead to exposure to the risk. In the case of the mailbox vandalism, rather than take a chance on someone smashing it, you simply choose not to have one and get a post office box instead.

One of the biggest problems with risk avoidance is that you are steering clear of activities from which you may benefit. The most effective risk-avoidance strategy to avoid computer crime, for example, would simply be to avoid using computers at all. Not only is that solution impractical, but it would also prevent companies from adding social value (not to mention monetary value) for their stakeholders.

The easiest way to think of *risk deterrence* is to think of a you-hit-me-and-I'll-hit-you-back-harder mentality. Deterrence involves understanding something about the enemy and letting them know the harm that can befall them if they cause harm to you. This can be as simple as posting prosecution policies on your login pages and convincing them that you have steps in place to identify intruders and take action against them. In the case of the mailbox vandalism, posting a sign on or near the mailbox warning of video surveillance and the threat of prosecution can serve as a deterrent that might convince the vandals to drive past your mailbox.

One common deterrence building block used today for physical security is the security camera. By placing these all about, you're making sure that a would-be attacker doesn't quite know when they are being monitored, what type of recording is taking place, or other related factors that will ideally turn their attention somewhere else.

When you take steps to reduce the risk, you engage in *risk mitigation* (occasionally referred to as *risk reduction*). Harm can still occur, but you've taken steps to reduce the impact it will have. Enclosing the mailbox in its own little fortress does not fully prevent someone from being able to destroy it—they could still take their bats to it for hours—but it greatly reduces the damage they can do, all other things remaining equal. Common steps in risk mitigation include installing antivirus software (the virus may still come in, but you'll isolate and stop it before it can do much harm), educating users about possible threats, monitoring network traffic, encrypting data to prevent its being of much value if it falls into the wrong hands, adding a firewall, and so on.

Some tools that can be helpful in risk mitigation include the Microsoft Security Assessment Tool (MSAT), which can identify risks; the Data Encryption Toolkit for Mobile PCs, which adds BitLocker and EFS to mobile devices; and the Windows Security Compliance Toolkit for rolling out BitLocker and EFS in enterprise environments. You can find these toolkits at the Microsoft Download Center (www.microsoft.com/downloads).

When you offload some of the risk to another party, you engage in *risk transference*. This does not mean that you are no longer exposed to risk, but rather that you have divested some of it (sharing the burden, so to speak) to the other party. A common "other party" is an insurance company that insures you for a cash amount if all steps were in place to reduce risk and your systems were still harmed. Because the harm is being distributed, risk transference is sometimes referred to as *risk sharing*. For example, moving from a standalone mailbox in the middle of nowhere to a grouping of communal boxes helps share the risk. If your mailbox is in the middle of the set of three shown here, your box can still be smashed but the odds of it happening are greatly reduced. Another alternative would be to rent a box at the post office, shifting some of the burden for maintaining the security and protection of your mailbox to a third party—the United States Postal Service.

The current push is to move many services to the cloud to be hosted by a third-party provider. If you do so, you are engaging in a form of risk transference by relying on that third-party provider for uptime, performance, and security measures. Another risk transference possibility involves employing external consultants for assistance with solutions in areas where internal IT is weak and requiring the external consultants to guarantee their work.

Risk strategies need not be thought of as either/or propositions. It is often possible to combine a bit of deterrence with mitigation or avoidance. You will often try to combine strategies to reduce your exposure as much as possible. You are then left to accept those issues that cannot be addressed otherwise. In the case of the mailbox analogy, the approach of grouping individual boxes together and placing them all in stone and concrete combines elements of both mitigation and transference.

Imagine that you are a junior administrator for a large IT department and you believe that one of the older servers should be replaced with a new one. There are no signs of failure now, but you believe that it would be prudent to upgrade before anything disastrous happens. The problem, however, is that all spending requires approval from your superior, who is focused on saving the company as much money as possible and, by doing so, hopes to be considered for a promotion. Thus, she does not want anyone coming up with ways to spend money unnecessarily. You know her well enough to realize that if a problem does occur, she will not hesitate to put all of the blame on you in order to save her own career. Table 1.2 shows how you would apply each of the possible risk actions to this scenario.

TABLE 1.2   Risk actions for the scenario

Risk action	Application
Risk avoidance	You begin moving services from the older server to other servers and remove the load to avoid the risk of any services being affected by its demise.
Risk transference	You write up the possibility of the server failing along with details of what you think should be done to prevent it and submit your findings to your boss while keeping a copy for yourself. If the server does fail, you have proof that you documented this possibility and made the appropriate parties aware of the situation.

Risk action	Application
Risk mitigation	You write up the possibility of failure and submit it to your boss while also moving crucial services from that server to others.
Risk deterrence	You write up the possibility of the server failing along with details of what you think should be done to prevent it and submit that document not only to your boss but also to her boss. You use quantitative analysis to show the logic in replacing the server *before* it fails rather than *after*.
Risk acceptance	You know the server could fail but hope that it doesn't. You neither write nor submit reports because you don't want to rock the boat and make your boss unhappy with you. With luck, you'll have transferred to another division before the server ever goes down.

Risk transference, mitigation, avoidance, and deterrence are all proactive solutions that require planning and implementation ahead of time. Risk acceptance, on the other hand, merely adopts a "do nothing" approach. These constitute the five strategies that CompTIA expects you to know for the risk management portion of the Security+ exam.

Risks Associated with Cloud Computing

The term *cloud computing* has grown in popularity recently, but few agree on what it truly means. For the purpose of the Security+ exam, cloud computing means hosting services and data on the Internet instead of hosting it locally. Some examples of this include running office suite applications such as Office 365 or Google Docs from the Web instead of having similar applications installed on each workstation; storing data on server space, such as Google Drive, SkyDrive, or Amazon Web Services; and using cloud-based sites such as Salesforce.com.

From an exam standpoint, there are three different ways of implementing cloud computing:

Platform as a Service   The *Platform as a Service (PaaS)* model is also known as *cloud platform services*. In this model, vendors allow apps to be created and run on their infrastructure. Two well-known models of this implementation are Amazon Web Services and Google Code.

Software as a Service   The *Software as a Service (SaaS)* model is the one often thought of when users generically think of cloud computing. In this model, applications are remotely run over the Web. The big advantage is that no local hardware is required (other than that needed to obtain web access) and no software applications need to be installed on the machine accessing the site. The best known model of this type is Salesforce.com. Costs are usually computed on a subscription basis.

Infrastructure as a Service   The *Infrastructure as a Service (IaaS)* model utilizes virtualization, and clients pay an outsourcer for resources used. Because of this, the IaaS model closely resembles the traditional utility model used by electric, gas, and water providers. GoGrid is a well-known example of this implementation.

A number of organizations have examined risk-related issues associated with cloud computing. These issues include the following:

Regulatory Compliance   Depending on the type and size of your organization, there are any number of regulatory agencies' rules with which you must comply. If your organization is publicly traded, for example, then you must adhere to Sarbanes–Oxley's demanding and exacting rules—which can be difficult to do when the data is not located on your servers. Make sure that whoever hosts your data takes privacy and security as seriously as you do.

User Privileges   Enforcing user privileges can be fairly taxing. If the user does not have least privileges (addressed later in this chapter), then their escalated privileges could allow them to access data to which they would not otherwise have access and cause harm to it— intentional or not. Be cognizant of the fact that you won't have the same control over user accounts in the cloud as you do locally, and when someone locks their account by entering the wrong password too many times in a row, you or they could be at the mercy of the hours that the technical staff is available at the provider.

Data Integration/Segregation   Just as web hosting companies usually put more than one company's website on a server in order to be profitable, data hosting companies can put more than one company's data on a server. To keep this from being problematic, you should use encryption to protect your data. Be aware of the fact that your data is only as safe as the data with which it is integrated. For example, assume that your client database is hosted on a server that another company is also using to test an application that they are creating. If their application obtains root-level access at some point (such as to change passwords) and crashes at that point, then the user running the application could be left with root permissions and conceivably be to access data on the server for which they are not authorized, such as your client database. Data segregation is crucial; keep your data on secure servers.

Data integration is equally important—make sure that your data is not comingled beyond your expectations. It is not uncommon in an extranet to pull information from a number of databases in order to create a report. Those databases can be owned by anyone connected to the extranet, and it is important to make certain that the permissions on your databases are set properly to keep other members from accessing more information than you intended to share.

Among the groups focused on cloud security issues, one worth noting is the Cloud Security Alliance (https://cloudsecurityalliance.org). Their most recent publications, "The Notorious Nine: Cloud Computing Top Threats in 2013" and "Security Guidance for Critical Areas of Focus in Cloud Computing," are both highly recommended reading for security administrators.

Risks Associated with Virtualization

If cloud computing has grown in popularity, *virtualization* has become the technology du jour. Virtualization consists of allowing one set of hardware to host multiple virtual machines. It is in use at most large corporations, and it is also becoming more common at smaller businesses.

Some of the possible security risks associated with virtualization include the following:

Breaking Out of the Virtual Machine   If a disgruntled employee could break out of the virtualization layer and were able to access the other virtual machines, they could access data that they should never be able to access.

Network and Security Controls Can Intermingle   The tools used to administer the virtual machine may not have the same granularity as those used to manage the network. This could lead to privilege escalation and a compromise of security.

Most virtualization-specific threats focus on the hypervisor. *Hypervisor* is the virtual machine monitor; that is, the software that allows the virtual machines to exist. If the hypervisor can be successfully attacked, the attacker can gain root-level access to all virtual systems. Although this is a legitimate issue, and one that has been demonstrated as possible in most systems (including VMware, Xen, and Microsoft Virtual Machine), it is one that has been patched each time it has arisen. The solution to most virtualization threats is always to apply the most recent patches and keep the system(s) up to date. Be sure to look for and implement suggestions that the vendor of your virtualization system may have published in a hardening guide.

Developing Policies, Standards, and Guidelines

The process of implementing and maintaining a secure network must first be addressed from a policies, standards, and guidelines perspective. This sets the tone, provides authority, and gives your efforts the teeth they need to be effective. Policies and guidelines set a standard of expectation in an organization. The process of developing these policies will help everyone in an organization become involved and invested in making security efforts successful. You can think of policies as providing high-level guidance on large issues. Standards tell people what is expected, and guidelines provide specific advice on how to accomplish a given task or activity.

There is a difference between "top-down policies" (those that use the support of upper management) and "bottom-up policies" (often generated by the IT department with little intradepartmental support).

The following sections discuss the policies, standards, and guidelines you'll need to establish in order for your security efforts to be successful.

Implementing Policies

Policies provide the people in an organization with guidance about their expected behavior. Well-written policies are clear and concise, and they outline the consequences when they aren't followed. A good policy contains several key areas besides the policy itself.

Scope Statement   A good policy has a *scope statement* that outlines what the policy intends to accomplish and which documents, laws, and practices the policy addresses. The scope statement provides background to help readers understand what the policy is about and how it applies to them.

> The scope statement is always brief—usually not more than a single sentence in length.

Policy Overview Statement   A *policy overview statement* provides the goal of the policy, why it's important, and how to comply with it. Ideally, a single paragraph is all you need to provide readers with a sense of the policy.

Policy Statement   Once the policy's readers understand its importance, they should be informed about the substance of the policy. A *policy statement* should be as clear and unambiguous as possible. The policy may be presented in paragraph form, as bulleted lists, or as checklists.

The presentation will depend on the policy's target audience as well as its nature. If the policy is intended to help people determine how to lock up the building at the end of the business day, for example, it might be helpful to provide a specific checklist of the steps that need to be taken to accomplish this task.

Accountability Statement   The policy should address who (usually expressed as a position, not the actual name of an individual) is responsible for ensuring that the policy is enforced. The *accountability statement* provides additional information to the reader about who to contact if a problem is discovered. It should also indicate the consequences of not complying with the policy.

> The accountability statement should be written in such a way as to leave no room for misinterpretation on the part of users.

Exception Statement   Sometimes, even the best policy doesn't foresee every eventuality. The *exception statement* provides specific guidance about the procedure or process that must be followed in order to deviate from the policy. This may include an escalation contact in the event that the person who is dealing with the situation needs to know whom to contact next.

The policy development process is often time consuming. The advantage of this process, though, is that the decisions can be made in advance and can be sent to all involved parties so that the policy doesn't have to be restated over and over again. In fact, formally developing policies saves time and provides structure: Instead of using valuable time trying to figure out what to do, employees will know exactly what to do.

Incorporating Standards

A *standard* deals with specific issues or aspects of a business. Standards are derived from policies. A standard should provide enough detail that an audit can be performed to determine whether the standard is being met. Standards, like policies, have certain structural aspects in common.

The following five points are the key aspects of standards documents:

Scope and Purpose   The *standards document* should explain or describe the intention. If a standard is developed for a technical implementation, the scope might include software, updates, add-ins, and any other relevant information that helps the implementer carry out the task.

Roles and Responsibilities   This section of the standards document outlines who is responsible for implementing, monitoring, and maintaining the standard. In a system configuration, this section would outline what the customer is supposed to accomplish and what the installer is supposed to accomplish. This doesn't mean that one or the other can't exceed those roles; it means that, in the event of confusion, it's clear who is responsible for accomplishing which tasks.

Reference Documents   This section of the standards document explains how the standard relates to the organization's different policies, thereby connecting the standard to the underlying policies that have been put in place. In the event of confusion or uncertainty, it also allows people to go back to the source and figure out what the standard means. You'll encounter many situations throughout your career where you're given a standard that doesn't make sense. Frequently, by referring to the policies, you can figure out why the standard was written as it was. Doing so may help you carry out the standard or inform the people responsible for the standard of a change or problem.

Performance Criteria   This part of the standards document outlines how to accomplish the task. It should include relevant baseline and technology standards. Baselines provide a minimum or starting point for the standard. Technology standards provide information about the platforms and technologies. Baseline standards spell out high-level requirements for the standard or technology.

An important aspect of performance criteria is benchmarking. You need to define what will be measured and the metrics that will be used to do so.

If you're responsible for installing a server in a remote location, for example, the standards spell out what type of computer will be used, what operating system will be installed, and any other relevant specifications.

Maintenance and Administrative Requirements   These standards outline what is required to manage and administer the systems or networks. For instance, in the case of a physical security requirement, the frequency with which locks or combinations are changed would be addressed.

As you can see, the standards documents provide a mechanism for both new and existing standards to be evaluated for compliance. The process of evaluation is called an *audit*. Increasingly, organizations are being required to conduct regular audits of their standards and policies.

Following Guidelines

Guidelines are slightly different from either policies or standards. Guidelines help an organization implement or maintain standards by providing information on how to accomplish the policies and maintain the standards.

Guidelines can be less formal than policies or standards because their nature is to help users comply with policies and standards. An example might be an explanation of how to install a service pack and what steps should be taken before doing so.

Guidelines aren't hard-and-fast rules. They may, however, provide a step-by-step process to accomplish a task. Guidelines, like standards and policies, should contain background information to help a user perform the task.

The following four items represent the minimum contents of a good guidelines document:

Scope and Purpose   The *scope and purpose* section provides an overview and statement of the guideline's intent. It is not uncommon to see the heading "Purpose and Scope" or "Scope and Purpose" at the beginning of a document followed by verbiage to the effect: "This document contains the guidelines and procedures for the assignment and use of *xyz* and establishes the minimum requirements for governing the acceptable use of…"

Where scope and purpose are two separate headings, the information beneath the "Purpose" section states why it exists (for example, "This policy establishes guidelines and minimum requirements governing…"), and the "Scope" section tells to whom it applies (for instance, "This policy applies to any employee who…").

Roles and Responsibilities   This section of the guidelines identifies which individuals or departments are responsible for accomplishing specific tasks. This may include implementation, support, and administration of a system or service. In a large organization, it's likely that the individuals involved in the process will have different levels of training and expertise. From a security perspective, it could be disastrous if an unqualified technician installed a system without guidelines.

Guideline Statements   The *guideline statements* provide the step-by-step instructions on how to accomplish a specific task in a specific manner. Again, these are guidelines—they may not be hard-and-fast rules.

Operational Considerations   A guideline's *operational considerations* specify and identify what duties are required and at what intervals. This list might include daily, weekly, and monthly tasks. Guidelines for systems backup, for example, might provide specific guidance as to which files and directories must be backed up and how frequently.

Guidelines help an organization in three ways:

- If a process or set of steps isn't performed routinely, experienced support and security staff will forget how to do them; guidelines will help refresh their memory.
- When you're trying to train someone to do something new, written guidelines can reduce the new person's learning curve.
- When a crisis or high-stress situation occurs, guidelines can keep you from coming unglued.

Business Policies to Implement

Business policies also affect the security of an organization. They address organizational and departmental business issues as opposed to corporate-wide personnel issues. When developing your business policy, you must consider these primary areas of concern.

Separation of Duties Policies

Separation of duties policies are designed to reduce the risk of fraud and to prevent other losses in an organization. A good policy will require more than one person to accomplish key processes. This may mean that the person who processes an order from a customer isn't the same person who generates the invoice or deals with the billing.

Separation of duties helps prevent various problems, such as an individual embezzling money from a company. To embezzle funds successfully, an individual would need to recruit others to commit an act of *collusion*—that is, an agreement between two or more parties established for the purpose of committing deception or fraud. Collusion, when part of a crime, is also a criminal act in and of itself.

In addition, separation-of-duties policies can help prevent accidents from occurring in an organization. Let's say that you're managing a software development project. You want someone to perform a quality assurance test on a new piece of code before it's put into production. Establishing a clear separation of duties prevents development code from entering production status until quality testing is accomplished.

Many banks and financial institutions require multiple steps and approvals to transfer money. This helps reduce errors and minimizes the likelihood of fraud.

Very small assaults are often called "salami attacks." In banking, various forms of salami attacks can occur, such as shaving a few cents from many accounts, rounding to whole numbers and compiling the remainder into one account, and so on.

Privacy Policies

Privacy policies define what controls are required to implement and maintain the sanctity of data privacy in the work environment. Many of the restrictions regarding privacy are addressed in legislation, and we cover them in Chapter 6. For now, however, think of the privacy policy as a legal document that outlines how data collected is secured. Google endorses a great example: www.google.com/privacy/privacy-policy.html. It outlines exactly what information the company collects, privacy choices you have based on your account, potential information sharing of your data with other parties, security measures in place, and enforcement. The last paragraph of the policy should appear in every privacy policy and addresses the fact that the policy may change. The verbiage, as currently written, is succinct and clear: "Please note that this Privacy Policy may change from time to time. We will not reduce your rights under this Privacy Policy without your explicit consent. We will post any Privacy Policy changes on this page and, if the changes are significant, we will provide a more prominent notice (including, for certain services, email notification of Privacy Policy changes). We will also keep prior versions of this Privacy Policy in an archive for your review."

Acceptable Use Policies

Acceptable use policies (AUPs) describe how the employees in an organization can use company systems and resources, both software and hardware. This policy should also outline the consequences for misuse. In addition, the policy (also known as a *use policy*) should address the installation of personal software on company computers and the use of personal hardware such as USB devices. When portable devices are plugged directly into a machine, they bypass the network security measures (such as firewalls) and allow data to be copied in what is known as *pod slurping*. This can also be done if employees start using free cloud drives instead, and that scenario should be addressed in the AUP.

Even secure workstations that do not contain traditional media devices (CD, DVD, and so forth) usually contain USB ports. Unless those ports are disabled, a user can easily connect a flash drive and copy files to and from it. Not only should you make every effort to limit USB ports, but you should also have the use of such devices spelled out in the acceptable use policy to circumvent the "I didn't know" defense.

 Real World Scenario

The Trouble with Not Having a Policy

A few years ago, an employee in a large company was using corporate computer systems to run a small accounting firm that he had started. He was using the computers on his own time. When this situation was discovered, he was immediately fired for the misuse of corporate resources. He sued the company for wrongful discharge and won the case. The company was forced to hire him back and pay his back wages, and he was even awarded damages. The primary reason the company lost the case was that its acceptable use policy didn't state that he couldn't use company computers for personal work, only that he couldn't use them for personal work during work hours. The company was unable to prove that he did the personal work during work hours.

Every acceptable use policy today should include a section on smartphone usage (and even presence) within the workplace. Although a smartphone is a convenience for employees (they can now more easily receive and make personal calls at work), it can be a headache for the security administrator. Most smartphones can store files in the same way as any USB device, and they can be used to copy files to and from a workstation. Additionally, the camera feature on most phones makes it possible for a user to take pictures of things such as company documents, servers, and physical security implementation, among many other things that the company may not want to share. For this reason, most secure facilities have stringent restrictions on the presence of smartphones within the vicinity.

> Make sure your acceptable use policies provide your company with adequate coverage regarding all acceptable uses of corporate resources.

Security Policies

Security policies define what controls are required to implement and maintain the security of systems, users, and networks. This policy should be used as a guide in system implementations and evaluations. Security policies will be discussed throughout this book, and you should be aware of their key aspects.

Mandatory Vacations

A *mandatory vacation policy* requires all users to take time away from work to refresh. As contradictory as it may seem, an employee who doesn't take their vacation time can be detrimental to the health, not only of the employee, but to the company's health as well. If the company becomes too dependent on one person, they can end up in a real bind if something should happen to that person. Not only does mandatory vacation give the employee a chance to refresh, but it also gives the company a chance to make sure that others can fill in any gaps in skills and satisfies the need to have replication or duplication at all levels. Mandatory vacations also provide an opportunity to discover fraud.

Job Rotation

A *job rotation policy* defines intervals at which employees must rotate through positions. Similar in purpose to mandatory vacations, it helps to ensure that the company does not become too dependent on one person (who then has the ability to do enormous harm). Rotate jobs on a frequent enough basis so that you are not putting yourself—and your data—at the mercy of any one administrator. Just as you want redundancy in hardware, you want redundancy in abilities.

When one person fills in for another, such as for mandatory vacations, it provides an opportunity to see what the person is doing and potentially uncover any fraud.

Least Privilege

A *least privilege policy* should be used when assigning permissions. Give users only the permissions that they need to do their work and no more. For example, a temporary employee should never have the right to install software, a receptionist does not need the right to make backups, and so on. Every operating system includes the ability to limit users based on groups and individual permissions, and your company should adhere to the policy of always applying only those permissions users need and blocking those that they do not.

Any time you see the phrase "least privilege," always equate it with giving only the minimum permissions needed to do the work that must be done.

Succession Planning

Succession planning outlines those internal to the organization who have the ability to step into positions when they open up. By identifying key roles that cannot be left unfilled and associating internal employees who can step into those roles, you can groom those employees to make sure that they are up to speed when it comes time for them to fill those positions.

Understanding Control Types and False Positives/Negatives

Risk assessment/analysis involves calculating potential risks and making decisions based on the variables associated with those risks (likelihood, ALE, impact, and so forth). Once you've identified risks that you want to address with actions other than avoidance, you put controls in place to address those risks.

The National Institute of Standards and Technology (NIST) places controls into various types. The control types fall into three categories: Management, Operational, and Technical, as defined in Special Publication 800-12. Table 1.3 lists the controls the control types and the controls they are associated with.

TABLE 1.3   Control Types and Controls

Control Type	Controls
Management	Risk Assessment
Management	Planning
Management	System and Services Acquisition
Management	Certification, Accreditation, and Security Assessment
Operational	Personnel Security
Operational	Physical and Environmental Protection
Operational	Contingency Planning
Operational	Configuration Management
Operational	Maintenance
Operational	System and Information Integrity
Operational	Media Protection
Operational	Incident Response
Operational	Awareness and Training
Technical	Identification and Authentication
Technical	Access Control
Technical	Audit and Accountability
Technical	System and Communication Protection

Another series of security controls worth examining is NIST 800-53, which are used by government and industry and viewed as more of a global standard:

http://csrc.nist.gov/publications/nistpubs/800-53-Rev3 /sp800-53-rev3-final_updated-errata_05-01-2010.pdf

Although we discussed risk assessment in this chapter, we address most of the other controls in subsequent chapters.

After you have implemented security controls based on risk, you must perform routine audits. These audits should include reviews of user rights and permissions as well as specific events. You should pay particular attention to false positives and negatives.

False positives are events that aren't really incidents. Event flagging is often based on established rules of acceptance (deviations from which are known as *anomalies*) and things such as attack signatures. If the rules aren't set up properly, normal traffic may set off an analyzer and generate an event. You don't want to declare an emergency unless you're sure that you have one. The opposite of a false positive is a *false negative*. With a false negative, you are not alerted to a situation when you should be alerted. In this case, you miss something crucial and it slips right by.

 Real World Scenario

Error Types

There are a number of error types that exist beyond what you need to know for the exam. Type I errors are those with false positives—that is, you think that evil is present when it is not. You have to be careful with them because if you erroneously raise a red flag and it turns out that nothing is wrong, then it becomes more difficult to get anyone to listen to you the next time you think you've uncovered something wrong because you've lost credibility.

Type II errors are those with false negatives, where you fail to notice a problem even though it is there—that is, you were looking directly at the evil and didn't recognize it. These errors are generally considered less harmful than Type Is, though they allow the wrongdoer to get away with the act and maybe even keep doing it.

Type III errors are those in which you come to the right conclusion for all of the wrong reasons. You may conclude that someone broke into your systems because users are having trouble logging in. Someone did indeed break into the system, but you should have noticed it because all of the valuable data is gone.

Risk Management Best Practices

One of the leading ways to address *business continuity* is to do a BIA and implement *best practices*. Best practices are based on what is known in the industry and those methods that have consistently shown superior results over those achieved by other means.

You need only a passing knowledge of business continuity issues for the Security+ exam. If you plan on taking the Project+ exam, also from CompTIA, you will need a more thorough knowledge of these topics.

Undertaking Business Impact Analysis

Business impact analysis (BIA) is the process of evaluating all of the critical systems in an organization to define impact and recovery plans. BIA isn't concerned with external threats or vulnerabilities; the analysis focuses on the impact a loss would have on the organization.

Here are the key components of a BIA:

Identifying Critical Functions   To identify critical functions, a company must ask itself, "What functions are necessary to continue operations until full service can be restored?" This identification process will help you establish which systems must be returned to operation in order for the business to continue. In performing this identification, you may find that a small or overlooked application in a department may be critical for operations. Many organizations have overlooked seemingly insignificant process steps or systems that have prevented business continuity planning (BCP) from being effective. Every department should be evaluated to ensure that no critical processes are overlooked.

Prioritizing Critical Business Functions   When business is continued after an event, operations must be prioritized as essential or nonessential functions. If the organization makes resources available to the recovery process, these resources may be limited. Furthermore, in a widespread outage full operation may not be possible for some time. What would happen, for example, if your data communications services went down? You can usually establish temporary services, but you probably won't be able to restore full network capability. You should be clear about which applications or systems have priority based on the resources available. For example, your company may find itself choosing to restore email before it restores its website.

Calculating a Timeframe for Critical Systems Loss   How long can the organization survive without a critical function? Some functions in an organization don't require immediate action whereas others do. Which functions must be reestablished and in what timeframe? If your business is entirely dependent on its web presence and is e-commerce oriented, how long can the website stay inoperable? Your organization may need to evaluate and attempt to identify the maximum time that a particular function can be unavailable. This component dictates the contingencies that must be established to minimize losses due to exceeding the allowable period.

Estimating the Tangible and Intangible Impact on the Organization   Your organization will suffer losses in an outage. These losses will be tangible in nature, such as lost production and lost sales. Intangible losses will also be a factor. For example, will customers lose faith in your service? Knowing the true cost of these impacts in advance will greatly increase the organization's effectiveness in responding to such outages.

A thorough BIA will accomplish several organizational goals:

- The true impact and damage that an outage can cause will be visible.

- Understanding the true loss potential may help you in your fight for a budget.

- Most important, perhaps, the process will document which business processes are being used, the impact they have on the organization, and how to restore them quickly.

The BIA will gain power in the organization as the true costs of an outage become known. People buy insurance not because they intend to have an accident but just in case they have one. A BIA can help identify what insurance is needed for the organization to feel safe.

Identifying Critical Systems and Components

Sometimes your systems are dependent on things that you would not normally consider. Basic utilities such as electricity, water, and natural gas are key aspects of business continuity. In the vast majority of cases, electricity and water are restored—at least on an emergency basis—fairly rapidly. The damage created by blizzards, tornadoes, and other natural disasters is managed and repaired by utility companies and government agencies. Other disasters, such as a major earthquake or hurricane, can overwhelm these agencies, and services may be interrupted for quite a while. When these types of events occur, critical infrastructure may be unavailable for days, weeks, or even months.

 Real World Scenario

The Importance of Utilities

When the earthquake of 1989 occurred in San Francisco, California, portions of the city were without electricity, natural gas, and water for several months. Entire buildings were left unoccupied because the infrastructure was badly damaged. This damage prevented many businesses whose information systems departments were located in those buildings from returning to operation for several weeks. Most of the larger organizations were able to shift the processing loads to other companies or divisions.

When you evaluate your business's sustainability, realize that disasters do indeed happen. If possible, build infrastructure that doesn't have a *single point of failure (SPOF)* or connection. After the September 11, 2001, terrorist attack on the World Trade Center (WTC), several ISPs and other companies became nonfunctional because the WTC housed centralized communications systems and computer departments. If you're the administrator for a small company, it is not uncommon for the SPOF to be a router/gateway. The best way to remove an SPOF from your environment is to add redundancy.

Consider the impact of weather on your *contingency plans*. What if you needed to relocate your facility to another region of the country due to a tornado hitting your server room? How would you get personnel there? What personnel would be relocated? How would they be housed and fed during the time of the crisis? You should consider these possibilities in advance. Although the possibility of a crippling disaster is relatively small, you still need to evaluate the risk.

🌐 Real World Scenario

Formulating Business Continuity Plans

As a security administrator, you'll need to think through a way to maintain business continuity should a crisis occur. Imagine that your company is involved in each of the following three scenarios:

Scenario 1   Your company is in the business of monitoring criminal offenders who are under electronic house arrest nationwide. Every offender wears an ankle bracelet that wirelessly communicates with a device in his or her home. The home device communicates to your site in real time over phone lines by calling a toll-free number to report if the offender is in or out of the home, and you alert local authorities immediately if someone isn't in compliance. The number of offenders, and the number of home devices that call your center, is in the tens of thousands. How could business be maintained if the trunk line for the toll-free phone carrier were disrupted in the middle of the night? How could you verify offender compliance if the problem took hours to correct?

Scenario 2   You're the administrator for a small educational company that delivers certification exams locally. The exams are downloaded the night before and delivered throughout the day as students—who have registered over the Internet—arrive. You show up at 8 a.m. on Friday, knowing that there are more than 20 exams to be administered that were downloaded Thursday night. What you find, however, is that someone has broken into the testing room and trashed all of the workstations and monitors. Some of those coming to take the exams are driving from far away. How will you approach the situation?

Scenario 3   You're the database administrator for a large grocery chain. When you leave on Wednesday, there are no problems. When you arrive on Thursday—the day a new sale starts—you learn that the DSL lines are down. They went down before the local stores could download the new sale prices. All scanned goods will ring up at the price they were last week (either sale or regular) and not at current prices. The provider says it's working on the DSL problem but can't estimate how long the repairs will take. How do you approach the problem?

Just like in the real world, there are no right or wrong answers for these scenarios. However, they all represent situations that have happened and for which administrators planned ahead of time.

There are several ways to plan for such scenarios, including implementing redundant technology, fault-tolerant systems, and RAID. A truly redundant system won't use just one of these methods, but rather it will support some aspect of all of them. The following sections address these topics in more detail.

As an administrator, you should always be aware of problems that can occur and have an idea of how you'll approach them. It's impossible to prepare for every emergency, but you can plan for those that could conceivably happen.

High Availability

High availability (HA) refers to the measures used to keep services and systems operational during an outage. In short, the goal is to provide all services to all users, where they need them and when they need them. With high availability, the goal is to have key services available 99.999 percent of the time (also known as *five nines availability*).

Redundancy

Redundancy refers to systems that either are duplicated or *fail over* to other systems in the event of a malfunction. *Failover* refers to the process of reconstructing a system or switching over to other systems when a failure is detected. In the case of a server, the server switches to a redundant server when a fault is detected. This strategy allows service to continue uninterrupted until the primary server can be restored. In the case of a network, this means processing switches to another network path in the event of a network failure in the primary path.

Failover systems can be expensive to implement. In a large corporate network or e-commerce environment, a failover might entail switching all processing to a remote location until your primary facility is operational. The primary site and the remote site would synchronize data to ensure that information is as up to date as possible.

Many operating systems, such as Linux, Windows Server 2012, and Novell Open Enterprise Server, are capable of *clustering* to provide failover capabilities. *Clustering* involves multiple systems connected together cooperatively (which provides *load balancing*) and networked in such a way that if any of the systems fail, the other systems take up the slack and continue to operate. The overall capability of the server cluster may decrease, but the network or service will remain operational.

To appreciate the beauty of clustering, contemplate the fact that this is the technology on which Google is built. Not only does clustering allow you to have redundancy, but it also offers you the ability to scale as demand increases.

Most ISPs and network providers have extensive internal failover capability to provide high availability to clients. Business clients and employees who are unable to access information or services tend to lose confidence. The tradeoff for reliability and trustworthiness, of course, is cost: Failover systems can become prohibitively expensive. You'll need to study your needs carefully to determine whether your system requires this capability. For example, if your environment requires a high level of availability, your servers should be clustered. This will allow the other servers in the network to take up the load if one of the servers in the cluster fails.

Fault Tolerance

Fault tolerance is the ability of a system to sustain operations in the event of a component failure. Fault-tolerant systems can continue operation even though a critical component, such as a disk drive, has failed. This capability involves overengineering systems by adding redundant components and subsystems.

Fault tolerance is discussed in more detail in Chapter 7, "Host, Data, and Application Security," but it appears here as it relates to risk.

Fault tolerance can be built into a server by adding a second power supply, a second CPU, and other key components. Several manufacturers (such as HP, Unisys, and IBM) offer fault-tolerant servers. These servers typically have multiple processors that automatically fail over if a malfunction occurs.

In addition to fault-tolerant servers, you can have fault-tolerant implementations such as Tandem, Stratus, and HP. In these settings, multiple computers are used to provide 100 percent availability of a single server.

There are two key components of fault tolerance that you should never overlook: spare parts and electrical power. Spare parts should always be readily available to repair any system-critical component if it should fail. The redundancy strategy N+1 means that you have the number of components you need, plus one to plug into any system should it be needed. For example, a small company with five standalone servers that are all the same model should have a power supply in a box nearby to install in any one of the servers should there be a failure. (The redundancy strategy 1+1 has one spare part for every component in use.)

Since computer systems cannot operate in the absence of electrical power, it is imperative that fault tolerance be built into your electrical infrastructure as well. At a bare minimum, an *uninterruptible power supply (UPS)*—with surge protection—should accompany every server and workstation. That UPS should be rated for the load it is expected to carry in the event of a power failure (factoring in the computer, monitor, and any other device connected to it) and be checked periodically as part of your preventive maintenance routine to make sure that the battery is operational. You will need to replace the battery every few years to keep the UPS operational.

A UPS will allow you to continue to function in the absence of power for only a short duration. For fault tolerance in situations of longer duration, you will need a *backup generator*. Backup generators run off of gasoline, propane, natural gas, or diesel and generate the electricity needed to provide steady power. Although some backup generators can come on instantly in the event of a power outage, most take a short time to warm up before they can provide consistent power. Therefore, you will find that you still need to implement UPSs within your organization.

Redundant Array of Independent Disks

Redundant Array of Independent Disks (RAID) is a technology that uses multiple disks to provide fault tolerance. There are several designations for RAID levels.

 RAID stands for not only *Redundant Array of Independent Disks* but also *Redundant Array of Inexpensive Disks.* Although the latter term has lost its popularity, you might still encounter it in some texts.

The most commonly implemented RAID levels are as follows:

RAID Level 0   RAID 0 is *disk striping*. It uses multiple drives and maps them together as a single physical drive. This is done primarily for performance, not for fault tolerance. If any drive in a RAID 0 array fails, the entire logical drive becomes unusable.

RAID Level 1   RAID 1 is *disk mirroring*. Disk mirroring provides 100 percent redundancy because everything is stored on two disks. If one disk fails, another disk continues to operate. The failed disk can be replaced, and the RAID 1 array can be regenerated. This system offers the advantage of 100 percent data redundancy at the expense of doubling the storage requirements. Each drive keeps an exact copy of all information, which reduces the effective storage capability to 50 percent of the overall rated storage. Some implementations of disk mirroring are called *disk duplexing* (*duplexing* is a less commonly used term). The difference between mirroring and duplexing is one more controller card. With mirroring, one controller card writes sequentially to each disk. With duplexing, the same data is written to both disks simultaneously. Disk duplexing has much faster write performance than disk mirroring. Many hardware implementations of RAID 1 are actually duplexing, but they are still generally referred to as mirrors.

 The data is intact in a RAID 1 array if either one of the two drives fails. After the failed drive is replaced with a new drive, you remirror the data from the good drive to the new drive to re-create the array.

RAID Level 3   RAID 3 is *disk striping with a parity disk*. RAID 3 arrays implement fault tolerance by using striping (RAID 0) in conjunction with a separate disk that stores parity information. *Parity information* is a value based on the value of the data stored in each disk location. This system ensures that the data can be recovered in the event of a failure. The process of generating parity information uses the arithmetic value of the data binary. This process allows any single disk in the array to fail while the system continues to operate. The failed disk is removed, a new disk is installed, and the new drive is then regenerated using the parity information. RAID 3 is common in older systems, and it's supported by most Unix systems.

RAID Level 5   RAID 5 is *disk striping with parity*, and it is one of the most common forms of RAID in use today. It operates similarly to disk striping, as in RAID 0. The parity information is spread across all of the disks in the array instead of being limited to a single disk, as in RAID 3. Most implementations require a minimum of three disks and support a maximum of 32.

These four types of RAID drives, or arrays, are illustrated in Figure 1.1.

 A RAID 5 array can survive the failure of any one drive and still be able to function. It can't, however, survive the failure of multiple drives.

 You aren't required to know the current RAID capabilities for the Security+ exam. They are presented here primarily for your edification. They are commonly used in highly reliable systems.

RAID levels 0, 1, 3, and 5 are the ones most commonly implemented in servers today. RAID 5 has largely replaced RAID 3 in newer systems. When two levels are combined for a more potent solution, the numbers simply move into double digits representing the two RAID levels combined. For example, combining RAID 1 with RAID 0 is now called RAID 10 (or RAID 0+1 in older documentation). Combining RAID 1 with RAID 5 is now known as RAID 15, and so on.

RAID levels are implemented either in software on the host computer or in the disk controller hardware. A RAID hardware-device implementation will generally run faster than a software-oriented RAID implementation because the software implementation uses the system CPU and system resources. Hardware RAID devices generally have their own processors, and they appear to the operating system as a single device.

You must do a fair amount of planning before you implement RAID. Within the realm of planning, you must be able to compute the number of disks needed for the desired implementation.

 Real World Scenario

How Many Disks Does RAID Need?

As a security administrator, you must determine how many RAID disks you'll need. Compute how many disks will be needed for each of the following scenarios or the amount of storage capacity that results. *(Answers appear at the end of each scenario.)*

Scenario 1 Your company has standardized on 500 GB disks. A new server will go online next month to hold the data files for a new division. The server will be disk-duplexed and needs to be able to store 800 GB of data. How many drives should you order?

Disk duplexing is the same as disk mirroring except there is also a second controller. Fifty percent of the overall storage capacity must be used for RAID, so you must purchase four 500 GB drives. This will give you excess data capacity of 200 GB.

Scenario 2   Your primary server is currently running four 300 GB disks in a RAID 5 array. Storage space is at a premium, and a purchase order has just been approved for four 500 GB disks. If you still use a RAID 5 array, what is the maximum data storage space this server will be able to host?

The solution that will generate the most data storage capacity is to install all eight drives (the four current ones and the four new ones) into the server. The array must use the same size storage on each drive; thus all eight drives will appear as if they are 300 GB drives. Under this scenario, 2100 GB can be used for data storage and 300 GB will be used for parity.

Scenario 3   Access speed is of the utmost importance on a web server. You want to purchase some fast 300 GB hard drives and install them in a RAID 0 array. How many drives will you need to purchase to host 900 GB of data?

RAID 0 doesn't perform any fault tolerance and doesn't require any extra disk space. You can obtain 900 GB of data by using three disks.

Disaster Recovery

Disaster recovery is the ability to recover system operations after a disaster. A key aspect of disaster recovery planning is designing a comprehensive backup plan that includes backup storage, procedures, and maintenance. Many options are available to implement disaster recovery. The following sections discuss backups and disaster recovery planning.

Disaster recovery is discussed in more detail in Chapter 12, "Disaster Recovery and Incident Response," but it appears here as it relates to risk.

It's important to recognize that, during a recovery, it may not always be necessary to bring all systems and services back up immediately. Critical systems should be the priority; extraneous services (such as an informational website for the public) can often be a lesser priority and can be addressed after everything else is up and running.

Types of Backups

Backups are duplicate copies of key information, ideally stored in a location other than the one where the information is stored currently. Backups include both paper and computer records. Computer records are usually backed up using a backup program, backup systems, and backup procedures.

FIGURE 1.1   The four primary RAID technologies used in systems

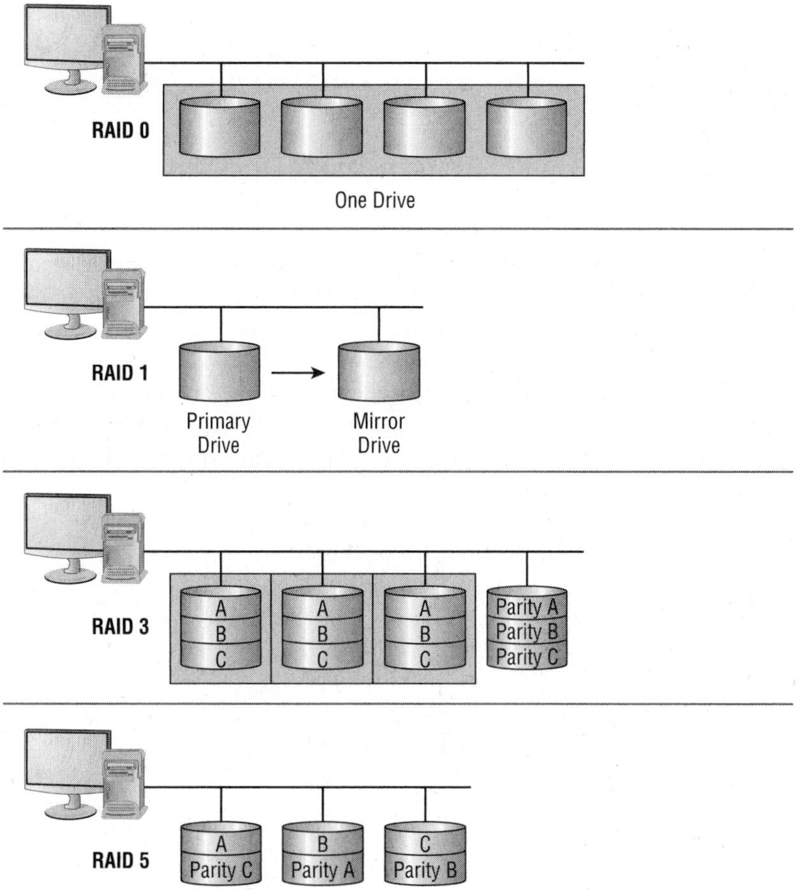

RAID 0

One Drive

RAID 1

Primary
Drive

Mirror
Drive

RAID 3

A
B
C

A
B
C

A
B
C

Parity A
Parity B
Parity C

RAID 5

A
Parity C

B
Parity A

C
Parity B

Disaster Recovery Planning

The primary starting point for a disaster recovery plan involves keeping current backup copies of key data files, databases, applications, and paper records available for use. Your organization must develop a solid set of procedures to manage this process and ensure that all key information is protected. A security professional can take several actions along with system administrators and business managers to protect this information. It's important to think of this problem as an issue that is larger than a single department.

As much as we live in an electronic age, it's impossible to get rid of all paper. For a number of reasons, some paper documents must be retained and carefully stored. The following are examples of key paper records that should be archived:

- Board minutes
- Board resolutions

- Papers of incorporation
- Critical contracts
- Financial statements
- Incorporation documents
- Loan documents
- Personnel information
- Tax records

This list, though not comprehensive, gives you a place to start when you evaluate your archival requirements. Most of these documents can easily be converted into an electronic format. However, keeping paper copies is strongly recommended because some government agencies don't accept electronic documentation as an alternative to paper documentation. Be sure to store the paper documents in a secure location where environmental conditions conducive to preserving paper are maintained. Storage facilities specifically intended for this purpose can be found in most large cities after the documents outgrow your capacity to store them on site.

Computer files and applications should also be backed up on a regular basis. Here are some examples of critical files that should be backed up:

- Applications
- Appointment files
- Audit files
- Customer lists
- Database files
- Email correspondence
- Financial data
- Operating systems
- Prospect lists
- Transaction files
- User files
- User information
- Utilities

Again, this list isn't all-inclusive, but it provides a place to start.

In most environments, the volume of information that needs to be stored is growing at a tremendous pace. Simply tracking this massive growth can create significant problems.

An unscrupulous attacker can glean as much critical information from copies as they can from original files. Make sure that your storage facilities are secure. It is also a good idea to add physical security to the backup media.

Tabletop Exercise

One of the tools that can be used to assess risk is known as a *tabletop exercise*. The name is appropriate, for it involves little more than individuals sitting around a table with a facilitator discussing situations that could arise and how best to respond to them. The advantage of this exercise is that there is very little cost to it (the time of the participants), and it allows key personnel to mentally walk through emergencies in a low-stress format. The biggest disadvantage of this exercise is its lack of realism.

Summary

Risk assessment is the process of evaluating and cataloging the threats, vulnerabilities, and weaknesses that exist in the systems being used. Risk assessment should ensure that all bases are covered.

Security models begin with an understanding of the business issues that an organization is facing. The following business matters must be evaluated:

- Policies
- Standards
- Guidelines

A good policy design includes scope statements, overview statements, accountability expectations, and exceptions. Each of these aspects of a well-crafted policy helps in setting expectations for everyone in a company. For a policy to be effective, it needs the unequivocal support of senior management and decision makers in an organization.

Exam Essentials

Know the three categories of control types.   The three types of controls that can be administered are Technical, Management, and Operational.

Know how to calculate risk.   Risk can be calculated either qualitatively (subjective) or quantitatively (objective). Quantitative calculations assign dollar amounts, and the basic formula is SLE × ARO = ALE, where SLE is the single loss expectancy, ARO is the annualized rate of occurrence, and ALE is the annual loss expectancy.

Know the five different approaches to risk.   The five risk strategies are avoidance (don't engage in that activity), transference (think insurance), mitigation (take steps to reduce the risk), deterrence (warn of harm to others if they affect you), and acceptance (be willing to live with the risk).

Know the importance of policies, standards, and guidelines.   The process of implementing and maintaining a secure network must first be addressed from a policies, standards, and guidelines perspective. Policies and guidelines set a standard of expectation in an organization. Standards tell people what is expected, and guidelines provide specific advice on how to accomplish a given task or activity.

Understand important elements of key levels of RAID.   RAID level 0 does not include any fault tolerance. RAID level 1 can be implemented as mirroring or duplexing, the difference being that the latter includes multiple controllers. RAID level 5 is known as disk striping with parity.

Understand tabletop exercises.   A tabletop exercise involves individuals sitting around a table with a facilitator discussing situations that could arise and how best to respond to them.

Review Questions

1. You're the chief security contact for MTS. One of your primary tasks is to document every-thing related to security and create a manual that can be used to manage the company in your absence. Which documents should be referenced in your manual as the ones that iden-tify the methods used to accomplish a given task?

   A. Policies

   B. Standards

   C. Guidelines

   D. BIA

2. Consider the following scenario: The asset value of your company's primary servers is $2 million, and they are housed in a single office building in Anderson, Indiana. Field offices are scattered throughout the United States, but the workstations located at the field offices serve as thin clients and access data from the Anderson servers. Tornados in this part of the country are not uncommon, and it is estimated that one will level the building every 60 years. Which of the following is the SLE for this scenario?

   A. $2 million

   B. $1 million

   C. $500,000

   D. $33,333.33

   E. $16,666.67

3. Refer to the scenario in question 2. Which of the following amounts is the ALE for this sce-nario?

   A. $2 million

   B. $1 million

   C. $500,000

   D. $33,333.33

   E. $16,666.67

4. Refer to the scenario in question 2. Which of the following is the ARO for this scenario?

   A. 0.0167

   B. 1

   C. 5

   D. 16.7

   E. 60

5. Which of the following strategies involves identifying a risk and making the decision to discontinue engaging in the action?

    A. Risk acceptance

    B. Risk avoidance

    C. Risk deterrence

    D. Risk mitigation

    E. Risk transference

6. Which of the following policy statements may include an escalation contact in the event that the person dealing with a situation needs to know whom to contact?

    A. Scope

    B. Exception

    C. Overview

    D. Accountability

7. Which of the following policies are designed to reduce the risk of fraud and prevent other losses in an organization?

    A. Separation of duties

    B. Acceptable use

    C. Least privilege

    D. Physical access control

8. What is the term used for events that were mistakenly flagged although they weren't truly events about which to be concerned?

    A. Fool's gold

    B. Non-incidents

    C. Error flags

    D. False positives

9. Which of the following is the structured approach that is followed to secure a company's assets?

    A. Audit management

    B. Incident management

    C. Change management

    D. Skill management

10. Which of the following strategies involves sharing some of the risk burden with someone else, such as an insurance company?

    A. Risk acceptance

    B. Risk avoidance

    C. Risk deterrence

    D. Risk mitigation

    E. Risk transference

11. The risk-assessment component, in conjunction with the _____, provides the organiza-tion with an accurate picture of the situation facing it.

    A. RAC

    B. ALE

    C. BIA

    D. RMG

12. Which of the following policy statements should address who is responsible for ensuring that the policy is enforced?

    A. Scope

    B. Exception

    C. Overview

    D. Accountability

13. Which of the following strategies is accomplished any time you take steps to reduce risk?

    A. Risk acceptance

    B. Risk avoidance

    C. Risk deterrence

    D. Risk mitigation

    E. Risk transference

14. If you calculate the SLE to be $4,000 and that there will be 10 occurrences a year (ARO), then the ALE is:

    A. $400

    B. $4,000

    C. $40,000

    D. $400,000

15. Which of the following policies describes how the employees in an organization can use company systems and resources, both software and hardware?

    A. Separation of duties

    B. Acceptable use

    C. Least privilege

    D. Physical access control

16. Separation of duties helps to prevent an individual from embezzling money from a company. To embezzle funds successfully, an individual would need to recruit others to commit an act of _____ (an agreement between two or more parties established for the purpose of committing deception or fraud).

   A. misappropriation

   B. misuse

   C. collusion

   D. fraud

17. Which of the following strategies involves understanding something about the enemy and letting them know the harm that can come their way if they cause harm to you?

   A. Risk acceptance

   B. Risk avoidance

   C. Risk deterrence

   D. Risk mitigation

   E. Risk transference

18. If you calculate SLE to be $25,000 and that there will be one occurrence every four years (ARO), then what is the ALE?

   A. $6,250

   B. $12,500

   C. $25,000

   D. $100,000

19. Which of the following policies should be used when assigning permissions, giving users only the permissions they need to do their work and no more?

   A. Separation of duties

   B. Acceptable use

   C. Least privilege

   D. Physical access control

20. Which of the following strategies necessitates an identified risk that those involved understand the potential cost/damage and agree to live with it?

   A. Risk acceptance

   B. Risk avoidance

   C. Risk deterrence

   D. Risk mitigation

   E. Risk transference

Chapter

2

Monitoring and Diagnosing Networks

THE FOLLOWING COMPTIA SECURITY+ EXAM OBJECTIVES ARE COVERED IN THIS CHAPTER:

✓ **3.6 Analyze a scenario and select the appropriate type of mitigation and deterrent techniques.**

  - Monitoring system logs: Event logs; Audit logs; Security logs, Access logs

  - Hardening: Disabling unnecessary services; Protecting management interfaces and applications; Password protection; Disabling unnecessary accounts

  - Network security: MAC limiting and filtering; 802.1x; Disabling unused interfaces and unused application service ports; Rogue machine detection

  - Security posture: Initial baseline configuration; Continuous security monitoring; Remediation

  - Reporting: Alarms; Alerts; Trends

The ability to monitor systems and networks is vital to security. If you cannot effectively monitor systems and networks, you'll find it impossible to detect security breaches and therefore address them.

Monitoring Networks

It is important to monitor the network and make sure that the traffic on it belongs there. In this section, we'll explore basic network monitors.

Network Monitors

Network monitors, also called *sniffers*, were originally introduced to help troubleshoot network problems. Simple network configuration programs like IPconfig don't get down on the wire and tell you what is physically happening on a network. Instead, examining the signaling and traffic that occurs on a network requires a network monitor.

Early monitors were bulky and required a great deal of expertise to use. Like most things in the computer age, they have gotten simpler, smaller, and less expensive. Network monitors are now available for most environments, and they're effective and easy to use.

Today, a network-monitoring system usually consists of a PC with a NIC (running in *promiscuous mode*) and monitoring software. *Promiscuous mode* simply means that the network card looks at any packet that it sees on the network, even if that packet is not addressed to that network card. The monitoring software is menu driven and easy to use, and it has a big help file. The traffic displayed by sniffers can become overly involved and require additional technical materials; you can buy these materials at most bookstores, or you can find them on the Internet for free. Essentially, you should have an in-depth understanding of the network protocols in order to understand the traffic that the sniffer is detecting. With a few hours in use, most people can make network monitors work efficiently and use the data they provide.

Windows Server products include a service called Network Monitor that you can use to gain basic information about network traffic. A more robust, detailed version of Network Monitor is included with Systems Management Server (SMS). When it comes to third-party products, Wireshark, available for most platforms, is a market leader (see www.wireshark.org for more information).

Sniffer is a trade name, like Kleenex. It's the best-known network monitor, so everyone started calling network-monitoring hardware *sniffers*.

Monitoring System Logs

In addition to network monitoring, you must monitor the *event logs*. *Event logs* are system logs that record various events that occur. Event logs comprise a broad category that includes some logs that are not relevant to security issues. But within that broad category are security and access logs that are clearly pertinent to security. Windows has several logs. The two most important logs for security purposes are the following:

Application Log   This log contains various events logged by applications or programs. Many applications will record their errors in this log. It can be useful particularly if the log is on a server that has database server software like SQL Server installed. Examining this log can provide clues that someone has been attempting to compromise the database.

Security Log   The most important things that you will find in the security log are successful and unsuccessful logon attempts. This log also records events related to resource use, such as creating, opening, or deleting files or other objects. Administrators can specify what events are recorded in the security log. Logon auditing can be turned off, but it never should be. In Windows a security log is the access log. Linux provides separate logs for successful and failed login attempts. By default, Windows does not log both successes and failures, but for security reasons this should be changed.

Although the Windows operating systems do not create audit logs by name, the logs they create are useful in auditing. If you add Sharepoint, SQL, or other services, then they will often call the application logs they create audit logs and you will want to carefully monitor them for security-related events.

Linux also has logs that are important to security:

`var/log/faillog`   This log file contains failed user logins. You'll find this log useful when tracking attempts to crack into your system.

`/var/log/apport.log`   This log records application crashes. Sometimes these can reveal attempts to compromise the system or the presence of a virus or spyware.

In Exercise 2.1, we'll show you how to view the event logs in Event Viewer.

EXERCISE 2.1

Viewing the Event Logs

Event Viewer has been the primary tool included with Windows for viewing log files for quite some time. The following exercise will walk you through using this tool on a Windows 7 workstation.

1.   Click Start ➢ Control Panel ➢ Administrative Tools ➢ Event Viewer to open Event Viewer.

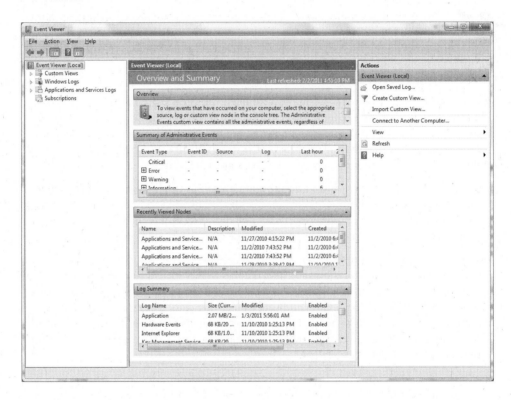

2. Expand Windows Logs and choose System.

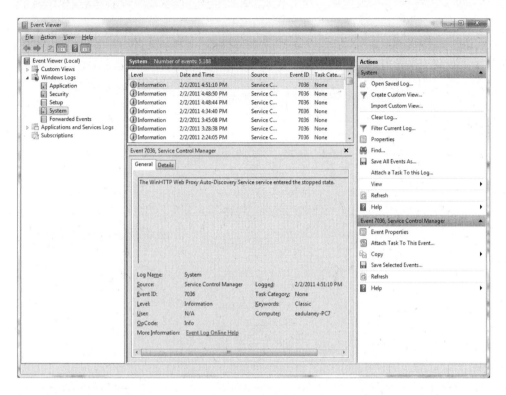

3. Click the heading for the Level field. This will alphabetize the list by the level type, and it should put error messages above information and other such messages.

4. Click an error message and read the details explaining it in the bottom part of the dialog box. If there is insufficient room to display all the details, double-clicking the event will open the properties for the event in a separate dialog box.

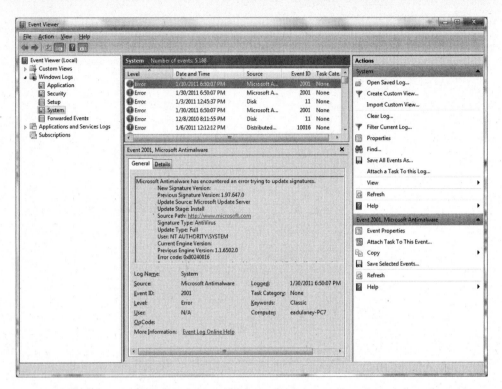

5.   Click the Event Log Online Help link. A dialog box appears asking if you want to send information across the Internet and displaying the information that will be sent. Click Yes.

Your browser will access the Microsoft TechNet site and display any other details about the event, including how to resolve it.

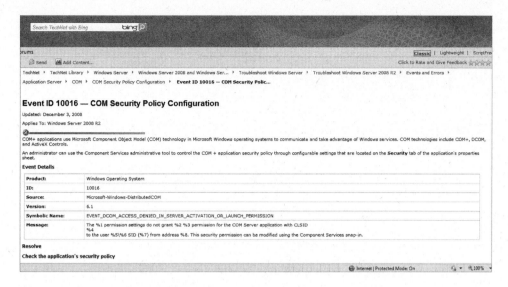

6. Exit the browser and exit Event Viewer.

The options within Event Viewer allow you to perform such actions as saving the log file (EVT, TXT, or CSV format), opening saved logs, filtering the log file, and viewing or changing properties. By clicking Properties, you can change the variables shown in Figure 2.1. The default is that the log files are overwritten as space is needed (the maximum size reached), but automatic archiving can be configured as well as the need for the administrator to clear logs manually.

The log files created by crucial network services such as DNS need to be routinely examined. The DNS service, when running on Windows Server (any version of Windows Server), for example, writes entries to the log file that can be examined using Event Viewer. Just as you set the size and overwrite options for the Security Log object, you should take those same actions for the DNS Server logs.

When enabled, a firewall, whether via software or hardware, often creates log files similar to most other services. Given the importance of the firewall and its purpose, you should hold the entries written to those logs in high esteem and evaluate them regularly. You can review these log files anywhere a firewall is running.

Most antivirus programs also create log files that you should check regularly. You want to verify not only that the program is running but also that the definition file(s) being used is current. Pay attention to the viruses that are found and deleted or quarantined and to any files that are being skipped.

FIGURE 2.1   Properties for the System log

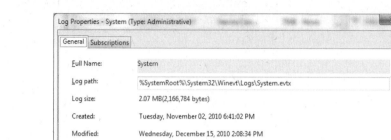

Understanding Hardening

The term *hardening* is usually applied to operating systems. The idea is to "lock down" the operating system as much as is practical. For example, ensure that all unneeded services are turned off, all unneeded software is uninstalled, patches are updated, user accounts are checked for security, and so forth. Hardening is a general process of making certain that the operating system itself is as secure as it can be. In fact, it could be said that if you have not hardened the operating system, then any other security measures are going to be far less effective (and possibly completely ineffective!).

In the following sections, we will look at the various aspects of operating system hardening. You must address each of these in order to harden your operating system.

Working with Services

Services are programs that run when the operating system boots, and they are often are running in the background without users interacting directly with them. Many services are quite important—even critical. However, a service can provide an attack vector that someone could exploit against your system, so be sure to enable only those services that are absolutely required. Part of operating system hardening is disabling unnecessary services. To display all the services on your Windows computer (any version—from XP to Windows 8 or Windows Server 2012), you first select the Control Panel and then select Administrative Tools, as shown in Figure 2.2.

In Figure 2.2, the Remote Registry service is shown. This service is used to allow technical support personnel to access that system's Registry remotely. The service can be quite useful in some situations, but it can also function as a means for an attacker to get into your system. If you don't need it, turn it off. The issue is not that a given service is "bad"; it is more of an issue of ensuring that you know what services are running on your system and that you make a conscious decision to allow the service to run (or not). Windows also provides a brief summary of what the service does and any services that depend on that service. If you don't know what a service does, then you should probably leave it at its default setting.

It is critical that you have a good understanding of any service you intend to disable. Some services depend on other services. Turning off one service could render others unusable. Fortunately, the Microsoft Services Console gives you information on dependencies.

As a security administrator, you should regularly check all servers and make certain that only necessary services are running on them. Here are some tips:

File and Print Servers   These are primarily vulnerable to *denial-of-service (DoS)* and access attacks. DoS attacks can be targeted at specific protocols and overwhelm a port with activity. Make sure that these servers run only the protocols that are needed to support the network.

Networks with PC-Based Systems   In a network that has PC-based systems, make sure that NetBIOS services are disabled on servers or that an effective firewall is in place between the server and the Internet. Many of the popular attacks that are occurring on systems today take place through the NetBIOS services via ports 135, 137, 138, and 139. On Unix systems, make sure that port 111, the *Remote Procedure Call (RPC)* port, is closed.

RPC is a programming interface that allows a remote computer to run programs on a local machine. It has created serious vulnerabilities in systems that have RPC enabled.

Directory Sharing   Directory sharing should be limited to what is essential to performing systems functions. Make sure that any root directories are hidden from browsing. It's better to designate a subfolder off the root directory and share it than to share a root directory.

FIGURE 2.2   Windows Services

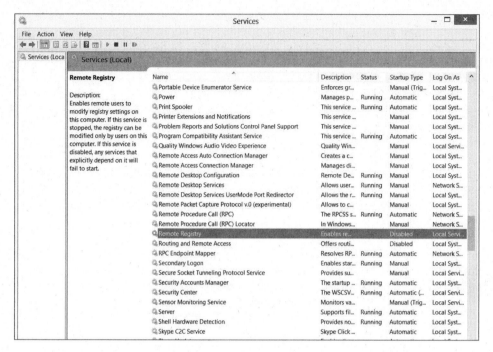

Protecting Management Interfaces and Applications

The ability to run the administrative interfaces within the operating system, and the applications associated with them, is often the difference between a standard user and an administrative user. The person running the administrative interfaces can make configuration changes to the system(s) and modify settings in ways that can have wide-ranging consequences. For example, a user who is able to gain access to the administrative tools could delete other users, set their own ID equal to the root user, change passwords, or delete key files.

> Even for administrators, it is a good idea to log in as a user and then right-click and choose Run As Administrator when needed. With Linux, most distributions will not allow you to log on as root (the Linux equivalent of administrator).

To protect against this, access to management and administrative interfaces should be restricted to only those administrators who need it. Not only should you protect server utilities, but you should also even go so far as to remove users' access to workstation utilities such as regedit and regedit32 that have administrative depth.

The System And Security applet beneath the Control Panel (known just as Security in operating systems earlier than Windows 7) is the main interface for security features in

Windows operating systems. From here, you can configure Windows Firewall, automatic scans of your computer, and Windows Defender.

> The Microsoft Safety & Security Center (www.microsoft.com/security/) is the first place to turn to for up-to-date information on Windows operating system issues.

One of the best tools to use when looking for possible illicit activity on a workstation is *Performance Monitor* (known as *System Monitor* in early versions of Windows). This utility can be used to examine activity on any counter. Excessive processor usage is one counter worth paying attention to if you suspect the workstation is affected or being illegitimately accessed.

It is important that you use password protection to protect the management functionality and consoles on a workstation or server. Just because users are authorized to use that machine does not mean they should be authorized to access all management functions.

Software

It is considered a security best practice to remove any software that is not needed. Obviously, this applies mainly to business computers. You can, of course, keep any software you wish on your home computer. However, in a work environment unnecessary software can be another venue for attack.

What is "unneeded" software? Frankly, in a work environment it is any software that is not essential to the function of that machine. Obviously, that means no games or similar extraneous software. Beyond that, even some business software is not required on all machines. For example, you probably don't need to have Microsoft Office installed on your web server. You certainly don't need accounting software on your domain controller.

A bigger issue is the Windows components that commonly come preinstalled on every machine. If you go to your Windows Control Panel and select Programs (it might have a slightly different name in different versions of Windows), select Programs And Features, and then select Windows Components, you will see something much like the screen shown in Figure 2.3.

From this screen, you can remove any component not needed. While the specific components to be removed will vary based on your environment, some components clearly should be removed from most systems. For example, you don't need IIS on any system that is not a web server. If you are not using PowerShell, remove it. If you are not running virtual machines, remove Hyper-V. You can easily go through the list and determine exactly what software your system needs.

> Ideally any server is dedicated to a single purpose, such as being a web server, database server, domain controller, DNS server, and so on. Although you can install multiple roles on one server, doing so is usually a bad idea. Thus, when you are removing software, any software not necessary for supporting that purpose should be removed.

FIGURE 2.3   Windows Features

Patches

A *patch* is an update to a system. Sometimes a patch adds new functionality; in other cases, it corrects a bug in the software. In Windows, you can select Control Panel ➢ Administrative Tools ➢ System Security and view updates. Doing so allows you to see updates that are currently installed, update settings, and any issues. If you are running a standalone system (a home system or perhaps a laptop used for travel), you should elect to have updates automatically installed.

However, in a network environment this is not the appropriate way to deal with patches. In a network environment, patches should first be applied to a single machine and tested. The reason for this is that it is possible for a patch to interfere with the functionality of some business-critical application. If that patch is not critical, you may choose not to apply it until some fix can be found. If you automatically patch all of the machines in your network and then discover that there is a problem, you can render all of your systems nonfunctional.

Microsoft TechNet describes three types of patches (http://technet.microsoft.com /en-us/library/cc526858.aspx):

> A service pack is a periodic update that corrects problems in one version of a product. In addition to correcting known problems, service packs provide tools, drivers, and updates that extend product functionality, including enhancements developed after the product was released. Specifically, service packs are designed to get software users to the current code base for the product in question. This is important because the current code base is where developers update the code.

> Updates are code fixes for products that are provided to individual customers when those customers experience critical problems for which no feasible workaround is available.

> Security updates address security vulnerabilities. Attackers wanting to break into systems can exploit such vulnerabilities. Security updates are analogous to updates, but should be considered mandatory, and they must be deployed quickly.

As you can see, service packs and updates usually don't need to be installed immediately. You have time to evaluate the impact that the update will have on your system. Under both PCI and HIPAA, there is a general expectation that critical security patches should be deployed within 30 days of release.

User Account Control

User account control is a very important part of operating system hardening. It is important that only active accounts be operational and that they be properly managed. This means disabling unnecessary accounts. Most network administrators focus on domain accounts. Nevertheless, operating system hardening requires that you pay attention to local accounts as well. A number of hacking techniques begin by compromising local accounts. It is also common practice for network administrators to configure a single machine to meet business needs and then to image that machine for other workstations. If the accounts on the model machine are not properly handled, issues will propagate throughout the network.

First and foremost, any accounts that are not needed should be disabled. That is simple enough. Second, all accounts must have passwords that meet your organization's standards. Password requirements are not just for domain passwords; they are also for local passwords. It is also important that you keep the principle of least privileges in mind: No account should have privileges in excess of the necessary job function.

Enabled accounts that are not needed on a system provide a door through which attackers can gain access. No matter how minimal the permissions of that user may be, they still provide a first stop from which the attacker can begin to gather information about the system and begin looking for ways to access it with elevated privileges.

You should disable all accounts that are not needed immediately—on servers and workstations alike. Here are some types of accounts that you should disable:

Employees Who Have Left the Company   Be sure to disable immediately accounts for any employee who has left the company. This should be done the minute employment is terminated. It does not matter why the employee left the company—whether they left on good terms after giving 2 weeks' notice, they were fired, or they retired after 30 years of loyal service—their accounts still get disabled immediately.

> Disable the accounts of employees who have left the company; don't delete them. There may be a need to access these accounts to retrieve some data, investigate some irregularity, and so forth.

Temporary Employees   It is not uncommon to create short-term accounts for brief periods of time for access by temporary employees. These also need to be disabled the moment they are no longer needed.

Default Guest Accounts   In many operating systems, a guest account is created during installation and intended for use by those needing only limited access and lacking their own account on the system. This account presents a door into the system that should not be there, and all who have worked with the operating system knows of its existence, thus making it a likely target for attackers.

Filesystems

Several filesystems are involved in the operating systems we've discussed, and from a network perspective, they have a high level of interoperability among them. Throughout the years, different vendors have implemented their own sets of file standards. Some of the more common filesystems in Windows are listed here:

Microsoft FAT   Microsoft's earliest filesystem was referred to as the *File Allocation Table (FAT)*. FAT was designed for relatively small disk drives. It was upgraded first to FAT-16 and finally to FAT-32. FAT-32 allows large disk systems to be used on Windows systems. FAT allows only two types of protection: share-level and user-level access privileges. If a user has Write or Change Access permissions to a drive or directory, they have access to any file in that directory. This is very unsecure in an Internet environment.

> It is rare to find FAT used in the corporate world these days (other than on some USB drives), but you should still know about it for the exam.

Microsoft NTFS   The *New Technology Filesystem (NTFS)* was introduced with Windows NT to address security problems. Before Windows NT was released, it had become apparent to Microsoft that a new filing system was required to handle growing disk sizes, security concerns, and the need for more file stability. NTFS was created to address these issues.

Although FAT was relatively stable if the systems that were controlling it kept running, it didn't do so well when the power went out or when the system crashed unexpectedly. One of the benefits of NTFS was a transaction-tracking system, which made it possible for Windows NT to back out of any disk operations that were in progress when Windows NT crashed or lost power.

With NTFS, files, directories, and volumes can each have their own security. NTFS's security is flexible and built in. Not only does NTFS track security in access control lists (ACLs), which can hold permissions for local users and groups, but each entry in the ACL can specify what type of access is given, such as Read-Only, Change, or Full Control. This allows a great deal of flexibility in setting up a network. In addition, special file-encryption programs were developed to encrypt data while it was stored on the hard disk drive (HDD).

Microsoft strongly recommends that all network shares be established using NTFS. As Microsoft has continued to refine NTFS, the versions have incremented, with 3.1 being the most commonly used as of this writing. To see the version installed on a particular workstation, at the command prompt with administrative privileges type `fsutil fsinfo ntfsinfo C:`, and the second line shown will be the NTFS version.

Windows systems often have hidden administrative shares with names that end with a dollar sign character (C$, admin$, and so on). These are created for use in managing the computer on the network, and they can be permanently disabled only through Registry edits. You can temporarily disable them with the Computer Management console, but they will return on reboot unless you permanently disable them with Group Policy. For the purpose of the Security+ exam, simply know that they exist and are needed for full network functionality.

Make sure that you periodically review the manufacturers' support websites and other support resources, which are available to apply current updates and security patches to your systems. Doing so on a regular basis will lower your exposure to security risks.

Although Windows is the focus here, know that other operating systems have their own filesystems. In Linux, for example, common choices include ext3, ext4, and XFS. Macs used HFS (Hierarchical File System) and later replaced it with HFS Plus (also known as HFS Extended).

Securing the Network

Obviously, network security is a broad topic, and it will be addressed throughout this book. However, there are some essential concepts identified on the CompTIA Security + exam that are discussed in this section:

MAC Limiting and Filtering   Limit access to the network to MAC addresses that are known, and filter out those that are not. Even in a home network, you can implement MAC filtering with most routers, and you typically have the option of choosing to allow or deny only those computers with MAC addresses that you list.

 If you don't know a workstation's MAC address, use ipconfig /all to find it in the Windows-based world (it is listed as *physical address*). Use ifconfig or ip a in Unix/Linux.

MAC filtering is not foolproof, and a quick look in a search engine will turn up tools that can be used to change the MAC address and help attackers circumvent this control.

802.1X   This is discussed in the following section, but adding port authentication to MAC filtering takes security for the network down to the switch port level and increases your security exponentially. The IEEE standard 802.1X defines port-based security for wireless network access control.

As such, it offers a means of authentication and defines the Extensible Authentication Protocol (EAP) over IEEE 802, discussed in Chapter 4, "Access Control, Authentication, and Authorization." It is often known as *EAP over LAN (EAPOL)*.

The biggest benefit of using 802.1X is that the access points and the switches do not need to do the authentication but instead rely on the authentication server to do the actual work.

Disable Unused Ports   Remember, a port is a connection, like a channel. For example, SMTP uses port 25. For that reason these are sometimes called application ports. All ports not in use should be disabled. Otherwise, they present an open door for an attacker to enter. Essentially, you disable a port by disabling the service and block the port with Windows Firewall (doing one and not the other can result in a single point of failure).

Rogue Machine Detection   On any sizable network it is always possible that someone has added an unauthorized machine. A rogue machine could be an intruder in a neighboring office connecting to your wireless network or an employee adding an unauthorized machine by plugging directly into a network RJ45 jack. Rogue machines pose a serious security risk. Part of your monitoring strategy must be to scan for rogue machines on your network.

Security Posture

It is impossible to evaluate your security without having a baseline configuration documented. The baseline must represent a secure state. In other words, it is not simply the state of your network when you decide to start monitoring. It is instead a baseline state you know to be secure. All future security reporting will be relative to this state, so it is rather important.

The National Institute of Standards and Technology has some guidelines on the issue of security baselines (http://csrc.nist.gov/publications /nistpubs/800-128/sp800-128.pdf):

> "Identifies the steps for creation of a baseline configuration, content of the baseline configuration, approval of the initial baseline configuration, maintenance of the baseline configuration (i.e., when it should be updated and by whom), and control of the baseline configuration. If applicable, requirements from higher regulatory bodies are considered and integrated when defining baseline configurations (e.g., requirements from OMB memos, laws such as Health Insurance Portability and Accountability Act (HIPAA), etc.)."

In other words, it is not just the current state of your network, but how it addresses specific compliance issues. Is your network in compliance with HIPAA, PCI, or other relevant regulatory standards? What is the configuration of network security devices (intrusion detection systems, antivirus, and so on)?

It is also a good idea to include network utilization statistics. Being aware of normal traffic flow on your network can be useful when identifying DoS attacks.

Continuous Security Monitoring

Once a baseline security configuration is documented, it is critical to monitor it to see that this baseline is maintained or exceeded. A popular phrase among personal trainers is "that which gets measured gets improved." Well, in network security, "that which gets monitored gets secure."

Continuous monitoring means exactly that: ongoing monitoring. This may involve regular measurements of network traffic levels, routine evaluations for regulatory compliance, and checks of network security device configurations.

Security Audits

Monitoring should take place on several levels. There should be basic, ongoing monitoring that is not labor intensive. Software solutions are available that will accomplish this for you. However, you should also implement scheduled, in-depth checks of security. These are usually called *security audits*.

A *security audit* is an integral part of continuous security monitoring. Security audits can be a check of any aspect of your security, including the following:

- Review of security logs
- Review of policies and compliance with policies
- A check of security device configuration
- Review of incident response reports

The scope of the audit and its frequency are determined by the organization. These parameters are determined by security needs and budget. For example, a high school network administrator does not have the budget or the security needs of a defense contractor. Therefore, you could expect the defense contractor to have more frequent and more comprehensive audits. However, every organization needs to have some type of audit policy as a part of continuous monitoring.

Setting a Remediation Policy

The monitoring of your system is very likely to uncover some gaps between the secure baseline that you established and the current state of the network. Those gaps might be quite significant or very minor. For example, you may have a requirement that all RSA cryptography be implemented with 2048-bit keys but discover one service is using 1024-bit keys. This is not a critical gap. This discrepancy will not render your system wide open to hackers, but it is a gap nonetheless.

Your policies must include a remediation policy. When a gap in the security posture is detected, it should first be classified, and then a remediation plan must be implemented. The specifics of how you classify and respond to a gap will vary from one organization to another. One possible classification system is given here:

Minor   This is a deviation from the security baseline that does not pose any immediate threat to security.

Serious   This is a deviation that could pose an immediate threat, but the threat is either so unlikely or so difficult to exploit as to minimize the danger.

Critical   This is a deviation that poses an immediate threat and that must be addressed as soon as possible.

This is just one possible classification system. An example of a minor threat would be the RSA issue previously mentioned. A serious threat might be the discovery of an obscure vulnerability in a database server that could be exploited but only by someone on the network. A critical threat might be finding out that your web application is vulnerable to SQL injection.

Reporting Security Issues

Security incidents will occur no matter how well you design your security system. Some of these incidents will be minor, whereas others will be quite serious. Regardless of the severity of the incident, it must be reported. A system must be in place to report all issues. In the following sections, we will look at ways you will be able to report these risks.

Alarms

Alarms are indications of an ongoing current problem currently. Think of a siren sounding when someone kicks in the door to a home. These are conditions to which you must respond right now.

Alarm rates can indicate trends that are occurring. Even after you solve the problem, you still need to look for indications that the condition may not be isolated. For example, if your IDS (discussed later in this chapter) or firewall has an alarm, how is this reported to network security staff? A notification system should be in place that immediately notifies appropriate staff. Once the issue is addressed, those staff members must have a procedure in place to report the specifics of the incident, and how it was addressed, to management.

The point is that your organization needs to have a system for reporting alarms. It cannot be an ad hoc process whereby each individual reports such alarms as they see fit. Incident response cannot occur without some reporting of alarms.

Alerts

Slightly below alarms in terms of security issues are *alerts*. Alerts are issues to which you need to pay attention but are not about to bring the system down at any moment. (Think of them as storm watches instead of storm warnings.) In Event Viewer, for example, system events are identified either as errors, information, or warnings. Although errors are the most critical, the others need attention too in order to keep them from eventually becoming errors.

Alerts can also refer to industry alerts. Many antivirus software vendors provide alert services that will email you when a new attack is found or is increasing. Sometimes, other organizations, such as Microsoft, will also send alerts. When a security professional receives such an alert, that information can be communicated both to management and to the staff, as appropriate.

Trends

Trends do not refer to the latest fad in security. Instead they refer to trends in threats. For example, there are more email-based phishing attempts in the last month than in previous months, or waterhole and spearphishing attacks have been increasing recently.

Though not often used in this fashion, the term can also refer to trends in your organizational security profile. Are audits finding an increase in compliance with software policies? Conversely, are you seeing an uptick in the violation of software installation policies?

Information about trends (both in the world at large and within your organization) can be invaluable for maintaining a proactive security posture. Seeing trends as they develop allows you to take action before a major issue occurs.

Differentiating between Detection Controls and Prevention Controls

Some security controls are implemented simply to detect potential threats. Others are designed to prevent or at least minimize such threats. For the CompTIA Security+ exam, it is important to know the difference. We will look at security controls here. An intrusion detection system (IDS), as the name implies, is focused on detecting intrusion. One step beyond this, an Intrusion Prevention System (IPS), again as the name implies, is focused on preventing an intrusion from occurring. There are various levels of both IDS and IPS as they can be based on a host (H-IDS, for example) or a network (N-IDS). Chapter 3, "Understanding Devices and Infrastructure," looks at these tools in more detail.

Not all approaches are so clear-cut as to include the term "detection" or "prevention" in the title, and many tools fall between the two. One such tool is a honeypot. A *honeypot* is a computer that has been designated as a target for computer attacks. The best way to visualize a honeypot is to think of Winnie the Pooh and the multiple times the character has become stuck while trying to get the honey out of the jugs in which it is stored. By getting stuck, he has incapacitated himself and become an easy target for anyone trying to find him.

 Two of the most popular honeypots for Linux are honeyd (http://honeyd .org) and Tiny Honeypot (thp) (http://freshmeat.net/projects/thp/).

The purpose of a honeypot is to allow itself to succumb to an attack. During the process of "dying," the system can be used to gain information about how the attack developed and what methods were used to institute the attack. The benefit of a honeypot system is that it draws attackers away from a higher-value system or allows administrators to gain intelligence about an attack strategy.

Honeypots aren't normally secured or locked down. If they come straight out of the box with an operating system and applications software, they may be configured as is. Elaborate honeypot systems can contain information and software that might entice an attacker to probe deeper and take over the system. If not configured properly, a honeypot system can be used to launch attacks against other systems. There are several initiatives in the area of honeypot technology. One of the more interesting involves the Honeynet Project, which created a synthetic network that can be run on a single computer system and is attached to a network using a normal network interface card (NIC). The system looks like an entire corporate network, complete with applications and data, all of which are fake. As part of the Honeynet Project, the network was routinely scanned, worms were inserted, and attempts were made to contact other systems to infest them—all over the course of a three-day period. At the end of day three, no fewer than three worms had infected the system. This infestation happened without any advertising by the Honeynet Project.

Additional information is available about the Honeynet Project at www .honeynet.org.

Before you even consider implementing a honeypot or a Honeynet-type project, you need to understand the concepts of enticement and entrapment:

Enticement   *Enticement* is the process of luring someone into your plan or trap. You might accomplish this by advertising that you have free software, or you might brag that no one can break into your machine. If you invite people to try, you're enticing them to do something that you want them to do.

Entrapment   *Entrapment* is the process in which a law enforcement officer or a government agent encourages or induces a person to commit a crime when the potential criminal expresses a desire not to go ahead. Entrapment is a valid legal defense in a criminal prosecution.

Although enticement is legally acceptable in the United States, entrapment is not. Your legal liabilities are probably small in either case, but you should seek legal advice before you implement a honeypot on your network. You may also want to contact law enforcement or the prosecutor's office if you want to pursue legal action against attackers.

Some security experts use the term *tar pit* in place of honeypot. The two terms are not completely interchangeable: a honey pot exists to trap so you can identify what their capabilities are while a tar pit only exists to slow them down and does not collect data.

Summary

In this chapter, we discussed network security, including network security posture, patches, updates, and reporting. These are all important concepts for the CompTIA Security+ exam.

Network monitors are primarily troubleshooting tools, and they can be used to eavesdrop on networks. Hardening the operating system has been a very important topic in this chapter. We have discussed patching, shutting down unneeded services, removing unnecessary software, and other OS hardening issues.

Exam Essentials

Be able to describe sniffers.   One of the primary tools used for network monitoring is sniffers. Sniffers are passive and can provide real-time displays of network traffic. They're intended primarily for troubleshooting purposes, but they're one of the tools used by attackers to determine what protocols and systems you're running.

Be able to explain the purpose of a honeypot.   A honeypot is a system that is used to gather information or designed to be broken. Honeypot systems are used to gather evidence in an investigation and to study attack strategies.

Be able to explain operating system hardening.   OS hardening is making the OS as secure as you can before adding in antivirus, firewalls, and so forth. It includes patching the system, shutting down unneeded services, and removing unneeded software.

Review Questions

1. In order for network monitoring to work properly, you need a PC and a network card running in what mode?

   A. Launch

   B. Exposed

   C. Promiscuous

   D. Sweep

2. Which of the following utilities can be used in Linux to view a list of users' failed authentication attempts?

   A. `badlog`

   B. `faillog`

   C. `wronglog`

   D. `killlog`

3. A periodic update that corrects problems in one version of a product is called a
   _____.

   A. Hotfix

   B. Overhaul

   C. Service pack

   D. Security update

4. Which device monitors network traffic in a passive manner?

   A. Sniffer

   B. IDS

   C. Firewall

   D. Web browser

5. What is a system that is intended or designed to be broken into by an attacker?

   A. Honeypot

   B. Honeybucket

   C. Decoy

   D. Spoofing system

6. How must user accounts for exiting employees be handled?

   A. Disabled, regardless of the circumstances

   B. Disabled if the employee has been terminated

   C. Deleted, regardless of the circumstances

   D. Deleted if the employee has been terminated

7. In intrusion detection system vernacular, which account is responsible for setting the security policy for an organization?

    A. Supervisor

    B. Administrator

    C. Root

    D. Director

8. Which of the following is the process in which a law enforcement officer or a government agent encourages or induces a person to commit a crime when the potential criminal expresses a desire not to go ahead?

    A. Enticement

    B. Entrapment

    C. Deceit

    D. Sting

9. Which of the following types of logs could provide clues that someone has been attempting to compromise the SQL Server database?

    A. Event

    B. SQL_LOG

    C. Security

    D. Access

10. Which of the following is another, more common, name for EAPOL?

    A. LDAP

    B. 802.1X

    C. LDAPS

    D. 802.12

11. If you don't know the MAC address of a Windows-based machine, what command-line utility can you use to ascertain it?

    A. `macconfig`

    B. `ifconfig`

    C. `ipconfig`

    D. `config`

12. In the Windows world, what tool is used to disable a port?

    A. System Manager

    B. System Monitor

    C. Performance Monitor

    D. Windows Firewall

13. Which of the following is an indication of an ongoing current problem?

    A. Alert

    B. Trend

    C. Alarm

    D. Trap

14. Which of the following a programming interface that allows a remote computer to run programs on a local machine?

    A. RPC

    B. RSH

    C. SSH

    D. SSL

15. Which of the following is the term for a fix for a known software problem?

    A. Skiff

    B. Patch

    C. Slipstream

    D. Upgrade

16. Which of the following file systems is from Microsoft and was included with their earliest operating systems?

    A. NTFS

    B. UFS

    C. MTFS

    D. FAT

17. The process of making certain that an entity (operating system, application, etc.) is as secure as it can be is known as:

    A. Stabilizing

    B. Reinforcing

    C. Hardening

    D. Toughening

18. What is the term for the process of luring someone in (usually done by an enforcement officer or a government agent)?

    A. Enticement

    B. Entrapment

    C. Deceit

    D. Sting

19. Which of the following is a notification that an unusual condition exists and should be investigated?

A. Alert

B. Trend

C. Alarm

D. Trap

20. If you don't know the MAC address of a Linux-based machine, what command-line utility can you use to ascertain it?

A. `macconfig`

B. `ifconfig`

C. `ipconfig`

D. `config`

Chapter 3

Understanding Devices and Infrastructure

THE FOLLOWING COMPTIA SECURITY+ EXAM OBJECTIVES ARE COVERED IN THIS CHAPTER:

✓ **1.1 Implement security configuration parameters on network devices and other technologies.**

- Firewalls
- Routers
- Switches
- Load balancers
- Proxies
- Web security gateways
- VPN concentrators
- NIDS and NIPS: Behavior based; Signature based; Anomaly based; Heuristic
- Protocol analyzers
- Spam filter
- UTM security appliances: URL filter; Content inspection; Malware inspection
- Web application firewall vs. network firewall
- Application aware devices: Firewalls; IPS; IDS; Proxies

✓ **1.2 Given a scenario, use secure network administration principles: Unified Threat Management**

✓ **1.3 Explain network design elements and components.**

- DMZ
- Subnetting
- VLAN

- NAT
- Remote access
- Telephony
- NAC

✓ **1.4 Given a scenario, implement common protocols and services.**

- Protocols: IPSec; SNMP; SSH; DNS; TLS; SSL; TCP/IP; FTPS; HTTPS; SCP; ICMP; IPv4; IPv6; iSCSI; Fibre Channel; FCoE; FTP; SFTP; TFTP; TELNET; HTTP; NetBIOS
- Ports: 21; 22; 25; 53; 80; 110; 139; 143; 443; 3389
- OSI relevance

✓ **3.6 Analyze a scenario and select the appropriate type of mitigation and deterrent techniques.**

- IDS vs. IPS

This chapter introduces the hardware used within the network. Your network is composed of a variety of *media* and *devices* that both facilitate communications and provide security. Many of these devices provide external connectivity from your network to other systems and networks, whereas others specialize in providing one form of security or another. To provide reasonable security to the entire network, you must know how these devices work and how they provide, or fail to provide, security.

This chapter deals with issues of infrastructure, network ports, and common protocols. They're key components of the Security+ exam, and it's necessary that you understand them in order to secure your network. Like many certification exams, though, the Security+ test requires you to not only know current technologies but to understand some legacy components as well.

Mastering TCP/IP

TCP/IP has been a salvation for organizations that need to connect different systems together to function as a unified structure. Unfortunately, the downside of an easy-to-use, well-documented network that has been around for many years is the presence of numerous holes. You can easily close most of these holes in your network, but you must first know about them.

You must have a good understanding of the processes TCP/IP uses in order to know how attacks on TCP/IP work. The emphasis in this section is on the types of connections and services. If you're weak in those areas, you'll do well to supplement your study with basic networking information that can be found on the Web.

The following sections delve into issues related to TCP/IP and security. Many of these issues will be familiar to you if you've taken the Network+ or Server+ exam from CompTIA. If there are any gaps in your knowledge of these topics, however, be sure to read these sections carefully.

OSI Relevance

When discussing networking, most experts refer to the seven-layer OSI model—long considered the foundation for how networking protocols should operate. This model is the most common one used, and the division between layers is well defined.

TCP/IP precedes the creation of the OSI model. Although it carries out the same operations, it does so with four layers instead of seven. Those four layers are discussed in the following section, but it is important to know that while TCP/IP is the most commonly used protocol suite, OSI is the most commonly referenced networking model.

Working with the TCP/IP Suite

The TCP/IP suite is broken into four architectural layers:

- Application layer
- Host-to-Host, or Transport layer
- Internet layer
- Network Access layer (also known as the Network Interface layer or the Link layer)

Computers using TCP/IP use the existing physical connection between the systems. TCP/IP doesn't concern itself with the network topology, or physical connections. The network controller that resides in a computer or host deals with the physical protocol, or topology. TCP/IP communicates with that controller and lets the controller worry about the network topology and physical connection.

In TCP/IP parlance, a computer on the network is a *host*. A host is any device connected to the network that runs a TCP/IP protocol suite, or stack. Figure 3.1 shows the four layers in a TCP/IP protocol stack. Note that this drawing includes the physical, or network topology. Although it isn't part of TCP/IP, the topology is essential to conveying information on a network.

FIGURE 3.1   The TCP/IP architecture layers

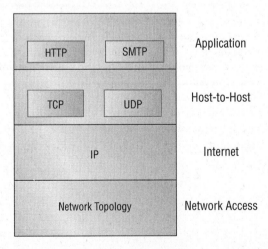

The four layers of TCP/IP have unique functions and methods for accomplishing work. Each layer talks to the layers that reside above and below it. Each layer also has its own rules and capabilities.

The following sections discuss the specific layers of TCP/IP as well as the common protocols used in the stack and how information is conveyed between the layers. Some common methods used to attack TCP/IP-based networks are also discussed.

Encapsulation, the process used to pass messages between the layers in TCP/IP, is briefly discussed in the next section after the layers have been covered.

The Application Layer

The *Application layer* is the highest layer of the suite. It allows applications to access services or protocols to exchange data. Most programs, such as web browsers, interface with TCP/IP at this level. The most commonly used Application layer protocols are as follows:

Hypertext Transfer Protocol   *Hypertext Transfer Protocol (HTTP)* is the protocol used for web pages and the World Wide Web. HTTP applications use a standard language called *Hypertext Markup Language (HTML)*. HTML files are normal text files that contain special coding that allows graphics, special fonts, and characters to be displayed by a web browser or other web-enabled applications. The default port is 80, and the URL begins with `http://`.

HTTP Secure   *HTTP Secure (HTTPS)* is the protocol used for "secure" web pages that users should see when they must enter personal information such as credit card numbers, passwords, and other identifiers. It combines HTTP with SSL/TLS to provide encrypted communication. The default port is 443, and the URL begins with `https://` instead of `http://`. Netscape originally created the protocol for use with their browser, and it became an accepted standard with RFC 2818 (`www.ietf.org/rfc/rfc2818.txt`).

> *Secure Sockets Layer (SSL)* is used to establish a secure communication connection between two TCP-based machines. This protocol uses the handshake method of establishing a session, and it was originally developed by Netscape to maintain a session using symmetric encryption.
>
> *Transport Layer Security (TLS)* is a security protocol that expands upon SSL. Many industry analysts predict that TLS will replace SSL, and it is also referred to as *SSL 3.1*. Despite its name, however, it doesn't interoperate with SSL. The TLS standard is supported by the Internet Engineering Task Force (IETF). For exam purposes, think of TLS as an updated version of SSL; TLS is based on SSL, and it is intended to supersede it.
>
> Chapter 8, "Cryptography," explores each of these protocols in greater detail.

File Transfer Protocol   *File Transfer Protocol (FTP)* is an application that allows connections to FTP servers for file uploads and downloads. FTP is a common application that uses ports 20 and 21 by default. It is used to transfer files between hosts on the Internet but is inherently insecure. A number of options have been released to try to create a more secure protocol, including *FTP over SSL (FTPS)*, which adds support for SSL cryptography, and *SSH File Transfer Protocol (SFTP)*, which is also known as *Secure FTP*.

An alternative utility for copying files is *Secure Copy (SCP)*, which uses port 22 by default and combines an old remote copy program (RCP) from the first days of TCP/IP with SSH. On the opposite end of the spectrum from a security standpoint is the *Trivial File Transfer Protocol (TFTP)*, which can be configured to transfer files between hosts without any user interaction (unattended mode). It should be avoided anywhere there are more secure alternatives.

Simple Mail Transfer Protocol   *Simple Mail Transfer Protocol (SMTP)* is the standard protocol for email communications. SMTP allows email clients and servers to communicate with each other for message delivery. The default port is 25.

Telnet   *Telnet* is an interactive terminal emulation protocol. It allows a remote user to conduct an interactive session with a Telnet server. This session can appear to the client as if it were a local session.

Domain Name System   *Domain Name System (DNS)* allows hosts to resolve hostnames to an Internet Protocol (IP) address. IP is discussed in the section "The Internet Layer" that follows. The default port used by name queries for this service is 53.

Remote Desktop Protocol   The *Remote Desktop Protocol (RDP)* is becoming more common in the workplace, and it allows Windows-based terminal servers to run on port 3389 by default.

Simple Network Management Protocol   *Simple Network Management Protocol (SNMP)* is a management tool that allows communications between network devices and a management console. Most routers, bridges, and intelligent hubs can communicate using SNMP.

Post Office Protocol   *Post Office Protocol (POP)* is a protocol used for receiving email. It enables the implementation of advanced features, and it is a standard interface in many email servers. The default port for version 3 (POP3) is 110. In its place, many systems now use the *Internet Message Access Protocol (IMAP)*, which uses port 143 by default. The primary difference between the two is that POP was originally created to move email to your client machine and not keep it on the server, whereas IMAP was intended to store the email on the server and allow you to access it from there. Although those remain default options, today you can configure POP not to delete from the server automatically and IMAP to do so. For this reason, most email providers allow you to use either POP or IMAP and even change between them.

One of the key things to know when securing any network is that you should run only the protocols needed for operations. Make certain that *antiquated protocols*—those that were once needed but now serve no purpose—are removed. If you do not remove them, you are leaving an opening for an attacker to access your system through weaknesses in that protocol.

The Host-to-Host or Transport Layer

The *Host-to-Host layer*, also called the *Transport layer*, provides the Application layer with session and datagram communications services. The *Transmission Control Protocol (TCP)* and *User Datagram Protocol (UDP)* operate at this layer. These two protocols provide a huge part of the functionality of the TCP/IP network:

TCP   TCP is responsible for providing a reliable, one-to-one, connection-oriented session. TCP establishes a connection and ensures that the other end receives any packets sent. Two hosts communicate packet results with each other. TCP also ensures that packets are decoded and sequenced properly. This connection is persistent during the session. When the session ends, the connection is torn down.

UDP   UDP provides an unreliable connectionless communication method between hosts. UDP is considered a best-effort protocol, but it's considerably faster than TCP. The sessions don't establish a synchronized session like the kind used in TCP, and UDP doesn't guarantee error-free communications. The primary purpose of UDP is to send small packets of information. The application is responsible for acknowledging the correct reception of the data.

The Internet Layer

The *Internet layer* is responsible for routing, IP addressing, and packaging. The Internet layer protocols accomplish most of the behind-the-scenes work in establishing the ability to exchange information between hosts. The following is an explanation of the four standard protocols of the Internet layer:

Internet Protocol   *Internet Protocol (IP)* is a routable protocol that is responsible for IP addressing. IP also fragments and reassembles message packets. IP only routes information; it doesn't verify it for accuracy. Accuracy checking is the responsibility of TCP. IP determines if a destination is known and, if so, routes the information to that destination. If the destination is unknown, IP sends the packet to the router, which sends it on.

Address Resolution Protocol   *Address Resolution Protocol (ARP)* is responsible for resolving IP addresses to Network Interface layer addresses, including hardware addresses. ARP can resolve an IP address to a *Media Access Control (MAC)* address. MAC addresses are used to identify hardware network devices, such as a network interface card (NIC).

> You'll notice the acronym *MAC* used a lot. It's also used to identify *Mandatory Access Control*, which defines how access control operates in an authentication model. You'll also see *MAC* used in cryptography, where it stands for *Message Authentication Code*. This MAC verifies that an algorithm is accurate.

Internet Control Message Protocol   *Internet Control Message Protocol (ICMP)* provides maintenance and reporting functions. The Ping program uses it. When a user wants to test connectivity to another host, they can enter the PING command with the IP address, and the user's system will test connectivity to the other host's system. If connectivity is good, ICMP will return data to the originating host. ICMP will also report if a destination is unreachable. Routers and other network devices report path information between hosts with ICMP.

The Network Access Layer

The lowest level of the TCP/IP suite is the *Network Access (or Interface) layer.* This layer is responsible for placing and removing packets on the physical network through communications with the network adapters in the host. This process allows TCP/IP to work with virtually any type of network topology or technology with little modification. If a new physical network topology were installed—say, a 10 GB Fiber Ethernet connection—TCP/IP would only need to know how to communicate with the network controller in order to function properly. TCP/IP can also communicate with more than one network topology simultaneously. This allows the protocol to be used in virtually any environment.

IPv4 and IPv6

The TCP/IP protocol suite in use today has been around since the earliest days of the Internet—prior to it even being known by that name. The remarkable fact that it has been able to scale to the level it is used at today is testament to the forward thinking of those involved in its creation.

Several years back, however, a panic arose amid fears that there would not be enough IP addresses to assign to every host needing to connect. The current numbering system, known as IP version 4 (IPv4) even though no prior versions were released publically, is what is described throughout this chapter and is still widely in use today. IP version 6 (IPv6) was introduced several years ago to replace IPv4, but it has not yet done so, and most systems currently support both at the Internet layer.

The key things to know for the exam are that IPv6 supports 128-bit addresses, whereas IPv4 supports 32-bit addresses (see "Network Address Translation" later in this chapter), and IPv6 includes mandatory IPSec security (see "Internet Protocol Security" later in this chapter).

Understanding Encapsulation

One of the key points in understanding this layering process is the concept of encapsulation. *Encapsulation* allows a transport protocol to be sent across the network and utilized by the equivalent service or protocol at the receiving host. Figure 3.2 shows how email is encapsulated as it moves from the application protocols through the transport and Internet protocols. Each layer adds header information as the email moves down the layers.

FIGURE 3.2   The encapsulation process of an email message

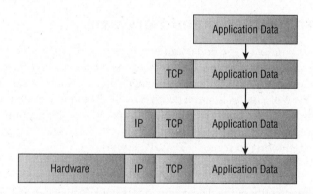

Transmission of the packet between the two hosts occurs through the physical connection in the network adapter. Figure 3.3 illustrates this process between two hosts. What's shown in the figure isn't comprehensive, but it illustrates the process of message transmission.

FIGURE 3.3   An email message that an email client sent to an email server across the Internet

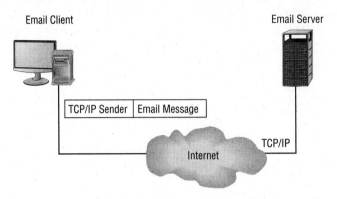

After it is encapsulated, the message is sent to the server. Notice that in Figure 3.3 the message is sent via the Internet; it could have just as easily been sent locally. The email client doesn't know how the message is delivered, and the server application doesn't care how the message got there. This makes designing and implementing services such as email possible in a global or Internet environment.

Working with Protocols and Services

It's imperative that you have a basic understanding of protocols and services to pass this exam. CompTIA recommends that you already hold the Network+ certification before undertaking this exam, although it isn't a requirement. In case you're weak in some areas, the following sections will discuss in more detail how TCP/IP hosts communicate with each other. We'll discuss the concepts of ports, handshakes, and application interfaces. The objective isn't to make you an expert on this subject but to help you understand what you're dealing with when attempting to secure a TCP/IP network.

The majority of the discussion in this book focuses on TCP/IP as the networking protocol since it is used in almost every implementation. Know, however, that TCP/IP is not the only networking protocol and Microsoft's implementation of *NetBIOS* (Network Basic Input Output System) was the default in early versions of Windows. Since then, NetBIOS has been adapted to run on top of TCP/IP, and it is still widely used for name resolution and registration in Windows-based environments.

Well-Known Ports

Simply stated, *ports* identify how a communication process occurs. Ports are special addresses that allow communication between hosts. A port number is added from the originator, indicating which port to communicate with on a server. If a server has a port defined and available for use, it will send back a message accepting the request. If the port isn't valid, the server will refuse the connection. The *Internet Assigned Numbers Authority (IANA)* has defined a list of ports called *well-known ports*.

> You can see the full description of the ports defined by IANA on this website: www.iana.org/assignments/service-names-port-numbers /service-names-port-numbers.xhtml. Many thousands of ports are available for use by servers and clients.

A port address or number is nothing more than a bit of additional information added either to the TCP or UDP message. This information is added in the header of the packet. The layer below it encapsulates the message with its header.

Many of the services you'll use in the normal course of using the Internet use the TCP port numbers identified in Table 3.1. Table 3.2 identifies some of the more common, well-known UDP ports. You will note that some services use both TCP and UDP ports, whereas many use only one or the other. (Those entries in the tables preceded by an asterisk [*] are ones to which CompTIA asks you pay particular attention when studying for this exam.)

TABLE 3.1   Well-known TCP ports

TCP Port Number	Service
20	FTP (data channel)
*21	FTP (control channel)
*22	SSH and SCP
23	Telnet
*25	SMTP
49	TACACS authentication service
*80	HTTP (used for the World Wide Web)
*110	POP3

TABLE 3.1   *Well-known TCP ports (continued)*

TCP Port Number	Service
115	SFTP
119	NNTP
137	NetBIOS name service
138	NetBIOS datagram service
*139	NetBIOS session service
*143	IMAP
389	LDAP
*443	HTTPS (used for secure web connections)
989	FTPS (data channel)
990	FTPS (control channel)
3389	MS WBT Server

TABLE 3.2   Well-known UDP ports

UDP Port Number	Service
*22	SSH and SCP
49	TACACS authentication service
*53	DNS name queries
69	Trivial File Transfer Protocol (TFTP)
*80	HTTP (used for the World Wide Web)
137	NetBIOS name service
138	NetBIOS datagram service
*139	NetBIOS session service
*143	IMAP

UDP Port Number	Service
161	SNMP
389	LDAP
989	FTPS (data channel)
990	FTPS (control channel)
3389	MS WBT Server

The early documentation for these ports specified that ports below 1024 were restricted to administrative uses. However, enforcement of this restriction has been voluntary, and it is creating problems for computer security professionals. As you can see, each of these ports potentially requires different security considerations, depending on the application to which it's assigned. All of the ports allow access to your network; even if you establish a firewall, you must have these ports open if you want to provide email or web services.

In Exercise 3.1, you'll learn how to view the active TCP and UDP ports.

EXERCISE 3.1

Viewing the Active TCP and UDP Ports

As an administrator, you should know what ports are active on your server. To view the active TCP and UDP ports, follow these steps:

1. Go to a command prompt. To do this in Windows, enter **CMD** at the Run prompt. On a Linux server, open a command window.

2. Enter the command **netstat**.

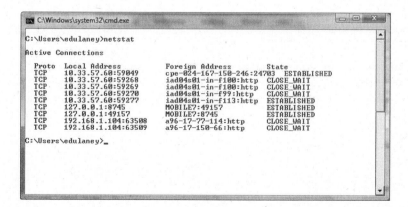

3. Few items should appear. Now enter the command **netstat -a**. The --a parameter tells the netstat command to display all of the information.

4. Note the ports that are listed.

5. View the services file (*systemroot*\system32\drivers\etc\services in Windows or /etc/services in Linux). Although the file is not actively read by the system, this file lists the services and the ports used for the most common network operations.

```
C:\Windows\system32\cmd.exe - more services
# Copyright (c) 1993-2004 Microsoft Corp.
#
# This file contains port numbers for well-known services defined by IANA
#
# Format:
#
# <service name>   <port number>/<protocol>   [aliases...]   [#<comment>]
#
echo              7/tcp
echo              7/udp
discard           9/tcp     sink null
discard           9/udp     sink null
systat            11/tcp    users                    #Active users
systat            11/udp    users                    #Active users
daytime           13/tcp
daytime           13/udp
qotd              17/tcp    quote                    #Quote of the day
qotd              17/udp    quote                    #Quote of the day
chargen           19/tcp    ttytst source            #Character generator
chargen           19/udp    ttytst source            #Character generator
ftp-data          20/tcp                             #FTP, data
ftp               21/tcp                             #FTP, control
ssh               22/tcp                             #SSH Remote Login Protocol
telnet            23/tcp
smtp              25/tcp    mail                     #Simple Mail Transfer Protoc
ol
time              37/tcp    timserver
time              37/udp    timserver
rlp               39/udp    resource                 #Resource Location Protocol
nameserver        42/tcp    name                     #Host Name Server
nameserver        42/udp    name                     #Host Name Server
nicname           43/tcp    whois
domain            53/tcp                             #Domain Name Server
domain            53/udp                             #Domain Name Server
bootps            67/udp    dhcps                    #Bootstrap Protocol Server
bootpc            68/udp    dhcpc                    #Bootstrap Protocol Client
tftp              69/udp                             #Trivial File Transfer
gopher            70/tcp
finger            79/tcp
http              80/tcp    www www-http             #World Wide Web
hosts2-ns         81/tcp                             #HOSTS2 Name Server
hosts2-ns         81/udp                             #HOSTS2 Name Server
kerberos          88/tcp    krb5 kerberos-sec        #Kerberos
kerberos          88/udp    krb5 kerberos-sec        #Kerberos
hostname          101/tcp   hostnames                #NIC Host Name Server
iso-tsap          102/tcp                            #ISO-TSAP Class 0
rtelnet           107/tcp                            #Remote Telnet Service
pop2              109/tcp   postoffice               #Post Office Protocol - Vers
ion 2
pop3              110/tcp                             #Post Office Protocol - Vers
ion 3
sunrpc            111/tcp   rpcbind portmap          #SUN Remote Procedure Call
sunrpc            111/udp   rpcbind portmap          #SUN Remote Procedure Call
auth              113/tcp   ident tap                #Identification Protocol
uucp-path         117/tcp
sqlserv           118/tcp                            #SQL Services
-- More (17%) --
```

TCP Three-Way Handshake

TCP, which is a *connection-oriented protocol*, establishes a session using a *three-way handshake*. A host called a *client* originates this connection. The client sends a TCP segment, or message, to the server. This client segment includes an *initial sequence number (ISN)* for the connection and a window size. The server responds with a TCP segment that contains its ISN and a value indicating its buffer, or window size. The client then sends back an acknowledgment of the server's sequence number.

Figure 3.4 shows this three-way handshake occurring between a client and a server. When the session or connection is over, a similar process occurs, using four steps to close the connection.

A web request uses the TCP connection process to establish the connection between the client and the server. After this occurs, the two systems communicate with each other; the server uses TCP port 80. The same thing occurs when an email connection is made, with the difference being that the client (assuming it's using POP3) uses port 110.

FIGURE 3.4   The TCP connection process

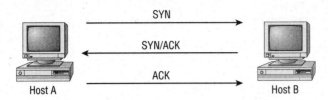

Host A   Host B

SYN

SYN/ACK

ACK

In this way, a server can handle many requests simultaneously. Each session has a different sequence number even though all sessions use the same port. All of the communications in any given session use this sequence number to keep from confusing the sessions.

Application Programming Interface

Interfacing to TCP/IP is much simpler than interfacing to earlier network models. A well-defined and well-established set of *application programming interfaces (APIs)* is available from most software companies. APIs allow programmers to create interfaces to the protocol suite. When a programmer needs to create a web-enabled application, they can call or use one of these APIs to make the connection, send or receive data, and end the connection. The APIs are prewritten, and they make the job considerably easier than manually coding all of the connection information.

Microsoft uses the *Windows Sockets (Winsock) API* to interface to the protocol suite. It can access either TCP or UDP protocols to accomplish the needed task. Figure 3.5 illustrates how Winsock connects to the TCP/IP protocol suite.

FIGURE 3.5   The Winsock interface

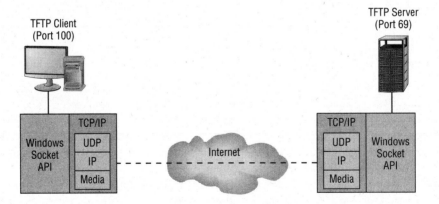

Other Protocols to Know

Although it would be nice if every exam objective fit neatly into a single discussion, there are often one or two that stand apart from the others. In the case of the Security+ exam objectives related to common protocols and services, two merit individual attention:

- *iSCSI (Internet Small Computer Systems Interface)* uses ports 860 and 3260, by default, for allowing data storage and transfers across the existing network. As such, it enables the creation of storage area networks (SANs).

- As opposed to iSCSI, *Fibre Channel* was originally created for the same purpose but intended to work only on fiber-based networks. The requirement of fiber has fallen by the wayside and, even though it is still called Fibre Channel, it uses SCSI to create a SAN across any existing network. One protocol commonly used with it is *FCoE (Fibre Channel over Ethernet)*. FCoE is not routable at the IP layer (iSCSI is), and thus it cannot work across large networks.

Designing a Secure Network

When you design the *security topology* of your network, you are concerned with the access methods, security, and technologies used. These issues have to be factored into the physical elements that comprise the network. Seven common elements that factor into the security topology and are primary areas of concern are the following:

- Demilitarized zones (DMZs)
- Subnetting
- VLANs
- Remote access
- NAT
- Telephony
- NACs

Demilitarized Zones

A *demilitarized zone (DMZ)* is an area where you can place a public server for access by people you might not trust otherwise. By isolating a server in a DMZ, you can hide or remove access to other areas of your network. You can still access the server using your network, but others aren't able to access further network resources. This can be accomplished using firewalls to isolate your network.

When establishing a DMZ, you assume that the person accessing the resource isn't necessarily someone you would trust with other information. Figure 3.6 shows a server placed in a DMZ. Notice that the rest of the network isn't visible to external users. This arrangement lowers the threat of intrusion in the internal network.

FIGURE 3.6 A typical DMZ

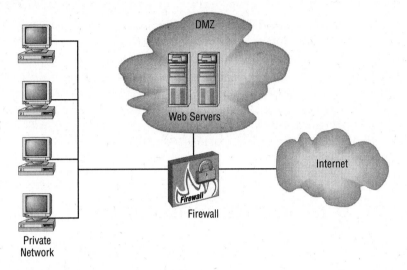

Any time you want to separate public information from private information, a DMZ is an acceptable option.

The easiest way to create a DMZ is to use a firewall that can transmit in three directions:

- To the internal network
- To the external world (Internet)
- To the public information you're sharing (the DMZ)

From there, you can decide what traffic goes where; for example, HTTP traffic would be sent to the DMZ, and email would go to the internal network.

A host that exists outside the DMZ and is open to the public is often called a *bastion host*. Routers and firewalls, because of where they must exist, often constitute bastion hosts.

Subnetting

When designing a network, one of the first issues you must consider is how to divide it. It can be divided logically, physically, topologically, and almost any other way you can think of. Such a division is based on the subnet values. *Subnetting* a network means using the subnet mask value to divide a network into smaller components. This gives you more networks but a smaller number of hosts available on each.

Subnetting uses bits from the node portion of the host address to create the additional networks, and there are two primary reasons for using it: to use IP addresses more effectively and, more importantly for this exam, to make the network more secure and manageable. It accomplishes the latter by confining traffic to the network that it needs to be on, reducing overall network traffic and creating more broadcast domains, thus reducing the range of network-wide broadcast traffic.

IP addressing is a subject on the Network+ exam and is just barely touched on in Security+, though CompTIA expects you to know the basics. In addition to understanding that subnetting is how networks are divided, you should read through RFCs 1466, www.faqs.org/rfcs/rfc1466.html, and 1918, www.faqs.org/rfcs/rfc1918.html.

Virtual Local Area Networks

A *virtual local area network (VLAN)* allows you to create groups of users and systems and segment them on the network. This segmentation lets you hide segments of the network from other segments and thereby control access. You can also set up VLANs to control the paths that data takes to get from one point to another. A VLAN is a good way to contain network traffic to a certain area in a network.

Think of a VLAN as a network of hosts that act as if a physical wire connects them, even though there is no such wire between them.

On a LAN, hosts can communicate with each other through broadcasts, and no forwarding devices, such as routers, are needed. As the LAN grows, so too does the number of broadcasts. Shrinking the size of the LAN by segmenting it into smaller groups (VLANs) reduces the size of the broadcast domains. The advantages of doing this include reducing the scope of the broadcasts, improving performance and manageability, and decreasing dependence on the physical topology. From the standpoint of this exam, however, the key benefit is that VLANs can increase security by allowing users with similar data sensitivity levels to be segmented together.

Figure 3.7 illustrates the creation of three VLANs in a single network.

FIGURE 3.7   A typical segmented VLAN

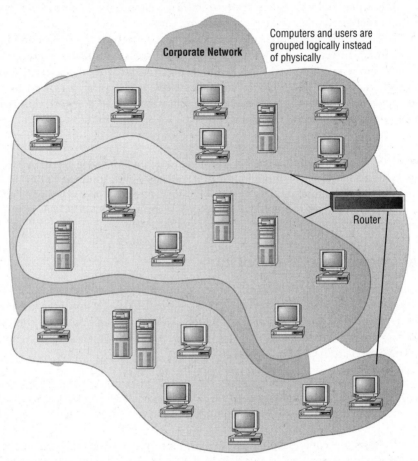

Tunneling protocols add a capability to the network: the ability to create tunnels between networks that can be more secure, support additional protocols, and provide virtual paths between systems. The best way to think of tunneling is to imagine sensitive data being encapsulated in other packets that are sent across the public network. Once they're received at the other end, the sensitive data is stripped from the other packets and recompiled into its original form.

The most common protocols used for tunneling are as follows:

Point-to-Point Tunneling Protocol   *Point-to-Point Tunneling Protocol (PPTP)* supports encapsulation in a single point-to-point environment. PPTP encapsulates and encrypts PPP packets. This makes PPTP a favorite low-end protocol for networks. The negotiation between the two ends of a PPTP connection is done in the clear. After the negotiation is performed, the channel is encrypted. This is one of the major weaknesses of PPTP. A *packet-capture device*, such as a sniffer, that captures the negotiation process can potentially use that information to determine the connection type and information about how the tunnel works. Microsoft developed PPTP and supports it on most of the company's products. PPTP uses port 1723 and TCP for connections.

Layer 2 Forwarding   *Layer 2 Forwarding (L2F)* was created by Cisco as a method of creating tunnels primarily for dial-up connections. It's similar in capability to PPP, and it shouldn't be used over WANs. L2F provides authentication, but it doesn't provide encryption. L2F uses port 1701 and TCP for connections.

Layer 2 Tunneling Protocol   Relatively recently, Microsoft and Cisco agreed to combine their respective tunneling protocols into one protocol: *Layer 2 Tunneling Protocol (L2TP)*. L2TP is a hybrid of PPTP and L2F. It's primarily a point-to-point protocol. L2TP supports multiple network protocols and can be used in networks besides TCP/IP. L2TP works over IPX, SNA, and IP, so it can be used as a bridge across many types of systems. The major problem with L2TP is that it doesn't provide data security: The information isn't encrypted. Security can be provided by protocols such as IPSec. L2TP uses port 1701 and UDP for connections.

Secure Shell   *Secure Shell (SSH)* is a tunneling protocol originally designed for Unix systems. It uses encryption to establish a secure connection between two systems. SSH also provides alternative, security-equivalent applications for such Unix standards as Telnet, FTP, and many other communications-oriented applications. SSH is now available for use on Windows systems as well. This makes it the preferred method of security for Telnet and other cleartext-oriented programs in the Unix environment. SSH uses port 22 and TCP for connections.

Internet Protocol Security   *Internet Protocol Security (IPSec)* isn't a tunneling protocol, but it's used in conjunction with tunneling protocols. IPSec is oriented primarily toward LAN-to-LAN connections, but it can also be used with dial-up connections. IPSec provides secure authentication and encryption of data and headers; this makes it a good choice for security. IPSec can work in either Tunneling mode or Transport mode. In Tunneling mode, the data or payload and message headers are encrypted. Transport mode encrypts only the payload.

 Real World Scenario

Connecting Remote Network Users

Your company wants to support network connections for remote users. These users will use the Internet to access desktop systems and other resources in the network. What would you advise the company to consider?

> *You should advise your organization to implement a tunneling protocol that supports security. A good solution would be a VPN connection that uses IPSec. You might also want to explore protocols like SSL, TLS, and SSH as alternatives. All of these protocols offer security as a part of their connection process.*

Remote Access

Tunneling refers to creating a virtual dedicated connection between two systems or networks. You create the tunnel between the two ends by encapsulating the data in a mutually agreed-upon protocol for transmission. In most tunnels, the data passed through the tunnel appears at the other side as part of the network.

Tunneling protocols usually include data security as well as encryption. Several popular standards have emerged for tunneling, with the most popular being the Layer 2 Tunneling Protocol (L2TP).

Tunneling sends private data across a public network by placing (encapsulating) that data into other packets. Most tunnels are virtual private networks (VPNs).

Figure 3.8 shows a connection being made between two networks across the Internet. To each end of the network, this appears to be a single connection.

FIGURE 3.8   A typical tunnel

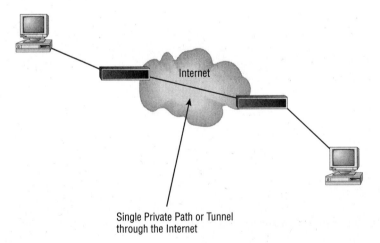

Single Private Path or Tunnel
through the Internet

Remote Access Services (RAS) refers to any server service that offers the ability to connect remote systems. The current Microsoft product for Windows-based clients is called

Routing and Remote Access Services (RRAS), but it was previously known as **Remote Access Services (RAS)**. Because of this, you'll encounter the term *RAS* used interchangeably to describe both the Microsoft product and the process of connecting to remote systems.

The RAS connection is accomplished via dial-up (*plain-old telephone service [POTS]* and a modem) or network technologies such as VPNs, ISDN, DSL, and cable modems. RAS connections may be secure or in the clear, depending on the protocols that are used in the connection.

A popular method of remote access that allows customer service technicians to take over the mouse and keyboard functions of a remote workstation is through the use of PC Anywhere and similar remote connection/virtual network programs. A major issue with Virtual Network Computing (VNC) is that you are leaving open a door into the network that anyone may stumble upon. By default, most of these programs start the server service automatically, and it is running even when it is not truly needed. We highly recommended that you configure the service as a manual start service and launch it *only* when needed to access the host. At all other times, that service should be shut down.

Network Address Translation

Network Address Translation (NAT) creates a unique opportunity to assist in the security of a network. Originally, NAT extended the number of usable Internet addresses. Now it allows an organization to present a single address to the Internet for all computer connections. The NAT server provides IP addresses to the hosts or systems in the network and tracks inbound and outbound traffic.

A company that uses NAT presents a limited number of connections to the network. These connections may be through a router or a NAT server. The only information that an intruder will be able to get is that the connection has a single address.

NAT effectively hides your network from the world, making it much harder to determine what systems exist on the other side of the router. The NAT server effectively operates as a firewall for the network. Most new routers support NAT; it provides a simple, inexpensive firewall for small networks.

 It's important to understand that NAT acts as a proxy between the local area network (which can be using private IP addresses) and the Internet. Not only can NAT save IP addresses, but it can also act as a firewall.

Most NAT implementations assign internal hosts private IP address numbers and use public addresses only for the NAT to translate to and communicate with the outside world. The private address ranges, all of which are non-routable, are as follows:

10.0.0.0–10.255.255.255

172.16.0.0–172.31.255.255

192.168.0.0–192.168.255.255

Figure 3.9 shows a router providing NAT services to a network. The router presents a single address for all external connections on the Internet.

FIGURE 3.9 A typical Internet connection to a local network

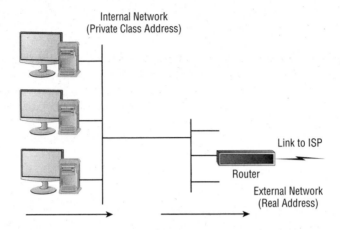

In addition to NAT, *Port Address Translation (PAT)* is possible. Whereas NAT can use multiple public IP addresses, PAT uses a single one and shares the port with the network. Because it is using only a single port, PAT is much more limited and is typically used only on small and home-based networks. Microsoft's Internet Connection Sharing is an example of a PAT implementation. Additionally, Destination NAT (DNAT) can be used to redirect traffic destined for a virtual host to the real host.

Telephony

When telephone technology is married with information technology, the result is known as *telephony*. A breach in your telephony infrastructure is just as devastating as any other violation and can lead to the loss of valuable data.

With the exodus from traditional landlines to Voice over IP (VoIP) in full swing to help companies save money, it is imperative that you treat this part of the network the same as you would any other. VoIP can be easily sniffed with tools such as Cain & Abel (www.oxid.it), and it is susceptible to denial-of-service (DoS) attacks because it rides on UDP. There is also an outage issue with VoIP in cases where the data network goes down and you lose the telephony as well. SecureLogix provides one source of available information on IP telephony security: www.securelogix.com/ip-telephony-security .html. Cisco also published a white paper titled "IP Telephony Security Operations Guide to Best Practices," which can be found here:

    www.cisco.com/en/US/netsol/ns340/ns394/ns165/ns391/networking_solutions
    _design_guidance09186a00801f8e47.html

From a security standpoint, the biggest problem with VoIP and data being on the same line is that they are then both vulnerable in the event of a PBX (private branch exchange) attack.

Network Access Control

Operational security issues include *network access control (NAC)*, authentication, and security topologies after the network installation is complete. Issues include the daily operations of the network, connections to other networks, backup plans, and recovery plans. In short, operational security encompasses everything that isn't related to design or physical security in your network. Instead of focusing on the physical components where the data is stored, such as the server, the focus is now on the topology and connections.

Some vendors use the acronym NAC to signify network *admission* control rather than the more commonly accepted network *access* control.

The best way to think of NAC is as a set of standards defined by the network for clients attempting to access it. Usually, NAC requires that clients be virus free and adhere to specified policies before allowing them on the network.

Understanding the Various Network Infrastructure Devices

Large multinational as well as small and medium-sized corporations are building networks of enormous complexity and sophistication. These networks work by using miles of both wired and wireless technologies. Whether the network is totally wire and fiber based or totally wireless, the method of transmitting data from one place to another opens up vulnerabilities and opportunities for exploitation. Vulnerabilities appear whenever an opportunity exists to intercept information from the media.

The devices briefly described here are the components you'll typically encounter in a network.

Many network devices contain firmware with which you interact during configuration. For security purposes, you must authenticate in order to make configuration changes and do so initially by using the default account(s). Make sure the default password is changed after installation on any network device; otherwise, you are leaving that device open for anyone recognizing the hardware to access it using the known factory password.

Firewalls

Firewalls are one of the first lines of defense in a network. There are different types of firewalls, and they can be either standalone systems or included in other devices such as routers or servers. You can find firewall solutions that are marketed as hardware only and others that are software only. Many firewalls, however, consist of add-in software that is available for servers or workstations.

> Although solutions are sold as "hardware only," the hardware still runs some sort of software. It may be hardened and in ROM to prevent tampering, and it may be customized—but software is present nonetheless.

The basic purpose of a firewall is to isolate one network from another. Firewalls are available as appliances, meaning they're installed as the primary device separating two networks. *Appliances* are freestanding devices that operate in a largely self-contained manner, requiring less maintenance and support than a server-based product.

> To understand the concept of a firewall, it helps to know where the term comes from. In days of old, dwellings used to be built so close together that if a fire broke out in one, it could easily destroy a block or more before it could be contained. To decrease the risk of this happening, firewalls were built between buildings. The firewalls were huge brick walls that separated the buildings and kept a fire confined to one side. The same concept of restricting and confining is true in network firewalls. Traffic from the outside world hits the firewall and isn't allowed to enter the network unless otherwise invited.

The firewall shown in Figure 3.10 effectively limits access from outside networks, while allowing inside network users to access outside resources. The firewall in this illustration is also performing proxy functions, discussed later.

FIGURE 3.10   A proxy firewall blocking network access from external networks

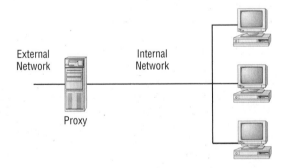

Firewalls function as one or more of the following:

- Packet filter
- Proxy firewall
- Stateful packet inspection firewall

 Although firewalls are often associated with outside traffic, you can place a firewall anywhere. For example, if you want to isolate one portion of your internal network from others, you can place a firewall between them.

Packet Filter Firewalls

A firewall operating as a *packet filter* passes or blocks traffic to specific addresses based on the type of application. The packet filter doesn't analyze the data of a packet; it decides whether to pass it based on the packet's addressing information. For instance, a packet filter may allow web traffic on port 80 and block Telnet traffic on port 23. This type of filtering is included in many routers. If a received packet request asks for a port that isn't authorized, the filter may reject the request or simply ignore it. Many packet filters can also specify which IP addresses can request which ports and allow or deny them based on the security settings of the firewall.

Packet filters are growing in sophistication and capability. A packet filter firewall can allow any traffic that you specify as acceptable. For example, if you want web users to access your site, you configure the packet filter firewall to allow data on port 80 to enter. If every network were exactly the same, firewalls would come with default port settings hard-coded, but networks vary, so the firewalls don't include such settings.

Decide Which Traffic to Allow Through

As an administrator, you need to survey your network and decide which traffic should be allowed through the firewall. What traffic will you allow in, and what will you block at the firewall?

The following is a list of only the most common TCP ports. Check the boxes indicating whether you'll allow data using this port through the firewall.

TCP Port Number	Service	Yes	No
20	FTP (data channel)	☐	☐
21	FTP (control channel)	☐	☐
23	Telnet	☐	☐

(continued)

TCP Port Number	Service	Yes	No
25	SMTP	☐	☐
49	TACACS & TACACS+ authentication service	☐	☐
80	HTTP (used for World Wide Web)	☐	☐
110	POP3	☐	☐
119	NNTP	☐	☐
137, 138, and 139	NetBIOS session service	☐	☐
143	IMAP	☐	☐
389	LDAP	☐	☐
443	HTTPS (used for secure web connections)	☐	☐
636	LDAP (SSL)	☐	☐

Proxy Firewalls

A *proxy firewall* can be thought of as an intermediary between your network and any other network. Proxy firewalls are used to process requests from an outside network; the proxy firewall examines the data and makes rule-based decisions about whether the request should be forwarded or refused. The proxy intercepts all of the packets and reprocesses them for use internally. This process includes hiding IP addresses.

 When you consider the concept of hiding IP addresses, think of Network Address Translation (NAT), discussed earlier in this chapter.

The proxy firewall provides better security than packet filtering because of the increased intelligence that a proxy firewall offers. Requests from internal network users are routed through the proxy. The proxy, in turn, repackages the request and sends it along, thereby isolating the user from the external network. The proxy can also offer caching, should the same request be made again, and it can increase the efficiency of data delivery.

A proxy firewall typically uses two network interface cards (NICs). This type of firewall is referred to as a *dual-homed firewall*. One of the cards is connected to the outside network, and the other is connected to the internal network. The proxy software manages the connection between the two NICs. This setup segregates the two networks from each other and offers increased security.

 Real World Scenario

Dual-Homed Proxy Firewall

You're the network administrator of a small network. You're installing a new firewall server. After you complete the installation, you notice that the network doesn't appear to be routing traffic through the firewall and that inbound requests aren't being blocked. This situation presents a security problem for the network because you've been getting unusual network traffic lately.

The most likely solution to this problem deals with the fact that the server offers the ability to use IP forwarding in a dual-homed server. IP forwarding bypasses your firewall and uses the server as a router. Even though the two networks are effectively isolated, the new router is doing its job well, and it's routing IP traffic.

You'll need to verify that IP forwarding and routing services aren't running on this server.

 Any time you have a system that is configured with more than one IP address, it can be said to be *multihomed*.

The proxy function can occur at either the application level or the circuit level.

Application-level proxy functions read the individual commands of the protocols that are being served. This type of server is advanced and must know the rules and capabilities of the protocol used. An implementation of this type of proxy must know the difference between GET and PUT operations, for example, and have rules specifying how to execute them.

A *circuit-level proxy* creates a circuit between the client and the server and doesn't deal with the contents of the packets that are being processed.

A unique application-level proxy server must exist for each protocol supported. Many proxy servers also provide full auditing, accounting, and other usage information that wouldn't normally be kept by a circuit-level proxy server.

Stateful Packet Inspection Firewalls

The last section on firewalls focuses on the concept of stateful inspection. To understand the terminology, you should know that what came before was referred to as *stateless*.

Stateless firewalls make decisions based on the data that comes in—the packet, for example—and not based on any complex decisions.

Stateful inspection is also referred to as *stateful packet inspection (SPI) filtering*. Most of the devices used in networks don't keep track of how information is routed or used. After a packet is passed, the packet and path are forgotten. In stateful inspection (or stateful packet filtering), records are kept using a state table that tracks every communications channel; it remembers where the packet came from and where the next one should come from.

> The real difference between SPI and simple packet filtering is that SPI tracks the entire conversation while packet filtering looks only at the current packet.

Stateful inspections occur at all levels of the network and provide additional security, especially in connectionless protocols, such as User Datagram Protocol and Internet Control Message Protocol. This adds complexity to the process. Denial-of-service attacks present a challenge because flooding techniques are used to overload the state table and effectively cause the firewall to shut down or reboot.

> For the exam, remember that pure packet filtering has no real intelligence. It allows data to pass through a port if that port is configured and otherwise discards it—it doesn't examine the packets. Stateful packet filtering, however, has intelligence in that it keeps track of every communications channel.

Routers

The primary instrument used for connectivity between two or more networks is the *router*. Routers work by providing a path between the networks. A router has two connections that are used to join the networks. Each connection has its own address (or more) and appears as a valid address in its respective network. Figure 3.11 illustrates a router connected between two LANs.

Routers are intelligent devices, and they store information about the networks to which they're connected. Most routers can be configured to operate as packet-filtering firewalls. Many of the newer routers also provide advanced firewall functions.

Routers, in conjunction with a Channel Service Unit/Data Service Unit (CSU/DSU), are also used to translate from LAN framing to WAN framing (for example, a router that connects a 100BaseT network to a T1 network). This is needed because the network protocols are different in LANs and WANs. Such routers are referred to as *border routers*. They serve as the outside connection of a LAN to a WAN, and they operate at the border of your network. Like the border patrols of many countries, border routers decide who can come in and under what conditions.

FIGURE 3.11   Router connecting two LANs

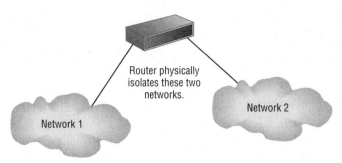

Router physically isolates these two networks.

Network 1

Network 2

Dividing internal networks into two or more subnetworks is a common use for routers. Routers can also be connected internally to other routers, effectively creating *zones* that operate autonomously. Figure 3.12 illustrates a corporate network that uses a combination of a border router for connection to an ISP and internal routers to create autonomous networks for communications. This type of connection keeps local network traffic off the backbone of the corporate network, and it provides additional security to internal users.

FIGURE 3.12   A corporate network implementing routers for segmentation and security

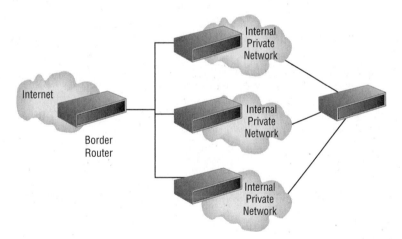

Internal Private Network

Internet

Internal Private Network

Border Router

Internal Private Network

 Because broadcasts don't traverse routers, network segmentation decreases traffic.

Routers establish communication by maintaining tables about destinations and local connections. A router contains information about the systems connected to it and where

to send requests if the destination isn't known. These tables grow as connections are made through the router.

Routers usually communicate routing and other information using one of three standard protocols: Routing Information Protocol (RIP), Border Gateway Protocol (BGP), or Open Shortest Path First (OSPF). Routing can occur interior to the network or exterior.

Routers are your first line of defense, and they must be configured to pass only traffic that is authorized by network administrators. In effect, a router can function as a firewall if it's configured properly. The best approach is layered; a router shouldn't take the place of a firewall but simply augment it.

The routes themselves can be configured as static or dynamic. If they are static, they are edited manually and stay that way until changed. If they are dynamic, they learn of other routers around them and use information about those routers to build their routing tables.

Switches

Switches are multiport devices that improve network efficiency.

A switch typically contains a small amount of information about systems in a network— a table of MAC addresses as opposed to IP addresses. Using switches improves network efficiency over hubs or routers because of the virtual circuit capability. Switches also improve network security because the virtual circuits are more difficult to examine with network monitors. You can think of a switch as a device that has some of the best capabilities of routers and hubs combined.

The switch maintains limited routing information about nodes in the internal network, and it allows connections to systems like a hub or router. Figure 3.13 shows a switch in action between two workstations in a LAN.

The connection isn't usually secure or encrypted; the need for that, however, is diminished since the data doesn't leave the switched area.

FIGURE 3.13   Switching between two systems

For the exam, know that switches are used only internally because the switching they do is based on MAC addresses that are not routable. Routers, on the other hand, route based on IP address.

Load Balancers

Load balancing refers to shifting a load from one device to another. Most often the device in question is a server, but the term could be used for a hard drive, a CPU, or almost any device that you want to avoid overloading. Using a server as the device in question, balancing the load between multiple servers instead of relying on only one reduces the response time, maximizes throughput, and allows better allocation of resources.

A *load balancer* can be implemented as a software or hardware solution, and it is usually associated with a device—a router, a firewall, NAT appliance, and so on. In its most common implementation, a load balancer splits the traffic intended for a website into individual requests that are then rotated to redundant servers as they become available. (If a server that should be available is busy or down, it is taken out of the rotation.)

Proxies

A proxy is a device that acts on behalf of other(s).

In the interest of security, all internal user interaction with the Internet should be controlled through a *proxy server*. The proxy server should automatically block known malicious sites. The proxy server should cache often-accessed sites to improve performance.

Web Security Gateway

One of the newest buzzwords is *web security gateway*, which can be thought of as a proxy server (performing proxy and caching functions) with web protection software built in. Depending on the vendor, the "web protection" can range from a standard virus scanner on incoming packets to monitoring outgoing user traffic for red flags as well.

Potential red flags that the gateway can detect and/or prohibit include inappropriate content, trying to establish a peer-to-peer connection with a file-sharing site, instant messaging, and unauthorized tunneling. You can configure most web security gateways to block known HTTP/HTML exploits, strip ActiveX tags, strip Java applets, and block/strip cookies.

VPNs and VPN Concentrators

A *virtual private network (VPN)* is a private network connection that occurs through a public network. A private network provides security over an otherwise unsecure environment. VPNs can be used to connect LANs together across the Internet or other public networks. With a VPN, the remote end appears to be connected to the network as if it were connected locally. A VPN requires either special hardware to be installed or a VPN software package running on servers and workstations.

VPNs typically use a tunneling protocol, such as Layer 2 Tunneling Protocol, IPSec, or Point-to-Point Tunneling Protocol (PPTP). Figure 3.14 shows a remote network connected to a LAN using the Internet and a VPN. This connection appears to be a local connection, and all message traffic and protocols are available across the VPN.

FIGURE 3.14   Two LANs connected using a VPN across the Internet

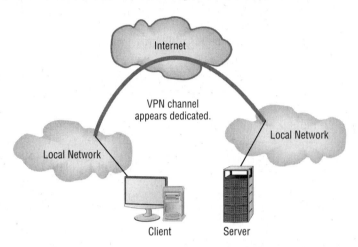

VPNs are becoming the connection of choice when establishing an extranet or intranet between two or more remote offices. The major security concern when using a VPN is encryption. PPTP offers some encryption capabilities, although they're weak. IPSec offers higher security, and it's becoming the encryption system used in many secure VPN environments.

 Even though a VPN is created through the Internet or other public network, the connection logically appears to be part of the local network. This is why a VPN connection that is used to establish a connection between two private networks across the Internet is considered a private connection or an extranet.

As mentioned earlier, VPNs are used to make connections between private networks across a public network, such as the Internet. These connections aren't guaranteed to be secure unless a tunneling protocol (such as PPTP) and an encryption system (such as IPSec) are used. A wide range of options, including proprietary technologies, is available for VPN support. Many of the large ISPs and data communications providers offer dedicated hardware with VPN capabilities. Many servers also provide software VPN capabilities for use between two networks.

VPN systems can be dedicated to a certain protocol, or they can pass whatever protocols they see on one end of the network to the other end. A pure VPN connection appears as a dedicated wired connection between the two network ends.

A *VPN concentrator* is a hardware device used to create remote access VPNs. The concentrator creates encrypted tunnel sessions between hosts, and many use two-factor authentication for additional security. Cisco models often incorporate Scalable Encryption Processing (SEP) modules to allow for hardware-based encryption and/or redundancy.

For purposes of the exam, whenever you see VPN, associate it with encryption and only allowing authorized remote users.

Intrusion Detection Systems

An *intrusion detection system (IDS)* is software that runs either on individual workstations or on network devices to monitor and track network activity. By using an IDS, a network administrator can configure the system to respond just like a burglar alarm. IDSs can be configured to evaluate system logs, look at suspicious network activity, and disconnect sessions that appear to violate security settings.

Many vendors have oversold the simplicity of these tools. They're quite involved and require a great deal of planning and maintenance to work effectively. Many manufacturers are selling IDSs with firewalls, and this area shows great promise. Firewalls by themselves will prevent many common attacks, but they don't usually have the intelligence or the reporting capabilities to monitor the entire network. In conjunction with a firewall, an IDS allows both a reactive posture with the firewall and a preventive posture with the IDS.

Figure 3.15 shows an IDS working in conjunction with a firewall to increase security.

FIGURE 3.15   An IDS and a firewall working together to secure a network

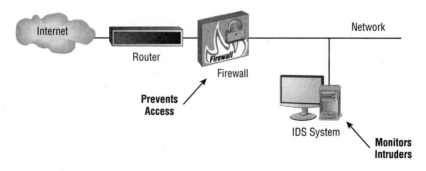

In the event that the firewall is compromised or penetrated, the IDS can react by disabling systems, ending sessions, and even potentially shutting down your network.

This arrangement provides a higher level of security than either device provides by itself. A section exploring IDS in more detail follows.

Understanding Intrusion Detection Systems

In the original *Walking Tall* movies, the sheriff puts small strips of clear tape on the hood of his car. Before getting in the vehicle, he would check the difficult-to-detect tape to see if it was broken. If it was, it tipped him off that someone had been messing beneath the hood and that saved his life. Do you have clear tape on your network?

IDSs are becoming integral parts of network monitoring. *Intrusion detection (ID)* is the process of monitoring events in a system or network to determine if an intrusion is occurring. An *intrusion* is defined as any activity or action that attempts to undermine or compromise the confidentiality, integrity, or availability of resources. Firewalls, as you may recall, were designed to prevent access to resources by an attacker. An IDS reports and monitors intrusion attempts.

Know the Resources Available in Linux

Security information is readily found at a number of Linux-related sites. The first to check is always the distribution vendor's site. Its pages usually provide an overview of Linux-related security issues with links to other relevant pages. You should also keep abreast of issues and problems posted at www.cert.org and www.linuxsecurity.com.

You can also find information on any Linux command through a number of utilities inherent in Linux:

- The man tool offers pages on each utility. For example, to find information about the setfacl tool, you can type **man setfacl**. It is a manual of commands and information.

- Most utilities have the built-in option of --help to offer information. From the command line, you can type **setfacl --help** to see a quick list of available options.

- The info utility shows the man pages as well.

- The whatis utility can show if there is more than one set of documentation on the system for the utility.

- The whereis utility lists all of the information it can find about locations associated with a file.

- The apropos utility uses the whatis database to find values and returns the short summary information.

It should be inherently understood that every network, regardless of size, should use a firewall. On a home-based network, a personal software firewall can be implemented to provide protection against attacks.

Several key terms are necessary to explain the technology behind intrusion detection:

Activity   An *activity* is an element of a data source that is of interest to the operator. This could include a specific occurrence of a type of activity that is suspicious. An example might be a TCP connection request that occurs repeatedly from the same IP address.

Administrator   The *administrator* is the person responsible for setting the security policy for an organization and is responsible for making decisions about the deployment and configuration of the IDS. The administrator should make decisions regarding alarm levels, historical logging, and session-monitoring capabilities. They're also responsible for determining the appropriate responses to attacks and ensuring that those responses are carried out.

Most organizations have an escalation chart. The administrator is rarely at the top of the chart but is always expected to be the one doing the most to keep incidents under control.

Alert   An alert is a message from the analyzer indicating that an event of interest has occurred. The alert contains information about the activity as well as specifics of the occurrence. An alert may be generated when an excessive amount of *Internet Control Message Protocol (ICMP)* traffic is occurring or when repeated logon attempts are failing. A certain level of traffic is normal for a network. Alerts occur when activities of a certain type exceed a preset threshold. For instance, you might want to generate an alert every time someone from inside your network pings the outside using the Ping program.

Analyzer   The *analyzer* is the component or process that analyzes the data collected by the sensor. It looks for suspicious activity among all of the data collected. Analyzers work by monitoring events and determining whether unusual activities are occurring, or they can use a rule-based process that is established when the IDS is configured.

Data Source   The *data source* is the raw information that the IDS uses to detect suspicious activity. The data source may include audit files, system logs, or the network traffic as it occurs.

Event   An *event* is an occurrence in a data source that indicates that a suspicious activity has occurred (once it's been analyzed and shown to be security-related, then it becomes known as an incident). It may generate an alert. Events are logged for future reference. They also typically trigger a notification that something unusual may be happening in the network. An IDS might begin logging events if the volume of inbound email connections suddenly spiked; this event might be an indication that someone was probing your network. The event might trigger an alert if a deviation from normal network traffic patterns occurred or if an activity threshold was crossed.

Manager   The *manager* is the component or process the operator uses to manage the IDS. The IDS console is a manager. Configuration changes in the IDS are made by communicating with the IDS manager.

Notification   *Notification* is the process or method by which the IDS manager makes the operator aware of an alert. This might include a graphic display highlighting the traffic or an email sent to the network's administrative staff.

Operator   The *operator* is the person primarily responsible for the IDS. The operator can be a user, administrator, and so on, as long as they're the primary person responsible.

Sensor   A *sensor* is the IDS component that collects data from the data source and passes it to the analyzer for analysis. A sensor can be a device driver on a system, or it can be an actual black box that is connected to the network and reports to the IDS. The important thing to remember is that the sensor is a primary data collection point for the IDS.

The IDS, as you can see, has many different components and processes that work together to provide a real-time picture of your network traffic. Figure 3.16 shows the various components and processes working together to provide an IDS. Remember that data can come from many different sources and must be analyzed to determine what's occurring. An IDS isn't intended as a true traffic-blocking device, though some IDSs can also perform this function; it's intended to be a traffic-auditing device.

FIGURE 3.16   The components of an IDS working together to provide network monitoring

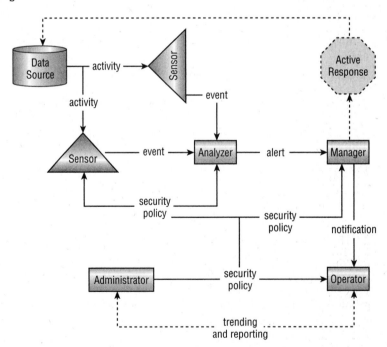

IDSs use four primary approaches:

Behavior-Based-Detection IDS   A *behavior-based system* looks for variations in behavior such as unusually high traffic, policy violations, and so on. By looking for deviations in behavior, it is able to recognize potential threats and to respond quickly to them.

Signature-Based-Detection IDS   A *signature-based system*, also commonly known as *misuse-detection IDS (MD-IDS)*, is primarily focused on evaluating attacks based on attack signatures and audit trails. Attack signatures describe a generally established method of attacking a system. For example, a TCP flood attack begins with a large number of incomplete TCP sessions. If the MD-IDS knows what a TCP flood attack looks like, it can make an appropriate report or response to thwart the attack.

Figure 3.17 illustrates a signature-based IDS in action. Notice that this IDS uses an extensive database to determine the signature of the traffic. This process resembles an antivirus software process.

FIGURE 3.17   A signature-based IDS in action

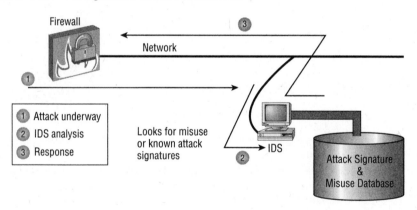

Anomaly-Detection IDS   An *anomaly-detection IDS (AD-IDS)* looks for anomalies, meaning it looks for things outside of the ordinary. Typically, a training program learns what the normal operation is and then spots deviations from it. An AD-IDS can establish the baseline either by being manually assigned values or through automated processes that look at traffic patterns. One method is *behavior based*, which looks for unusual behavior and then acts accordingly.

Heuristic IDS   A *heuristic system* uses algorithms to analyze the traffic passing through the network. As a general rule, heuristic systems require more tweaking and fine-tuning than the other types of detection systems to prevent false positives in your network.

IDSs are primarily focused on reporting events or network traffic that deviate from historical work activity or network traffic patterns. For this reporting to be effective, administrators should develop a baseline or history of typical network traffic. This baseline activity provides a stable, long-term perspective on network activity. An example might be a report generated when a higher-than-normal level of ICMP responses is received in a specified time period. Such activity may indicate the beginning of an ICMP flood attack. The system may also report when a user who doesn't normally access the network using a VPN suddenly requests administrative access to the system. Figure 3.18 demonstrates an AD-IDS tracking and reporting excessive traffic in a network. The AD-IDS process frequently uses artificial intelligence or expert system technologies to learn about normal traffic for a network.

FIGURE 3.18   AD-IDS using expert system technology to evaluate risks

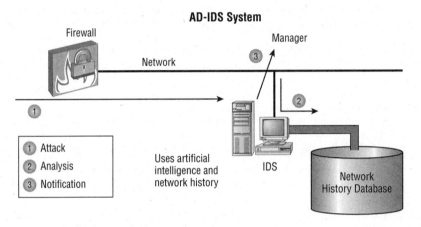

Whenever there is an attack, there is almost always something created that identifies it—an entry in the login report, an error in a log, and so forth. These items (frequently called Indicators of Compromise) represent intrusion signatures, and you can learn from them and instruct an IDS to watch for and prevent repeat performances.

MD-IDS and AD-IDS are merging in most commercial systems. They provide the best opportunity to detect and thwart attacks and unauthorized access. Unlike a firewall, the IDS exists to detect and report unusual occurrences in a network, not to block them.

The next sections discuss network-based and host-based implementations of IDS and the capabilities they provide.

IDS vs. IPS

Although IDSs have been popular for a long time, *intrusion prevention systems (IPSs)* have become prevalent in the past few years.

What is now called an IPS was formally known as an active IDS.

This type of system is an IDS that reacts to the intrusion that has been detected, most often by blocking communication from the offending IP address. The problem with this approach is the issue of false positives. No system is perfect—at some point you will have a situation where network activity is anomalous and the IDS indicates an intrusion, but in reality it is not an intrusion. For example, if the IDS is set up to react to traffic outside normal bounds, excessive traffic from a given system could indicate an attack. However, it could also indicate an unusually high workload.

Working with a Network-Based IDS

A *network-based IDS (NIDS)* approach to IDS attaches the system to a point in the network where it can monitor and report on all network traffic. This can be in front of or behind the firewall, as shown in Figure 3.19.

FIGURE 3.19   NIDS placement in a network determines what data will be analyzed.

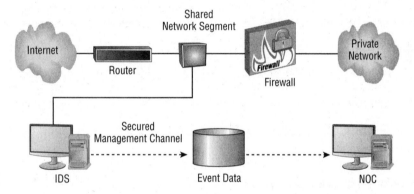

 The best solution for creating a secure network is to place an IDS in front of and behind the firewall. This dual-security approach provides as much defense as possible.

Placing the NIDS in front of the firewall enables monitoring of all traffic going into the network and can give you data on the attacks that your firewall is blocking. This approach allows a huge amount of data to be processed, and it lets you see all of the traffic coming into the network. Putting the NIDS behind the firewall only allows you to see the traffic that penetrates the firewall. Although this approach reduces the amount of data processed, it doesn't let you see all of the attacks that might be developing.

The NIDS can be attached to a switch or a hub, or it can be attached to a tap. Many hubs and switches provide a monitoring port for troubleshooting and diagnostic purposes. This port may function in a manner similar to a tap. The advantage of the tap approach is that the IDS is the only device that will be using the tap. Figure 3.20 illustrates a connection to the network using a hub or tap.

FIGURE 3.20 A hub being used to attach the NIDS to the network

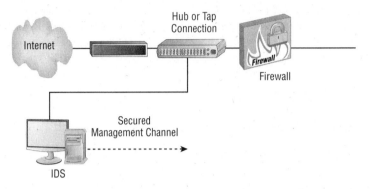

 Port spanning, also known as *port mirroring,* copies the traffic from all ports to a single port and disallows bidirectional traffic on that port. Cisco's Switched Port Analyzer (SPAN) is one example of a port-spanning implementation.

In either case, the IDS monitors and evaluates all the traffic to which it has access.

Two basic types of responses can be formulated at the network level: passive and active. They're briefly explained in the following sections.

 Real World Scenario

Working with Network Audit Files

You're the network administrator of a relatively busy network. Your company has gone through a couple of cutbacks, and your staffing is limited. You want to make sure that your network stays as secure as you can make it. What can you do to ease your workload?

You have three possibilities. There are two you should consider to protect your network: Either install an IDS or reduce the logging levels of your network audit files. An alternative is to install an audit log-collection system with filtering.

You might be able to reduce the amount of logged traffic in your audit files by changing the settings that determine what you audit. However, changing audit rules would prevent you from seeing what's happening on your network because most events wouldn't be logged.

Installing an IDS would allow you to establish rules that would provide a higher level of automation than you could achieve by reviewing audit files. Your best solution might be to convince your company to invest in an IDS. An IDS could send you an email or alert you when an event is detected.

Implementing a Passive Response

A *passive response* is the most common type of response to many intrusions. In general, passive responses are the easiest to develop and implement. The following list includes some passive response strategies:

Logging   *Logging* involves recording that an event has occurred and under what circumstances. Logging functions should provide sufficient information about the nature of the attack to help administrators determine what has happened and to assist in evaluating the threat. This information can then be used to devise methods to counter the threat.

Notification   *Notification* communicates event-related information to the appropriate personnel when an event has occurred. This includes relaying any relevant data about the event to help evaluate the situation. If the IDS is manned full time, messages can be displayed on the manager's console to indicate that the situation is occurring.

Shunning   *Shunning* or ignoring an attack is a common response. This might be the case if your IDS notices an Internet Information Services (IIS) attack occurring on a system that's running another web-hosting service, such as Apache. The attack won't work because Apache doesn't respond the same way as IIS, so why pay attention to it? In a busy network, many different types of attacks can occur simultaneously. If you aren't worried about an attack succeeding, why waste energy or time investigating it or notifying someone about it? The IDS can make a note of it in a log and move on to other more pressing business.

 The difference between a passive response and an active response is much like the difference between a security guard and a security camera. All a security camera can do is record what occurs, it cannot react to any incident. A security guard can take action. This is the same with IDSs. A passive IDS simply records what occurs, an active IDS takes action.

Implementing an Active Response

An *active response* involves taking an action based on an attack or threat. The goal of an active response is to take the quickest action possible to reduce an event's potential impact. This type of response requires plans for how to deal with an event, clear policies, and intelligence in the IDS in order to be successful. An active response will include one of the reactions briefly described here:

Terminating Processes or Sessions   If a flood attack is detected, the IDS can cause the subsystem, such as TCP, to force resets to all of the sessions that are under way. Doing so frees up resources and allows TCP to continue to operate normally. Of course, all valid TCP sessions are closed and will need to be reestablished—but at least this will be possible, and it may have little effect on end users. The IDS evaluates the events and determines the best way to handle them. Figure 3.21 illustrates TCP being directed to issue RST commands from the IDS to reset all open connections to TCP. This type of mechanism can also terminate user sessions or stop and restart any process that appears to be operating abnormally.

FIGURE 3.21   An IDS instructing TCP to reset all connections

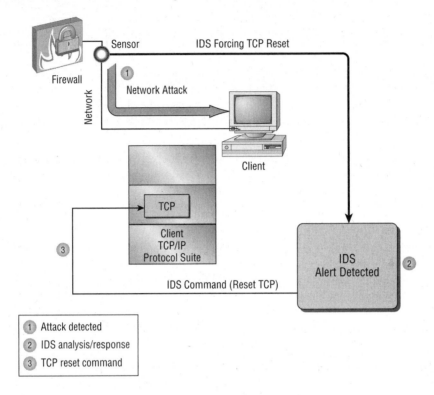

1. Attack detected
2. IDS analysis/response
3. TCP reset command

Network Configuration Changes   If a certain IP address is found to be causing repeated attacks on the network, the IDS can instruct a border router or firewall to reject any requests or traffic from that address. This configuration change can remain in effect permanently or for a specified period. Figure 3.22 illustrates the IDS instructing the firewall to close port 80 for 60 seconds to terminate an IIS attack.

If the IDS determines that a particular socket or port is being attacked, it can instruct the firewall to block that port for a specified amount of time. Doing so effectively eliminates the attack but may also inadvertently cause a self-imposed DoS situation to occur by eliminating legitimate traffic. This is especially true for port 80 (HTTP or web) traffic.

Deception   A *deception active response* fools the attacker into thinking that the attack is succeeding while the system monitors the activity and potentially redirects the attacker to a system that is designed to be broken. This allows the operator or administrator to gather data about how the attack is unfolding and the techniques being used in the attack. This process is referred to as *sending them to the honeypot*. Figure 3.23 illustrates a honeypot where a deception has been successful.

FIGURE 3.22 An IDS instructing the firewall to close port 80 for 60 seconds to thwart an IIS attack

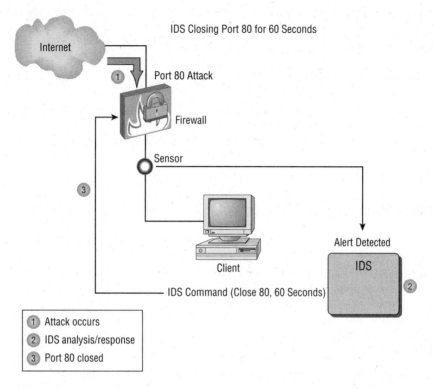

IDS Closing Port 80 for 60 Seconds

Internet

Port 80 Attack

Firewall

Sensor

Client

Alert Detected

IDS

IDS Command (Close 80, 60 Seconds)

1 Attack occurs
2 IDS analysis/response
3 Port 80 closed

FIGURE 3.23 A network honeypot deceives an attacker and gathers intelligence.

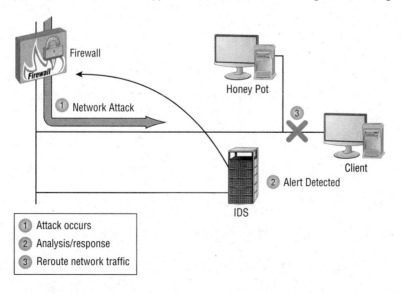

Firewall

Honey Pot

Network Attack

Client

Alert Detected

IDS

1 Attack occurs
2 Analysis/response
3 Reroute network traffic

The advantage of this type of response is that all activities are watched and recorded for analysis when the attack is completed. This is a difficult scenario to set up, and it's dangerous to allow a hacker to proceed into your network, even if you're monitoring the events.

This approach is frequently used when an active investigation is under way by law enforcement and they're gathering evidence to ensure a successful prosecution of the attacker. Deception allows you to gather documentation without risking live data.

Remember that active responses are the least commonly implemented. Those that are the most effective are the most costly and the hardest to put into practice, not to mention the trouble you can get into following a we-attack-those-who-attack-us strategy.

Working with a Host-Based IDS

A *host-based IDS (HIDS)* is designed to run as software on a host computer system. These systems typically run as a service or as a background process. An HIDS examines the machine logs, system events, and applications interactions; it normally doesn't monitor incoming network traffic to the host. An HIDS is popular on servers that use encrypted channels or channels to other servers.

Figure 3.24 illustrates an HIDS installed on a server. Notice that the HIDS interacts with the logon audit and kernel audit files. The kernel audit files are used for process and application interfaces.

FIGURE 3.24 A host-based IDS interacting with the operating system

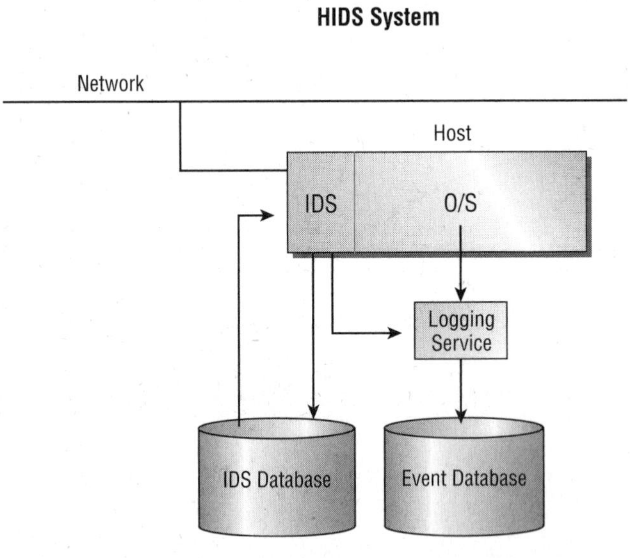

HIDS System

Network

Host

IDS | O/S

Logging Service

IDS Database Event Database

Two major problems with HIDS aren't easily overcome. The first problem involves a compromise of the system. If the system is compromised, the log files to which the IDS reports may become corrupt or inaccurate. This may make fault determination difficult or it may make the system unreliable. The second major problem with an HIDS is that it must be deployed on each system that needs it. This can create a headache for administrative and support staff.

One of the major benefits of HIDSs is the potential to keep checksums on files. These checksums can be used to inform system administrators that files have been altered by an attack. Recovery is simplified because it's easier to determine where tampering has occurred. The other advantage is that HIDS can read memory when NIDS can not.

HIDSs typically respond in a passive manner to an incident. An active response would theoretically be similar to those provided by a network-based IDS.

Working with NIPSs

As opposed to NIDSs, *network intrusion prevention systems (NIPSs)* focus on *prevention*. These systems focus on signature matches and then take a course of action. For example, if it appears as though an attack might be under way, packets can be dropped, ignored, and so forth. To do this, the NIPS must be able to ***detect*** the attack occurring, and thus it can be argued that NIPS is a subset of NIDS.

 The line continues to blur between technologies. For example, NIST now refers to these systems as Intrusion Detection and Prevention Systems (IDPSs). Though it is important to stay current with the terminology in the real world, know that the exam is frozen in time and you should be familiar with the older terminology for the questions that you will face on it.

Log Files in Linux

You should check a number of logs for entries that might indicate an intrusion. The primary ones you should examine are listed here:

/var/log/faillog   Open a shell prompt, and use the `faillog` utility to view a list of users' failed authentication attempts.

/var/log/lastlog   Open a shell prompt, and use the **lastlog** utility to view a list of all users and when they last logged in.

/var/log/messages   Use `grep`, or a derivative thereof, to find login-related entries in this file.

/var/log/wtmp   Open a shell prompt, and use the `last` command to view a list of users who have authenticated to the system.

Protocol Analyzers

The terms *protocol analyzing* and *packet sniffing* are interchangeable. They refer to the process of monitoring the data that is transmitted across a network. The software that performs the operation is called either an *analyzer* or a *sniffer*. Sniffers are readily available on the Internet. These tools were initially intended for legitimate network-monitoring processes, but they can also be used to gather data for illegal purposes.

IM traffic, for example, uses the Internet and is susceptible to packet-sniffing activities. Any information contained in an IM session is potentially vulnerable to interception. Make sure that users understand that sensitive information should not be sent using this method.

One of the best-known tools for analyzing network traffic in real time is Snort (www. snort.org). Exercise 3.2 walks you through the installation of this tool.

EXERCISE 3.2

Installing Snort in Linux

The de facto standard for intrusion detection in Linux is Snort. To install the package on an openSUSE server, follow these steps:

1. Log in as root and start YaST.

2. Choose Software and then Install And Remove Software. Search for **snort**.

3. Check the box when the package appears.

4. Click Accept. If any dependency messages appear, click Continue to add them as well.

5. Swap CDs as prompted, and exit YaST upon completion.

To use the Snort utility, open a terminal session and type **snort**. This generates an error message that lists all of the options that you can use with this utility.

Spam Filters

Spam filters can be added to catch unwanted email and filter it out before it gets delivered internally. The filtering is done based on established rules, such as blocking email coming from certain IP addresses, email that contains particular words in the subject line, and the like. Although spam filters are usually used to scan incoming messages, they can also be used to scan outgoing messages as well and thus act as a quick identifier of internal PCs that may have contracted a virus.

It is estimated that over 90 percent of incoming email is spam. SpamAssassin is one of the best-known open source spam filters. You can find more information about it here: http://spamassassin.apache.org/.

A number of vendors make all-in-one security devices that combine spam filters with firewalls, load balancers, and several other services.

UTM Security Appliances

In the broadest sense of the term, any freestanding device that operates in a largely self-contained manner is considered to be an *appliance*. An *all-in-one appliance*, also known as Unified Threat Management (UTM) and Next Generation Firewall (NGFW), is one that provides a good foundation for security. A variety are available; those that you should be familiar with for the exam fall under the categories of providing URL filtering, content inspection, or malware inspection and are discussed further in the sections that follow. When you combine a firewall with other abilities (intrusion prevention, antivirus, content filtering, etc.), what used to be called an all-in-one appliance is now known as a UTM. The advantages of combining everything into one include a reduced learning curve (you only have one product to learn), a single vendor to deal with, and—typically—reduced complexity. The disadvantages of combining everything into one include a potential single point of failure, and the dependence on the one vendor.

URL Filters

URL filtering involves blocking websites (or sections of websites) based solely on the URL, restricting access to specified websites and certain web-based applications. This is in contrast to content filters, which block data based on its content rather than from where the data originates. Within Internet Explorer, the Phishing Filter included with earlier versions acted as a URL filter. The Phishing Filter was replaced with the SmartScreen Filter in IE8 and subsequent releases.

SmartScreen Filter runs in the background and sends the address of the website being visited to the SmartScreen Filter server, where it is compared against a list that is maintained of phishing and malware sites. If a match is found, a blocking web page appears (in red), and it encourages you to not continue. You can continue to the site (not recommended) or abort the operation. You can control the operations of the SmartScreen Filter in IE from the Safety menu. From there, you can toggle it on/off, report an unsafe site, and check to see if a site is in the database. Figure 3.25 shows the results of a check that did not find any threats.

FIGURE 3.25 A website that does not appear in the URL filter list

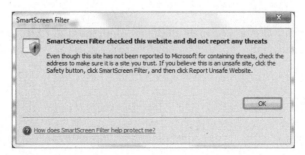

Content Inspection

Instead of relying on a website to be previously identified as questionable as URL filtering does, *content inspection* works by looking at the data that is coming in. In the most recent versions of Internet Explorer, content filtering can be configured using Content Advisor. In Exercise 3.3, you'll see how to configure content filtering in Internet Explorer.

EXERCISE 3.3

Configuring Web Filtering

In Internet Explorer, Content Advisor performs content inspection. This can be turned on and configured by following these steps:

1. In Internet Explorer, choose Internet Options from the Tools menu.

2. Click the Content tab.

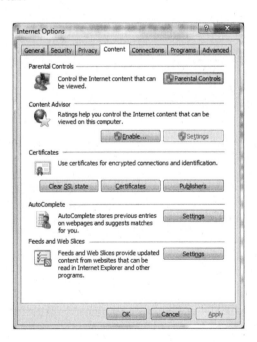

3. Click Enable beneath Content Advisor. Click Yes when the UAC (User Account Control) prompts you to continue. The Content Advisor dialog box will appear.

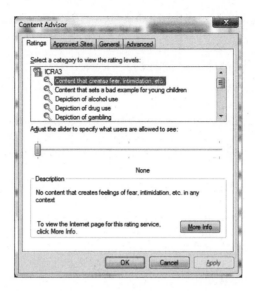

4. For each of the categories that appear in the box, use the slider to choose a setting. Options include None, Limited, Some, and Unrestricted. Definitions of what will appear for each setting are shown in the bottom portion of the dialog box.

5. After making a selection for each category, click OK.

6. Click OK again to exit Internet Options.

Internet content filters, though not included with every operating system by default, are plentiful and can be readily found for any operating system with a simple web search. We highly recommend that you place content filters on all servers (NAT, proxy, and so on) facilitating client access as well as on the workstations themselves. This provides two levels of security that can keep errant pages out.

Malware Inspection

It is important to stop malware before it ever gets hold of a system. Although tools that identify malware when they find it on a system are useful, real-time tools that stop it from ever making it to the system are much better. One of the available tools for Windows is Microsoft Security Essentials, and it runs on Windows 7 as well as Windows Vista and Windows XP SP2. A beefed-up Windows Defender replaced Microsoft Security Essentials in Windows 8.

Also note that another free tool from Microsoft is the Malicious Software Removal Tool, which helps remove any infection found but is not intended to be a full anti-malware suite.

An updated version of this tool is released on the second Tuesday of each month, and once installed, it is included, by default, in Microsoft Update and Windows Update.

Web Application Firewall vs. Network Firewall

A *web application firewall (WAF)* is a real-time appliance that applies a set of rules to block traffic to and from web servers and to try to prevent attacks. The rules of blocking can be customized, and WAFs are gaining popularity along with the movement to put everything on the cloud. Among the main threats a WAF is trying to protect against are cross-site scripting (XSS), injection attacks (such as those using SQL), and forged HTTP requests.

Operating at the highest level of the OSI model, WAFs can not only detect known problems but react to suspected problems as well—making them similar to, though superior than, intrusion protection systems. A traditional network firewall was discussed earlier in this chapter, and it differs from a WAF in terms of the focus of the latter on web-based servers/services and the degree of rule-based logic applied.

Application-Aware Devices

An *application-aware device* is one that has the ability to respond to traffic based on what is there. Often, such devices combine SNMP and quality of service to be able to prioritize traffic based on the importance and value of the content. This functionality can be added to such devices as a firewall, IPSs, IDSs, and proxies—all of which have been described in this chapter.

Summary

This chapter focused on the key elements of network infrastructure and some of the hardware components involved in networking. Your infrastructure is the backbone of your network and the key to all of its security capabilities.

Your total network infrastructure includes the hardware and software necessary to run your network. Two key components related to security are routers and firewalls. Proper configuration of these components is the key to providing services in the way that your network needs them. If your network security devices are improperly configured, you may be worse off than if you didn't have them at all. It's a dangerous situation when you think that you're secure but in reality you are not.

Networks are becoming more complicated, and they're being linked to other networks at an accelerated speed. Several tools are available to help you both link and secure your networks:

- VPNs
- VLANs
- Remote access

The connections you make using TCP/IP are based primarily on IP addresses. When coupled with a port, these addresses form a socket. Sockets are the primary method used to communicate with services and applications such as the Web and Telnet. Changing default ports requires that users know which ports provide which services.

Exam Essentials

Be able to describe the various components and the purpose of an infrastructure.   Your network's infrastructure is the backbone of your systems and network operations. The infrastructure includes all of the hardware, software, physical security, and operational security methods in place. The key components of your infrastructure include devices such as routers, firewalls, switches, and the other devices used in the network.

Know the characteristics of the connectivity technologies available to you and the security capabilities associated with each.   Remote access, PPP, tunneling protocols, and VPNs are your primary tools. PPTP and L2TP are two of the most common protocols used for tunneling. IPSec, though not a tunneling protocol, provides encryption to tunneling protocols; it's often used to enhance tunnel security.

Familiarize yourself with the technologies used by TCP/IP and the Internet.   IP addresses and port numbers are combined to create an interface called a socket. Most TCP and UDP protocols communicate using this socket as the primary interface mechanism. Clients and servers communicate using ports. Ports can be changed to enhance security. Web services use HTML and other technologies to allow rich and animated websites. These technologies potentially create security problems because they may have individual vulnerabilities.

Review Questions

1. Which of the following devices is the most capable of providing infrastructure security?

   A. Hub

   B. Switch

   C. Router

   D. Modem

2. Upper management has decreed that a firewall must be put in place immediately, before your site suffers an attack similar to one that struck a sister company. Responding to this order, your boss instructs you to implement a packet filter by the end of the week. A packet filter performs which function?

   A. Prevents unauthorized packets from entering the network

   B. Allows all packets to leave the network

   C. Allows all packets to enter the network

   D. Eliminates collisions in the network

3. Which device stores information about destinations in a network (choose the best answer)?

   A. Hub

   B. Modem

   C. Firewall

   D. Router

4. As more and more clients have been added to your network, the efficiency of the network has decreased significantly. You're preparing a budget for next year, and you specifically want to address this problem. Which of the following devices acts primarily as a tool to improve network efficiency?

   A. Hub

   B. Switch

   C. Router

   D. PBX

5. Most of the sales force has been told that they should no longer report to the office on a daily basis. From now on, they're to spend the majority of their time on the road calling on customers. Each member of the sales force has been issued a laptop computer and told to connect to the network nightly through a dial-up connection. Which of the following protocols is widely used today as a transport protocol for Internet dial-up connections?

   A. SMTP

   B. PPP

   C. PPTP

   D. L2TP

6. Which protocol is unsuitable for WAN VPN connections?

   A. PPP

   B. PPTP

   C. L2TP

   D. IPSec

7. You've been notified that you'll soon be transferred to another site. Before you leave, you're to audit the network and document everything in use and the reason why it's in use. The next administrator will use this documentation to keep the network running. Which of the following protocols isn't a tunneling protocol but is probably used at your site by tunneling protocols for network security?

   A. IPSec

   B. PPTP

   C. L2TP

   D. L2F

8. A socket is a combination of which components?

   A. TCP and port number

   B. UDP and port number

   C. IP and session number

   D. IP and port number

9. You're explaining protocols to a junior administrator shortly before you leave for vacation. The topic of Internet mail applications comes up, and you explain how communications are done now as well as how you expect them to be done in the future. Which of the following protocols is becoming the standard for Internet mail applications?

   A. SMTP

   B. POP

   C. IMAP

   D. IGMP

10. Which protocol is primarily used for network maintenance and destination information?

   A. ICMP

   B. SMTP

   C. IGMP

   D. Router

11. IPv6, in addition to having more bits allocated for each host address, has mandatory requirements built in for which security protocol?

   A. TFTP

   B. IPSec

   C. SFTP

   D. L2TP

12. Which ports are, by default, reserved for use by FTP? (Choose all that apply.)

    A. 20 and 21 TCP

    B. 20 and 21 UDP

    C. 22 and 23 TCP

    D. 22 and 23 UDP

13. Which of the following services use only TCP ports and not UDP?

    A. IMAP

    B. LDAP

    C. FTPS

    D. SFTP

14. Which of the following can be implemented as a software or hardware solution and is usually associated with a device—a router, a firewall, NAT, and so on—used to shift a load from one device to another?

    A. Proxy

    B. Hub

    C. Load balancer

    D. Switch

15. Which of the following are multiport devices that improve network efficiency?

    A. Switches

    B. Modems

    C. Gateways

    D. Concentrators

16. Which service(s), by default, use TCP and UDP port 22? (Choose all that apply.)

    A. SMTP

    B. SSH

    C. SCP

    D. IMAP

17. What protocol, running on top of TCP/IP, is often used for name registration and resolution with Windows-based clients?

    A. Telnet

    B. SSL

    C. NetBIOS

    D. TLS

18. How many bits are used for addressing with IPv4 and IPv6, respectively?

    A. 32, 128

    B. 16, 64

    C. 8, 32

    D. 4, 16

19. Which IDS system uses algorithms to analyze the traffic passing through the network?

    A. Arithmetical

    B. Algebraic

    C. Statistical

    D. Heuristic

20. Which device monitors network traffic in a passive manner?

    A. Sniffer

    B. IDS

    C. Firewall

    D. Web browser

Chapter

4

Access Control, Authentication, and Authorization

THE FOLLOWING COMPTIA SECURITY+ EXAM OBJECTIVES ARE COVERED IN THIS CHAPTER:

✓ **1.2 Given a scenario, use secure network administration principles.**

- Rule-based management
- Firewall rules
- VLAN management
- Secure router configuration
- Access control lists
- Port Security
- 802.1x
- Flood guards
- Loop protection
- Implicit deny
- Network separation
- Log analysis

✓ **1.3 Explain network design elements and components.**

- Layered Security / Defense in Depth

✓ **5.1 Compare and contrast the function and purpose of authentication services.**

- RADIUS
- TACACS+

- Kerberos
- LDAP
- XTACACS
- SAML
- Secure LDAP

✓ **5.2 Given a scenario, select the appropriate authentication, authorization, or access control.**

- Identification vs. authentication vs. authorization
- Authorization: Least privilege; Separation of duties; ACLs; Mandatory access; Discretionary access; Rule-based access control; Role-based access control; Time of day restrictions
- Authentication: Tokens; Common access card; Smart card; Multifactor authentication; TOTP; HOTP; CHAP; PAP; Single sign-on; Access control; Implicit deny; Trusted OS
- Authentication factors: Something you are; Something you have; Something you know; Somewhere you are; Something you do
- Identification: Biometrics; Personal identification verification card; Username
- Federation
- Transitive trust/authentication

✓ **5.3 Install and configure security controls when performing account management, based on best practices.**

- Mitigate issues associated with users with multiple account/roles and/or shared accounts
- Account policy enforcement: Credential management; Group policy; Password complexity; Expiration; Recovery; Disablement; Lockout; Password history; Password reuse; Password length; Generic account prohibition
- Group based privileges
- User assigned privileges
- User access reviews
- Continuous monitoring

This chapter covers a critical topic in security, that of controlling who can access your system, what resources they can access, and how to ensure that individuals are who they claim to be. At the most basic level, you can consider authentication and access control to be the two foundations of security. If you don't do a good job on these tasks, it is unlikely that the rest of your security strategy will be effective.

This chapter starts by looking at the basics of access control and then explores remote access and authentication services. It concludes by examining access control implementation and best practices.

Understanding Access Control Basics

Quite simply, *access control* means allowing the correct users into a system (those who are authorized) and keeping others out (those who are *not* authorized). You can employ a great many tools and technologies to make this happen, all of which are discussed in this chapter. The fundamental principle, however, remains the same: Let the right ones in.

In the following sections, we will explore the differences between identification and authentication, authentication and authorization, multifactor authentication, and operational security. We will also look at tokens and issues to watch for.

Identification vs. Authentication

Understanding the difference between identification and authentication is critical to correctly answering access control questions on the Security+ exam. *Identification* means finding out who someone is. *Authentication* is a mechanism of verifying that identification. Put another way, identification is claiming an identity; authentication is proving it.

In the physical world, the best analogy would be that any person can claim to be anyone (identification). To prove it (authentication), however, that person needs to provide some evidence, such as a driver's license, passport, and so forth.

Authentication systems or methods are based on one or more of these five factors:

- Something you know, such as a password or PIN

- Something you have, such as a smart card, token, or identification device

- Something you are, such as your fingerprints or retinal pattern (often called biometrics)

- Something you do, such as an action you must take to complete authentication

- Somewhere you are (this is based on geolocation)

Because of the use of mobile computing, "somewhere you are" authentication is not often used, since users are likely to log in from diverse locations. In fact, many sources do not include "somewhere you are" as an authentication factor.

Systems authenticate each other using similar methods. Frequently, systems pass private information between each other to establish identity. Once authentication has occurred, two systems can communicate in the manner specified in the design. Several common methods are used for authentication, and they fall within the categories of either single factor or multifactor. Each offers something in terms of security and should be considered when you're evaluating authentication schemes or methods.

Another method that is becoming popular is out-of-band authentication. This is a process whereby the system you are authenticating gets information from public records and asks you questions to help authenticate you. For example, the system might retrieve your credit report and then query you about specific entries in it.

Authentication (Single Factor) and Authorization

The most basic form of authentication is known as *single-factor authentication (SFA)*, because only one type of authentication is checked. SFA is most often implemented as the traditional username/password combination. A *username* and *password* are unique identifiers for a logon process. Here's a synopsis for how SFA works: When users sit down in front of a computer system, the first thing a security system requires is that they establish who they are. Identification is typically confirmed through a logon process. Most operating systems use a user ID (username) and password to accomplish this. These values can be sent across the connection as plain text or they can be encrypted.

The logon process identifies that you are who you say you are to the operating system and possibly the network. Figure 4.1 illustrates the logon and password process. Notice that the operating system compares this information to the stored information from the security processor, and it either accepts or denies the logon attempt. The operating system might establish privileges or permissions based on stored data about that particular user ID.

Whenever two or more parties authenticate each other, it is known as *mutual authentication*. A client may authenticate to a server and a server may authenticate to a client when there is a need to establish a secure session between the two and employ encryption. Mutual authentication ensures that the client is not unwittingly connecting and providing its credentials to a rogue server, which can then turn around and steal the data from the real server.

Commonly, mutual authentication will be implemented when the data to be sent during the session is of a critical nature, such as financial or medical records.

FIGURE 4.1   A logon process occurring on a workstation

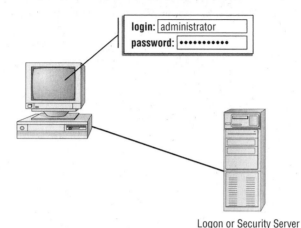

Logon or Security Server

Multifactor Authentication

When two or more access methods are included as part of the authentication process, you're implementing a *multifactor* authentication system. A system that uses smart cards and passwords is referred to as a *two-factor authentication* system. Two-factor authentication is shown in Figure 4.2. This example requires both a smart card and a logon password process.

A multifactor system can consist of a two-factor system, three-factor system, and so on. As long as more than one factor is involved in the authentication process, it is considered a multifactor system.

For obvious reasons, the two or more factors employed should not be from the same category. Although you do increase difficulty in gaining system access by requiring the user to enter two sets of username/password combinations, it is much preferred to pair a single username/password combination with a biometric identifier or other security check.

When taking the Security+ exam, keep in mind the number of authentication factors in each type. For example, using a smart card and a password is two-factor authentication. However, using a password and a PIN is one-factor authentication because both involve "something you know."

Layered Security and Defense in Depth

Two terms synonymous with each other are *layered security* and *defense in depth*. All these terms mean is that you should not rely on a single entity for protection but instead implement multiple layers of security. In a physical environment, for example, it is all well and good to have a guard posted at the entrance of the office building, but to keep the servers secure, you should also put a lock on the server room door. From a technology standpoint, a firewall is a great thing to restrict traffic into the network from the outside, but you will also want to have antivirus software, intrusion detection, and as many other layers of security as you can to truly protect the systems.

FIGURE 4.2 Two-factor authentication

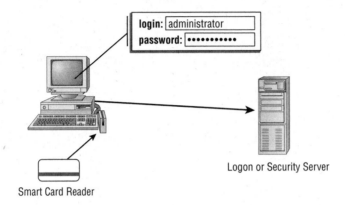

Smart Card Reader

Logon or Security Server

Both factors must be valid:
• User ID and Password
• Smart Card

Network Access Control

Operational security focuses on how an organization achieves its goals. It is also part of a security triad that also includes physical and management security. As such, operational security issues include *network access control (NAC)*, authentication, and security topologies after the network installation is complete. Issues include the daily operations of the network, connections to other networks, backup plans, and recovery plans. In short, operational security encompasses everything that isn't related to design or physical security in your network. Instead of focusing on the physical components where the data is stored, such as the server, the focus is now on the topology and connections.

 Some vendors use the acronym NAC to signify *network admission control* rather than the more commonly accepted *network access* control. Regardless of which word appears mid-acronym, the concept is the same.

The issues you address in an operational capacity may seem overwhelming at first. Many of the areas on which you'll focus are vulnerabilities in the systems you use or weak or inadequate security policies. For example, if you implement a comprehensive password expiration policy, you can require that users change their passwords every 30 or 60 days. If the system doesn't require password rotation, though (it allows the same passwords to be reused), you have a vulnerability that you may not be able to eliminate. A user can go through the motions of changing their password only to reenter the same value and keep it in use.

From an operational perspective, this type of system has weak password-changing capabilities. There is nothing you can do short of installing a higher-security logon process or replacing the operating system. Either solution may not be feasible given the costs, conversion times, and possible unwillingness of an organization—or its partners—to make this switch.

Such dependence on a weak system usually stems from the fact that most companies use software that was developed by third parties in order to save costs or meet compatibility requirements. These packages may require the use of a specific operating system. If that operating system has significant security problems or vulnerabilities, your duties will be immense as you'll still be responsible for providing security in such an environment. Your secure corporate network, for example, should never be connected to the Internet, where it can become subject to a seemingly endless number of potential vulnerabilities. You must install hardware and software solutions to improve security, and you must convince management that these measures are worth the cost to implement.

Tokens

Security tokens are similar to certificates in that they are used to identify and authenticate the user. They contain the rights and access privileges of the token bearer as part of the token. Think of a token as a small piece of data that holds a sliver of information about the user.

Many operating systems generate a token that is applied to every action taken on the computer system. If your token doesn't grant you access to certain information, then either that information will not be displayed or your access will be denied. The authentication system creates a token every time a user connects or when a session begins. At the completion of a session, the token is destroyed. Figure 4.3 shows the security token process.

Federations

A *federation* is a collection of computer networks that agree on standards of operation, such as security standards. Normally, these are networks that are related in some way. In some cases, it could be an industry association that establishes such standards.

Another example of a federation would be an instant messaging (IM) federation. In this scenario, multiple IM providers form common communication standards, thus allowing users on different platforms with different clients to communicate freely.

In other situations, a group of partners might elect to establish common security and communication standards, thus forming a federation. This would facilitate communication between employees in each of the various partners.

A *federated identity* is a means of linking a user's identity with their privileges in a manner that can be used across business boundaries (for example, Microsoft Passport or Google checkout). This allows a user to have a single identity that they can use across different business units and perhaps even entirely different businesses.

FIGURE 4.3   Security token authentication

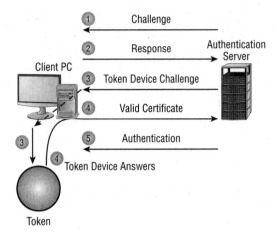

   A federated identity sounds similar to a single sign-on, but do not confuse the two. Single sign-on is about having one password for all resources on a given network. Federated identities relate to being able to access resources on diverse networks.

Potential Authentication and Access Problems

There are two problem areas you should know about for the Security+ exam as they apply to authentication/access issues: transitive access and client-side attacks. Let's address both of these.

Transitive Access

The word *transitive* means involving transition—keep this in mind as you learn how *transitive access* problems occur. With transitive access, one party (A) trusts another party (B). If the second party (B) trusts another party (C), then a relationship can exist where the first party (A) also may trust the third party (C).

In early operating systems, this process was often exploited. In current operating systems, such as Windows Server 2012, the problems with transitive access are solved by creating *transitive trusts*, which are a type of relationship that can exist between domains (the opposite is *nontransitive trusts*). When the trust relationship is transitive, the relationship between party (A) and party (B) flows through as described earlier (for instance, A now trusts C). In all versions of Active Directory, the default is that all domains in a forest trust each other with two-way, transitive trust relationships.

Although this process makes administration much easier when you add a new child domain (no administrative intervention is required to establish the trusts), it leaves open the possibility of a hacker acquiring more trust than they should by virtue of joining the domain. In Exercise 4.1, we'll explore how to validate the trust relationship in Windows Server 2012, which is a step toward addressing this problem.

EXERCISE 4.1

Validating a Trust Relationship

As an administrator, you should know what trust relationships exist between domains. To validate a trust relationship in Windows Server 2012, follow these steps:

1. Open Active Directory Domains and Trusts.

2. Right-click your domain name, and choose Properties from the menu.

3. Click the Trusts tab, and select the name of the domain, or forest, that you want to validate.

4. Click Properties. The Properties dialog box for that trust appears.

5. Approximately two-thirds of the way down the dialog box, the Transitivity Of Trust item appears. Click Validate.

6. A confirmation message appears. Click OK.

7. Exit Active Directory Domains and Trusts.

Authentication Issues to Consider

You can set up many different parameters and standards to force the people in your organization to conform. In establishing these parameters, it's important that you consider the capabilities of the people who will be working with these policies. If you're working in an environment where people aren't computer savvy, you may spend a lot of time helping them remember and recover passwords. Each organization has its own quirks, and many have had to reevaluate their security guidelines only after they've already invested a great deal of time and expense to implement high-security systems to accommodate such quirks. Remember that it is always better to educate users and raise their awareness than to lower security.

Setting authentication security, especially when supporting users, can become a high-maintenance activity for network administrators. On one hand, you want people to be able to authenticate themselves easily; on the other hand, you want to establish security that protects your company's resources. Here are some tips for making this process easier:

- Be wary of popular names or current trends that make certain passwords predictable. For example, every January, Super Bowl teams become likely passwords, as do variations on players' names and numbers. This can create a security problem for computer centers.

- Use *identity proofing* whenever an issue arises between identification and authentication. The identification process starts when a user ID or logon name is typed into a sign-on screen. Authentication is accomplished by challenging the claim of who is accessing the resource. In other words, you start by claiming to be some specific user (perhaps an administrator); then authentication asks you to prove it (perhaps by providing the proper password).

▪ Incorporate a second value, such as mother's maiden name, to prove a user's identity. This is helpful when identity proofing is invoked—for example, in the case of a lost password and a person claims that they are a given user but cannot be authenticated.

 Real World Scenario

Multifactor Authentication and Security

The IT manager of your company is becoming increasingly concerned about the laxness of users when it comes to computer security. She reports that users regularly leave the office at the end of the day without signing out of their accounts.

The company is attempting to win a contract that involves government work, which will require additional security measures. What would you suggest?

First and foremost, you should recommend that the company implement a multifactor authentication system. This system could consist of a smart card and a logon/password process. Most smart card readers can be configured to require that the card remain inserted in the reader while the user is logged on. If the smart card is removed, say at the end of the day, the workstation will automatically log the user out. By requiring a logon/ password process, you can still provide security if the smart card is stolen. This solution provides a reasonable level of security, and it doesn't significantly increase security costs. It works best if the smart card is also required to exit the building, otherwise you run the risk of people leaving their cards at their desk when they go home.

Other suggestions are to consider additional access controls, such as perimeter alarms and physical access control of sensitive areas. The government would probably require these anyway, although such measures won't force users to log out when they leave their workstations.

An inherent problem with many identity-proofing implementations is that they ask questions that someone other than the user could easily guess or learn (for example, what color are your eyes?). To increase the difficulty of someone fraudulently using identity proofing, you should use only questions that are difficult to guess, or implement biometrics such as voice identification. Under no circumstances should the person proofing be allowed access immediately; instead, their access information should be sent to their email account of record.

Authentication Protocols

A variety of authentication protocols are used to aid in authenticating a user (or another system) to a system:

- *PAP (Password Authentication Protocol)* is an older system that is no longer used. PAP sends the username and password to the authentication server in plain text.

- *SPAP (Shiva Password Authentication Protocol)* replaced PAP. The main difference is that SPAP encrypts the username and password.

- *CHAP (Challenge Handshake Authentication Protocol)* was designed to stop man-in-the-middle attacks. During the initial authentication, the connecting machine is asked to generate a random number (usually a hash) and send it to the server. Periodically the server will challenge the client machine, demanding to see that number again. If an attacker has taken over the session, they won't know that number and won't be able to authenticate.

- The *TOTP (Time-Based One-Time Password)* algorithm uses a time-based factor to create unique passwords.

- The *HOTP (HMAC-Based One-Time Password)* algorithm is based on using a Hash Message Authentication Code (HMAC) algorithm. HMAC will be discussed in Chapter 7, "Host, Data, and Application Security."

Account Policy Enforcement

The account policy determines the security parameters regarding who can and cannot access the system. As mentioned earlier, there is a fine line between lax security (which keeps users happy) and stringent security. When you impose stringent security—long passwords that must be changed every few days and accounts locked as soon as wrong entries are given—you create unhappy users who will often start jeopardizing the very security you are trying to create by writing down values on slips of paper that can fall in the wrong hands.

In this section, we will look at the best practices related to key components of account policy enforcement that you need to know for the exam. These include the issues of password length and complexity, password expiration, password recovery, and, finally, password disablement and lockout.

Password Length and Complexity

The more difficult a user's password is, the more difficult it becomes for a miscreant to break it and log in as that user, and the more difficult it becomes, as well, for the user to remember it. Thus, you need to obtain a fine balance between the two extremes.

Eight characters (upper and lowercase) are generally considered the minimum for password length, and most systems today encourage the use of at least one non-alpha character—punctuation, special characters, numbers, and so on. On Windows-based systems, the password value can be set to 0 to not require passwords.

Windows 8 (as well as older Windows versions such as Windows 7 and Vista)—through the Local Security Policy (which is overridden by Group Policy values on a domain controller)—allows you to choose to enable password complexity. Choosing this option requires users to create passwords that meet the following requirements:

- They cannot contain the user's account name or parts of the user's full name that exceed two consecutive characters.

- They must be at least eight characters long.

- They have to contain characters from at least three of the following four sets:

  - A–Z

  - a–z

  - 0–9

  - Non-alpha characters (!, $, #, %, and so forth)

 There are methods that will allow a person with physical access to a Windows machine to retrieve the password regardless of complexity. You can find tools such as Ophcrack freely available on the Web for this purpose. For this reason, many experts recommend longer passphrases with complexity. For example, !L!k3Ch33s3Burg3rsFromBurg3rK!ng would be something the user can remember but would be difficult to guess or crack.

Password Expiration

Every password must expire because the longer the same value is used, the more likely it is to be broken. Ninety days is acceptable for many organizations, but Microsoft often recommends setting this value to 42 days if you want to enforce strong password usage throughout the organization. For more information on this topic, go to http://technet .microsoft.com/en-us/library/cc875814.aspx.

To keep users from changing their password to the same value as the old one, or to one they used the last time around, you should enable *password history*. Most Microsoft OSs allow you to set this to a number between 0 (disabled) and 24. For the best security, set it to 24 so that 24 unique passwords must be used by any given user before they can begin to reuse them.

Along with the expiration date, you should configure a minimum number of days that can exist between password changes. If this setting is disabled or set too low, users can immediately change new passwords to other values—something a hacker may want to do. We recommended that you not set it to anything lower than 2 days.

Password Recovery

One of the certainties in life is that users will occasionally forget their password. This often occurs shortly after they've changed it from one value to another, but it can often occur after a long weekend. Since a user's password isn't stored on most operating systems (only a hash value is kept), most operating systems allow the administrator to change the value for a user who has forgotten theirs. This new value allows the user to log in and then immediately change it to another value that they can (ideally) remember.

Password Disablement and Lockout

When a user will be gone from a company for a while (maternity leave, for example), their account should be disabled until they return. When a user will be gone from a company forever (termination), their account should be removed from the system immediately.

> If there is the possibility that the terminated employee may come back as a contractor, then consider suspending the account as opposed to removing it. This action is preferable since relative identifiers (RIDs) are not reused after they are deleted.

Between the two extremes lies the need to lock an account. This occurs when a user is attempting to log in but giving incorrect values; locking this account is necessary to prevent a would-be attacker from repeatedly guessing at password values until they find a match. You can configure the lockout policies at the local level on the workstation (Local Security Policy) as well as at the domain level (Group Policies), and the values you configure are the same:

Account Lockout Duration   When the system locks the account, this is the duration before it is unlocked. With Windows, this value can range from 0 minutes to 99,999 minutes. Setting it to 0 does not disable the feature but rather requires an administrator to explicitly unlock the account before it can be used again.

Account Lockout Threshold   This setting determines how many incorrect attempts a user can give before the account is locked. In Windows, this value can range from 0 to 999 failed attempts. If it is set at 0, the account will never be locked out. Note that attempts to enter values at the password-protected screensaver count just the same as attempts to log in after the system has booted and Ctrl+Alt+Delete has been pressed.

Reset Account Lockout Counter After   This value specifies the number of minutes to wait between counting failed login attempts that are part of the same batch of attempts. For example, Account Lockout Threshold may be set to 3 to lock the account after three bad tries, but this value can be set to 5 so that if the user tries once and then waits more than five minutes to try again, they have another three attempts before the account is locked. The values here can range from 0 to 99,999 minutes. This value can be set (or have meaning) only if the Account Lockout Threshold is set, and the reset time must be less than or equal to the Account Lockout Duration value.

Users with Multiple Accounts/Roles

As we mentioned when discussing least privilege, of particular concern is users who have multiple accounts and/or act in multiple roles. An example of this is any administrator who has an account they use for administrative purposes and one they use when performing another role (editor, author, etc.). In most organizations, it is not possible to not have a number of users who operate in multiple capacities. The key then becomes education and policies.

Education is needed to show why employees should use the elevated accounts only when necessary and to make them understand the security risks inherent in operating at those levels. Policies are needed to put into action and enforce the common sense that these users should possess. The policy should be understood—and signed off on—by those operating in this group.

Generic Account Prohibition

A generic account is any account that is shared—allowing multiple users to log in and use the system/network/resource. Not only can these be guest accounts, but they can also be anonymous accounts, accounts created for temporary users, and a plethora of other possibilities. While such generic accounts can make it easy to grant access to the system, they suffer from two significant problems. The first is the password is shared, and that goes against normal security procedures. The second significant problem is that since the account is being shared, auditing it can be a nightmare. As a general rule, therefore, generic accounts should not be used where they can be avoided.

Group-based and User-assigned Privileges

Two methods of privilege assignment prevalent today are group-based and user-assigned. As the name implies, group-based privileges are those acquired as a result of belonging to a group. This topic is touched on in several locations throughout this chapter (with the discussion of group policy, and role-based access control), but the easiest way to think of it is that if you are member of the editors' group, then you have access to resources needed by editors and it is easier for the administrator to grant permissions to all members of that group than to individually assign them to each.

User-assigned privileges are those that can be assigned by the user. For example, when you create a file in most operating systems, you can change the permissions associated with that file. It is possible, for example, to give others the privilege of only being able to read it, or to read and write to it.

Understanding Remote Access Connectivity

One of the primary purposes of having a network is the ability to connect systems. As networks have grown, many technologies have come on the scene to make this process easier and more secure. A key area of concern relates to the connection of systems and other networks that aren't part of your network. The following sections discuss the more common protocols used to facilitate connectivity among remote systems.

Ancient History: The Serial Line Internet Protocol

Serial Line Internet Protocol (SLIP) is an older protocol that was used in early remote access environments and serves as the starting point for most remote discussions. SLIP was originally designed to connect Unix systems in a dial-up environment, and it only supported serial communications.

A very simple protocol, SLIP could only be used to pass TCP/IP traffic and wasn't secure or efficient. Although some systems today still support SLIP, it is strictly there for legacy systems and should be avoided whenever possible.

Any authentication done for a remote user is known as *remote authentication*. This authentication is commonly done using TACACS, TACACS+, XTACACS, or RADIUS.

Using the Point-to-Point Protocol

Introduced in 1994, the *Point-to-Point Protocol (PPP)* offers support for multiple protocols, including AppleTalk, IPX, and DECnet. PPP works with POTS, Integrated Services Digital Network (ISDN), and other faster connections, such as T1. PPP doesn't provide data security, but it does provide authentication using the *Challenge Handshake Authentication Protocol (CHAP)*.

Except for CHAP, the aforementioned protocols are just given for background information and are not on the Security+ exam. CHAP is described in more detail elsewhere in this chapter.

Figure 4.4 shows a PPP connection over an ISDN line. In the case of ISDN, PPP would normally use one 64 Kbps B channel for transmission. PPP allows many channels in a network connection (such as ISDN) to be connected or bonded together to form a single virtual connection.

PPP works by encapsulating the network traffic in a protocol called the *Network Control Protocol (NCP)*. Authentication is handled by the *Link Control Protocol (LCP)*. A PPP connection allows remote users to log on to the network and have access as though they were local users on the network. PPP doesn't provide for any encryption services for the channel.

As you may have guessed, the unsecure nature of PPP makes it largely unsuitable for WAN connections. To counter this issue, other protocols have been created that take advantage of PPP's flexibility and build on it. You should make sure that all of your PPP connections use secure channels, dedicated connections, or high-speed connections.

Remote users who connect directly to a system don't necessarily need to have encryption capabilities enabled. If the connection is direct, the likelihood that anyone would be able to tap an existing phone line is relatively small. However, you should make sure that connections through a network use an encryption-oriented tunneling system.

FIGURE 4.4 PPP using a single B channel on an ISDN connection

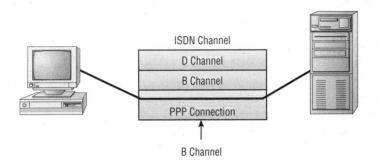

Working with Tunneling Protocols

Tunneling protocols add the ability to create tunnels between networks that can be more secure, support additional protocols, and provide virtual paths between systems. The best way to think of tunneling is to imagine sensitive data being encapsulated in other packets that are sent across the public network. Once they're received at the other end, the sensitive data is stripped from the other packets and recompiled into its original form.

The most common protocols used for tunneling are as follows:

Point-to-Point Tunneling Protocol *Point-to-Point Tunneling Protocol (PPTP)* supports encapsulation in a single point-to-point environment. PPTP encapsulates and encrypts PPP packets. This makes PPTP a favorite low-end protocol for networks. The negotiation between the two ends of a PPTP connection is done in the clear. After the negotiation is performed, the channel is encrypted. This is one of the major weaknesses of PPTP. A *packet-capture device*, such as a sniffer, that captures the negotiation process can potentially use that information to determine the connection type and information about how the tunnel works. Microsoft developed PPTP and supports it on most of its products. PPTP uses port 1723 and TCP for connections.

Layer 2 Forwarding *Layer 2 Forwarding (L2F)* was created by Cisco as a method of creating tunnels primarily for dial-up connections. It's similar in capability to PPP and shouldn't be used over WANs. L2F provides authentication, but it doesn't provide encryption. L2F uses port 1701 and TCP for connections.

Layer 2 Tunneling Protocol Microsoft and Cisco agreed to combine their respective tunneling protocols into one: *Layer 2 Tunneling Protocol (L2TP)*. L2TP is a hybrid of PPTP and L2F. It's primarily a point-to-point protocol. L2TP supports multiple network protocols and can be used in networks beside TCP/IP. L2TP works over IPX, SNA, and IP, so it can be used as a bridge across many types of systems. The major problem with L2TP is that it doesn't provide data security—the information isn't encrypted. Security can be provided by protocols such as IPSec. L2TP uses port 1701 and UDP for connections.

Secure Shell   *Secure Shell (SSH)* is a tunneling protocol originally designed for Unix systems. It uses encryption to establish a secure connection between two systems. SSH also provides alternative, security-equivalent programs for such Unix standards as Telnet, FTP, and many other communications-oriented applications. SSH is available for use on Windows systems as well. This makes it the preferred method of security for Telnet and other cleartext-oriented programs in the Unix environment. SSH uses port 22 and TCP for connections.

Internet Protocol Security   *Internet Protocol Security (IPSec)* isn't a tunneling protocol, but it's used in conjunction with tunneling protocols. IPSec is oriented primarily toward LAN-to-LAN connections, but it can also be used with remote connections. IPSec provides secure authentication and encryption of data and headers, which makes it a good choice for security. IPSec can work in either Tunneling mode or Transport mode. In Tunneling mode, the data or payload and message headers are encrypted. Transport mode encrypts only the payload. IPSec is an add-on to IPv4 and built into IPv6.

Working with RADIUS

Remote Authentication Dial-In User Service (RADIUS) is a mechanism that allows authentication of remote and other network connections. Originally intended for use on dial-up connections, it has moved well beyond that and offers many state-of the-art features. The RADIUS protocol is an IETF standard, and it has been implemented by most of the major operating system manufacturers. A RADIUS server can be managed centrally, and the servers that allow access to a network can verify with a RADIUS server whether an incoming caller is authorized. In a large network with many connections, this allows a single server to perform all authentications.

 The term *caller* may seem outdated, but Windows Server 2012 (and 2008 as well as 2003) all refer to the ability to remotely access a system as *dial-in privileges*. Although few people are actually "dialing" or calling in, the terms have stuck.

Figure 4.5 shows an example of a RADIUS server communicating with an ISP to allow access to a remote user. Notice that the remote ISP server is functioning as a client to the RADIUS server. This allows centralized administration of access rights.

You should use RADIUS when you want to improve network security by implementing a single service to authenticate users who connect remotely to the network. Doing so gives you a single source for the authentication to take place. Additionally, you can implement auditing and accounting on the RADIUS server.

The major difficulty with a single-server RADIUS environment is that the entire network may refuse connections if the server malfunctions. Many RADIUS systems allow multiple servers to be used to increase reliability. All of these servers are critical components of the infrastructure, and they must be protected from attack.

FIGURE 4.5 The RADIUS client manages the local connection and authenticates against a central server.

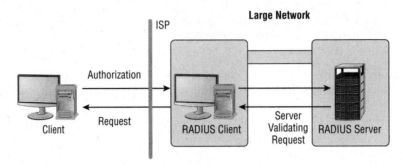

TACACS/TACACS+/XTACACS

Terminal Access Controller Access-Control System (TACACS) is a client/server-oriented environment, and it operates in a manner similar to RADIUS. Extended TACACS (XTACACS) replaced the original version and combined authentication and authorization with logging to enable auditing.

The most current method, or level, of TACACS is TACACS+. It replaces the previous two incarnations. TACACS+ allows credentials to be accepted from multiple methods, including Kerberos. The TACACS client/server process occurs in the same manner as the RADIUS process illustrated in Figure 4.5.

Cisco has widely implemented TACACS+ for connections. TACACS+ has become a widely accepted as an alternative to RADIUS.

Remember, RADIUS and TACACS (or any of its variations such as TACACS+ or XTACACS) can be used to authenticate connections.

VLAN Management

A *virtual local area network (VLAN)* allows you to create groups of users and systems and segment them on the network. This segmentation lets you hide segments of the network from other segments and thereby control access. You can also set up VLANs to control the paths that data takes to get from one point to another. A VLAN is a good way to contain network traffic to a certain area in a network.

Think of a VLAN as a network of hosts that act as if they're connected by a physical wire even though there is no such wire between them.

On a LAN, hosts can communicate with each other through broadcasts, and no forwarding devices, such as routers, are needed. As the LAN grows, so too does the number of broadcasts. Shrinking the size of the LAN by segmenting it into smaller groups (VLANs) reduces the size of the broadcast domains. The advantages of doing this include reducing the scope of the broadcasts, improving performance and manageability, and decreasing dependence on the physical topology. From the standpoint of this exam, however, the key benefit is that VLANs can increase security by allowing users with similar data sensitivity levels to be segmented together.

SAML

Security Assertion Markup Language (SAML) is an open standard based on XML that is used for authentication and authorization data. Service providers often use SAML to prove the identity of someone connecting to the service provider. The current version is SAML v2.0.

Understanding Authentication Services

Authentication services are the implementation of the specific technology in question. For this part of the exam, the focus is on LDAP and Kerberos, though many other possibilities exist, such as Internet Authentication Service (IAS) and Central Authentication Service (CAS), which are outside the scope of this exam. Single sign-on initiatives round out the discussion in this section.

LDAP

Lightweight Directory Access Protocol (LDAP) is a standardized directory access protocol that allows queries to be made of directories (specifically, pared-down X.500-based directories). If a directory service supports LDAP, you can query that directory with an LDAP client, but it's LDAP itself that is growing in popularity and is being used extensively in online white and yellow pages.

LDAP is the main access protocol used by Active Directory. It operates, by default, at port 389. The LDAP syntax uses commas between names.

Because a breach of LDAP can be quite serious, some organizations use secure LDAP. With *secure LDAP* (LDAPS), all LDAP communications are encrypted with SSL/TLS, and port 636 is used.

Throughout this book you will see various port numbers mentioned. These port numbers are often the subject of questions on the Security+ exam (as well as other security-related certifications), so it is a good idea for you to get to know them.

Kerberos

Kerberos is an authentication protocol named after the mythical three-headed dog that stood at the gates of Hades. Originally designed by MIT, Kerberos is very popular as an authentication method. It allows for a single sign-on to a distributed network.

Kerberos authentication uses a *key distribution center (KDC)* to orchestrate the process. The KDC authenticates the *principal* (which can be a user, program, or system) and provides it with a ticket. After this ticket is issued, it can be used to authenticate against other principals. This process occurs automatically when another principal performs a request or service.

Kerberos is quickly becoming a common standard in network environments. Its only significant weakness is that the KDC can be a single point of failure. If the KDC goes down, the authentication process will stop. Figure 4.6 illustrates the Kerberos authentication process and the ticket being presented to systems that are authorized by the KDC.

When using Kerberos, the user authenticates to the KDC and is given a *ticket granting ticket (TGT)*. This ticket is encrypted and has a time limit of up to 10 hours. The ticket lists the privileges of that user (much like a token). Each time the user wishes to access some resource on the network, the user's computer presents the KDC with the TGT; the TGT then sends that user's computer a *service ticket*, granting the user access to that service. Service tickets are usually only good for up to 5 minutes. The user's computer then sends the service ticket to the server the user is trying to access. As a final authentication check, that server then communicates with the TGT to confirm and validate the service ticket.

FIGURE 4.6   Kerberos authentication process

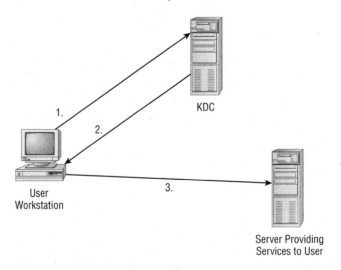

1. User requests access to service running on a different server.
2. KDC authenticates user and sends a ticket to be used between the user and the service on the server.
3. User's workstation sends a ticket to the service.

Single Sign-On Initiatives

One of the big problems that larger systems must deal with is the need for users to access multiple systems or applications. This may require a user to remember multiple accounts and passwords. The purpose of a *single sign-on (SSO)* is to give users access to all the applications and systems they need when they log on. This is becoming a reality in many environments, including Kerberos, Microsoft Active Directory, Novell eDirectory, and some certificate model implementations.

> Single sign-on is both a blessing and a curse. It's a blessing in that once the user is authenticated, they can access all of the resources on the network and browse multiple directories. It's a curse in that it removes the doors that otherwise exist between the user and various resources.

In the case of Kerberos, a single token allows any "Kerberized" applications to accept a user as valid. The important thing to remember in this process is that each application that wants to use SSO must be able to accept and process the token presented by Kerberos.

Active Directory (AD) uses a slightly different method. A server that runs AD retains information about all access rights for all users and groups in the network. When a user logs on to the system, AD issues the user a globally unique identifier (GUID). Applications that support AD can use this GUID to provide access control.

Figure 4.7 illustrates this process in further detail. In this instance, the database application, email client, and printers all authenticate with the same logon. Like Kerberos, this process requires all applications that want to take advantage of AD to accept AD controls and directives.

FIGURE 4.7   AD validating a user

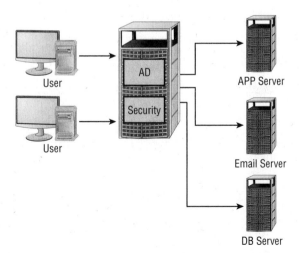

In this way, the user doesn't have to have separate sign-on, email, and application passwords. Using AD simplifies the sign-on process for users and lowers the support requirements for administrators. Access can be established through groups, and it can be enforced through group memberships. For example, the domain administrator can place all the tech support people in a group named techsupport and assign privileges to the entire group.

On a decentralized network, SSO passwords are stored on each server and can represent a security risk. It's important to enforce password changes and make certain that passwords are updated throughout the organization on a frequent basis.

Although single sign-on has its own security issues, it is perhaps the simplest way to mitigate the issue of users with multiple roles and multiple accounts. If a user is required to manage a plethora of accounts/login credentials, the natural tendency is to write down usernames and passwords, which is a major security risk. Single sign-on, if managed properly, can be an excellent answer to this issue.

 Single sign-on is not the opposite of multifactor authentication, but it is often mistakenly thought of this way. One-, two-, and three-factor authentication merely refer to the number of items a user must supply to authenticate. Authentication can be based on something they have (a smart card), something they know (a password), something unique (biometric), and so forth. Once factor authentication is done, single sign-on can still apply throughout a user's session.

Understanding Access Control

The four primary methods of access control are as follows:

Mandatory Access Control (MAC)   All access is predefined.

Discretionary Access Control (DAC)   Incorporates some flexibility.

Role-Based Access Control (RBAC)   Allows the user's role to dictate access capabilities.

Rule-Based Access Control (RBAC)   Rule-Based Access Control (which also uses the RBAC acronym) is gaining in popularity and limits the user to settings in preconfigured policies.

Each of these methods has advantages and disadvantages to the organization from a security perspective—that's why they all still exist. Each is appropriate for some environment.

There has been some recent discussion of something called *Lattice-Based Control (LBAC)*. LBAC is a variation of Mandatory Access Control, and it isn't addressed separately on the Security+ exam. It involves a lattice composed of subjects (users, systems, and so forth) and resources, and the resources are labeled to provide access control.

The method you choose will be greatly affected by your organization's philosophy on the sharing of information. In a high-security environment, the tendency is to implement either a MAC or RBAC (in this case Role-Based Access Control) method. In a traditional business environment or educational institution, the tendency is to implement a DAC method. You should do some consulting within the organization to understand how particular departments and the organization as a whole want to implement access control models. Doing so will allow you to gather input from all concerned parties about how to establish access guidelines and how to implement security.

In the following sections, we will look at each of these methods from a business perspective.

Mandatory Access Control

Mandatory Access Control (MAC) is a relatively inflexible method for how information access is permitted. In a MAC environment, all access capabilities are predefined. Users can't share information unless their rights to share it are established by administrators. Consequently, administrators must make any changes that need to be made to such rights. This process enforces a rigid model of security. However, it is also considered the most secure security model.

For a MAC model to work effectively, administrators and network designers must think relationships through carefully in advance of implementation. The advantage of this model is that security access is well established and well defined, making security breaches easier to investigate and correct. A well-designed MAC model can make the job of information control easier and can essentially lock down a network. The major disadvantages of this model are its lack of flexibility and the fact that it requires change over time. The inability of administrative staff to address these changes can sometimes make the model hard to maintain.

This model is used in environments where confidentiality is a driving force. It often employs government and military classifications (labels), such as Top Secret and others.

Discretionary Access Control

In a *Discretionary Access Control (DAC)* model, network users have some flexibility regarding how information is accessed. This model allows users to share information dynamically with other users. The method allows for a more flexible environment, but it increases the risk of unauthorized disclosure of information. Administrators have a more difficult time ensuring that information access is controlled and that only appropriate access is issued.

A classic example of DAC is the permission structure that exists for "other" with files in the Unix/Linux environment. All permissions in this operating system fall within three groups of users: owner, group, and other. The permissions associated with the owner and the group to which the owner belongs are based on their roles, but all of those who are not the owner, or a member of the owner's group, fall within the category of other.

The permissions for this group are set separately from the other two and, with very few special exceptions, are a combination of read, write, and execute. Within this environment, you can create a database and give yourself (owner) permission to read and write, give other admins (group) only read permission, and not give any permission to those not in admin (other).

You could just as easily create a script file that cleans up log files and frees space on a workstation. To do this, you would give yourself (owner) all rights, give other admins (group) the ability to read and execute, and give basic users (other) the right only to execute.

Role-Based Access Control

Role-Based Access Control (RBAC) models approach the problem of access control based on established roles in an organization. RBAC models implement access by job function or by responsibility. Each employee has one or more roles that allow access to specific information. If a person moves from one role to another, the access for the previous role will no longer be available. RBAC models provide more flexibility than the MAC model and less flexibility than the DAC model. They do, however, have the advantage of being strictly based on job function as opposed to individual needs.

Instead of thinking "Denise needs to be able to edit files," RBAC uses the logic "Editors need to be able to edit files" and "Denise is a member of the Editors group." This model is always good for use in an environment in which there is high employee turnover.

This is also sometimes called *group-based control* or *group-based permissions*. Essentially, Windows operating systems work in this fashion. Your permissions on a Windows-based domain are determined by the group(s) into which you are placed. These groups are, in effect, roles.

Rule-Based Access Control

Rule-Based Access Control (RBAC) uses the settings in preconfigured security policies to make all decisions. These rules can be to:

- Deny all but those who specifically appear in a list (an allow list)
- Deny only those who specifically appear in the list (a true deny list)

Entries in the list may be usernames, IP addresses, hostnames, or even domains. Rule-Based models are often being used in conjunction with Role-Based to add greater flexibility.

The easiest way to implement Rule-Based Access Control is with access control lists (ACLs), discussed later in this chapter. The ACLs create the rules by which the access control model functions.

Implementing Access Controlling Best Practices

How you implement access control makes all the difference in the security of your systems. In this section, we will look at smart cards, access control lists, trusted operating systems, secure router configuration, and a few others.

Least Privileges

This is one of the most critical concepts in access control. Implementing *least privileges* means that any given user (or system) is given the minimum privileges necessary to accomplish his or her job. For example, if sales managers need to run reports from a database, they will be given privileges only allowing the running of reports. They won't be given privileges to delete data, alter the database tables, add users, and so forth.

Any privilege could be used to cause some harm to the system, even inadvertently, for example, the deletion of important data. This is particularly true when users have more privileges than they really need. Also, *privilege escalation* is a common attack on systems. Giving each user the minimum privileges to accomplish their job reduces this risk.

In the real world, you will find some resistance to this idea. Some employees will perceive it as a lack of trust. For example, a software engineer, who may have more experience and more training than the security administrator, might be upset to learn that she does not have unrestricted access to the database. One way to address this is to educate end users. One fact that tends to be compelling to users is this: If they don't have access to a given system/resource and if something goes awry with that resource, they cannot be held responsible.

Separation of Duties

Almost every operating system in use today employs the concept of differentiation between users and groups at varying levels. As an example, there is always a system administrator (SA) account that has godlike control over everything: root in Unix/Linux, admin (or a deviation of it) in Windows, administrator in Apple OS X, supervisor in Novell NetWare, and so on. Once you move beyond that user, you move to administrative accounts, then regular users, and all the way down to restricted accounts, which can barely do more than log in.

As a security administrator, you need to use that as a baseline and then go beyond that and make certain that you have as many different levels of permissions and privileges as possible. At a minimum, you should do the following:

- Separate the SA account from regular accounts. *Never* log in as the SA and use the system to perform routine functions. Use the SA account only to do those operations that require those privileges.

- Limit the SA account to as small a group as possible.

- Separate the audit and logging responsibilities from the SA.

Again, using the ISO standard as an example, it recommends the segregation of duties and separation of environments as a way to reduce the likelihood of misuse of systems or information (either intentional or accidental).

Time of Day Restrictions

One of the easiest policies to enforce is time of day restrictions. Almost every operating system—server and workstation—allows you to configure when an account can have access to the system. While it may seem pedantic, it can increase the security of the system significantly. For example, if you are the administrator for an office, and workers use the systems only from 8:00 to 5:00 Monday through Friday, then you can configure their accounts to allow access only from 7:00 to 6:00 (offering an extra hour at each end for work they need to do outside of normal) on those days and not allow access outside of those parameters. What you have accomplished by making the accounts valid for only 55 hours each week is to prevent them from being used by attackers the other 113 hours. As simple as it is, it is also effective.

Restrictions can be applied as policies for groups or users in Active Directory, set locally, or set through a number of add-on packages.

User Access Review

In addition to assigning user access properly, it is important to review that access periodically. *Access review* is a process to determine whether a user's access level is still appropriate. People's roles within an organization can change over time. It is important to review user accounts periodically and determine if they still require the access they currently have. An example of such a scenario would be a network administrator who was responsible for the domain controller but then moved over to administer the remote access servers. The administrator's access to the domain controller should now be terminated. This concept of access review is closely related to the concept of least privileges. It is important that users do not have "leftover" privileges from previous job roles.

Another closely related topic is continuous monitoring. *Continuous monitoring* implies an ongoing audit of what resources a user actually accesses. This can be critical for stopping insider threats. For example, a human resources employee would need access to employee files. However, if that employee is accessing a given employee's file without a valid work-related reason, this is a security breach. Only by continuously monitoring access can you detect such breaches.

It turns out that Edward Snowden was using other users' accounts to access tremendous amounts of data at the National Security Administration (NSA). It was also learned that the NSA location where Snowden was working lacked continuous monitoring. One has to wonder, if they had such monitoring, would they have detected his anomalous activities and prevented a massive security breach?

Smart Cards

Smart cards are generally used for access control and security purposes. The card itself usually contains a small amount of memory that can be used to store permissions and access information.

Smart cards are difficult to counterfeit, but they're easy to steal. Once a thief has a smart card, they have access to all that the card allows. To prevent this, many organizations don't put any identifying marks on their smart cards, making it harder for someone to use them. A password or PIN is required to activate most smart cards, and encryption is employed to protect the contents. With many smart cards, if you enter the wrong PIN number multiple times (usually three), the card will shut down to enhance security further.

Many European countries are beginning to use smart cards instead of magnetic-strip credit cards because they offer additional security and can contain more information.

 Real World Scenario

Working with Smart Cards

You've been asked to help troubleshoot a problem that is occurring in your school's computer lab. Students are complaining about viruses that are infecting the flash drives they bring to school. How can you help remedy this situation?

Make sure that all of the systems in your school lab computers are running antivirus software and that this software is kept up to date. Doing so will prevent known viruses from entering the school's system and being transferred to student files.

You may also want to evaluate whether the school's computers should have removable media installed on their systems. Several manufacturers sell systems called *thin clients*, which don't provide any disk storage or removable media on their workstations. Thin clients access servers to download applications, data, and any other information they need to have in order to run. This eliminates the danger of viruses being introduced from student disks.

There are two main types of smart cards: Common Access Cards and Personal Identification Verification Cards. We will discuss these smart cards in the following sections.

Common Access Card

One type of smart card is the *Common Access Card (CAC)*. These cards are issued by the Department of Defense (DoD) as a general identification/authentication card for military personnel, contractors, and non-DoD employees. A picture appears on the front of the card with an integrated chip beneath and a barcode. On the back of the card is a magnetic strip and another barcode.

A CAC is used for accessing DoD computers, signing email, and implementing PKI. In 2008, the most recent year for which data is available, over 17 million cards had been issued. You can find current information on the CAC here: www.cac.mil.

Personal Identification Verification Card

What the CAC is for military employees, the *Personal Identity Verification (PIV)* (referenced by CompTIA as Personal Identification Verification Card) is to federal employees and contractors. Per Homeland Security Presidential Directive number 12 (HSPD-12), the PIV will eventually be required of all U.S. government employees and contractors. The PIV will be required to gain access (physical and logical) to government resources.

Access Control Lists

Access control lists (ACLs) enable devices in your network to ignore requests from specified users or systems or to grant them access to certain network capabilities. You may find that a certain IP address is constantly scanning your network, and you can block this IP address at the router and the IP address will automatically be rejected any time it attempts to utilize your network.

ACLs allow a stronger set of access controls to be established in your network. The basic process of ACL control allows the administrator to design and adapt the network to deal with specific security threats.

The following sections look at approaches to ACLs, including implicit deny and firewall rules.

Implicit Deny

Within ACLs exists a condition known as implicit deny. An *implicit deny* clause is implied at the end of each ACL, and it means that if the proviso in question has not been explicitly granted, then access is denied.

 Real World Scenario

The Implicit Deny Bouncer

Suppose you're hosting a party at your home and you give the guest list to a strong friend of yours. As each guest arrives, your friend examines the list to see if their name appears on it. If their name is not on the list, then the "party crasher" is denied entry (access). You don't have to tell your friend not to let in specific people; only if those attempting entry are not on the guest list, they are implicitly denied access.

The same principle holds true in the ACL. The entity denied access because it does not appear on a list can be a source address, a destination address, a packet type, or almost anything else for which you want to deny access.

Firewall Rules

Firewall rules act like ACLs, and they are used to dictate what traffic can pass between the firewall and the internal network. Three possible actions can be taken based on the rule's criteria:

- Block the connection
- Allow the connection
- Allow the connection only if it is secured

The rules can be applied to inbound traffic or outbound traffic and any type of network (LAN, wireless, VPN, or remote access). You should audit the firewall rules on a regular basis, verify that you are obtaining the results you want, and make modifications as necessary.

Port Security

Port security involves the Coast Guard keeping our seaports safe from terrorism. Not really. In the realm of IT, port security works at level 2 of the OSI model and allows an administrator to configure switch ports so that only certain MAC addresses can use the port. This is a common feature on both Cisco's Catalyst as well as Juniper's EX Series switches and essentially differentiates so-called dumb switches from managed (or intelligent) switches. Similarly, Dynamic ARP Inspection (DAI) works with these and other smart switches to protect ports from ARP spoofing.

Three areas of port security that CompTIA wants you to be familiar with for the Security+ exam are as follows:

MAC Limiting and Filtering   Limit access to the network to MAC addresses that are known, and filter out those that are not. Even in a home network, you can implement MAC filtering with most routers and typically have an option of choosing to allow only computers with MAC addresses that you list or deny only computers with MAC addresses that you list.

> If you don't know a workstation's MAC address, use `ipconfig /all` to find it in the Windows-based world (it is listed as *physical address*) and use `ip a` or `ifconfig` in Unix/Linux.

MAC filtering is not foolproof, and a quick look in a search engine will turn up tools that can be used to change the MAC address and help miscreants circumvent this control.

802.1X   As discussed in the following section, adding port authentication to MAC filtering takes security for the network down to the switch port level and increases your security exponentially.

Unused Ports   All ports not in use should be disabled. Otherwise, they present an open door for an attacker to enter.

Working with 802.1X

The IEEE standard 802.1X defines port-based security for wireless network access control. As such, it offers a means of authentication and defines the Extensible Authentication Protocol (EAP) over IEEE 802—discussed in Chapter 12, "Disaster Recovery and Incident Response"—and is often known as *EAP over LAN* (EAPOL). The biggest benefit of using 802.1X is that the access points and the switches do not need to do the authentication but instead rely on the authentication server to do the actual work.

Flood Guards and Loop Protection

A *flood guard* is a protection feature built into many firewalls that allows the administrator to tweak the tolerance for unanswered login attacks. Reducing this tolerance makes it possible to lessen the likelihood of a successful DoS attack.

If a resource—inbound or outbound—appears to be overused, then the flood guard kicks in. With many Cisco firewalls, to protect subgroups and devices you can configure the same protection you apply at an upper level to be inherited by children as well.

Loop protection is a similar feature that works in layer 2 switching configurations and is intended to prevent broadcast loops. When configuring it in most systems, you can choose to disable broadcast forwarding and protect against duplicate ARP requests (those having the same target protocol address). The *Spanning Tree Protocol (STP)* is intended to ensure loop-free bridged Ethernet LANs. It operates at the Data Link layer and ensures only one active path exists between two stations.

Preventing Network Bridging

Network bridging occurs when a device has more than one network adapter card installed and the opportunity presents itself for a user on one of the networks to which the device is attached to jump to the other. Although multiple cards have been used in servers (known as multihomed hosts) for years, it is not uncommon today to find multiple cards in laptops (wired and wireless) and the bridging to occur without the user truly understanding what is happening.

To prevent network bridging, you can configure your network such that when bridging is detected, you shut off/disable that jack. You can also create profiles that allow for only one interface.

At a micro level, you can configure workstations to disable unused connections. In Windows 8, for example, you can accomplish this by choosing Control Panel ➤ Network And Internet ➤ Network Sharing Center and then clicking Change Adapter Settings.

It is not uncommon for a network bridge to appear in the Network Sharing Center. If it does appear, you will want to delete it. Windows Internet Connection is often identified as a cause of unintended bridging and should be disabled.

Log Analysis

Log analysis is crucial to identifying problems that occur related to security. As an administrator, you have the ability to turn on logging at many different locations and levels. The next step, however, is the most important—what you do with the log information collected. Far too many administrators turn on logging and then fail to properly (if ever) analyze what they collect because it is a lot of information and a lot of work.

A number of programs are available that can automate the log analysis. One such program is ManageEngine (www.manageengine.com/it-compliance-suite.html).

Not only do you need to collect and analyze the logs, but you also need to store them for the future when you want to compare what is happening now to then (baselining). The logs should be stored in a format that you can quickly access and understand without having to convert them to a document each time you want to look at them.

Trusted OS

A *trusted operating system (TOS)* is any operating system that meets the government's requirements for security. The most common set of standards for security is *Common Criteria (CC)*. This document is a joint effort among Canada, France, Germany, the Netherlands, the United Kingdom, and the United States. The standard outlines a comprehensive set of evaluation criteria, broken down into seven *Evaluation Assurance Levels (EALs)*. EAL 1 to EAL 7 are discussed here:

As of this writing, the latest version of the standard is 3.1 Release 4, and it's available for viewing at www.commoncriteriaportal.org. The website also maintains a registry of products certified by CC.

EAL 1   EAL 1 is primarily used when the user wants assurance that the system will operate correctly but threats to security aren't viewed as serious.

EAL 2   EAL 2 requires product developers to use good design practices. Security isn't considered a high priority in EAL 2 certification.

EAL 3   EAL 3 requires conscientious development efforts to provide moderate levels of security.

EAL 4   EAL 4 requires positive security engineering based on good commercial development practices. It is anticipated that EAL 4 will be the common benchmark for commercial systems.

EAL 5   EAL 5 is intended to ensure that security engineering has been implemented in a product from the early design phases. It's intended for high levels of security assurance. The EAL documentation indicates that special design considerations will most likely be required to achieve this level of certification.

EAL 6   EAL 6 provides high levels of assurance of specialized security engineering. This certification indicates high levels of protection against significant risks. Systems with EAL 6 certification will be highly secure from penetration attackers.

EAL 7   EAL 7 is intended for extremely high levels of security. The certification requires extensive testing, measurement, and complete independent testing of every component.

EAL certification has replaced the Trusted Computer Systems Evaluation Criteria (TCSEC) system for certification, which was popular in the United States. It has also replaced the Information Technology Security Evaluation Criteria (ITSEC), which was popular in Europe. The recommended level of certification for commercial systems is EAL 4.

Currently, only a few operating systems have been approved at the EAL 4 level, and even though an operating system straight out of the box may be, that doesn't mean your own individual implementation of it is functioning at that level. If your implementation doesn't use the available security measures, then you're operating below that level.

As an administrator, you should know and thoroughly understand that just because the operating system you have is capable of being certified at a high level of security doesn't mean that your implementation is at that level.

Secure Router Configuration

One of the most important things you can do to secure your network is to secure the router. Though this is basic common sense, it is too often overlooked in the rush to finish the router configuration and move on to the next job. To configure the router securely, you must do the following:

Change the default password.   The password for the administrator is set before the router leaves the factory. You have to assume that every intruder wanting unauthorized access to your network knows the default passwords set by the factory. Employ good password principles (alphanumeric, more than eight characters, and so on), and change it to a value that is known only by those who must.

Walk through the advanced settings.   These settings will differ based on the router manufacturer and type, but they often include settings to block ping requests, perform MAC filtering, and so on. All of these issues are discussed elsewhere in this book, and they need to be applied to the router configuration as well.

Keep the firmware upgraded.   Router manufacturers often issue patches when problems are discovered. Those patches need to be applied to the router to remove any security gaps that may exist.

Always remember to back up your router configuration before making any significant changes—in particular a firmware upgrade—in order to provide a fallback in case something goes awry.

> Cisco routers often use one of two different types of passwords for their accounts: Type 7 and MD5. Type 7 passwords use weak encryption and are considered only slightly above Type 0, which is cleartext. As such, Type 7 passwords are easily decrypted with readily available shareware/freeware and should be avoided. MD5 password encryption uses a one-way hash, and this is configured in IOS (Cisco Internetwork Operating System) using the command enable secret.

Summary

The chapter focused on access control and identity management. The key difference between authentication and identification is that authentication means someone has accurate information, whereas identification means that accurate information is proven to be in possession of the correct individual.

The most basic form of authentication is known as single-factor authentication (SFA) because only one set of values is checked. To increase security, it is necessary to use multi-factor authentication, which involves two or more values that are checked.

This chapter examined the various types of authentication services in use, including RADIUS and different variations of TACACS. It also looked at tunneling protocols, smart cards, and other means of access control.

ACLs are being implemented in network devices and systems to enable the control of access to systems and users. ACLs allow individual systems, users, or IP addresses to be ignored.

Exam Essentials

Be able to describe the roles of access control.   The four primary roles are MAC, DAC, and RBAC (both types of RBAC). Mandatory Access Control (MAC) establishes rigid access control methods in the organization. Discretionary Access Control (DAC) allows for flexibility in access control. Role-Based Access Control (RBAC) is based on the role the individual or department has in the organization. In a fourth type, Rule-Based Access Control (RBAC) settings in preconfigured security policies are used to make all decisions.

Know the characteristics of the connectivity technologies available to you and the security capabilities associated with each.   Remote access, PPP, tunneling protocols, and VPNs are your primary tools. PPTP and L2TP are two of the most common protocols used for tunneling. IPSec, although not a tunneling protocol, provides encryption to tunneling protocols; it's often used to enhance tunnel security.

Know how ACLs work.   Access control lists (ACLs) are used to identify systems and specify which users, protocols, or services are allowed. ACL-based systems can be used to prevent unauthorized users from accessing vulnerable services.

Explain the relative advantages of the technologies available to you for authentication.   You have many tools available to you to help establish authentication processes. Some of these tools start with a password and user ID. Others involve physical devices or the physical characteristics of the person who is requesting authentication.

Know how to deal with users having multiple roles.   Users who have multiple accounts and/or act in multiple roles, such as an administrator who has an account for administrative purposes and one for performing another role, require attention and education. Users need to understand why they should use the elevated accounts only when necessary and the security risks inherent in operating at those levels.

Understand least privilege.   Least privilege states that when assigning permissions, you should give users only the permissions they need to do their work and no more. The biggest benefit to following this policy is the reduction of risk.

Review Questions

1. Which of the following is the basic premise of least privilege?

    A. Always assign responsibilities to the administrator who has the minimum permissions required.

    B. When assigning permissions, give users only the permissions they need to do their work and no more.

    C. Regularly review user permissions and take away one that they currently have to see if they will complain or even notice that it is missing.

    D. Do not give management more permissions than users.

2. Which of the following is a protection feature built into many firewalls that allows the administrator to tweak the tolerance for unanswered login attacks?

    A. MAC filter

    B. Flood guard

    C. MAC limiter

    D. Security posture

3. Which of the following is not a tunneling protocol, but is used in conjunction with tunneling protocols?

    A. IPSec

    B. PPTP

    C. L2TP

    D. L2F

4. The present method of requiring access to be strictly defined on every object is proving too cumbersome for your environment. The edict has come down from upper management that access requirements should be slightly reduced. Which access model allows users some flexibility for information-sharing purposes?

    A. DAC

    B. MAC

    C. RBAC

    D. MLAC

5. A newly hired junior administrator will assume your position temporarily while you attend a conference. You're trying to explain the basics of security to her in as short a period of time as possible. Which of the following best describes an ACL?

    A. ACLs provide individual access control to resources.

    B. ACLs aren't used in today's systems.

    C. The ACL process is dynamic in nature.

    D. ACLs are used to authenticate users.

6. LDAP is an example of which of the following?

    A. Directory access protocol

    B. IDS

    C. Tiered model application development environment

    D. File server

7. Upper management has suddenly become concerned about security. As the senior network administrator, you are asked to suggest changes that should be implemented. Which of the following access methods should you recommend if the technique to be used is one that is primarily based on preestablished access and can't be changed by users?

    A. MAC

    B. DAC

    C. RBAC

    D. Kerberos

8. Your office administrator is being trained to perform server backups. Which authentication method would be ideal for this situation?

    A. MAC

    B. DAC

    C. RBAC

    D. Security tokens

9. You've been assigned to mentor a junior administrator and bring him up to speed quickly. The topic you're currently explaining is authentication. Which method uses a KDC to accomplish authentication for users, programs, or systems?

    A. CHAP

    B. Kerberos

    C. Biometrics

    D. Smart cards

10. After a careful risk analysis, the value of your company's data has been increased. Accordingly, you're expected to implement authentication solutions that reflect the increased value of the data. Which of the following authentication methods uses more than one authentication process for a logon?

    A. Multifactor

    B. Biometrics

    C. Smart card

    D. Kerberos

11. You're the administrator for Mercury Technical. Due to several expansions, the network has grown exponentially in size within the past two years. Which of the following is a popular method for breaking a network into smaller private networks that can coexist on the same wiring and yet be unaware of each other?

    A. VLAN

    B. NAT

    C. MAC

    D. Security zone

12. Which technology allows a connection to be made between two networks using a secure protocol?

    A. Tunneling

    B. VLAN

    C. Internet

    D. Extranet

13. Your company provides medical data to doctors from a worldwide database. Because of the sensitive nature of the data, it's imperative that authentication be established on each session and be valid only for that session. Which of the following authentication methods provides credentials that are valid only during a single session?

    A. Tokens

    B. Certificate

    C. Smart card

    D. Kerberos

14. Which of the following is the term used whenever two or more parties authenticate each other?

    A. SSO

    B. Multifactor authentication

    C. Mutual authentication

    D. Tunneling

15. Which of the following security areas encompasses network access control (NAC)?

    A. Physical security

    B. Operational security

    C. Management security

    D. Triad security

16. You have added a new child domain to your network. As a result of this, the child has adopted all of the trust relationships with other domains in the forest that existed for its parent domain. What is responsible for this?

    A. LDAP access

    B. XML access

    C. Fuzzing access

    D. Transitive access

17. What is invoked when a person claims that they are the user but cannot be authenticated, such as with a lost password?

    A. Identity proofing

    B. Social engineering

    C. Directory traversal

    D. Cross-site requesting

18. Which of the following is a client/server-oriented environment that operates in a manner similar to RADIUS?

    A. HSM

    B. TACACS+

    C. TPM

    D. ACK

19. What is implied at the end of each access control list?

    A. Least privilege

    B. Separation of duties

    C. Implicit deny

    D. Explicit allow

20. Which of the following is a type of smart card issued by the Department of Defense as a general identification/authentication card for military personnel, contractors, and non-DoD employees?

    A. PIV

    B. POV

    C. DLP

    D. CAC

Chapter

5

Protecting Wireless Networks

THE FOLLOWING COMPTIA SECURITY+ EXAM OBJECTIVES ARE COVERED IN THIS CHAPTER:

✓ **1.5 Given a scenario, troubleshoot security issues related to wireless networking.**

- WPA
- WPA2
- WEP
- EAP
- PEAP
- LEAP
- MAC filter
- Disable SSID broadcast
- TKIP
- CCMP
- Antenna placement
- Power level controls
- Captive portals
- Antenna types
- Site surveys
- VPN (over open wireless)

✓ **3.4 Explain types of wireless attacks.**

- Rogue access points
- Jamming/Interference
- Evil twin
- War driving

- Bluejacking
- Bluesnarfing
- War chalking
- IV attack
- Packet sniffing
- Near field communication
- Replay attacks
- WEP/WPA attacks
- WPS attacks

Wireless systems, plainly put, are systems that don't use wires to send information but rather transmit data through the air. The growth of wireless systems creates many opportunities for attackers. These systems are relatively new, they use well-established communications mechanisms, and they're easily intercepted.

This chapter discusses the various types of wireless systems that you'll encounter, and it examines some of the security issues associated with this technology. Specifically, the systems deal with the IEEE 802 wireless standards, WPA2, and WEP/WAP applications.

Working with Wireless Systems

The days of running Ethernet cable through a room are fading. We are increasingly moving to an environment where wireless is *the* networking topology of choice. To make that environment successful, and to pass the CompTIA Security+ exam, you need to understand the 802.11 standards that are applicable, as well as the technologies—that is, the implementations of those standards—in use today.

This section examines the security protocols that you need to know as well as the transport layer implementation.

IEEE 802.11*x* Wireless Protocols

The *IEEE 802.11x* family of protocols provides for wireless communications using radio frequency transmissions. The frequencies in use for the 802.11 standards are the 2.4 GHz and the 5 GHz frequency spectrum. Several standards and bandwidths have been defined for use in wireless environments and (with the exception of 802.11a) are compatible with each other.

Although the standards may be compatible, there is always a default available of running at the slower speed in a mixed protocol environment.

802.11 The *802.11* standard defines wireless LANs transmitting at 1 Mbps or 2 Mbps bandwidths using the 2.4 GHz frequency spectrum.

802.11a The *802.11a* standard provides wireless LAN bandwidth of up to 54 Mbps in the 5 GHz frequency spectrum.

802.11b The *802.11b* standard provides for bandwidths of up to 11 Mbps (with fallback rates of 5.5, 2, and 1 Mbps) in the 2.4 GHz frequency spectrum. This standard is also called *Wi-Fi* or *802.11 high rate*.

802.11g The *802.11g* standard provides for bandwidths of up to 54 Mbps in the 2.4 GHz frequency spectrum. Though able to obtain faster speeds, it also suffers from the same interference problem of having to share the spectrum with other devices using that frequency, which are inherent with 802.11b.

802.11i The *802.11i* standard provides for security enhancements to the wireless standard with particular focus on authentication. The standard is often referenced as WPA2, the name given to it by the Wi-Fi Alliance.

802.11n The *802.11n* standard is one of the most popular today. It can operate in both the 5 GHz and the 2.4 GHz (for compatibility) ranges. Under the right conditions, it can reach speeds of 600 Mbps, but actual speeds are much slower. The advantage of this standard is that it offers higher speed and a frequency that does not have as much interference.

An amendment to 802.11n was published several years after its initial release that focuses on the use of multiple antennas to increase data speeds (throughput rates).

Most of the time, a wireless access point will work with more than just one 802.11 standard. (We will discuss wireless access points in greater detail later in the chapter.) For example, in Figure 5.1, the Dell Wireless WLAN Card Utility shows that most of the networks from which this client is able to pick up a signal are using 802.11b, 802.11g, and 802.11n.

FIGURE 5.1 A number of wireless networks are found, and most are using more than one 802.11 standard.

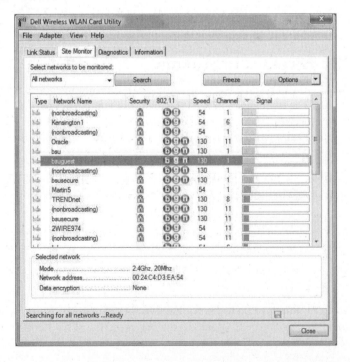

WEP/WAP/WPA/WPA2

Wired Equivalent Privacy (WEP) was intended to provide basic security for wireless networks, whereas wireless systems frequently use the *Wireless Application Protocol (WAP)* for network communications. Over time, WPA and WPA2 have replaced WEP in most implementations. The following sections briefly discuss these technologies and provide you with an understanding of their relative capabilities.

Wired Equivalent Privacy

Wired Equivalent Privacy (WEP) is a wireless protocol designed to provide a privacy equivalent to that of a wired network. WEP was implemented in a number of wireless devices, including smartphones and other mobile devices. WEP was vulnerable because of weaknesses in the way its encryption algorithms (RC4) are employed. These weaknesses allowed the algorithm to be cracked potentially in as little as five minutes using available PC software. This made WEP one of the more vulnerable security protocols.

As an example, the initialization vector (IV) that WEP uses for encryption is 24-bit, which is quite weak and means that IVs are reused with the same key. By examining the repeating result, it was easy for attackers to crack the WEP secret key. This is known as an *IV attack*.

Since the IV is shorter than the key, it must be repeated when used. To put it in perspective, the attack happened because the algorithm used is RC4, the IV is too small, the IV is static, and the IV is part of the RC4 encryption key.

Figure 5.2 shows the configuration settings on a very simple wireless router and sums up the situation best: The only time to use WEP is when you must have compatibility with older devices that do not support new encryption.

FIGURE 5.2   Wireless security settings for a simple router

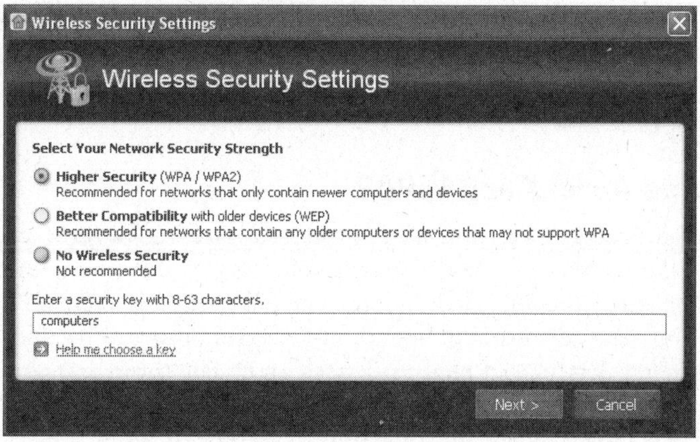

To strengthen WEP encryption, a *Temporal Key Integrity Protocol (TKIP)* was employed. This placed a 128-bit wrapper around the WEP encryption with a key that is based on things such as the MAC address of the destination device and the serial number of the packet. TKIP was designed as a backward-compatible replacement to WEP, and it could work with all existing hardware. Without the use of TKIP, WEP, as mentioned earlier in this chapter, was considered weak. It is worth noting, however, that even TKIP has been broken.

Wireless Application Protocol

Wireless Application Protocol (WAP) is a technology designed for use with wireless devices. WAP has become a data transmission standard adopted by many manufacturers, including Motorola and Nokia. WAP functions are equivalent to TCP/IP functions in that they're attempting to serve the same purpose for wireless devices. WAP uses a smaller version of HTML called *Wireless Markup Language (WML)*, which is used for Internet displays. WAP-enabled devices can also respond to scripts using an environment called *WMLScript*. This scripting language is similar to the Java programming language.

The ability to accept web pages and scripts allows malicious code and viruses to be transported to WAP-enabled devices.

WAP systems communicate using a WAP gateway system, as illustrated in Figure 5.3. The gateway converts information back and forth between HTTP and WAP as well as encodes and decodes between the protocols.

FIGURE 5.3   A WAP gateway enabling a connection to WAP devices by the Internet

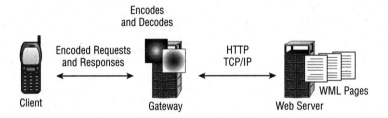

This structure provides reasonable assurance that WAP-enabled devices can be secured. If the interconnection between the WAP server and the Internet isn't encrypted, packets between the devices may be intercepted, referred to as *packet sniffing*, creating a potential vulnerability. This vulnerability is called a *gap in the WAP* (the security concern that exists when converting between WAP and SSL/TLS and exposing plain text). It was prevalent in versions of WAP prior to 2.0.

Wi-Fi Protected Access and WPA2

The Wi-Fi Protected Access (WPA) and *Wi-Fi Protected Access 2 (WPA2)* technologies were designed to address the core, easy-to-crack problems of WEP. These technologies were created to implement the 802.11i standard. The difference between WPA and WPA2 is that the former implements most, but not all, of 802.11i in order to be able to communicate with older wireless devices that might still need an update through their firmware in order to be compliant. WPA uses the RC4 encryption algorithm with TKIP, whereas WPA2 implements the full standard and is not compatible with older devices.

Although WPA mandates the use of TKIP, WPA2 requires *Counter Mode with Cipher Block Chaining Message Authentication Code Protocol (CCMP)*. CCMP uses 128-bit AES encryption with a 48-bit initialization vector. With the larger initialization vector, it increases the difficulty in cracking and minimizes the risk of a *replay attack*.

Replay attacks are discussed in greater detail in Chapter 9, "Malware, Vulnerabilities, and Threats." They essentially amount to capturing portions of a session to play back later to convince a host that it is still talking to the original connection.

As a simplified timeline useful for exam study, think of WEP as coming first. It was fraught with errors and WPA (with TKIP) was used as an intermediate solution, implementing a portion of the 802.11i standard. The ultimate solution, a full implementation of the 802.11i standard, is WPA2 (with CCMP).

Wireless Transport Layer Security

Wireless Transport Layer Security (WTLS) is the security layer of the Wireless Application Protocol, discussed in the section "WEP/WAP/WPA/WPA2" earlier. WTLS provides authentication, encryption, and data integrity for wireless devices. It's designed to use the relatively narrow bandwidth of these types of devices and is moderately secure. WTLS provides reasonable security for mobile devices, and it's being widely implemented in wireless devices.

WTLS provides an encrypted and authenticated connection between a wireless client and a server. It is similar in function to TLS, but it uses a lower bandwidth and less processing power. WTLS is used to support wireless devices that don't yet have extremely powerful processors.

Figure 5.4 illustrates WTLS as part of the WAP environment. WAP provides the functional equivalent of TCP/IP for wireless devices. Many devices, including newer smartphones, include support for WTLS as part of their networking protocol capabilities.

FIGURE 5.4   WTLS used between two WAP devices

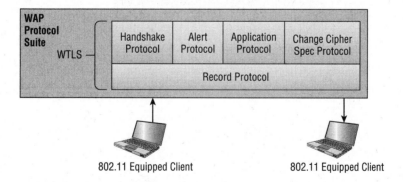

Communication between a WAP client and WAP server is protected by WTLS. Once on the Internet, a connection is typically protected by the Secure Sockets Layer (SSL), an Internet standard for encrypting data between points on the network.

Understanding Wireless Devices

Mobile devices, including smartphones, e-book readers, and tablet computers, are popular. Many of these devices use either RF signaling or cellular technologies for communication. Figure 5.5 shows the results of an Amazon Kindle's search for wireless networks.

FIGURE 5.5   Wireless scanning is done by a wide variety of devices, such as the Amazon Kindle.

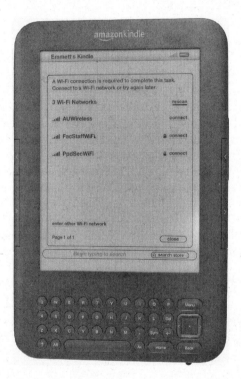

If the device uses WAP, in all likelihood it doesn't have security enabled. Several levels of security exist in WAP:

Anonymous Authentication   This allows virtually anyone to connect to the wireless portal.

Server Authentication   This requires the workstation to authenticate against the server.

Two-Way (Client and Server) Authentication   This requires both ends of the connection (client and server) to authenticate to confirm validity.

Many new wireless devices are also capable of using certificates to verify authentication. Figure 5.6 shows a mobile system's network. This network uses both encryption and authentication to increase security.

FIGURE 5.6 A mobile environment using WAP security

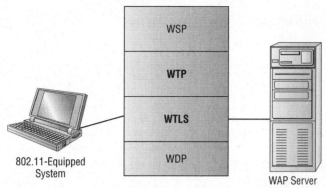

Security is managed at the WTLS layer.

WSP

WTP

WTLS

WDP

802.11-Equipped
System

WAP Server

Following are the technologies used to provide services between the devices:

Wireless Session Protocol (WSP) WSP manages the session information and connection between the devices.

Wireless Transaction Protocol (WTP) WTP provides services similar to TCP and UDP for WAP.

Wireless Transport Layer Security (WTLS) WTLS is the security layer of WAP.

Wireless Datagram Protocol (WDP) WDP provides the common interface between devices.

Wireless Access Points

It doesn't take much to build a wireless network. On the client side, you need a wireless network interface card (NIC) in place of the standard wired NIC. On the network side, you need something to communicate with the clients.

The primary method of connecting a wireless device to a network is via a wireless portal. A *wireless access point* (commonly just called an access point or *AP*) is a low-power transmitter/receiver, also known as a *transceiver*, which is strategically placed for access. The portable device and the access point communicate using one of several communications protocols, including IEEE 802.11 (also known as *Wi-Fi*).

Wireless communications, as the name implies, do not use wires as the basis for communication. Most frequently, they use a portion of the radio frequency (RF) spectrum called *microwave*. Wireless communication methods are becoming more prevalent in computing because the cost of the transmitting and receiving equipment has fallen drastically over the last few years. Wireless also offers mobile connectivity within a campus, a building, or even a city. Most wireless frequencies are shared frequencies in that more than one person may be using the same frequency for communication.

Figure 5.7 illustrates a wireless portal being used to connect a computer to a company network. Notice that the portal connects to the network and is treated like any other connection used in the network.

FIGURE 5.7   Wireless access portal and workstation

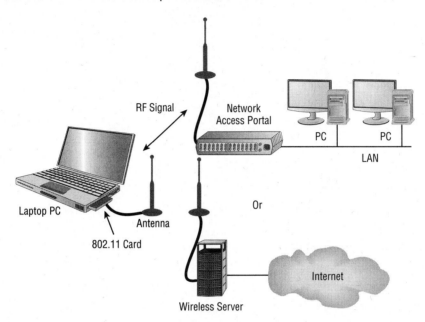

Wireless communications, although convenient, can also be less than secure. Although many APs now ship with encryption turned on, you will still want to verify that this is the case with your network and change the default password. Back in Figure 5.1, it is possible to see that bsu and bsuguest are not using security. Figure 5.8 shows a received packet from an unsecure network, and Figure 5.9 shows the information received from a network that has security enabled. Notice the list of protocols in the lower half of Figure 5.9.

FIGURE 5.8   Data from an unsecure network

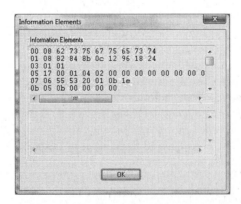

FIGURE 5.9 Data from a secure network

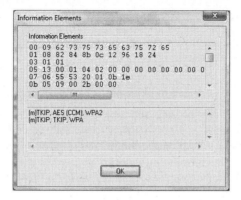

Antenna Placement

Antenna placement can be crucial in allowing clients to reach the access point. There isn't a universal solution to this issue, and it depends on the environment in which the access point is placed. As a general rule, the greater the distance the signal must travel, the more it will attenuate, but you can lose a signal quickly over a short distance as well if the building materials reflect or absorb the signal. You should try to avoid placing access points near metal (which includes appliances) or near the ground. Placing them in the center of the area to be served and high enough to get around most obstacles is recommended. On the chance that the signal is actually traveling too far, some access points include *power level controls*, which allow you to reduce the amount of output provided.

 Real World Scenario

Estimating Signal Strength

One of the most troublesome aspects of working with wireless networks is trying to compute the strength of the signal between the wireless AP and the client(s). It is a common joke that a hacker can stand outside a building and tap into your network but a user within the building can't get a strong enough signal to stay on the network.

Think of a wireless signal in terms of any other radio signal—cinderblock walls, metal cabinets, and other barriers will significantly reduce its strength. However, the signal can pass through glass windows and thin walls with no difficulty.

When you're laying out a network, it's highly recommended that you install a strength meter on a workstation—many are free to download—and use it to evaluate the intensity of the signal you're receiving (perform what is known as a *site survey*). If the signal is weak, you can add additional APs and repeaters to the network, just as you would on a wired network.

A great source for information on RF power values and antenna can be found on the Cisco site at:

www.cisco.com/en/US/tech/tk722/tk809/technologies_tech_note09186a00800e90fe.shtml

Antenna Types

Just as important as antenna placement is the type of antenna used. The default antenna on many (but not all) APs can be replaced to increase or decrease transmission range. The proper antenna can work around obstacles, minimize the effects of interference, increase signal strength, and focus the transmission (which can increase signal speed).

The antenna can be completely internal on an AP, or it can consist of one, two, or three external poles.

An *omnidirectional* antenna is designed to provide a 360-degree pattern and an even signal in all directions, so you usually want to locate the AP in the middle of the area to be covered. A *directional* antenna, on the other hand, forces the signal in one direction, and since it is focusing the signal, it can cover a greater distance with a stronger signal.

All antennas are rated in terms of *gain value*, which is expressed in dBi numbers. A wireless antenna advertised with a 20 dBi would be 20 times stronger than the base of 0 dBi. As a general rule, every 3 dB added to an antenna effectively doubles the power output.

MAC Filtering

Most APs offer the ability to turn on *MAC filtering*, but it is off by default. The MAC address is the unique identifier that exists for each network card (part of the hexadecimal address identifies the manufacturer, and the other part acts as a serial number). In the default stage, if MAC filtering is turned off, any wireless client that knows the values looked for (MAC addresses) can join the network. When MAC filtering is used, the administrator compiles a list of the MAC addresses associated with users' computers and enters those addresses. When a client attempts to connect and other values have been correctly entered, an additional check of the MAC address is done. If the address appears in the list, the client is allowed to join; otherwise, it is forbidden from doing so. On a number of wireless devices, the term *network lock* is used in place of MAC filtering, and the two are synonymous.

The weakness with MAC filtering is that the MAC address is a value that an attacker could spoof in order to gain entry. By making it look as if the illegitimate host is legitimate, it will pass through the filter and be allowed access.

In Exercise 5.1, we'll show you how to change the order of preferred networks in Windows. Preferred networks are limited in Windows 7 to networks to which you have successfully connected.

EXERCISE 5.1

Changing the Order of Preferred Networks

Most wireless clients can receive signals from, and connect to, more than one wireless network. If a wireless network is not available, the connection will often drop down to the next one in this list, and thus it is important to have the wireless networks on the client in the order in which you want connection to be attempted. The following exercise will show you how to change this order:

1. On a Windows client, click the Windows button, type **Network and Sharing Center** into the search bar, and press Enter.

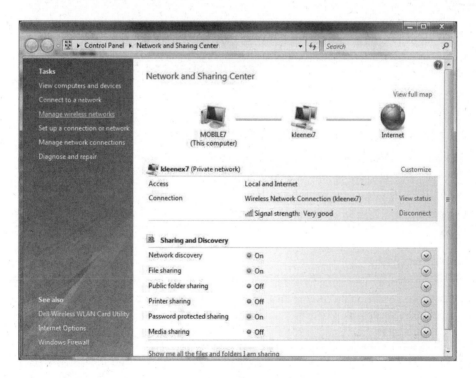

2. Choose Manage Wireless Networks.

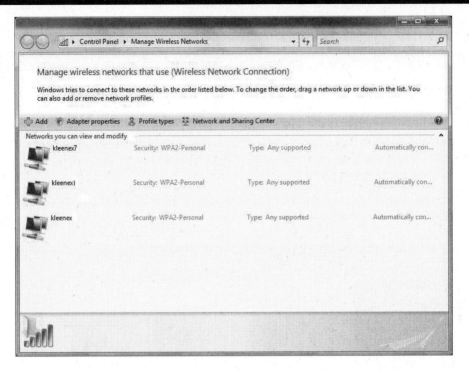

3. Click any network that appears in the list, and drag it up or down to change the order of the preferred networks.

4. Exit Manage Wireless Networks.

5. Exit the Network and Sharing Center.

Captive Portals

Most public networks, including Wi-Fi hotspots, use a *captive portal*, which requires users to agree to some condition before they use the network or Internet. The condition could be to agree to the acceptable use policy, payment charges for the time they are using the network, and so forth.

One of the most popular implementations of captive portals is a Cisco application in their Identity Services Engine. However, there have been vulnerabilities identified with it, which allow attackers to intercept cleartext values:

```
http://web.nvd.nist.gov/view/vuln/detail?vulnId=CVE-2013-3471
```

Working with VPNs

It may seem pointless to create a virtual private network (VPN) over an open wireless channel since one of the primary purposes for using a VPN is to enhance security, but one of the downsides of using open wireless is that there are so many susceptibilities to it that it makes these two traits seemingly incompatible. Though it may seem questionable at first, the technology is currently considered secure. A VPN can be configured at either the Network or Data Link layer of the network, and it is the existence of the VPN that enhances the security of the wireless network. For the tunneling you can use either IPSec or SSL, both discussed in earlier chapters, just as you would with a wired network. To put it simply, the security of a VPN can supplement the insecurity of open wireless.

 The NIST recommends that the VPN use Federal Information Processing Standards (FIPS)–validated encryption algorithms.

Extensible Authentication Protocol

Extensible Authentication Protocol (EAP) provides a framework for authentication that is often used with wireless networks. Among the five EAP types adopted by the WPA/WPA2 standard are EAP-TLS, EAP-PSK, EAP-MD5, and two that you need to know for the exam: LEAP and PEAP. Figure 5.10 shows the configuration information for a WLAN card that uses EAP-TTLS. This is a form of EAP-TLS that adds tunneling (Extensible Authentication Protocol—Tunneled Transport Layer Security).

FIGURE 5.10   Using EAP-TTLS on a wireless network

By adding the tunneling, TTLS adds one more layer of security against man-in-the-middle attacks or eavesdropping.

To simplify network setup, a number of small office and home office (SOHO) routers use a series of EAP messages to allow new hosts to join the network and use WPA/WPA2. Known as *Wi-Fi Protected Setup (WPS)*, this often requires the user to do something in order to complete the enrollment process: press a button on the router within a short time period, enter a PIN, or bring the new device close-by (so that near field communication can take place).

> *Near field communication (NFC)* is a technology that requires a user to bring the client close to the AP in order to verify (often through RFID or Wi-Fi) that the device is present. It can also be used to "bump" phones and send data from one to another.

Unfortunately, *WPS attacks* have become commonplace, as the technology is susceptible to brute-force attacks used to guess the user's PIN. Once an attacker gains access, they are then on the Wi-Fi network. For that reason, we suggest that you disable WPS in devices that allow it (and update firmware in those where it is a possibility).

Lightweight Extensible Authentication Protocol

Lightweight Extensible Authentication Protocol (LEAP) was created by Cisco as an extension to EAP, but it's being phased out in favor of PEAP. Because it is a proprietary protocol to Cisco and created solely as a quick fix for problems with WEP, it lacks native Windows support.

LEAP requires mutual authentication to improve security, but it's susceptible to dictionary attacks. It is considered a weak EAP protocol, and Cisco does not currently recommend using it.

> Here is the URL of an excellent white paper from Cisco on wireless LAN security, which discusses LEAP architecture:
>
> www.cisco.com/en/US/prod/collateral/wireless/ps5678/ps430
> /ps4076/prod_white_paper09186a00800b469f_ps4570_Products
> _White_Paper.html

Protected Extensible Authentication Protocol

Cisco, RSA, and Microsoft worked together to create *Protected Extensible Authentication Protocol (PEAP)*. It replaces LEAP, and there is native support for it in Windows (which previously favored EAP-TLS) beginning with Windows XP. There is support for it in all Windows operating systems since then, including the current versions of Windows.

Although many consider PEAP and EAP-TTLS to be similar options, PEAP is more secure because it establishes an encrypted channel between the server and the client.

> The same Cisco white paper mentioned earlier on wireless LAN security also outlines the PEAP authentication process:
>
> www.cisco.com/en/US/prod/collateral/wireless/ps5678/ps430
> /ps4076/prod_white_paper09186a00800b469f_ps4570_Products
> _White_Paper.html

Wireless Vulnerabilities to Know

Wireless systems are vulnerable to all the same attacks as wired networks. However, because these protocols use radio frequency signals for data emanation, they have an additional weakness: All radio frequency signals can be easily intercepted. To intercept 802.11*x* traffic, all you need is a PC with an appropriate 802.11x card installed. Many networks will regularly broadcast their name (known as an *SSID broadcast*) to announce their presence. Simple software on the PC can capture the link traffic in the wireless AP and then process this data in order to decrypt account and password information.

> One method of protecting the network that is often recommended is to disable, or turn off, the SSID broadcast (also known as *cloaking*). The access point is still there, and it is still accessible by those who have been told of its existence by the administrator, but it prevents those who are just scanning from finding it. This is considered a *very* weak form of security, because there are still other ways, albeit a bit more complicated, to discover the presence of the access point besides the SSID broadcast.

In Exercise 5.2, we'll show you how to configure Windows to connect to a network not broadcasting an SSID.

EXERCISE 5.2

Configuring a Wireless Connection Not Broadcasting

To configure the client to connect to a network even when the SSID is not broadcasting, follow these steps:

1. On a Windows client, right-click the network icon and choose Connect To A Network.

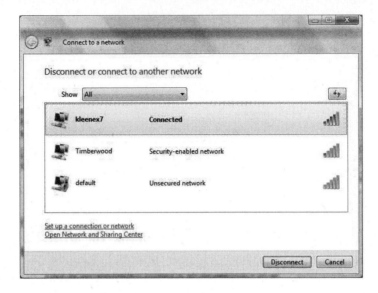

2. Right-click the network to which you are connected and choose Properties.

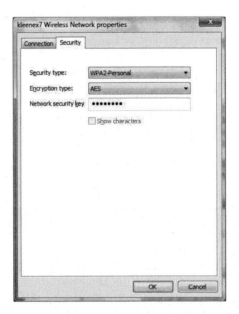

3. Click the Connection tab, and check the Connect Even If The Network Is Not Broadcasting box.

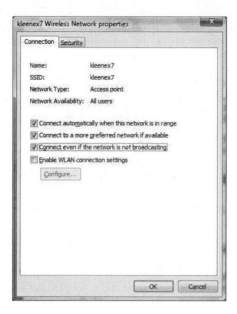

4. Click OK.

5. Exit the Connect To A Network dialog box.

An additional aspect of wireless systems is the site survey. *Site surveys* involve listening in on an existing wireless network using commercially available technologies. Doing so allows intelligence, and possibly data capture, to be performed on systems in your wireless network.

The term *site survey* initially meant determining whether a proposed location was free from *interference*. When used by an attacker, a site survey can determine what types of systems are in use, the protocols used, and other critical information about your network. It's the primary method used to gather information about wireless networks. Virtually all wireless networks are vulnerable to site surveys.

As for interference, it can be unintentional (caused by other devices in the vicinity, for example) or intentional. When it is intentional, then it is referred to as *jamming*, as the intent is to jam the signal and keep the legitimate device from communicating.

If wireless APs are installed in a building, the signals will frequently radiate past the inside of the building, and they can be detected and decoded outside the building using inexpensive equipment. The term *war driving* refers to driving around town with a laptop looking for APs to communicate with. The network card on the intruder's laptop is set to promiscuous mode, and it looks for signals coming from anywhere. After intruders gain access, they may steal Internet access or corrupt your data.

Once weaknesses have been discovered in a wireless network, *war chalking* can occur. War chalking involves those who discover a way into the network leaving signals (often written in chalk) on, or outside, the premise to notify others that a vulnerability exists there. The marks can be on the sidewalk, the side of the building, a nearby signpost, and so on and resemble those shown in Figure 5.11.

FIGURE 5.11   The war chalking symbols

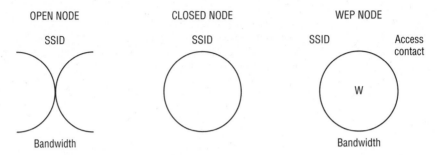

Weak encryption was an issue with earlier access points, but most of the newer wireless APs use special ID numbers (SSIDs) and must be configured in network cards to allow communication. However, using ID number configurations doesn't necessarily prevent wireless networks from being monitored, and one particularly mischievous undertaking involves taking advantage of *rogue access points*. Any wireless access point added to your network that has not been authorized is considered a rogue.

The rogue may be added by an attacker or could have been innocently added by a user wanting to enhance their environment. The problem with a user doing so is that there is a good chance they will not implement the same level of security that you would, and this could open up the system for a man-in-the-middle attack or evil twin attack. An *evil twin attack* is one in which a rogue wireless access point poses as a legitimate wireless service provider to intercept information that users transmit.

Educate and train users about a wireless network and the need to keep it secure, just as you would train and educate them about any other security topic. They may think that there is no harm in them joining any wireless network they can find as they travel, such as those shown in Figure 5.12, but they should question whether the administrators for all such networks have the best interest of your company data at heart.

Be sure to change the default password settings on all wireless devices. Never assume that a wireless connection is secure. The emissions from a wireless portal may be detectable through walls and for several city blocks from the portal. Interception is easy to accomplish, given that RF is the medium used for communication. Newer wireless devices offer data security, and you should use it. You can set newer APs and wireless routers to non-broadcast in addition to configuring WPA2 and a higher encryption level.

Bluetooth technology is often used for creating personal area networks (PANs or WPANs), and most Bluetooth devices come with a factory default PIN that you will want to change to more secure values. With the popularity of Bluetooth on the rise, two additional vulnerabilities have been added: bluejacking and bluesnarfing. *Bluejacking* is the sending of unsolicited messages (think spam) over a Bluetooth connection. While annoying, it is basically considered harmless.

FIGURE 5.12   Examples of some questionable wireless networks

Bluesnarfing is the gaining of unauthorized access through a Bluetooth connection. This access can be obtained through a smartphone or any Bluetooth device. Once access has been achieved, the attacker can copy data in the same way they could with any other type of unauthorized access.

The Bluetooth standard has addressed weaknesses in the technology, and it continues to become more secure. One of the simplest ways to secure Bluetooth devices is to not set their attribute to Discoverable.

Wireless Attack Analogy

Imagine that you've decided to go to a sandwich shop for lunch and that you want to eat and return back to work as quickly as possible. Problems lurk with the lunch, however, as illustrated by Table 5.1. Not every type of attack fits this scenario, and only those that do are examined.

TABLE 5.1   Sandwich shop attacks

Attack	Analogy
Rogue access point	While standing in line to place your order, an employee who is on a break recognizes you as a regular customer and offers to make you a sandwich from ingredients in the back room rather than making you wait. This will circumvent the cash register and short the owner.
Jamming	While trying to place your order, a co-worker who knows you keeps mimicking what you are saying. Their attempt at humor is keeping the sandwich preparer from correctly hearing your order.
Interference	While trying to place your order, an obnoxious businessman stands behind you in line and shouts into his cell phone. He is so loud that he keeps the sandwich preparer from correctly hearing your order.
Bluejacking	As you're ordering, someone in line behind you keeps anonymously mentioning things to be added to the sandwich, and the sandwich preparer adds them to your order thinking you are the one who wants them.
Evil twin	Distracted by the rain, you get out of your car and run into what you think is your favorite sandwich shop only to find out that you went in one door too soon and are in a rival sandwich shop that charges twice as much and gives half as much meat.
Replay attack	The person behind you in line tells the sandwich preparer that they will have the exact same thing you had, and it should be added to your bill.

It would be great if your obnoxious co-workers did not know the shop existed because you never mentioned it (disable the SSID broadcast), if the sandwich preparer only placed items on the sandwich that they knew for certain that you ordered (near field communication), and if they only allowed in new people recommended by current customers (Wi-Fi Protected Setup).

Summary

Wireless systems have become increasingly popular and standardized. The most common protocol implemented in wireless systems is WAP. The security layer for WAP is WTLS. WAP is equivalent to TCP/IP for wireless systems.

The IEEE develops the standards for wireless systems. The most common standards are 802.11, 802.11a, 802.11b, 802.11i, 802.11g, and 802.11n. These standards use the 2.4 GHz or 5 GHz frequency spectrum, with the exception of 802.11i, which is a security standard often referred to as WPA2. Several communications technologies are available to send messages between wireless devices.

Wireless networks are vulnerable to site surveys. Site surveys can be accomplished using a PC and an 802.11x card. The term *site survey* is also used in reference to detecting interference in a given area that might prevent 802.11x from working.

There have been a number of security standards for wireless networking. WEP (Wired Equivalent Privacy) was the first widely used standard. It was fraught with errors, and WPA (Wi-Fi Protected Access), which used TKIP, replaced it in most implementations, which used TKIP. This was an intermediate solution that implemented only a portion of the 802.11i standard. The ultimate solution—a full implementation of the 802.11i standard—is WPA2, which uses CCMP.

Vulnerabilities exist because of weaknesses in the protocols. As an example, WEP is vulnerable because of weaknesses in the way that the encryption algorithms are employed; the initialization vector (IV) that WEP uses for encryption is 24-bit and IVs are reused with the same key. By examining the repeating result, it is easy for intruders to crack the WEP secret key, known as an IV attack.

Mobile devices use either RF signaling or cellular technologies for communication. If the device uses WAP, several levels of security exist: anonymous authentication (anyone can connect), server authentication (the workstation must authenticate against the server), and two-way authentication (both the client and server must authenticate with each other).

Exam Essentials

Know the protocols and components of a wireless system.   The backbone of most wireless systems is WAP. WAP can use WEP and WPA with TKIP and WPA2 to provide security in a wireless environment. WTLS is the security layer of WAP. WAP and TCP/IP perform similarly.

Know the hardware used in a wireless network.   The wireless access point (AP) sits on the wired network and then acts as the router for the wireless clients. Most wireless access points will work with more than one 802.11 standard. Wireless clients, using a wireless NIC card, and mobile devices connect to the access point.

Know the capabilities and limitations of the 802.11x network standards.   The current standards for wireless protocols are 802.11, 802.11a, 802.11b, 802.11g, and 802.11n.

Know the vulnerabilities of wireless networks.   The primary method of gaining information about a wireless network is a site survey. Site surveys can be accomplished with a PC and an 802.11 card. Wireless networks are subject to the same attacks as wired networks.

Know the wireless security protocols.   The 802.11i standard is often referenced as WPA2. It is an enhancement to earlier standards such as WEP (Wired Equivalent Privacy) and WPA (Wi-Fi Protected Access), which were much weaker.

Review Questions

1. Which protocol is mainly used to enable access to the Internet from a mobile device or smartphone?

   A. WEP

   B. WTLS

   C. WAP

   D. WPO

2. Which protocol operates on 2.4 GHz and has a bandwidth of 1 Mbps or 2 Mbps?

   A. 802.11

   B. 802.11a

   C. 802.11b

   D. 802.11g

3. You're outlining your plans for implementing a wireless network to upper management. Suddenly, a vice president brings up the question of security. Which protocol was designed to provide security for a wireless network and is considered equivalent to the security of a wired network?

   A. WAP

   B. WTLS

   C. WPA2

   D. IR

4. Which of the following is a primary vulnerability of a wireless environment?

   A. Decryption software

   B. IP spoofing

   C. A gap in the WAP

   D. Site survey

5. Which of the following is synonymous with MAC filtering?

   A. TKIP

   B. Network lock

   C. EAP-TTLS

   D. MAC secure

6. Which of the following 802.11 standards is often referenced as WPA2?

   A. 802.11a

   B. 802.11b

   C. 802.11i

   D. 802.11n

7. Which of the following 802.11 standards provides for bandwidths of up to 300 Mbps?

    A. 802.11n

    B. 802.11i

    C. 802.11g

    D. 802.11b

8. An IV attack is usually associated with which of the following wireless protocols?

    A. WEP

    B. WAP

    C. WPA

    D. WPA2

9. Which type of encryption does CCMP use?

    A. EAP

    B. DES

    C. AES

    D. IV

10. Which encryption technology is associated with WPA?

    A. TKIP

    B. CCMP

    C. WEP

    D. LDAP

11. What is the size of the initialization vector (IV) that WEP uses for encryption?

    A. 6-bit

    B. 24-bit

    C. 56-bit

    D. 128-bit

12. Which of the following authentication levels with WAP requires both ends of the connection to authenticate to confirm validity?

    A. Relaxed

    B. Two-way

    C. Server

    D. Anonymous

13. Which of the following provides services similar to TCP and UDP for WAP?

    A. WTLS

    B. WDP

    C. WTP

    D. WFMD

14. Packets between the WAP server and the Internet may be intercepted. What is this vulnerability known as?

  A. Packet sniffing

  B. Minding the gap

  C. Middle man

  D. Broken promise

15. What is the size of the wrapper TKIP places around the WEP encryption with a key that is based on things such as the MAC address of your machine and the serial number of the packet?

  A. 128-bit

  B. 64-bit

  C. 56-bit

  D. 12-bit

16. The system administrator for Bill Steen Moving comes back from a conference intent on disabling the SSID broadcast on the single AP the company uses. What will the effect be on client machines?

  A. They will no longer be able to use wireless networking.

  B. They will no longer see the SSID as a Preferred Network when they are connected.

  C. They will no longer see the SSID as an available network.

  D. They will be required to make the SSID part of their HomeGroup.

17. Tammy is having difficulty getting a signal from the AP on the second floor of her home office to the basement. You recommend that she replace the antenna on the AP. What measurement should she use to compare gain between possible antenna options?

  A. ios

  B. GB/s

  C. MHz

  D. dBi

18. What should a VPN over wireless use for tunneling?

  A. TKIP

  B. SSL or IPSec

  C. CCMP

  D. PEAP

19. What technology is used to send data between phones that are in close proximity to each other?

  A. NFC

  B. IBI

  C. IBJ

  D. IFNC

20. What technology is used to simplify network setup by allowing a router to have the administrator push a button on it to allow a new host to join?

   A. WEP

   B. WPA

   C. WTLS

   D. WPS

Chapter

6

Securing the Cloud

THE FOLLOWING COMPTIA SECURITY+ EXAM OBJECTIVES ARE COVERED IN THIS CHAPTER:

✓ **1.3 Explain network design elements and components.**

- Virtualization
- Cloud computing: Platform as a Service; Software as a Service; Infrastructure as a Service; Private; Public; Hybrid; Community

✓ **4.3 Given a scenario, select the appropriate solution to establish host security.**

- Virtualization: Snapshots; Patch compatibility; Host availability/elasticity; Security control testing; Sandboxing

✓ **4.4 Implement the appropriate controls to ensure data security.**

- Cloud storage

If there were such a thing as a word-of-the-day for information technology, the one that would have to be the most popular recently would be "cloud." Vendors have come to embrace the word in their marketing materials for everything from tablets to servers and a lot of odd devices in between. As a security professional, you are likely to be pulled into discussions about the cloud by many who don't fully understand the meaning of what they are saying.

CompTIA has not one but two certifications available on the cloud: CompTIA Cloud Essentials and CompTIA Cloud+. The purpose of this chapter is to define just what the cloud—and its necessary cousin, virtualization—really are and what you need to know about this topic for the Security+ exam and to be able to keep your systems secure.

Working with Cloud Computing

One of the reasons "the cloud" can be so confusing in discussions is that there are many instances in which the phrase has been improperly used in marketing hype. To find a meaning that all can agree upon, let's turn to the National Institute of Standards and Technology (NIST). Three service models are defined in Special Publication 800-145: Software as a Service (SaaS), Platform as a Service (PaaS), and Infrastructure as a Service (IaaS). Each of these service models are explored in the sections that follow. Following that, we will take a look at the four possible delivery models: private, public, community, and hybrid.

So important is NIST when it comes to cloud computing definitions that the objectives for the Cloud+ certification from CompTIA include the phrase "according to NIST" after the first six topics in the first subdomain.

Software as a Service (SaaS)

According to NIST, *Software as a Service (SaaS)* is defined as:

> The capability provided to the consumer is to use the provider's applications running on a cloud infrastructure. The applications are accessible from various client devices through either a thin client interface, such as a web browser (e.g., web-based email), or a program interface. The consumer does not manage or control the underlying cloud infrastructure including network, servers, operating systems, storage, or even individual application capabilities, with the possible exception of limited user-specific application configuration settings.
>
> *National Institute of Standards and Technology, Special Publication 800-145*

Although the description may seem verbose, the words used are very important. The ones to focus on in this definition are that the consumer can "use" the provider's applications and that they do not "manage or control" any of the underlying cloud infrastructure. Figure 6.1 graphically depicts the responsibilities of each party in this model.

FIGURE 6.1   The SaaS service model

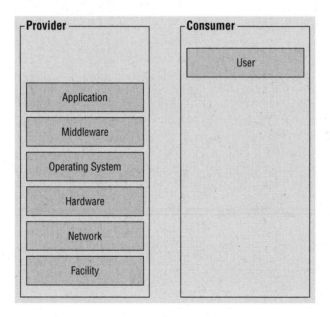

Platform as a Service (PaaS)

According to NIST, *Platform as a Service (PaaS)* is defined as:

> The capability provided to the consumer is to deploy onto the cloud infrastructure consumer-created or acquired applications created using programming languages, libraries, services, and tools supported by the provider. The consumer does not manage or control the underlying cloud infrastructure including network, servers, operating systems, or storage, but has control over the deployed applications and possible configuration settings for the application-hosting environment."
>
> *National Institute of Standards and Technology, Special Publication 800-145*

To understand the difference between this model and the others, the key words to focus on in this definition are that the consumer can "deploy," that they do not "manage or control" any of the underlying cloud infrastructure, but that they can have "control over the deployed applications." Figure 6.2 graphically depicts the responsibilities of each party in this model.

FIGURE 6.2 The PaaS service model

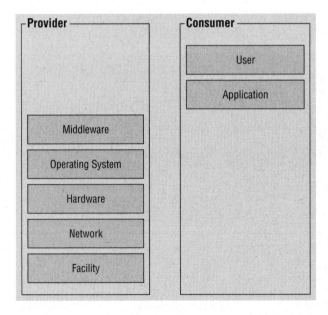

Infrastructure as a Service (IaaS)

The third service model defined by NIST, *Infrastructure as a Service (IaaS)*, is defined as:

> The capability provided to the consumer is to provision processing, storage, networks, and other fundamental computing resources where the consumer is able to deploy and run arbitrary software, which can include operating systems and applications. The consumer does not manage or control the underlying cloud infrastructure but has control over operating systems, storage, and deployed applications; and possible limited control of select networking components (e.g., host firewalls).
>
> *National Institute of Standards and Technology, Special Publication 800-145*

The relevant wording here is that the consumer can "provision," is able to "deploy and run," but still does not "manage or control" the underlying cloud infrastructure, but now they can be responsible for some aspects. Figure 6.3 graphically depicts the responsibilities of each party in this model.

FIGURE 6.3   The IaaS service model

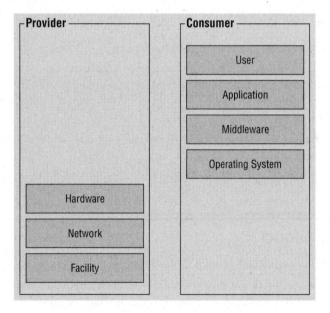

Regardless of the service model used, the characteristics of each are that they must include on-demand self-service, broad network access, resource pooling, rapid elasticity, and measured service. Once you have a service model selected, both CompTIA and NIST recognize four different delivery models and those are explored in the sections that follow.

When multiple models are combined—mixing IaaS, PaaS, and/or SaaS into a hybrid—this is referred to as *Anything as a Service (XaaS)*.

Private Cloud

According to NIST, a *private cloud* is defined as follows:

> The cloud infrastructure is provisioned for exclusive use by a single organization comprising multiple consumers (e.g., business units). It may be owned, managed, and operated by the organization, a third party, or some combination of them, and it may exist on or off premises.
>
> *National Institute of Standards and Technology, Special Publication 800-145*

Under most circumstances, a private cloud is owned by the organization and they act as both the provider and the consumer. They have an advantage in not needing to put their data on the Internet.

Public Cloud

As opposed to a private cloud, the *public cloud* is defined as follows:

> The cloud infrastructure is provisioned for open use by the general public. It may be owned, managed, and operated by a business, academic, or government organization, or some combination of them. It exists on the premises of the cloud provider.
>
> *National Institute of Standards and Technology, Special Publication 800-145*

Under most circumstances, the cloud provider owns a public cloud, and it will use a pay-as-you-go model. Examples include webmail and online document sharing/collaboration.

Community Cloud

According to NIST, a *community cloud* is defined as follows:

> The cloud infrastructure is provisioned for exclusive use by a specific community of consumers from organizations that have shared concerns (e.g., mission, security requirements, policy, and compliance considerations). It may be owned, managed, and operated by one or more of the organizations in the community, a third party, or some combination of them, and it may exist on or off premises.
>
> *National Institute of Standards and Technology, Special Publication 800-145*

The key to distinguishing between a community cloud and other types of cloud delivery is that it serves a *similar* group. There must be joint interests and limited enrollment. For an analogy, think of a private cloud as a house (you own it; you're responsible for the maintenance, utilities, and all of it; and so forth), a public cloud as a hotel (you're using only a small part of it, you have very little responsibility for the structure), and a community cloud as a condominium (you own a portion, you share maintenance of common areas, and so on).

Hybrid Cloud

The last of the delivery models, the *hybrid cloud*, is defined as follows:

> The cloud infrastructure is a composition of two or more distinct cloud infrastructures (private, community, or public) that remain unique entities, but are bound together by standardized or proprietary technology that enables data and application portability (e.g., cloud bursting for load balancing between clouds).

National Institute of Standards and Technology, Special Publication 800-145

Although a hybrid can be any combination of public, private, and community clouds, under most circumstances it is an amalgamation of private and public clouds. When you start mixing in community clouds, it often becomes more of an extension of the community cloud rather than a hybrid cloud.

One common implementation of cloud computing is to take advantage of *cloud bursting.* This means that when your servers become too busy, you offload traffic to resources from a cloud provider. Technologies that make much of the load balancing/prioritizing possible employ the *QoS (Quality of Service)* protocols.

Working with Virtualization

An equally popular—and complementary—buzzword to "the cloud" is *virtualization.* The cost savings promised by virtualization are often offset by the threats to security should the hypervisor be compromised. One reason for the popularity of virtualization is that in order to have cloud computing, you must have virtualization—it is the foundation on which cloud computing is built. At the core of virtualization is the hypervisor, which is the software/hardware combination that makes it possible. There are two methods of implementation: Type I and Type II. The *Type I hypervisor* model, also known as *bare metal*, is independent of the operating system and boots before the OS. The *Type II hypervisor* model, also known as *hosted*, is dependent on the operating system and cannot boot until the OS is up and running. It needs the OS to stay up so that it can boot.

Figure 6.4 illustrates the Type I model. From a performance and scalability standpoint, this model is superior to Type II. Type II is considered more complex to manage.

FIGURE 6.4   Type I hypervisor model

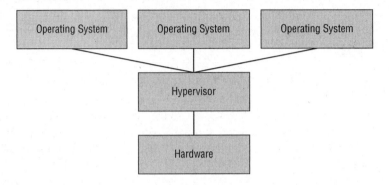

Figure 6.5 illustrates the Type II model. This is the model commonly found in use in consumer implementations.

FIGURE 6.5   Type II hypervisor model

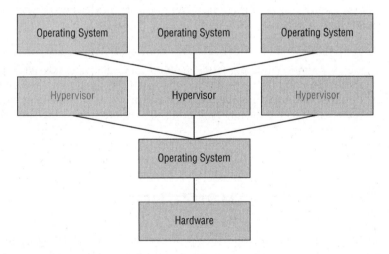

The machine on which virtualization software is running is known as a *host* whereas the virtual machines are known as *guests*.

Both proprietary and open source implementations of both types are available, and sometimes it can be confusing as to which type of implementation is in use. Xen, for example, forks into both proprietary and open source solutions. As a general rule, Xen is considered to be both free and open source; ESX, from VMware, is free but not open source (proprietary); KVM is free and open source; and Hyper-V, from Microsoft, is usually free (depending on the implementation) but definitely not open source (proprietary).

From the standpoint of the Security+ certification, there are five primary virtualization topics that CompTIA wants you to know, and the following sections focus on them.

Snapshots

Snapshots allow you to take an image of a system at a particular point in time. With most virtual machine implementations, you can take as many snapshots as you want (provided you have enough storage space) in order to be able to revert a machine to a "saved" state. Snapshots contain a copy of the virtual machine settings (hardware configuration), information on all virtual disks attached, and the memory state of the machine at the time of the snapshot.

Snapshots can also be used for virtual machine cloning, allowing the machine to be copied once—or multiple times—for testing.

Patch Compatibility

As with any server implementation, *patch compatibility* needs to be factored in before systems are updated. With VMware, patch releases are based on the code from the immediately preceding update, and compatibility for patches is assumed to have the same compatibility as the preceding update release. Although this approach differs for each vendor, most follow similar guidelines.

Always verify the source of patches and test the patches on lab machines before applying them to production machines. It is possible for one patch not to be compatible with another, and you want to discover any problems on non-mission-critical systems first, if at all possible.

Host Availability/Elasticity

Host availability is a topic that needs to be addressed in the *Service Level Agreement (SLA)* with any vendor with whom you contract for cloud services. The goal is always to have minimal downtime: five 9s, or 99.999 percent uptime, is the industry standard. According to NIST, one of the five essential characteristics of the cloud is not just *elasticity*, but rapid elasticity. This is defined as:

> Capabilities can be elastically provisioned and released, in some cases automatically, to scale rapidly outward and inward commensurate with demand. To the consumer, the capabilities available for provisioning often appear to be unlimited and can be appropriated in any quantity at any time.
>
> *National Institute of Standards and Technology, Special Publication 800-145*

The key words to focus on in this definition are "provisioned and released," "scale," and "appear to be unlimited."

Security Control Testing

Security control testing (SCT) often includes interviews, examinations, and testing of systems to look for weaknesses. It should also include contract reviews of SLAs, a look at the history of prior breaches that a provider has had, a focus on shared resources as well as dedicated servers, and so on.

If this sounds a lot like penetration testing, that is because it is a subset of it. In some organizations, security can be pushed aside in favor of design, and there is a great opportunity for this to happen when transitioning to virtualization and/or cloud computing. As a security professional, it is your responsibility to see that design does not overwhelm security.

Never underestimate the power of creativity. As an example, the IT department of a major hospital became concerned about Health Insurance Portability and Accountability Act of 1996 (HIPAA) data security, and they used group policy management to restrict the ability of users to write to any USB drive device. During a security audit, they found that users were getting around the intended protection of the data by writing their work data to various personal clouds provided by Google and Amazon.

Sandboxing

Sandboxing involves running apps in restricted memory areas. By doing so, it is possible to limit the possibility of an app's crash, allowing a user to access another app or the data associated with it. Without sandboxing, the possibility exists that a crash in another customer's implementation could expose a path by which a user might hop ("server hop") to your data. It is important to know that though this possibility exists—and you should test extensively to keep it from happening—the possibility of it occurring has been greatly exaggerated by some in the media.

Security and the Cloud

Since this is a certification exam on security and not just on memorization of cloud-based terminology, it is important to recognize the security issues associated with cloud computing. Two you should know for the exam are multitenancy and laws and regulations:

Multitenancy   One of the ways cloud computing is able to obtain cost efficiencies is by putting data from various clients on the same machines. This "multitenant" nature means that workloads from different clients can be on the same system, and a flaw in implementation could compromise security. In theory, a security incident could originate with another customer at the cloud provider and bleed over into your data. Because of this, data needs to be protected from other cloud consumers and from the cloud provider as well.

Laws and Regulations   The consumer retains the ultimate responsibility for compliance. Per NIST:

> The main issue centers on the risks associated with moving important applications or data from within the confines of the organization's computing center to that of another organization (i.e., a public cloud), which is readily available for use by the general public. The responsibilities of both the organization and the cloud provider vary depending on the service model. Reducing cost and increasing efficiency are primary motivations for moving towards a public cloud, but relinquishing responsibility for security should not be. Ultimately, the organization is accountable for the choice of public cloud and the security and privacy of the outsourced service.

> *National Institute of Standards and Technology, Special Publication 800-144*

Cloud computing holds great promise when it comes to scalability, cost savings, rapid deployment, and empowerment. As with any technology where so much is removed from your control, though, risks are involved. Each risk should be considered carefully in order to identify ways to help mitigate it. Data segregation, for example, can help reduce some of the risks associated with multitenancy.

Software and services not necessary for the implementation should be removed or at least disabled. Patches and firmware updates should be kept current, and log files should be carefully monitored. You should find the vulnerabilities in the implementation before others do and work with your service provider(s) to close any holes.

When it comes to data storage on the cloud, encryption is one of the best ways to protect it (keeping it from being of value to unauthorized parties), and VPN routing and forwarding can help. Backups should be performed regularly (and encrypted and stored in safe locations), and access control should be a priority.

> For a good discussion of cloud computing and data protection, visit http://whoswholegal.com/news/features/article/18246/cloud-computing-data-protection.

Cloud Storage

The first couple of PCs that this author owned booted from media (tape with one and floppies with another) and did not include hard drives. After saving up for quite a while, I bought and installed my first hard drive—costing more than $600. It had a capacity of 20 MB, and I could not fathom what I would possibly do with all of that space.

Today that number is so small, it's laughable. The trend for both individuals and enterprises has been to collect and store as much data as possible. This has led to large local hard drives—DAS (direct attached storage), NAS (network area storage), SANs (storage area networks), and now the cloud.

Just as the cloud holds such promise for running applications, balancing loads, and a plethora of other options, it also offers the ability to store more and more data on it and to let a provider worry about scaling issues instead of local administrators. From an economic perspective, this can be a blessing, but from a security standpoint, this can be troublesome—and it is from that perspective that we focus throughout this book.

First and foremost, it is imperative that you understand and accept that you are responsible for the protection of your data (legally, morally, and so forth), even if another party hosts it. The SLA needs to spell out how the provider will protect the data (sandboxing and/or other methods) as well as redundancy, disaster recovery, and so on. Make sure that you encrypt the data, back it up, and implement as much control as possible.

Summary

Cloud computing holds great promise. It offers the ability to decrease costs, increase efficiency, and make the world a better place. There are three service models available (SaaS, PaaS, and IaaS), and four delivery models (private, public, community, and hybrid).

Virtualization is a key component of cloud computing. It makes it possible by abstracting the hardware and making it available to the virtual machines. The abstraction is done through the use of a hypervisor, which can be either Type I (bare metal) or Type II (hosted).

Just as cloud computing holds great promise, it also introduces new security risks. It is imperative that design considerations not overshadow the need for securing the data and keeping security a priority.

Exam Essentials

Know the three cloud service models.   NIST (National Institute of Standards and Technology) recognizes three possible cloud service models: Software as a Service (SaaS), Platform as a Service (PaaS), and Infrastructure as a Service (IaaS).

Know the four different cloud delivery models.   NIST recognizes four possible cloud delivery models: private, public, community, and hybrid.

Know the purpose of the hypervisor.   The hypervisor is the element (software/hardware) that allows a virtual machine to exist. Without the hypervisor, it would not be possible to have multiple operating systems running on one physical machine.

Know the hypervisor types.   A Type I hypervisor is known as bare metal and runs as both hypervisor and operating system. A Type II hypervisor is known as hosted, and it runs on top of another operating system.

Review Questions

1. In which cloud service model can the consumer "provision" and "deploy and run"?

    A. SaaS

    B. PaaS

    C. IaaS

    D. CaaS

2. Which cloud delivery model is implemented by a single organization, enabling it to be implemented behind a firewall?

    A. Private

    B. Public

    C. Community

    D. Hybrid

3. Which cloud service model provides the consumer the infrastructure to create applications and host them?

    A. SaaS

    B. PaaS

    C. IaaS

    D. CaaS

4. Which cloud delivery model could be considered a pool of services and resources delivered across the Internet by a cloud provider?

    A. Private

    B. Public

    C. Community

    D. Hybrid

5. Which cloud service model gives the consumer the ability to use applications provided by the cloud provider over the Internet?

    A. SaaS

    B. PaaS

    C. IaaS

    D. CaaS

6. Which cloud delivery model has an infrastructure shared by several organizations with shared interests and common IT needs?

    A. Private

    B. Public

    C. Community

    D. Hybrid

7. Which cloud delivery model could be considered an amalgamation of other types of delivery models?

    A. Private

    B. Public

    C. Community

    D. Hybrid

8. Which of the following is a method of capturing a virtual machine at a given point in time?

    A. Snapshot

    B. Photograph

    C. Syslog

    D. WMI

9. Which of the following is an industry standard for host availability?

    A. Eight 9s

    B. Seven 9s

    C. Six 9s

    D. Five 9s

10. Which feature of cloud computing involves dynamically provisioning (or de-provisioning) resources as needed?

    A. Multitenancy

    B. Elasticity

    C. CMDB

    D. Sandboxing

11. What is the term for restricting an application to a safe/restricted resource area?

    A. Multitenancy

    B. Fencing

    C. Securing

    D. Sandboxing

12. Which of the following terms implies hosting data from more than one consumer on the same equipment?

    A. Multitenancy

    B. Duplexing

    C. Bastioning

    D. Fashioning

13. When going with a public cloud delivery model, who is accountable for the security and privacy of the outsourced service?

    A. The cloud provider and the organization

    B. The cloud provider

    C. The organization

    D. No one

14. There are some implementations of cloud computing where multiple service models (IaaS, SaaS, PaaS) are combined into a hybrid. This is known as what?

    A. DBaaS

    B. HaaS

    C. XaaS

    D. ZaaS

15. Although a hybrid cloud could be any mixture of cloud delivery models, it is usually a combination of which of the following?

    A. Public and community

    B. Public and private

    C. Private and community

    D. Two or more communities

16. Which type of hypervisor implementation is known as "bare metal"?

    A. Type I

    B. Type II

    C. Type III

    D. Type IV

17. Which type of hypervisor implementation is known as "hosted"?

    A. Type I

    B. Type II

    C. Type III

    D. Type IV

18. When your servers become too busy, you can offload traffic to resources from a cloud provider. This is known as which of the following?

    A. Latency

    B. Cloud bursting

    C. Multitenancy

    D. Peaking

19. What protocol is used by technologies for load balancing/prioritizing traffic?

    A. ESX

    B. QoS

    C. IBJ

    D. IFNC

20. What is the machine on which virtualization software is running known as?

    A. Node

    B. Workstation

    C. Host

    D. Server

Chapter

7

Host, Data, and Application Security

THE FOLLOWING COMPTIA SECURITY+ EXAM OBJECTIVES ARE COVERED IN THIS CHAPTER:

✓ **2.8 Summarize risk management best practices.**

- Fault tolerance: Hardware; RAID; Clustering; Load balancing; Servers

✓ **4.1 Explain the importance of application security controls and techniques.**

- Fuzzing

- Secure coding concepts: Error and exception handling; Input validation

- Application configuration baseline (proper settings)

- Application hardening

- Application patch management

- NoSQL databases vs. SQL databases

- Server-side vs. Client-side validation

✓ **4.2 Summarize mobile security concepts and technologies.**

- Application security: Key management; Credential management; Authentication; Geo-tagging; Encryption; Application white-listing; Transitive trust/authentication

✓ **4.3 Given a scenario, select the appropriate solution to establish host security.**

- Operating system security and settings

- OS hardening

- Antimalware: Antivirus; Anti-spam; Anti-spyware; Pop-up blockers

- Patch management

- White listing vs. black listing applications

- Trusted OS

- Host-based firewalls

- Host-based intrusion detection

- Host software baselining

✓ **4.4 Implement the appropriate controls to ensure data security.**

- SAN

- Handling big data

- Data in-transit, data at-rest, data in-use

- Permissions/ACL

Computers (servers and clients), data, and applications are best secured by implementing them properly. That is not perfect security, but it is the foundation of security. However, once you start reducing security settings to increase interoperability with other operating systems or applications, you introduce weaknesses that may be exploited. This chapter deals with the process of ensuring that the products you use are as secure as they can be.

In this chapter, we'll begin by discussing how to secure an application. As you'll see, a number of security threats are based on exploiting flaws in applications, particularly web applications. Next we'll discuss methods to secure the computer, or the host, itself. We explored operating system hardening in Chapter 2, "Monitoring and Diagnosing Networks," and we won't repeat that material here. Finally, we'll discuss methods to protect the data itself.

Application Hardening

As we've explained, a good way to begin securing a network is to make sure that every system in the network is up-to-date and to verify that only those protocols you need are enabled. Unfortunately, these steps aren't enough. Your servers and workstations also run applications and services. Server services (especially web, email, and media servers) are particularly vulnerable to exploitation and attack. These applications must also be hardened to make them as difficult as possible to exploit.

The following sections deal with hardening your applications, both on the desktop and at the server, to provide maximum security.

Databases and Technologies

One key reason why computers are installed is for their ability to store, access, and modify data. The primary tool for data management is the database. Databases have become increasingly sophisticated, and their capabilities have grown dramatically over the last 10 years. This growth has created opportunities to view data in new ways; it has also created problems for both designers and users of these products.

This section briefly discusses database technologies and some of the common issues associated with vulnerabilities in database systems.

The *relational database* has become the most common approach to database implementation. This technology allows data to be viewed in dynamic ways based on the user's or administrator's needs. The most common language used to speak to databases is *Structured*

Query Language (SQL). SQL allows queries to be configured in real time and passed to database servers. This flexibility causes a major vulnerability when it isn't implemented securely.

 Don't confuse the acronym *SQL* with Microsoft's database product *SQL Server.* SQL Server implements Structured Query Language, or SQL, as do most other databases.

For example, you might want to get the phone numbers of all of the customers who live in a certain geographic area and have purchased products from you in the last two years. In a manual system, you would first need to determine which customers live in the area you want. You would perform a manual search of customer records, and then you would identify which customers have made purchases. This type of process could be very involved and time consuming.

In a relational database environment, you could query the database to find all of the records that meet your criteria and then print them. The command to do this might be a single line of code, or it might require thousands of instructions. Obviously, the increase in productivity is a worthwhile investment.

Corporate or organizational data is one of an organization's most valuable assets. It usually resides either in desktop systems or in large centralized database servers. This information makes the servers tempting targets for industrial espionage and damage.

Database servers suffer from all of the vulnerabilities we've discussed to this point. Additionally, the database itself is a complex set of programs that work together to provide access to data.

Early database systems connected the end user directly to the data through applications programs. These programs were intended to allow easy data access and to allow transactions to be performed against the database. In a private network, physical security was usually all that was needed to protect the data.

As the Internet has grown, businesses have allowed customer access to such data as tracking orders, reviewing purchases, wiring funds, and virtually any other capabilities they wanted. This increased interoperability has added more coding, more software, and more complexity to databases.

Software manufacturers work hard to keep up with customer demands. Unfortunately, they frequently release software that is prone to security problems. The increase in demand for database-oriented systems and the security problems introduced by software developers and manufacturers have been the biggest areas of vulnerability for database servers.

 Databases need patching just like other applications. You should configure them to use access controls and provide their own levels of security.

To improve system performance, as well as to improve the security of databases, companies have implemented the tiered systems model. Three different models are explained here:

One-Tier Model In a *one-tier model*, or *single-tier environment*, the database and the application exist on a single system. This is common on desktop systems running a standalone database. Early Unix implementations also worked in this manner; each user would sign on to a terminal and run a dedicated application that accessed the data.

Two-Tier Model   In a *two-tier model,* the client workstation or system runs an application that communicates with the database that is running on a different server. This is a common implementation, and it works well for many applications.

Three-Tier Model   The *three-tier model* effectively isolates the end user from the database by introducing a *middle-tier server.* This server accepts requests from clients, evaluates them, and then sends them on to the database server for processing. The database server sends the data back to the middle-tier server, which then sends the data to the client system. This approach is becoming common in business today. The middle server can also control access to the database and provide additional security.

These three models provide increasing capability and complexity. You must manage each system and keep it current in order for it to provide security.

NoSQL

NoSQL is a relatively new concept. Most commercial relational database management systems (Oracle, Microsoft SQL Server, MySQL, PostGres, and so forth) use SQL. A *NoSQL database* is not a relational database and does not use SQL. These databases are less common than relational databases but often used where scaling is important. Table 7.1 compares NoSQL vs. SQL databases:

TABLE 7.1   NoSQL Databases vs. SQL Databases

Feature	NoSQL Database	SQL Database
Database Type	Non-Relational/Distributed	Relational
Schema Type	Dynamic	Pre-defined
Data Storage	Stores everything in a single nested document, often in XML format (document-based)	Individual records are stored as rows in tables (table-based)
Benefits	Can handle large volumes of structured, semi-structured, and unstructured data	Widely supported and easy to configure for structured data
Typical Scaling Model	Horizontal – add more servers	Vertical – beef up the server
Popular Vendors/ Implementations	MongoDB, CouchDB, and others	Oracle, Microsoft, MySQL, and others
Susceptible to SQL Injection Attacks	No, but susceptible to similar injection-type attacks	Yes

Big Data

Increasingly, organizations have to store extremely large amounts of data, often many terabytes. This is sometimes referred to simply as *Big Data*. This data normally cannot fit on a single server, and it is instead stored on a storage area network (SAN)—discussed next. One of the issues with Big Data is that it reaches a size where it becomes difficult to search, to store, to share, to back up, and to truly manage.

SAN

A *storage area network (SAN)* is a separate network set up to appear as a server to the main organizational network. For example, multiple servers, network storage devices, and switches might be configured to store several terabytes of data. This mini-network has one purpose: to store data. It is then connected to the main organizational network. Users can access the data in the SAN without being concerned about the complexities involved in the SAN. SANs usually have redundant servers, and they are connected via high-speed fiber-optic connections or iSCSI running on copper.

Security for a SAN is similar to that for any server, with the exception of network isolation. There needs to be a firewall, perhaps an intrusion detection system (IDS), user access control, and all of the other security features that you would expect on many networks. SANS are primarily used when there is a large amount of data to store that must be accessible to users on the network.

For more details beyond what is covered on the Security+ exam, visit the following site:

www.sans.org/reading-room/whitepapers/storage/storage-area-network-secure-overview-storage-area-network-security-perspective-516

Fuzzing

Most applications that are written to accept input expect a particular type of data—string values, numerical values, and so on. Sometimes, it is possible to enter unexpected values and cause the application to crash. When that happens, the user may be left with elevated privileges or access to values they should not have. *Fuzzing* is the technique of providing unexpected values as input to an application in order to make it crash. Those values can be random, invalid, or just unexpected. A common method is to flood the input with a stream of random bits.

The best way to prevent fuzzing from occurring on your systems is to validate all input to ensure that input is of the expected type.

Secure Coding

Secure coding can best prevent many of the attacks discussed in this chapter. Cross-site scripting and SQL injection are discussed in detail in this chapter, and proper/secure coding is the only prevention for these attacks. Buffer overflows are examined elsewhere in this book, but again, secure coding is the only real defense against this attack.

Secure coding is a broad area, but for the Security+ exam, you only need to know the general concepts. If you are a programmer, or supervise application security, we recommend that you delve deeper into this topic with the URLs that are provided in this section.

OWASP

The Open Web Application Security Project (`https://www.owasp.org/index.php/OWASP_Secure_Coding_Practices_-_Quick_Reference_Guide`) is a voluntary group dedicated to forming secure coding practices for web-based applications as well as mobile and client applications along with back-end design issues. The focus on web-based is important since web applications are among the most vulnerable to attack. This organization has a range of coding standards; the most fundamental (and the most critical for the Security+ exam) is input validation.

As you will see later in this chapter, some attacks, such as SQL injection, depend entirely on unfiltered input being sent through a web application. OWASP recommends that all data input by a user be validated before it is processed. There are two primary ways to do input validation: client-side validation and server-side validation.

Client-side validation usually works by taking the input that a user enters into a text field and, on the client side, checking for invalid characters or input. This process can be as simple as verifying that the input does not exceed the required length, or it can be a complete check for SQL injection characters. In either case, the validation is accomplished on the client web page before any data is sent to the server.

Server-side validation involves validating data after the server has received it. This process can include checking business logic to see if the data sent conforms to expected parameters. It is unusual to have just server-side validation. You may have systems with only client-side validation, but server-side validation is normally done in conjunction with client-side validation.

CERT Secure Coding Standards

The *Computer Emergency Response Team (CERT)* at Carnage Mellon University (`www.cert.org/secure-coding/`) also details standards for secure coding. CERT standards cover many of the same issues as OWASP, but they also have complete language-specific standards for Java, Perl, C, and C++.

One item that CERT addresses is the issue of exception handling. The fact is that programs encounter errors. How those errors are handled is critical to security. For example, some programmers present detailed error information to the end user. Not only is this not very helpful for most end users, it might provide information that is useful to a hacker at the same time. A better idea is to have a simple but helpful message displayed to the end user and simply to log the detailed information.

Application Configuration Baselining

Baselining always involves comparing performance to a metric. That metric is a historical measurement that you can point to and identify as coming before a configuration change, before the site became busy, before you added new services, and so on. Baselining can be done with any metric, such as network performance or CPU usage, as well as with applications.

It is advisable to do baselining with key applications prior to major configuration changes. Make certain that applications have proper settings to work at their optimal values and provide security protection as well.

Operating System Patch Management

In Chapter 2, we discussed patches. There are three types of operating system patches, each with a different level of urgency.

Hotfix   A *hotfix* is an immediate and urgent patch. In general, these represent serious security issues and are not optional; they must be applied to the system.

Patch   A *patch*, as we discussed in Chapter 2, provides some additional functionality or a non-urgent fix. These are sometimes optional.

Service Pack   *Service packs* are a cumulative assortment of the hotfixes and patches to date. These should always be applied but tested first to be sure that no problems are caused by the update.

Application Patch Management

Just as you need to keep operating system patches current, as they often fix security problems discovered within the OS, you need to do the same with application patches. Once an exploit in an application becomes known, an attacker can take advantage of it to enter or harm a system. Most vendors post patches on a regular basis, and you should routinely scan for any available ones.

A large number of attacks today are targeted at client systems for the simple reason that clients do not always manage application patching well. When you couple that with the fact that most clients have many applications running, the odds of being able to find a weakness to exploit are increased dramatically.

Host Security

We have said it before, but it is worth repeating: The entire network is only as strong as the weakest host. Given that, you should focus on keeping all hosts current in terms of malware protection and baselining. All of these areas are covered in the following sections.

Permissions

User permissions may be the most basic aspect of security. Remember the concept of *least privileges*, which means that any given user will be granted only the privileges necessary to perform their job function.

Microsoft describes five file permissions and one additional folder permission:

Full Control   This means the user cannot only read, execute, and write, but they can also assign permissions to other uses.

Modify   This is the same as read and write, with delete added.

Read and Execute   Not all files are documents. For example, programs are files, and the Read and Execute privilege is needed to run the program.

Read   This permission allows the user to read the file but not to modify it.

Write   This permission allows the user to modify the file.

Folders have the same permissions, with one added permission: *list folder contents*. This permission allows the user to see what is in a folder but not to read the files.

Access Control Lists

Related to permissions is the concept of the *access control list (ACL)*. An ACL is literally a list of who can access what resource and at what level. It can be an internal part of an operating system or application. For example, a custom application might have an ACL that lists which users have what permissions (access levels) in that system.

An ACL can also be a physical list of who is allowed to enter a room or a building. This is a much less common definition for ACL, but it is relevant to physical security.

Related to ACLs are white lists and black lists. In fact, you could consider these to be special types of access control lists. Essentially, a white list is a list of items that are allowed. It could be a list of websites that are okay to visit with company computers, or it could be a list of third-party software that is authorized to be installed on company computers. Black lists are the opposite. They are lists of things that are prohibited. It could be specific websites that employees should not visit or software that is forbidden to be installed on client computers.

In the case of black lists, many companies block access to hacking websites, network scanners, and steganography tools (see Chapter 8, "Cryptography," for details) to prevent a rogue employee from using those resources on a company network.

Antimalware

To keep all hosts safe from malware, there are a number of actions you should take at minimum:

Install antivirus software.   Antivirus software, discussed in depth in Chapter 4, "Access Control, Authentication, and Authorization," should be installed and definitions kept current on all hosts. Antivirus software should run on the server as well as on every workstation. In addition to active monitoring of incoming files, scans should be conducted regularly to catch any infections that have slipped through.

Install antispam filters.   Although exact numbers are hard to acquire, it is clear that a great deal of email traffic is spam. Spam filters are needed to keep the majority of this unwanted email from reaching the users.

Install antispyware software.   Some antispyware software is combined with antivirus packages, whereas other programs are available as standalones. Regardless of the type you use, you must regularly look for spyware, often identified by the presence of tracking cookies on hosts, and remove those that get installed.

Use pop-up blockers.   Not only are pop-ups irritating, but they are also a security threat. Pop-ups (including pop-unders) represent unwanted programs running on the system, and they can jeopardize the system's well-being. In Exercise 7.1, we'll show you how to configure a pop-up blocker in Microsoft Internet Explorer.

Use host-based firewalls.   A *firewall* is the first line of defense against attackers and malware. Almost every current operating system includes a firewall, and most are turned on by default. In Exercise 7.2, we'll show you how to configure Windows Firewall to notify you when a program is blocked.

Use host-based IDSs.   IDSs are also available for individual hosts. In fact, the standard way SNORT (www.snort.org) installs is as a host-based IDS. Usually, you will come across host-based IDS on critical servers, but they can be installed on any machine.

EXERCISE 7.1

Configuring a Pop-up Blocker

Pop-ups represent a security risk that often bypasses other forms of security. To configure a pop-up blocker in Internet Explorer, follow these steps:

1.   In Internet Explorer, choose Tools ➤ Internet Options ➤ Privacy ➤ Settings.

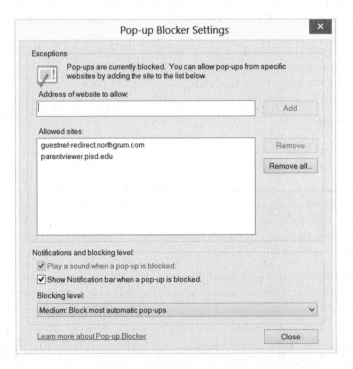

2. Add Google to the list of allowed pop-ups by entering the address **http://google .com** and clicking Add. This URL should now appear in the list of allowed sites as `*.google.com`.

3. Note the three possible settings for blocking levels:

   - Low allows pop-ups from sites considered to be secure.

   - Medium (the default) blocks most pop-ups.

   - High blocks all (but Ctrl+Alt will override).

   Click Close to exit the settings.

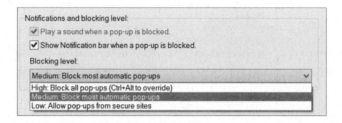

4. Click OK.

5. Click OK again to exit Internet Options.

EXERCISE 7.2

Configuring Windows Firewall

Windows Firewall is used to block access to a system from attackers and malware. You can configure it in a number of different ways, including sending a notification when a program is blocked. To configure Windows Firewall to send a notification, follow these steps.

Note that different versions of Windows will have slight variations in where things are found. For example, in Windows 8, you don't launch the Control Panel by clicking Start; you do so by moving your mouse to the bottom right of the screen and waiting for a pop-up menu. Then you go to Settings and click Control Panel. However, once you get to the individual item (firewall, services, and so forth), they are all virtually identical in Windows 7, 8, and 8.1. This example is for Windows 7:

1. Click Start ➢ Control Panel ➢ System And Security ➢ Windows Firewall.

2. Click Change Notification Settings. Beneath Allow An App Or Feature Through Windows Firewall, click Change Notification Settings.

EXERCISE 7.2 *(continued)*

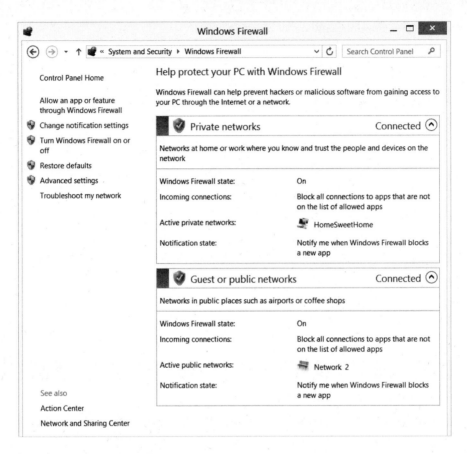

3. You can now choose whether or not to be notified when Windows Firewall blocks a new application.

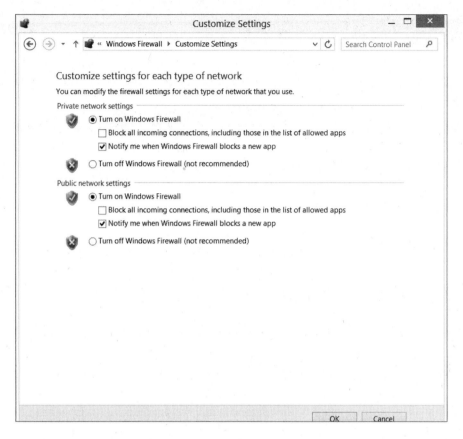

4. If you return to the main firewall screen and select Advanced, you will see the screen that allows you to set up rules and monitoring.

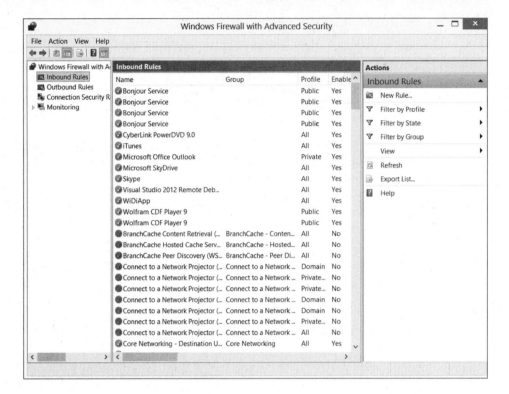

5. Click OK. Click OK again to exit the properties. Exit the dialog boxes and Control
    Panel.

Although software-based firewalls included with the operating system are a great
defense, they should not be considered the only necessary solution. A *web application fire-wall (WAF)* can look at every request between a web client and a web server and identify
possible attacks.

Host Software Baselining

One of the first steps in developing a secure environment is to develop a baseline of the
minimum security needs of your organization. A *security baseline* defines the level of
security that will be implemented and maintained. You can choose to set a low baseline by
implementing next to no security or a high baseline that doesn't allow users to make any
changes at all to the network or their systems. In practice, most implementations fall some-where between these two extremes; you must determine what is best for your organization.

A security baseline, which can also be called a *performance baseline*, provides the input needed to design, implement, and support a secure network. Developing the baseline includes gathering data on the specific security implementation of the systems with which you'll be working.

Microsoft Baseline Security Analyzer is a free tool that can be downloaded and run on Windows to create security reports and scan for errors (`http://technet.microsoft.com/en-us/security/cc184923`). Figure 7.1 shows the interface for this tool.

FIGURE 7.1   The opening interface for Microsoft Baseline Security Analyzer

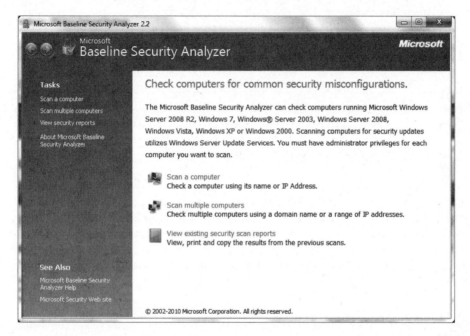

To keep your network secure, you need to harden its individual components. In the sections that follow, we will look at hardening web servers, email servers, FTP servers, DNS servers, NNTP servers, and DHCP servers.

Hardening Web Servers

Web servers are one of the favorite areas for attackers to exploit because of the reach they have. If an attacker can gain access to a popular web server and take advantage of a weakness there, they have the opportunity to reach thousands, if not hundreds of thousands, of users who access the site. By targeting a web server, the attacker can actually affect all the connections from users' web browsers and inflict harm far beyond the one machine they compromised.

Web servers were originally simple in design and used primarily to provide HTML text and graphics content. Modern web servers allow database access, chat functionality, streaming media, and virtually every other type of service that can be contemplated. This diversity gives websites the ability to provide rich and complex capabilities to web surfers.

Every service and capability supported on a website is potentially a target for exploitation. Make sure that they're kept up with the most current software standards. You must also make certain that you're allowing users to have only the minimal permissions necessary to accomplish their tasks. If users are accessing your server via an anonymous account, then common sense dictates that you must make certain that the anonymous account has only the permissions needed to view web pages and nothing more.

Two particular areas of interest with web servers are filters and controlling access to executable scripts. *Filters* allow you to limit the traffic that is allowed through. Limiting traffic to only that which is required for your business can help ward off attacks.

A good set of filters can also be applied to your network to prevent users from accessing sites other than those that are business related. Not only does this increase productivity, but it also decreases the likelihood of users obtaining a virus from a questionable site.

Executable scripts, such as those written in PHP, Python, various flavors of Java, and Common Gateway Interface (CGI) scripts, often run at elevated permission levels. Under most circumstances this isn't a problem because the user is returned to their regular permission level at the conclusion of the execution. Problems arise, however, if the user can break out of the script while at the elevated level. From an administrator's standpoint, the best course of action is to verify that all scripts on your server have been thoroughly tested, debugged, and approved for use.

On all web servers, one account is created when services are installed that is used to represent the anonymous user. Rights assigned to this account apply to all anonymous web users. With IIS, for example, that account is *IUSR_computername*, whereas in Apache it can be any account that you choose to assign as the anonymous user (often *nobody*, *apache*, or *webuser*).

Hardening Email Servers

Email servers provide the communications backbone for many businesses. They typically run either as an additional service on an existing server or as dedicated systems.

Putting an active virus scanner on email servers can reduce the number of viruses introduced into your network and prevent viruses from being spread by your email server. It is worth noting, though, that most scanners can't read Microsoft's open files, so to scan Exchange mail stores, you need a specific email AV scanner. Figure 7.2 illustrates an email virus scanner being added to a server. In this implementation, the scanner filters incoming emails that are suspicious and informs email users of a potential system compromise. This feature is very effective in preventing the spread of viruses via email.

FIGURE 7.2   Email virus scanner being added to a server

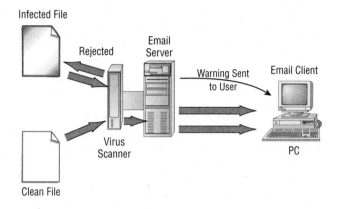

 Real World Scenario

Using ACLs to Address Spam

You've been observing repeated attempts by a TCP/IP address to connect to your email server. These failed connection attempts appear in your email system logs. The intruder continually attempts to access port 25.

Email servers are being inundated by automated systems that attempt to use them to send spam. Most email servers have implemented measures to prevent this. The threats, however, are becoming increasingly more sophisticated. You may be able to reduce these attempts to access your system by entering the TCP/IP addresses in your router's ACL Deny list. Doing so will cause your router to ignore connection requests from these IP addresses, effectively improving your security.

Hardening FTP Servers

File Transfer Protocol (FTP) servers aren't intended for high-security applications because of their inherent weaknesses. Most FTP servers allow you to create file areas on any drive on the system. You should create a separate drive or subdirectory on the system to allow file transfers. If possible, use virtual private network (VPN) or Secure Shell (SSH) connections for FTP-type activities. FTP isn't notable for security, and many FTP systems send account and password information across the network unencrypted. FTP is one of the tools frequently used to exploit systems.

From an operational security perspective, you should use separate logon accounts and passwords for FTP access. Doing so will prevent system accounts from being disclosed to unauthorized individuals. Also, make sure that all files stored on an FTP server are scanned for viruses.

You should *always* disable the anonymous user account. To make FTP use easier, most servers default to allowing anonymous access. However, from a security perspective the last thing you want is to allow anonymous users to copy files to and from your servers. Disabling anonymous access requires the user to be a known, authenticated user in order to access the FTP server.

As mentioned in the web access discussion, an account is created on servers that offer FTP service for representing the anonymous user. For example, the *IUSR_computername* account is created in versions of IIS when services are installed. Rights assigned to this account apply to all anonymous users.

The best way to secure FTP is to replace it altogether. Instead of using FTP, the same functionality can be found in more secure services such as Secure File Transfer Protocol (SFTP), which was discussed in Chapter 3, "Understanding Devices and Infrastructure."

Hardening DNS Servers

Domain Name Service (DNS) servers resolve hostnames to IP addresses. This service allows a website name such as www.sybex.com to be resolved to an IP address such as 192.168.1.110.

A registrar manages your domain name, and most require an annual renewal fee. If these fees aren't paid, another company will be able to hijack your domain name. Such hijacking has embarrassed many organizations.

DNS servers can be used internally for private functions and externally for public lookups. Though DNS-related attacks aren't common, they are generally of three types:

Domain Name Service Denial-of-Service Attacks   Domain Name Service Denial-of-Service (DNS DoS) attacks are primarily aimed at DNS servers. The intention is to disrupt the operations of the server, thereby making the system unusable. To address these attacks, make sure that your DNS server software and the operating system software are kept up-to-date and that you're using two-factor authentication with your registrar. Doing so will tend to minimize the impact of DNS DoS attacks.

Network Footprinting   *Footprinting* is the act of gathering data about a network in order to find ways that someone might intrude. When you footprint, you're looking for vulnerabilities and any means of entry. A great deal of information about your network is stored in DNS servers. By using one of the common DNS lookup programs, such as NSLOOKUP, an attacker can learn about your network configuration. DNS entries typically include information pertaining to domain names and mail, web, commerce, and other key servers in your network. Keep the amount of information stored about your network in external DNS servers to a bare minimum.

A good recommendation is to use two DNS servers: one on the internal network and one on the external network.

Compromising Record Integrity   DNS lookup systems usually involve either a primary or a primary and a secondary DNS server. If you make a change to a primary or secondary server, the change propagates to other trusted DNS servers. If a bogus record is inserted into a DNS server, the record will point to the location the attacker intends to compromise rather than to a legitimate site. Imagine the embarrassment to a corporation when its website visitors are redirected to a competitor or, even worse, to a porn site. Make sure that all DNS servers require authentication before updates are made or propagated. Doing so will help ensure that unauthorized records aren't inserted into your servers.

As DNS was originally designed, it did not include security because it was never thought to be a possible weakness in the network. Once it was realized that DNS could be exploited, however, the Domain Name System Security Extensions (DNSSEC) were created by the IETF (Internet Engineering Task Force) to add security and maintain backward compatibility. DNSSEC checks digital signatures and can protect information by digitally signing records. Specifically, DNSSEC was designed to protect against forged DNS data. More information on DNSSEC can be found at www.dnssec.net.

DNS poisoning is a problem that existed in early implementations of DNS. It hasn't been a serious problem for a while, but you should be aware of it for the exam. With DNS poisoning (also known as *cache poisoning*), a daemon caches DNS reply packets, which sometimes contain other information (data used to fill the packets). The extra data can be scanned for information useful in a break-in or man-in-the-middle attack.

A similar attack, *Address Resolution Protocol (ARP) poisoning*, tries to convince the network that the attacker's MAC address is the one associated with an IP address so that traffic sent to that IP address is wrongly sent to the attacker's machine.

Hardening DHCP Services

Dynamic Host Configuration Protocol (DHCP) is used in many networks to automate the assignment of IP addresses to workstations. DHCP services can be provided by many different types of devices, including routers, switches, and servers. The DHCP process involves leasing a TCP/IP address to a workstation for a specified time. DHCP can also provide other network configuration options to a workstation.

In a given network or segment, only one DHCP server should be running. If more than one is running, they will clash with each other over which one provides the address. This can cause duplication of TCP/IP addresses and potentially lead to addressing conflicts.

A Network Address Translation (NAT) server can service DHCP-enabled clients. (See the section "Network Address Translation" in Chapter 3 for a discussion of NAT servers.) DHCP usage should be limited to workstation systems.

 Real World Scenario

Dealing with Strange IP Addresses

Some of your computer users have suddenly started calling you to indicate that, after rebooting their systems, they can no longer access network services or the Internet. After investigating the situation, you discover that the IP addresses they're using are invalid for your network. The IP addresses are valid, but they aren't part of your network. You've inspected your DHCP server and can't find a reason for this. What should you investigate next?

You should investigate whether someone has configured another server or device in your network with an active DHCP server. If so, the illicit DHCP server is now leasing addresses to the users instead of the addresses coming from your server, or the systems can't reach your DHCP server and are getting an Automatic Private IP Addressing (APIPA) address.

This happens when administrators or developers are testing pilot systems. Make sure that all test systems are isolated from your production network either by a router or by some other mechanism. These servers are referred to as *rogue servers*, and they can cause much confusion in a DHCP environment.

Many devices, such as routers and modems, have the ability to act also as DHCP servers. A user trying to skirt IT and add their own wireless router to their computer could potentially add a rogue DHCP server to the network that an intruder could use to gain access. Use IDSs to look for rogue servers, and disable them immediately.

An exception to having only one DHCP server running in the network would be if you were implementing redundant DHCP services without overlapping scopes.

Protecting Data Through Fault Tolerance

The fact is that equipment fails. At some point, all equipment fails, so fault tolerance is important.

Backups

At the most basic level, fault tolerance for a server means a data backup. *Backups* are simply the periodic archiving of the data so that if there is a server failure you can retrieve the data. Although database administrators may use a number of different types of data backups (for example, transaction log backups), from a security point of view there are three primary backup types with which we are concerned:

Full   All changes to the data are archived.

Differential   All changes since the last full backup are archived.

Incremental   All changes since the last backup of any type are archived.

So consider a scenario where you do a full backup at 2 a.m. each morning. You are concerned about the possibility of a server crash before the next full backup, so you want to do a backup every two hours. The type of backup you choose will determine the efficiency of doing those frequent backups and the time needed to restore data. Let's consider each scenario and what would happen if the system crashes at 10:05 a.m.

Full Backup   In this scenario, assume a full backup is done every two hours beginning at 2 a.m. When the system crashes at 10:05 a.m., you simply need to restore the 10:00 a.m. full backup. However, running a full backup every two hours is very time consuming and resource intensive, and it will have a significant negative impact on your server's performance.

Differential Backup   In this scenario, you do a full backup at 2 a.m. and then perform a differential every two hours thereafter. When the system crashes at 10:05 a.m., you have to restore the full backup from 2 a.m. and the differential backup from 10 a.m. This takes just one more step than restoring the full backup. Keep in mind, however, that the differential backups are going to get larger each time you do them and thus more time consuming and resource intensive. Although they won't have the impact of the full backups, they will still slow down your network.

Incremental Backup   In this scenario you do a full backup at 2 a.m. and then an incremental backup every two hours. When the system crashes at 10:05 a.m., you need to restore the last full backup done at 2 a.m and then each incremental backup done since then—and they must be restored in order. This is much more complex to restore, but each incremental backup is small and does not take much time, nor do they consume many resources.

Which backup should you use? Unfortunately, there is no single, correct choice. The proper choice depends on your organization's needs. Which one you select will depend on your organization's needs. Whatever backup strategy you choose, you must periodically test it. The only effective way to test your backup strategy is to restore the backup data to a test machine.

Hierarchical storage management (HSM) provides continuous online backup by using optical or tape jukeboxes. It appears as an infinite disk to the system, and you can configure it to provide the closest version of an available real-time backup.

RAID

The other fundamental aspect of fault tolerance is RAID, or *redundant array of independent disks (RAID)*. RAID allows your servers to have more than one hard drive so that if the main hard drive fails, the system keeps functioning. The primary RAID levels are described here:

RAID 0 (Striped Disks)   This RAID level distributes data across multiple disks in a way that provides improved speed (read/write performance) at any given instant but does not offer any fault tolerance. A minimum of two disks are needed.

RAID 1   This RAID level introduces fault tolerance as it mirrors the contents of the disks; it is also called *mirroring*. For every disk you need for operations, there is an identical disk in the system. A minimum of two disks are needed and 50 percent of your total capacity is used for data and the other 50 percent for the mirror. So if you have a server with two hard drives, it would actually only be able to store data equal to the size of one of the disks. With RAID 1, if the primary drive(s) fails, the system keeps running on the backup drive. If you add another controller to the system, it is still RAID 1, but now called *duplexing*.

RAID 3 or 4 (Striped Disks with Dedicated Parity)   This RAID level combines three or more disks with the data distributed across the disks. This RAID level also uses one dedicated disk to store parity information. The storage capacity of the array is reduced by one disk (the one used for parity). If a disk fails, that is only a partial loss of data. The data remaining on the other disks, along with the parity information, allows the data to be recovered.

RAID 5 (Striped Disks with Distributed Parity)   This RAID level combines three or more disks in a way that protects data against the loss of any one disk. It is similar to RAID 3, but the parity is distributed across the drive array. This way, you don't forego an entire disk for storing parity bits.

RAID 6 (Striped Disks with Dual Parity)   This RAID level combines four or more disks in a way that protects data against the loss of any two disks. It accomplishes this by adding an additional parity block to RAID 5. Each of the parity blocks is distributed across the drive array so parity is not dedicated to any specific drive.

RAID 1+0 (or 10)   This RAID level is a mirrored data set (RAID 1), which is then striped (RAID 0), which is the reason for the "1+0" name. Think of it as a "stripe of mirrors."

A RAID 1+0 array requires a minimum of four drives: two mirrored drives to hold half of the striped data, plus another two mirrored drives for the other half of the data.

RAID 0+1   This RAID level is the opposite or RAID 1+0. Here, the stripes are mirrored (think of it as a "mirror of the stripes"). A RAID 0+1 array requires a minimum of four drives: two mirrored drives to replicate the data on the RAID 0 array.

Backups and RAID are examples of protecting *data at rest*. This means data that is not currently being transmitted. *Data in transit*, on the other hand, is information that is being sent over some network connection—active data.

Clustering and Load Balancing

RAID does a fantastic job of protecting data on systems (which you then protect further with regular backups), but sometimes you need to grow beyond single systems. Anytime you connect multiple computers to work/act together as a single server, it is known as *clustering*. Clustered systems utilize parallel processing (improving performance and availability) and add redundancy (but also add costs).

High availability can also be obtained through *load balancing*. This allows you to split the workload across multiple computers. Those computers are often *Servers* answering HTTP requests (often called a server farm), which may or may not be in the same geographic location. If you split locations, this is usually called a mirror site, and the mirrored copy can add geographic redundancy (allowing requests to be answered quicker) and help prevent downtime.

Application Security

There are a number of issues to be cognizant of when it t comes to application security. Many of these have been addressed—or will be addressed—in other chapters where the discussion is more relevant, but the following is a list of those issues that CompTIA wants you to be aware of:

Key Management   Key management is an area of importance that is continuing to grow as PKI services increase and expand to mobile. Chapter 8 focuses on cryptography and issues associated with keys.

Credential Management   Credentials allow usernames and passwords to be stored in one location and then used to access websites and other computers. Newer versions of Windows include Credential Manager (beneath the Control Panel) to simplify management.

Authentication   Authentication has always been an issue, but now that mobile is expanding and the need for authentication with applications associate with it has grown, the issue has become even more important. Users should be taught best practices and should never configure any application to automatically log them in.

Geo-Tagging   Geo-tagging (usually written as GeoTagging) allows GPS coordinates (latitude, longitude, etc.) to accompany a file such as an image. This is a common practice with pictures taken using a smartphone or digital camera. While it can be useful if you are trying to remember details of a family vacation, it can also raise security concerns in a business environment. As an example, suppose a picture is taken of your server room and posted—the geotagged information accompanying it would allow anyone to know the precise location of your server room and that could easily be something you would rather protect.

Encryption   Encryption, the subject of Chapter 8, opens up a lot of possibilities for increasing security, but brings it with issues that company policies should be created to address: for example, what is the procedure when a user forgets their password to an application/data?

Application White-Listing   As was mentioned with the ACL discussion earlier in the chapter, "white lists" are lists of those items that are allowed (as opposed to a black list—things that are prohibited). A white list of applications should exist to identify what applications are approved and accepted on your network.

Transitive Trust/Authentication   Transitive access and transitive trust are addressed in Chapter 4. Anytime one entity accepts a user without requiring additional authentication on the behalf of another entity, the possibility is introduced for problems to occur. As much of a pain as it is for users, the more stops that you have requiring them to authenticate before passing through, the safer you make you make your environment.

This section has focused on security related to applications and relevant mostly to mobile security concepts. In the next section, the best practices relevant to security overall will be examined.

Best Practices for Security

In the preceding sections of this chapter, some of the basics of operating system and application hardening were given. These gave you a good foundation for security, but there are several technologies and practices that you, as a security administrator, should also be aware of in order to implement the best security in your environment. These technologies are covered in this section, and you should be familiar with them for the exam.

Data Loss Prevention

Data loss prevention (DLP) systems monitor the contents of systems (workstations, servers, and networks) to make sure that key content is not deleted or removed. They also monitor who is using the data (looking for unauthorized access) and transmitting the data. DLP systems share commonality with network intrusion prevention systems, discussed in Chapter 3.

One of the best-known DLP systems is MyDLP, an open source solution that runs on most Windows platforms. You can find MyDLP at www.mydlp.org. A large number of commercial programs are available for purchase, including Microsoft Forefront (www.microsoft.com/forefront/). RSA is another popular DLP product and there are others available from McAfee, Palisade Systems and Global Velocity.

> Tripwire is a great system for data protection. Tripwire monitors specific files to see if they have changed. If they have, the Tripwire system can either restore them or simply alert an administrator. There is both a commercial and an open source version of Tripwire.

Hardware-Based Encryption Devices

In addition to software-based encryption, hardware-based encryption can be applied. Within the advanced configuration settings on some BIOS configuration menus, for example, you can choose to enable or disable TPM. A *Trusted Platform Module (TPM)* can be used to assist with hash key generation. TPM is the name assigned to a chip that can store cryptographic keys, passwords, or certificates. TPM can be used to protect smartphones and devices other than PCs as well. It can also be used to generate values used with whole disk encryption such as BitLocker, which will be discussed in more detail in Chapter 8. BitLocker can be used with or without TPM. It is much more secure when coupled with TPM (preferable, in fact) but does not require it.

The TPM chip may be installed on the motherboard. When it is, in many cases it is set to off in the BIOS by default. In Exercise 7.3, you'll look for a TPM chip in Windows 7 (note the process is pretty much the same in Windows 8). Windows 7 is used as the example here merely because the support for TPM is included with most versions of it, whereas with Windows 8, that support is limited.

EXERCISE 7.3

Verifying the Presence of a TPM Chip in Windows 7

The following steps will allow you to verify whether or not a TPM chip is installed on your computer:

1. In Windows 7, open Control Panel and choose Security.

2. Under Security, choose BitLocker Drive Encryption.

3. A dialog box will appear. The contents of the box do not matter. What does matter is a link in the lower-left corner that reads TPM Administration. If the link is there, TPM is installed and active. If you don't see the link but are certain that your computer contains such a chip, you may need to boot into your BIOS Setup menu and enable TPM before trying this again.

More information on TPM can be found at the Trusted Computing Group's website: https://www.trustedcomputinggroup.org/home.

In addition to TPM, *HSM (Hardware Security Module)* is a cryptoprocessor that can be used to enhance security. HSM is commonly used with PKI systems (discussed in Chapter 8) to augment security with certification authorities (CAs). As opposed to being mounted on the motherboard like TPMs, HSMs are traditionally packaged as PCI adapters.

There is an open source product called TrueCrypt (www.Truecrypt.org) that is free; available for Windows, Linux, or Macintosh; and uses 256-bit AES encryption. TrueCrypt is an excellent choice for encrypting hard drives and partitions.

Summary

This chapter introduced you to the concept of hardening. To secure a network, each of the elements in its environment must be individually evaluated. Remember, your network is no more secure than its weakest link. The process of making a server or an application resistant to an attack is called hardening. One of the major methods of hardening is to disable anything that isn't needed in the system. Keeping systems updated also helps improve security.

Product updates are often used to improve security and to fix errors. The three primary methods of upgrading systems are hotfixes, service packs, and patches. Hotfixes are usually meant as immediate fixes, whereas service packs usually contain multiple fixes. Patches are used to fix a program temporarily until a permanent fix can be applied.

Application hardening helps to ensure that vulnerabilities are minimized. Make sure you run only the applications and services that are needed to support your environment. Attackers can target application protocols. Many of the newer systems offer a rich environment for end users, and each protocol increases your risk.

Database technologies are vulnerable to attacks because of the nature of the flexibility they provide. Make sure that database servers and applications are kept up-to-date. To provide increased security, many environments have implemented multitiered approaches to data access.

Exam Essentials

Be able to discuss the weaknesses and vulnerabilities of the various applications that run on a network.   Web, email, and other services present unique security challenges that must be considered. Turn off services that aren't needed. Make sure that applications are kept up-to-date with security and bug fixes. Implement these services in a secure manner as the manufacturer intended. This is the best method for securing applications.

Review Questions

1. Which of the following terms refers to the process of establishing a standard for security?

    A. Baselining

    B. Security evaluation

    C. Hardening

    D. Methods research

2. You've been chosen to lead a team of administrators in an attempt to increase security. You're currently creating an outline of all the aspects of security that will need to be examined and acted on. Which of the following terms describes the process of improving security in a NOS?

    A. Common Criteria

    B. Hardening

    C. Encryption

    D. Networking

3. Which of the following statements is *not* true?

    A. You should never share the root directory of a disk.

    B. You should share the root directory of a disk.

    C. You should apply the most restrictive access necessary for a shared directory.

    D. Filesystems are frequently based on hierarchical models.

4. Users are complaining about name resolution problems suddenly occurring that were never an issue before. You suspect that an intruder has compromised the integrity of the DNS server on your network. What is one of the primary ways in which an attacker uses DNS?

    A. Network footprinting

    B. Network sniffing

    C. Database server lookup

    D. Registration counterfeiting

5. Which of the following is the technique of providing unexpected values as input to an application to try to make it crash?

    A. DLP

    B. Fuzzing

    C. TPM

    D. HSM

6. Which systems monitor the contents of systems (workstations, servers, networks) to make sure key content is not deleted or removed?

    A. DLP

    B. PKM

    C. XML

    D. GSP

7. You're redesigning your network in preparation for putting the company up for sale. The network, like all aspects of the company, needs to perform at its best in order to benefit the sale. Which model is used to provide an intermediary server between the end user and the database?

    A. One-tiered

    B. Two-tiered

    C. Three-tiered

    D. Relational database

8. The administrator at MTS was recently fired, and it has come to light that he didn't install updates and fixes as they were released. As the newly hired administrator, your first priority is to bring all networked clients and servers up-to-date. What is a bundle of one or more system fixes in a single product called?

    A. Service pack

    B. Hotfix

    C. Patch

    D. System install

9. Your company does electronic monitoring of individuals under house arrest around the world. Because of the sensitive nature of the business, you can't afford any unnecessary downtime. What is the process of applying a repair to an operating system while the system stays in operation?

    A. Upgrading

    B. Service pack installation

    C. Hotfix

    D. File update

10. Which of the following security features are not needed in a SAN?

    A. Firewall

    B. Antivirus

    C. User access control

    D. None of the above

11. Your company has grown at a tremendous rate, and the need to hire specialists in various IT areas has become apparent. You're helping to write an online advertisement that will be used to recruit new employees, and you want to make certain that applicants possess the necessary skills. One knowledge area in which your organization is weak is database intelligence. What is the primary type of database used in applications today that you can mention in the ads?

    A. Hierarchical

    B. Relational

    C. Network

    D. Archival

12. What is the process of applying manual changes to a program called?

    A. Hotfix

    B. Service pack

    C. Patching

    D. Replacement

13. You want to assign privileges to a user so that she can delete a file but not be able to assign privileges to others. What permissions should you assign?

    A. Full Control

    B. Delete

    C. Administrator

    D. Modify

14. What types of systems monitor the contents of workstations, servers, and networks to make sure that key content is not deleted or removed?

    A. Backup systems

    B. DLP

    C. DoS

    D. HSM

15. Which level of RAID is a "stripe of mirrors"?

    A. RAID 1+0

    B. RAID 0+1

    C. RAID 0

    D. RAID 1

16. A list of applications approved for use on your network would be known as which of the following?

    A. Black list

    B. Red list

    C. White list

    D. Orange list

17. What is the term for files including GPS-relevant information with them?

    A. Backdating

    B. GPS-linking

    C. RDF-feeding

    D. Geo-tagging

18. What types of systems utilize parallel processing (improving performance and availability) and add redundancy?

   A. Loaded

   B. Collected

   C. Clustered

   D. Dispersed

19. There is a term used for extremely large amounts of data owned by an organization. What is it officially known as?

   A. VMFS

   B. NAS

   C. SAN

   D. Big Data

20. Which RAID level writes parity to two different drives, thus providing fault tolerance to the system even in the event of the failure of two drives in the array?

   A. RAID 0+1

   B. RAID 6

   C. RAID 5

   D. RAID 1+0

Chapter 8

Cryptography

THE FOLLOWING COMPTIA SECURITY+ EXAM OBJECTIVES ARE COVERED IN THIS CHAPTER:

✓ **4.4 Implement the appropriate controls to ensure data security.**

- Data encryption: Full disk; Database; Individual files; Removable media; Mobile devices
- Hardware based encryption devices: TPM; HSM; USB encryption; Hard drive

✓ **6.1 Given a scenario, utilize general cryptography concepts.**

- Symmetric vs. asymmetric
- Session keys
- In-band vs. out-of-band key exchange
- Fundamental differences and encryption methods: Block vs. stream
- Transport encryption
- Non-repudiation
- Hashing
- Key escrow
- Steganography
- Digital signatures
- Use of proven technologies
- Elliptic curve and quantum cryptography
- Ephemeral key
- Perfect forward secrecy

✓ **6.2 Given a scenario, use appropriate cryptographic methods.**

- WEP vs. WPA/WPA2 and preshared key
- MD5

- SHA
- RIPEMD
- AES
- DES
- 3DES
- HMAC
- RSA
- Diffie-Hellman
- RC4
- One-time pads
- NTLM
- NTLMv2
- Blowfish
- PGP/GPG
- TwoFish
- DHE
- ECDHE
- Comparative strengths and performance of algorithms
- Use of algorithms/protocols with transport encryption: SSL; TLS; IPSec; SSH; HTTPS
- Cipher suites: Strong vs. weak ciphers
- Key stretching: PBKDF2; Bcrypt

✓ **6.3 Given a scenario, use appropriate PKI, certificate management and associated components.**

- Certificate authorities and digital certificates: CA; CRLs; OCSP; CSR
- PKI
- Recovery agent
- Public key
- Private key
- Registration
- Key escrow
- Trust models

Cryptography is the science of altering information so that it cannot be decoded without a key. It is the practice of protecting information through encryption and transformation. As data becomes more valuable, it is an area of high interest to governments, businesses, and, increasingly, individuals. People want privacy when it comes to their personal and other sensitive information. Corporations want—and need—to protect financial records, trade secrets, customer lists, and employee information. The government uses cryptography to help ensure the safety and well-being of its citizens. Entire governmental agencies have been created to help ensure secrecy, and millions of dollars have been spent trying to protect national secrets and attempting to learn the secrets of other countries.

The study of cryptographic algorithms is called *cryptography*. The study of how to break cryptographic algorithms is called *cryptanalysis*. The two subjects taken together are generally referred to as *cryptology*. All of these disciplines require a strong mathematics background, particularly in number theory.

Many people, even many textbooks, tend to use the terms *cryptography* and *cryptology* interchangeably.

An Overview of Cryptography

Cryptography is a field almost as old as humankind. The first recorded cryptographic efforts occurred 4,000 years ago. These early efforts included translating messages from one language into another or substituting characters. Since that time, cryptography has grown to include a plethora of possibilities.

The only part of historical cryptography you may be tested on in the Security+ exam are the Caesar cipher, ROT13, and the Vigenère cipher, all of which will be discussed in this section.

Historical Cryptography

Historical methods of cryptography predate the modern computer age. These methods did not depend on mathematics, as many modern methods do, but rather on some technique for scrambling the text.

A *cipher* is a method used to encode characters to hide their value. *Ciphering* is the process of using a cipher to encode a message. The two primary types of nonmathematical cryptography, or ciphering methods, are substitution and transposition. We will discuss both of these methods in this section.

Substitution Ciphers

A *substitution cipher* is a type of coding or ciphering system that changes one character or symbol into another. Character substitution can be a relatively easy method of encrypting information. One of the oldest known substitution ciphers is called the *Caesar cipher*. It was purportedly used by Julius Caesar. The system involves simply shifting all letters a certain number of spaces in the alphabet. Supposedly, Julius Caesar used a shift of 3 to the right. He was working in Latin, of course, but the same thing can be done with any language, including English. Here is an example:

I will pass the Security plus test.

If you shift each letter three to the right, you get the following:

L zloo sdvv wkh Vhfxulwb soxv whvw.

Substitution ciphers are not adequate for modern uses, and a computer would crack one almost instantly. The issue involved is letter and word frequency. All languages have certain words and letter combinations that appear more often than others. In English, if you see a three-letter word, it is most likely to be *the* or *and*. If you see a single-letter word, it is most likely to be *I* or *a*. So using this information, you can guess that the first L is really an I, that the *wkh* is actually the word *the*, and then use that information to decrypt the rest of the message. The more ciphertext you have to work with, the easier it is to decrypt.

The Caesar cipher is only one of many, among them Atbash, PlayFair, and Scytale. One of the authors of this book has a website devoted to cryptology where you can learn more. You can visit this site at www.cryptocorner.com.

Multi-Alphabet Substitution

One of the problems with substitution ciphers is that they did not change the underlying letter and word frequency of the text. One way to combat this was to have multiple substitutions. For example, you might shift the first letter by 3 to the right, the second letter by 2 to the right, and the third letter by 1 to the left, then repeat this formula with the next three letters. The most famous example of a multi-alphabet substitution from historical times was the *Vigenère cipher*. It used a keyword to look up the cipher text in a table. The user would take the first letter in the text they wanted to encrypt, go to the Vigenère table, and match that with the letter from the keyword in order to find the ciphertext letter. This would be repeated until the entire message was encrypted. Each letter in the keyword generated a different substitution alphabet.

Transposition Ciphers

A *transposition cipher* involves transposing or scrambling the letters in a certain manner. Typically, a message is broken into blocks of equal size, and each block is then scrambled.

In the simple example shown in Figure 8.1, the characters are transposed by changing the order of the group. In this case, the letters are rotated three places in the message. You could change the way Block 1 is transposed from Block 2 and make it a little more difficult, but it would still be relatively easy to decrypt.

The Rail Fence Cipher is a classic example of a transposition cipher. With this cipher, you write message letters out diagonally over a number of rows and then read off cipher row by row. For example, you write the message out as:

    m e m a t r h t g p r y
    e t e f e t e o a a t

yielding the ciphertext:

    MEMATRHTGPRYETEFETEOAAT

You can also see an example of a transposition cipher in Figure 8.1

FIGURE 8.1   A simple transposition cipher in action

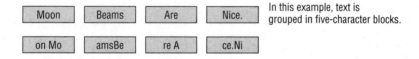

Moon beams are nice.

| Moon | Beams | Are | Nice. |

In this example, text is grouped in five-character blocks.

| on Mo | amsBe | re A | ce.Ni |

In this example, each character (including the spaces) is moved to the right three positions.

 Real World Scenario

Working with rot13

One of the oldest known encoding algorithms is *ROT13*—and one commonly asked about on the Security+ exam. This simple algorithm rotates every letter 13 places in the alphabet. Thus, an *A* becomes an *N*, a *B* becomes an *O*, and so forth. The same rotation of 13 letters that is used to encrypt the message is also used to decrypt the message. Many newsgroups offer a ROT13 option that allows you to encrypt or decrypt postings.

See if you can solve these encryptions:

1.   Neg snve qrohgf urer Fngheqnl.

2.   Gevcyr pbhcbaf ng Xebtre!

3.   Gel lbhe unaq ng chmmyrf.

One of the easiest ways to solve ROT13 text messages is to take a sheet of paper and write the letters from *A to M* in one column and from *N* to *Z* in a second. To decipher, replace the letter in the encrypted message with the one that appears beside it in the other column.

Here are the answers:

1. Art fair debuts here Saturday.

2. Triple coupons at Kroger!

3. Try your hand at puzzles.

The Enigma Machine

No discussion of the history of cryptography would be complete without discussing the Enigma machine. The *Enigma machine* was essentially a typewriter that implemented a multi-alphabet substitution cipher. When each key was hit, a different substitution alphabet was used. The Enigma machine used 26 different substitution alphabets. Prior to computers, this was extremely hard to break.

Steganography

Steganography is the process of hiding a message in a medium such as a digital image, audio file, or other file. In theory, doing this prevents analysts from detecting the real message. You could encode your message in another file or message and use that file to hide your message.

The most common way this is done today is called the *least significant bit (lsb) method*. As you know, everything on a computer is stored in bits that are organized into bytes. For example, a single pixel on a Windows computer screen is stored in 3 bytes/24 bits. If you changed the very last bit (the least significant bit in each byte), then that would not make a noticeable change in the image. In other words, you could not tell that anything had been changed. Using this fact, you can store data by putting it in the least significant bits of an image file. Someone observing the image would see nothing out of the ordinary.

It is also possible to hide data in audio files, video files, or literally any digital file type. There are even programs available on the Web for doing steganography. QuickStego (http://quickcrypto.com) is a free and easy-to-use program. Invisible Secrets (www.invisiblesecrets.com) is fairly inexpensive and quite robust.

Steganography can also be used to accomplish *electronic watermarking*. Mapmakers and artists have used watermarking for years to protect copyrights. If an image contains a watermark placed there by the original artist, proving that copyright infringement has occurred in a copy is relatively easy.

In Exercise 8.1, we will show you how to encrypt a filesystem in SUSE Linux.

EXERCISE 8.1

Encrypting a Filesystem in Linux

This lab requires access to a server running SUSE Linux Enterprise Server or OpenSUSE. To encrypt a filesystem, follow these steps:

1. Log in as root and start YaST.
2. Choose System ➤ Partitioner.
3. Answer Yes to the prompt that appears. Select a filesystem and click Edit.
4. Select the Encrypt File System check box and click OK.

Transport Encryption

Encryption can be done in either tunneling or transport mode. In tunneling mode, the data or payload and message headers are encrypted. Transport mode encrypts only the payload.

Modern Cryptography

With the advent of computers, older methods of cryptography are no longer viable. A computer can quickly and easily crack substitution and transposition ciphers. Even Vigenère and the Enigma machine are not able to withstand modern cryptographic attacks.

Modern cryptography is divided into three major areas: symmetric cryptography, asymmetric cryptography, and hashing algorithms. All three of these are covered extensively on the Security+ certification exam and are discussed in detail in this section.

Working with Symmetric Algorithms

Symmetric algorithms require both ends of an encrypted message to have the same key and processing algorithms. Symmetric algorithms generate a secret key that must be protected. A *symmetric key*, sometimes referred to as a *secret key* or *private key*, is a key that isn't disclosed to people who aren't authorized to use the encryption system. The disclosure of a private key breaches the security of the encryption system. If a key is lost or stolen, the entire process is breached. These types of systems are common, but the keys require special handling. Figure 8.2 illustrates a symmetric encryption system; in this example, the keys are the same on each end.

FIGURE 8.2:   Symmetric encryption system

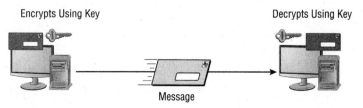

The other issue surrounding symmetric cryptography is key distribution. If you wish to encrypt messages with a friend in another city, how do you exchange keys?

 A few basic facts to know about symmetric cryptography for the test are that symmetric cryptographic algorithms are always faster than asymmetric, and they can be just as secure with a smaller key size. For example, RSA (an asymmetric algorithm) uses keys of a minimum length of 2048 bits, whereas AES (a symmetric algorithm) uses key sizes of 128, 192, or 256 bits.

Symmetric methods use either a block or stream cipher. As the name implies, with a *block cipher* the algorithm works on chunks of data—encrypting one and then moving to the next. With a *stream cipher*, the data is encrypted one bit, or byte, at a time.

Several successful encryption systems use symmetric algorithms. A strong algorithm can be difficult to break. Here are some of the common standards that use symmetric algorithms:

Data Encryption Standard   The *Data Encryption Standard (DES)* has been used since the mid-1970s. It was the primary standard used in government and industry until it was replaced by AES. It's based on a 56-bit key and has several modes that offer security and integrity. It is now considered insecure because of the small key size.

Triple-DES   *Triple-DES (3DES)* is a technological upgrade of DES. 3DES is still used, even though AES is the preferred choice for government applications. 3DES is considerably harder to break than many other systems, and it's more secure than DES. It increases the key length to 168 bits (using three 56-bit DES keys).

Advanced Encryption Standard   *Advanced Encryption Standard (AES)* has replaced DES as the current standard, and it uses the Rijndael algorithm. It was developed by Joan Daemen and Vincent Rijmen. AES is the current product used by U.S. governmental agencies. It supports key sizes of 128, 192, and 256 bits, with 128 bits being the default.

 For more background/historical information about Rijndael (AES), visit this website: http://csrc.nist.gov/archive/aes/index.html.

AES256   *AES256* (also often written as AES-256) uses 256 bits instead of 128. This qualifies for U.S. government classification as Top Secret.

CAST   *CAST* is an algorithm developed by Carlisle Adams and Stafford Tavares (hence the name). It's used in some products offered by Microsoft and IBM. CAST uses a 40-bit to 128-bit key, and it's very fast and efficient. Two additional versions, CAST-128 and CAST-256, also exist.

Ron's Cipher   RC is an encryption family produced by RSA laboratories. RC stands for *Ron's Cipher* or Ron's Code. (Ron Rivest is the author of this algorithm.) The current levels are RC4, RC5, and RC6. RC5 uses a key size of up to 2048 bits. It's considered to be a strong system.

RC4 is popular with wireless and WEP/WPA encryption. It is a streaming cipher that works with key sizes between 40 and 2048 bits, and it is used in SSL and TLS. It is also popular with utilities used for downloading BitTorrent files since many providers limit the download of these, and by using RC4 to obfuscate the header and the stream, it makes it more difficult for the service provider to realize that they are indeed BitTorrent files being moved about.

Blowfish and Twofish   *Blowfish* is an encryption system invented by a team led by Bruce Schneier that performs a 64-bit block cipher at very fast speeds. It is a symmetric block cipher that can use variable-length keys (from 32 bits to 448 bits). Twofish is quite similar and works on 128-bit blocks. The distinctive feature of the latter is that it has a complex key schedule.

International Data Encryption Algorithm   *International Data Encryption Algorithm (IDEA)* was developed by a Swiss consortium. It's an algorithm that uses a 128-bit key. This product is similar in speed and capability to DES, but it's more secure. IDEA is used in Pretty Good Privacy (PGP), a public domain encryption system used by many for email. Currently, Ascom AG holds the right to market IDEA.

One-Time Pads   *One-time pads* are the only truly completely secure cryptographic implementations. They are so secure for two reasons. First, they use a key that is as long as a plaintext message. That means there is no pattern in the key application for an attacker to use. Also, one-time pad keys are used only once and then discarded. So even if you could break a one-time pad cipher, that same key would never be used again, so knowledge of the key would be useless.

Key Exchange

Key exchange is an important topic in relation to symmetric cryptography. There are two primary approaches to key exchange: in-band key exchange and out-of-band key exchange. In-band key exchange essentially means that the key is exchanged within the same communications channel that is going to be encrypted. IPSec, which will be discussed later in this chapter, uses in-band key exchange. Out-of-band key exchange means that some other channel, other than the one that is going to be secured, is used to exchange the key.

   Forward secrecy is a property of any key exchange system, which ensures that if one key is compromised, subsequent keys will not also be compromised. *Perfect forward secrecy* occurs when this process is unbreakable. A common approach uses ephemeral keys, discussed later in this chapter.

Working with Asymmetric Algorithms

Asymmetric algorithms use two keys to encrypt and decrypt data. These asymmetric keys are referred to as the *public key* and the *private key*. The sender uses the public key to encrypt a message, and the receiver uses the private key to decrypt the message; what one key does, the other one undoes. As you may recall, symmetrical systems require the key to be private between the two parties. With asymmetric systems, each circuit has one key.

The public key may be truly public or it may be a secret between the two parties. The private key is kept private, and only the owner (receiver) knows it. If someone wants to send you an encrypted message, they can use your public key to encrypt the message and then send you the message. You can use your private key to decrypt the message. The private key is always kept protected. If both keys become available to a third party, the encryption system won't protect the privacy of the message.

The real "magic" of these systems is that the public key cannot be used to decrypt a message. If Bob sends Alice a message encrypted with Alice's public key, it does not matter if everyone else on Earth has Alice's public key, which cannot decrypt the message. Only Alice's private key can do that, as illustrated in Figure 8.3. All asymmetric algorithms are based on number theory.

FIGURE 8.3: A two-key system in use

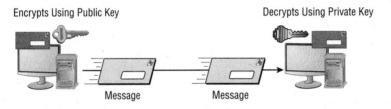

Encrypts Using Public Key   Decrypts Using Private Key

Message   Message

> Two-key systems are referred to as *public-key cryptography (PKC)*. Don't confuse this with public-key infrastructure (PKI), which uses PKC as a part of the process.

Four popular asymmetric systems are in use today:

RSA *RSA* is named after its inventors Ron Rivest, Adi Shamir, and Leonard Adleman. The RSA algorithm is an early public-key encryption system that uses large integers as the basis for the process. It's widely implemented, and it has become a de facto standard. RSA works with both encryption and digital signatures, which are discussed later in the chapter. RSA is used in many environments, including Secure Sockets Layer (SSL), and it can be used for key exchange.

> The Security+ exam does not require you to know the details of any cryptographic algorithms. However, many people are confused by the concept of asymmetric cryptography, and the RSA algorithm is rather simple, so we present it here for your edification.

Key generation is actually pretty simple, as shown in the following example:

1. Generate two large random primes, *p* and *q*, of approximately equal size such that their product, *n = pq*, is of the required bit length (such as 2048 bits, 4096 bits, and so forth).

   Let n = pq

   Let m = (p-1)(q-1)

2. Choose a small number *e*, co-prime to *m* (note: Two numbers are co-prime if they have no common factors).

3. Find *d*, such that

   de % m = 1

4. Publish *e* and *n* as the public key. Keep *d* and *n* as the secret key. Encrypt as follows:

   C= M^e % n

   or, put another way, compute the ciphertext:

   c = m^e mod n

5. Decrypt as follows:

   P = C^d % n

   or, put another way, use this private key (*d,n*) to compute:

   m = c^d mod n

Diffie-Hellman   Whitfield Diffie and Martin Hellman conceptualized the *Diffie-Hellman key exchange*. They are considered the founders of the public/private key concept; their original work envisioned splitting the key into two parts. This algorithm is used primarily to send keys across public networks. The process isn't used to encrypt or decrypt messages; it's used merely for the creation of a symmetric key between two parties.

An interesting twist is that the method had actually been developed a few years earlier by Malcolm J. Williamson of the British Intelligence Service, but it was classified.

On the Security+ exam, if you are asked about an algorithm for exchanging keys over an insecure medium, unless the context is IPSec, the answer is always Diffie-Hellman.

Elliptic Curve Cryptography   *Elliptic Curve Cryptography (ECC)* provides similar functionality to RSA but uses smaller key sizes to obtain the same level of security. ECC encryption systems are based on the idea of using points on a curve combined with a point at infinity and the difficulty of solving discrete logarithm problems.

Many vendors have implemented, or are implementing, the ECC system for security. The National Security Agency has also recommended several implementations of ECC. You can expect that ECC will be commonly implemented in cellular devices in the near future.

There are many variations of Elliptic Curve, such as:

- Elliptic Curve Diffie-Hellman (ECC-DH)
- Elliptic Curve Digital Signature Algorithm (ECC-DSA)

ElGamal   *ElGamal* was developed by Taher Elgamal in 1984. It is an asymmetric algorithm, and several variations of ElGamal have been created, including Elliptic Curve ElGamal. ElGamal and related algorithms use what is called an ephemeral key. An *ephemeral key* is simply a key that exists only for that session. Essentially, the algorithm creates a key to use for that single communication session and it is not used again.

> Adding an ephemeral key to Diffie-Hellman turns it into *DHE* (which, despite the order of the acronym, stands for Ephemeral Diffie-Hellman). Adding an ephemeral key to Elliptic Curve Diffie-Hellman turns it into *ECDHE* (again, overlook the order of the acronym letters, it is called Ephemeral Elliptic Curve Diffie-Hellman). It is the ephemeral component of each of these that provides the perfect forward secrecy.

Not as many asymmetric algorithms were discussed as symmetric encryption algorithms, but it can still be difficult keeping all of them straight. Table 8.1 provides an alphabetic list of the most popular asymmetric algorithms, and it should be useful for Security+ exam preparation.

TABLE 8.1:   Asymmetric algorithms

Algorithm	Common use
Diffie-Hellman	Key agreement.
ElGamal	Transmitting digital signatures and key exchanges.
Elliptic Curve (ECC)	An option to RSA that uses less computing power than RSA and is popular in smaller devices like smartphones.
RSA	The most commonly used public-key algorithm, RSA is used for encryption and digital signatures.

What Cryptography Should You Use?

Whether you are using asymmetric or symmetric cryptography, it is important to use only proven cryptography technologies. In cryptology, one of the key principles is called Kerckhoffs's principle. This principle was first stated by Auguste Kerckhoffs in the nineteenth century. Essentially, *Kerckhoffs's principle* states that the security of an algorithm should depend only on the secrecy of the key and not on the secrecy of the algorithm itself.

This literally means that the algorithm can be public for all to examine, and the process will still be secure as long as you keep the specific key secret.

Allowing the algorithm to be public might seem counterintuitive. Nevertheless, all of the major algorithms discussed in this chapter are public, and the entire set of algorithms is published in many books and articles and on numerous websites. This allows researchers to examine the algorithm for flaws. Usually, secret algorithms have not been properly vetted. The cryptology community has not been given the opportunity to examine the algorithm for flaws. This all leads to a basic principle: You should only use proven cryptography technology—that is, avoid new, and "secret," methods.

Hashing Algorithms

The hashes used to store data, such as hash tables, are very different from cryptographic hashes. In cryptography, a hash function must have three characteristics:

- *It must be one-way.* This means that it is not reversible. Once you hash something, you cannot unhash it.

- *Variable-length input produces fixed-length output.* This means that whether you hash two characters or two million, the hash size is the same.

- *The algorithm must have few or no collisions.* This means that hashing two different inputs does not give the same output.

The following is a list of hashing algorithms you should be familiar with:

Secure Hash Algorithm   The *Secure Hash Algorithm (SHA)* was designed to ensure the integrity of a message. SHA is a one-way hash that provides a hash value that can be used with an encryption protocol. This algorithm produces a 160-bit hash value. SHA-2 has several sizes: 224, 256, 334, and 512 bit. SHA-2 is the most widely used, but SHA-3 has been released. Although SHA3 is now a standard, there simply are no known issues with SHA2, so it is still the most widely used and recommended hashing algorithm. The algorithm was originally named *Keccak* and designed by Guido Bertoni, Joan Daemen, Michaël Peeters, and Gilles Van Assche.

Message Digest Algorithm   The *Message Digest Algorithm (MD)* also creates a hash value and uses a one-way hash. The hash value is used to help maintain integrity. There are several versions of MD; the most common are MD5, MD4, and MD2. MD4 was used by NTLM (discussed in a moment) to compute the NT Hash.

MD5 is the newest version of the algorithm. It produces a 128-bit hash, but the algorithm is more complex than its predecessors and offers greater security. Its biggest weakness is that it does not have strong collision resistance, and thus it is no longer recommended for use. SHA (1 or 2) are the recommended alternatives.

RIPEMD   The *RACE Integrity Primitives Evaluation Message Digest (RIPEMD)* algorithm was based on MD4. There were questions regarding its security, and it has been replaced by RIPEMD-160, which uses 160 bits. There are versions in existence that use 256 and 320 bits (RIPEMD-256 and RIPEMD-320, respectively), but all versions of RIPEMD remain.

GOST   *GOST* is a symmetric cipher developed in the old Soviet Union that has been modified to work as a hash function. GOST processes a variable-length message into a fixed-length output of 256 bits.

LANMAN   Prior to the release of Windows NT, Microsoft's operating systems used the *LANMAN protocol* for authentication. While functioning only as an authentication protocol, LANMAN used LM Hash and two DES keys. It was replaced by the NT LAN Manager (NTLM) with the release of Windows NT.

NTLM   Microsoft replaced the LANMAN protocol with *NTLM (NT LAN Manager)* with the release of Windows NT. NTLM uses MD4/MD5 hashing algorithms. Several versions of this protocol exist (NTLMv1, *NTLMv2*), and it is still in widespread use despite the fact that Microsoft has pointed to Kerberos as being its preferred authentication protocol. Although LANMAN and NTLM both employ hashing, they are used primarily for the purpose of authentication.

Rainbow Tables and Salt

Since a hashing algorithm is not reversible, you might think it is impossible to break a hash. However, there are methods to do so. This is particularly important since passwords are often stored as a hash. Rainbow tables are one such method. With a *rainbow table*, all of the possible hashes are computed in advance. In other words, you create a series of tables; each has all the possible two-letter, three-letter, four-letter, and so forth combinations and the hash of that combination, using a known hashing algorithm like SHA-2. Now if you search the table for a given hash, the letter combination in the table that produced the hash must be the password you are seeking.

Popular password cracking tools, such as OphCrack, use rainbow tables. A countermeasure, called *Salt*, refers to the addition of bits at key locations, either before or after the hash. So if you type in the password letmein, bits are added by the operating system before it is hashed. Using Salt, should someone apply a rainbow table attack, the hash they search for will yield a letter combination other than what you actually typed in.

Key Stretching

Key stretching refers to processes used to take a key that might be a bit weak and make it stronger, usually by making it longer. The key (or password/passphrase) is input into an algorithm that will strengthen the key and make it longer, thus less susceptible to brute-force attacks. There are many methods for doing this; two are discussed here:

PBKDF2   *PBKDF2* (Password-Based Key Derivation Function 2) is part of PKCS #5 v. 2.01. It applies some function (like a hash or HMAC) to the password or passphrase along with Salt to produce a derived key.

Bcrypt   *bcrypt* is used with passwords, and it essentially uses a derivation of the Blowfish algorithm, converted to a hashing algorithm, to hash a password and add Salt to it.

Understanding Quantum Cryptography

Quantum cryptography is a relatively new method of encryption. At one time, its application was limited to laboratory work and possibly to secret governmental applications. This method is based on the characteristics of the smallest particles known. The details of quantum physics are not required for the Security+ exam and won't be covered in this book.

Although there are many theoretical uses for quantum cryptography, the only method currently practical is quantum key exchange (QKE). The process is dependent on quantum physics, and it is not covered on the Security+ certification exam.

Cryptanalysis Methods

If time has taught us anything, it is that people frequently do things that other people thought were impossible. Every time a new code or process is invented that is thought to be unbreakable, someone comes up with a method of breaking it.

The following list includes some common code-breaking techniques:

Frequency Analysis   *Frequency analysis* involves looking at blocks of an encrypted message to determine if any common patterns exist. Initially, the analyst doesn't try to break the code but looks at the patterns in the message. In the English language, the letters *e* and *t* and words like the, *and, that, it*, and is are very common. Single letters that stand alone in a sentence are usually limited to *a* and *I*.

A determined cryptanalyst looks for these types of patterns and, over time, may be able to deduce the method used to encrypt the data. This process can sometimes be simple, or it may take a lot of effort. This method works only on the historical ciphers we discussed at the beginning of this chapter. It does not work on modern algorithms.

Chosen Plaintext   In this attack, the attacker obtains the ciphertexts corresponding to a set of plaintexts of their own choosing. This allows the attacker to attempt to derive the key used and thus decrypt other messages encrypted with that key. This can be difficult, but it is not impossible. Advanced methods such as differential cryptanalysis are chosen plaintext attacks.

Related Key Attack   This is like a chosen-plaintext attack, except the attacker can obtain ciphertexts encrypted under two different keys. This is actually a very useful attack if you can obtain the plaintext and matching ciphertext.

Brute-Force Attacks   *Brute-force attacks* can be accomplished by applying every possible combination of characters that could be the key. For example, if you know that the key is three characters long, then you also know that there is a finite number of possibilities of what the key could be. Although it may take a long time to find the key, it can indeed be found.

Exploiting Human Error   Human error is one of the major causes of encryption vulnerabilities. If an email is sent using an encryption scheme, someone else may send it *in the clear* (unencrypted). If a cryptanalyst gets ahold of both messages, the process of decoding future messages will be considerably simplified. A code key might wind up in the wrong hands, giving insights into what the key consists of. Many systems have been broken into as a result of these types of accidents.

A classic example involved the transmission of a sensitive military-related message using an encryption system. Most messages have a preamble that informs the receiver who the message is for, who sent it, how many characters are in the message, the date and time it was sent, and other pertinent information. In this case, the preamble was sent in cleartext, and this information was also encrypted and put into the message. As a result, the cryptanalysts gained a key insight into the message contents. They were given approximately 50 characters that were repeated in the message in code. This error caused a relatively secure system to be compromised.

Wi-Fi Encryption

Wi-Fi encryption requires a short discussion of its own. In such an environment, the clients and the access point share the same key, using symmetric encryption, and RC4 was mentioned for this purpose earlier in this chapter. Since all of the clients and the access point share the same key, this is known as a *preshared key*.

WEP (Wired Equivalent Privacy) encryption was an early attempt to add security, but it fell short because of weaknesses in the way the encryption algorithms are employed. The *Wi-Fi Protected Access (WPA)* and *Wi-Fi Protected Access 2 (WPA2)* technologies were designed to address the core problems with WEP.

WPA couples the RC4 encryption algorithm with TKIP, whereas WPA2 favors *Counter Mode with Cipher Block Chaining Message Authentication Code Protocol (CCMP)*. CCMP uses 128-bit AES.

The Security+, as well as other security-related tests, discusses the fact that WPA2 uses Counter Mode with Cipher Block Chaining but doesn't discuss what Cipher Block Chaining is. It is actually simple, but effective. As you encrypt text with any block cipher (including AES) if you encrypt the same block in different places in the message, it is likely to come out exactly the same in the ciphertext. AES 128 uses a 128-bit block that is 16 characters. So if the same 16 characters appear more than once in your plaintext, they may come out exactly the same in the cipher text, giving attackers a clue that they can use. The answer to this is to take the output of block i-1 and exclusively Or it with the plaintext of block i before encrypting it. Basically the output of each block is combined with the plaintext of the next block before that next block is encrypted. This guarantees that even if you have the same plaintext in various places in your text, it won't come out the same in the ciphertext.

Using Cryptographic Systems

A *cryptographic system* is a system, method, or process that is used to provide encryption and decryption. It may be a hardware, software, or manually performed process. Cryptographic systems exist for the same reasons that security exists: to provide confidentiality, integrity, authentication, nonrepudiation, and access control. The following sections discuss these issues within the framework of cryptographic systems.

> Confidentiality, integrity, and availability are the three most important concepts in security. You should know and understand them well before taking the Security+ certification exam. Confidentiality and integrity are discussed here. Availability relates to disaster recovery and system redundancy.

Confidentiality and Strength

One of the major reasons to implement a cryptographic system is to ensure the confidentiality of the information being used. Confidentiality may be intended to prevent the unauthorized disclosure of information in a local network or to prevent the unauthorized disclosure of information across a network. A cryptographic system must do this effectively in order to be of value.

The need to keep records secure from internal disclosure may be just as great as the need to keep records secure from outside attacks. The effectiveness of a cryptographic system in preventing unauthorized decryption is referred to as its *strength*: A strong cryptographic system is difficult to crack. Strength is also referred to as the algorithm's *work factor*: The *work factor* describes an estimate of the amount of time and effort that would be needed to break a system.

The system may be considered weak if it allows weak keys, has defects in its design, or is easily decrypted. Many systems available today are more than adequate for business and personal use, but they are inadequate for sensitive military or governmental applications.

Cipher suites, for example, work with SSL/TLS to combine authentication, encryption, and message authentication. Most vendors allow you to set cipher suite preferences on a server to determine the level of strength required by client connections. With Sybase, for example, you set the cipher suite preference to Weak, Strong, FIPS, or All. If you choose Strong, you are limiting the choices to only encryption algorithms that use keys of 64 bits or more. Choosing Weak adds all the encryption algorithms that are less than 64 bits, while choosing FIPS requires encryptions, hash and key exchange algorithms to be FIPS-compliant (AES, 3DES, DES, and SHA1). Apache offers similar choices but instead of the words Strong and Weak, the names are changed to High, Medium, and Low.

Integrity

The second major reason for implementing a cryptographic system involves providing assurance that a message wasn't modified during transmission. Modification may render a message unintelligible or, even worse, inaccurate. Imagine the consequences if record alterations weren't discovered in medical records involving drug prescriptions. If a message is tampered with, the encryption system should have a mechanism to indicate that the message has been corrupted or altered.

Integrity can be accomplished by adding information such as redundant data that can be used as part of the decryption process. Figure 8.4 provides a simple example of how integrity can be validated in a message. Notice that data about the message's length and the number of vowels in the message are included in the message.

FIGURE 8.4: A simple integrity-checking process for an encrypted message

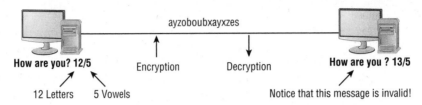

These two additions to the message provide a two-way check on the integrity of the message. In this case, the message has somehow become corrupted or invalidated. The original message had 12 characters; the decrypted message has 13 characters. Of course, the processes used in a real system are much more complicated. The addition of this information could be considered a signature of some sort.

A common method of verifying integrity involves adding a *message authentication code (MAC)* to the message. The MAC is derived from the message and a shared secret key. This process ensures the integrity of the message. The MAC would be encrypted with the message, adding another layer of integrity checking. From the MAC, you would know that the message came from the originator and that the contents haven't been altered. Figure 8.5 illustrates the MAC value being calculated from the message and included with the message. The receiver also calculates the MAC value and compares it to the value sent in the message. If the values are equal, the message can be assumed to be intact and genuine.

FIGURE 8.5: The MAC value is calculated by the sender and receiver using the same algorithm.

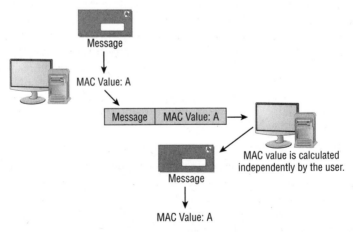

HMAC (Hash-Based Message Authentication Code) uses a hashing algorithm along with a symmetric key.

Digital Signatures

A *digital signature* is similar in function to a standard signature on a document. It validates the integrity of the message and the sender. The message is encrypted using the encryption system, and a second piece of information, the digital signature, is added to the message. Figure 8.6 illustrates this concept.

Let's say that the sender in Figure 8.6 wants to send a message to the receiver. It's important that this message not be altered. The sender uses the private key to create a digital signature. The message is, in effect, signed with the private key. The sender then sends the message to the receiver. The receiver uses the public key attached to the message to validate the digital signature. If the values match, the receiver knows the message is authentic.

The receiver uses a key provided by the sender—the public key—to decrypt the message. Most digital signature implementations also use a hash to verify that the message has not been altered, intentionally or accidently, in transit.

The receiver compares the signature area referred to as a *message digest* in the message with the calculated value. If the values match, the message hasn't been tampered with and the originator is verified as the person they claim to be. This process provides message integrity, nonrepudiation, and authentication.

FIGURE 8.6:   Digital signature processing steps

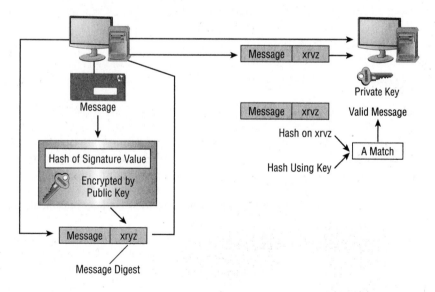

Authentication

Authentication is the process of verifying that the sender is who they say they are. This is critical in many applications. A valid message from an invalid source isn't authentic.

One of the common methods of verifying authenticity is the addition of a digital signature. Authenticity can also be established using secret words that have been mutually agreed on in advance.

Nonrepudiation

Nonrepudiation prevents one party from denying actions they carried out. To use an analogy, imagine coming home to find your house's picture window broken. All three of your kids say they didn't do it, and the babysitter says it must have been broken when she arrived. All the parties who could be guilty are "repudiating" the fact that they did it, and it's their word against common sense. Now, imagine that you had a nanny-cam running and were able to review the video and see who actually broke it. The video cancels out their saying that they knew nothing about the broken window and offers "nonrepudiation" of the facts.

In the electronic world, a similar type of proof can be achieved in a two-key system. The problem is that anyone can claim to be a legitimate sender, and if they have access to this type of system, they can send you a public key. So although you have received the message, you would have no way of verifying that the sender is really who they say they are, and you need nonrepudiation to verify that the sender is who they say they are.

Third-party organizations called *certificate authorities (CAs)* manage public keys and issue certificates verifying the validity of a sender's message. The verifying aspect serves as nonrepudiation; a respected third party vouches for the individual. The goal of any effective cryptography system must include nonrepudiation. However, the implementation is a little more difficult than the concept.

Key Features

Key escrow addresses the possibility that a third party may need to access keys. Under the conditions of key escrow, the keys needed to encrypt/decrypt data are held in an escrow account (think of the term as it relates to home mortgages) and made available if that third party requests them. The third party in question is generally the government, but it could also be an employer if an employee's private messages have been called into question.

A *key recovery agent* is an entity that has the ability to recover a key, key components, or plaintext messages as needed. As opposed to escrow, recovery agents are typically used to access information that is encrypted with older keys.

Key registration is the process of providing certificates to users, and a registration authority (RA) typically handles this function when the load must be lifted from a certificate authority (CA).

There is also the issue of keys that are no longer to be used. A key may have expired, it may have been canceled due to some breach of security, or it may have been replaced. In any case, there must be some mechanism to find out if a key is still valid. The most widely used method is the *certificate revocation list (CRL)*. This is literally a list of certificates that a specific CA states should no longer be used. CRLs are now being replaced by a real-time protocol called *Online Certificate Status Protocol (OCSP)*.

Trust models exist in PKI implementations and come in a number of types. The four main types of trust models that are used with PKI are bridge, hierarchical, hybrid, and mesh.

Understanding Cryptography Standards and Protocols

Numerous standards are available to establish secure services. Some of the standards that will be presented in the following sections have already been discussed in greater detail in earlier chapters. Here we will remind you of them and introduce you to a few more standards.

The movement from proprietary governmental standards toward more unified global standards is a growing trend that has both positive and negative implications. Higher interoperability between disparate systems will also mean that these standards will be widely used. The more that standards are used, the more that attackers will focus on them to try to break them.

As a security administrator, you have to weigh the pros and cons of the various standards and evaluate them against your organization's needs. The following sections introduce you to the major standards, discuss their focus, and describe how they were developed.

The Origins of Encryption Standards

As mentioned at the beginning of the chapter, early cryptography standards were primarily designed to secure communications for the government and the military. Many different standards groups exist today, and they often provide standards that are incompatible with the standards of other groups. These standards are intended to address the specific environments in which these groups exist.

The following sections describe key U.S. government agencies, a few well-known industry associations, and public-domain cryptography standards.

The Role of Government Agencies

Several U.S. government agencies are involved in the creation of standards for secure systems. They either directly control specific sectors of government or provide validation, approval, and support to government agencies. We'll look at each of these agencies in the following sections.

National Security Agency

The *National Security Agency (NSA)* is responsible for creating codes, breaking codes, and coding systems for the U.S. government. The NSA was chartered in 1952. It tries to keep a low profile; for many years, the government didn't publicly acknowledge its existence.

The NSA is responsible for obtaining foreign intelligence and supplying it to the various U.S. government agencies that need it. It's said to be the world's largest employer of mathematicians. The NSA's missions are extremely classified, but its finger is in everything involving cryptography and cryptographic systems for the U.S. government, government contractors, and the military.

 The NSA's website is www.nsa.gov.

National Security Agency/Central Security Service

The *National Security Agency/Central Security Service (NSA/CSS)* is an independently functioning part of the NSA. It was created in the early 1970s to help standardize and support Department of Defense (DoD) activities. The NSA/CSS supports all branches of the military. Each branch of the military used to have its own intelligence activities. Frequently, these branches didn't coordinate their activities well. NSA/CSS was created to help coordinate their efforts.

National Institute of Standards and Technology

The *National Institute of Standards and Technology (NIST)*, which was formerly known as the National Bureau of Standards (NBS), has been involved in developing and supporting standards for the U.S. government for over 100 years. NIST has become very involved in cryptography standards, systems, and technology in a variety of areas. It's primarily concerned with governmental systems, and it exercises a great deal of influence on them. NIST shares many of its findings with the security community because business needs are similar to government needs.

NIST publishes information about known vulnerabilities in operating systems and applications. You'll find NIST very helpful in your battle to secure your systems.

    You can find NIST on the Web at www.nist.gov.

Industry Associations and the Developmental Process

The need for security in specific industries, such as the banking industry, has driven the development of standards. Standards frequently begin as voluntary or proprietary efforts.

The *Request for Comments (RFC)*, originated in 1969, is the mechanism used to propose a standard. It's a document-creation process with a set of practices. An RFC is categorized as standard (draft or standard), best practice, informational, experimental, or historic.

Draft documents are processed through a designated RFC editor, who makes sure that the document meets publication standards. Editors play a key role in the RFC process; they are responsible for making sure that proposals are documented properly, and they manage the discussion. The RFC is then thrown open to the computer-user community for comments and critique. This process ensures that all interested parties have the opportunity to comment on an RFC.

The RFC process allows open communications about the Internet and other proposed standards. Virtually all standards relating to the Internet that are adopted go through this process.

Several industrial associations have assumed roles that allow them to address specific environments. The following sections briefly discuss some of the major associations and the specific environments they address.

American Bankers Association

The *American Bankers Association (ABA)* has been very involved in the security issues facing the banking and financial industries. Banks need to communicate with each other in a secure manner. The ABA sponsors and supports several key initiatives regarding financial transactions.

You can find out more about the ABA at www.aba.com/default.htm.

Internet Engineering Task Force

The *Internet Engineering Task Force (IETF)* is an international community of computer professionals that includes network engineers, vendors, administrators, and researchers. The IETF is mainly interested in improving the Internet; it's also very interested in computer security issues. The IETF uses working groups to develop and propose standards.

IETF membership is open to anyone. Members communicate primarily through mailing lists and public conferences.

You can find additional information about the IETF on its website at www.ietf.org.

Internet Society

The *Internet Society (ISOC)* is a professional group whose membership consists primarily of Internet experts. The ISOC oversees a number of committees and groups, including the IETF.

You can find a history of ISOC and IETF at www.isoc.org/internet /history/ietfhis.shtml.

World Wide Web Consortium

The *World Wide Web Consortium (W3C)* is an association concerned with the interoperability, growth, and standardization of the World Wide Web (WWW). It's the primary sponsor of XML and other web-enabled technologies. Although not directly involved in cryptography, the W3C recently published a proposed standard for encryption in XML.

The W3C's website is located at www.w3.org.

International Telecommunications Union

The *International Telecommunications Union (ITU)* is responsible for virtually all aspects of telecommunications and radio communication standards worldwide. The ITU is broken into three main groups that are targeted at specific areas of concern: ITU-R is concerned with radio communication and spectrum management, ITU-T is concerned with telecommunications standards, and ITU-D is concerned with expanding telecommunications throughout undeveloped countries. The ITU is headquartered in Switzerland, and it operates as a sponsored agency of the United Nations.

For more information on the ITU, visit www.itu.int.

Institute of Electrical and Electronics Engineers

The *Institute of Electrical and Electronics Engineers (IEEE)* is an international organization focused on technology and related standards. Pronounced "I Triple-E," the IEEE is organized into several working groups and standards committees. IEEE is actively involved in the development of PKC, wireless, and networking protocol standards.

You can find information on the IEEE at www.ieee.org.

Public-Key Infrastructure X.509/Public-Key Cryptography Standards

The *Public-Key Infrastructure X.509 (PKIX)* is the working group formed by the IETF to develop standards and models for the PKI environment. The PKIX working group is responsible for the X.509 standard, which is discussed in the next section.

The *Public-Key Cryptography Standards (PKCS)* is a set of voluntary standards created by RSA and security leaders. Early members of this group included Apple, Microsoft, DEC (now HP), Lotus, Sun, and MIT.

Currently, there are 15 published PKCS standards:

- PKCS #1: RSA Cryptography Standard
- PKCS #2: Incorporated in PKCS #1
- PKCS #3: Diffie-Hellman Key Agreement Standard
- PKCS #4: Incorporated in PKCS #1
- PKCS #5: Password-Based Cryptography Standard
- PKCS #6: Extended-Certificate Syntax Standard
- PKCS #7: Cryptographic Message Syntax Standard

- PKCS #8: Private-Key Information Syntax Standard
- PKCS #9: Selected Attribute Types
- PKCS #10: Certification Request Syntax Standard
- PKCS #11: Cryptographic Token Interface Standard
- PKCS #12: Personal Information Exchange Syntax Standard
- PKCS #13: Elliptic Curve Cryptography Standard
- PKCS #14: Pseudorandom Number Generators
- PKCS #15: Cryptographic Token Information Format Standard

These standards are coordinated through RSA; however, experts worldwide are welcome to participate in the development process.

X.509

The *X.509 standard* defines the certificate formats and fields for public keys. It also defines the procedures that should be used to distribute public keys. The X.509 version 2 certificate is still used as the primary method of issuing CRL certificates. The current version of X.509 certificates is version 3, and it comes in two basic types:

End-Entity Certificate The most common is the *end-entity certificate*, which is issued by a CA to an end entity. An *end entity* is a system that doesn't issue certificates but merely uses them.

CA Certificate The CA certificate is issued by one CA to another CA. The second CA can, in turn, then issue certificates to an end entity.

 For the exam, remember X.509 v2 for CRL and v3 for certificate.

All X.509 certificates have the following:

- Signature, which is the primary purpose for the certificate
- Version
- Serial number
- Signature algorithm ID
- Issuer name
- Validity period
- Subject name
- Subject public-key information
- Issuer unique identifier (relevant for versions 2 and 3 only)

- Subject unique identifier (relevant for versions 2 and 3 only)
- Extensions (in version 3 only)

SSL and TLS

Secure Sockets Layer (SSL) is used to establish a secure communication connection between two TCP-based machines. This protocol uses the handshake method of establishing a session. The number of steps in the handshake depends on whether steps are combined and/or mutual authentication is included. The number of steps is always between four and nine, inclusive, based on who is doing the documentation.

One of the early steps will always be to select an appropriate cipher suite to use. A *cipher suite* is a combination of methods, such as an authentication, encryption, and message authentication code (MAC) algorithms used together. Many cryptographic protocols such as TLS use a cipher suite.

Netscape originally developed the SSL method, which has gained wide acceptance throughout the industry. SSL establishes a session using asymmetric encryption and maintains the session using symmetric encryption.

Regardless of which vendor's implementation is being discussed, the steps can be summarized as illustrated in Figure 8.7. When a connection request is made to the server, the server sends a message back to the client indicating that a secure connection is needed. The client sends the server a certificate indicating the capabilities of the client. The server then evaluates the certificate and responds with a session key and an encrypted key. The session is secure at the end of this process.

FIGURE 8.7: The SSL connection process

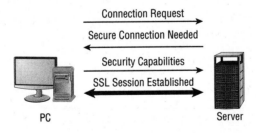

This session will stay open until one end or the other issues a command to close it. The command is typically issued when a browser is closed or another URL is requested.

As a security administrator, you will occasionally need to know how to configure SSL settings for a website running on your operating system. You should also know that, in order for SSL to work properly, the clients must be able to accept the level of encryption that you apply. Modern browsers can work with 128-bit encrypted sessions/certificates. Earlier browsers often needed to use 40- or 56-bit SSL encryption. As an administrator, you should push for the latest browsers on all clients.

VeriSign used a clever advertising strategy that makes this point readily comprehensible: It mailed flyers in a clear bag with the lines "Sending sensitive information over the Web without the strongest encryption is like sending a letter in a clear envelope. Anyone can see it." This effectively illustrates the need for the strongest SSL possible.

Transport Layer Security (TLS) is a security protocol that expands upon SSL. Many industry analysts predict that TLS will replace SSL in the future. Figure 8.8 illustrates the connection process in the TLS network.

FIGURE 8.8: The TLS connection process

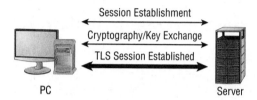

Session Establishment

Cryptography/Key Exchange

TLS Session Established

PC   Server

The TLS protocol is also referred to as *SSL 3.1*, but despite its name, it doesn't interoperate with SSL. The TLS standard is supported by the IETF.

Think of TLS as an updated version of SSL. TLS is based on SSL, and it is intended to supersede it.

In Exercise 8.2, we will show you how to configure the SSL port in Windows Server 2012.

EXERCISE 8.2

SSL Settings in Windows Server 2012

This lab requires a test machine (nonproduction) running Windows Server 2012. To configure the SSL port setting, follow these steps:

1. Open Internet Information Services Manager by choosing Start ➢ Administrative Tools ➢ Internet Information Services (IIS) Manager.

2. Expand the left pane entries until your website becomes an option. Right-click the website, and choose Properties from the context menu.

3. Select the Web Site tab. Check whether the port number for SSL is filled in. If it isn't, enter a number here.

4. Click OK and exit Internet Information Services Manager.

Notice that the SSL port field is blank by default, and any port number can be entered here—this differs from the way some previous versions of IIS worked. The default SSL port is 443; if you enter a number other than that in this field, then clients must know and request that port in advance in order to connect.

Certificate Management Protocols

Certificate Management Protocol (CMP) is a messaging protocol used between PKI entities. This protocol is used in some PKI environments.

XML Key Management Specification (XKMS) is designed to allow XML-based programs access to PKI services. XKMS is being developed and enhanced as a cooperative standard of the W3C. XKMS is a standard that is built on CMP and uses it as a model.

CMP is expected to be an area of high growth as PKI usage grows.

Secure Multipurpose Internet Mail Extensions

Secure Multipurpose Internet Mail Extensions (S/MIME) is a standard used for encrypting email. S/MIME contains signature data. It uses the PKCS #7 standard (Cryptographic Message Syntax Standard), and it is the most widely supported standard used to secure email communications.

MIME is the de facto standard for email messages. S/MIME, which is a secure version of MIME, was originally published to the Internet as a standard by RSA. It provides encryption, integrity, and authentication when used in conjunction with PKI. S/MIME version 3, the current version, is supported by IETF.

> S/MIME is defined by RFC 2633. For the exam, know that it's a secure version of MIME used for encrypting email. Know, as well, that it uses asymmetric encryption algorithms for confidentiality and digital certificates for authentication.

Secure Electronic Transaction

Secure Electronic Transaction (SET) provides encryption for credit card numbers that can be transmitted over the Internet. Visa and MasterCard developed it.

> SET is most suited for transmitting small amounts of data.

SET works in conjunction with an electronic wallet that must be set up in advance of the transaction. An *electronic wallet* is a device that identifies you electronically in the same way as the cards you carry in your wallet.

Figure 8.9 illustrates the process used in a SET transaction. The consumer must establish an electronic wallet that is issued by the consumer or issuing bank. When the consumer wants to make a purchase, they communicate with the merchant. The wallet is accessed to provide credit or payment information. The merchant then contacts the credit processor to complete the transaction. The credit processor interfaces with the existing credit network. In this situation, the transactions between the issuing bank, the consumer, the merchant, and the credit processor all use SET.

FIGURE 8.9: The SET transaction in process

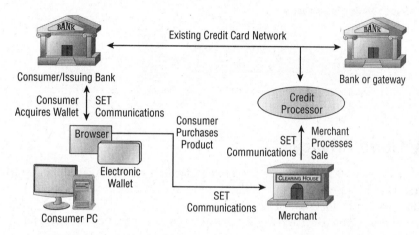

Secure Shell

Secure Shell (SSH) is a tunneling protocol originally used on Unix systems. It's now available for both Unix and Windows environments. The handshake process between the client and server is similar to the process described in SSL. SSH is primarily intended for interactive terminal sessions. Figure 8.10 illustrates the SSH connection process.

> SSH can be used in place of the older Remote Shell (RSH) utility that used to be a standard in the Unix world. It can also be used in place of rlogin and Telnet.

Notice that SSH connections are established in two phases:

Phase 1 The first phase is a secure channel to negotiate the channel connection.

Phase 2 The second phase is a secure channel used to establish the connection.

FIGURE 8.10: The SSH connection-establishment process

Phase 1: Secure Channel Negotiation

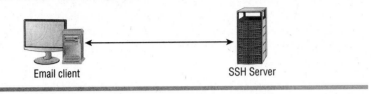

Email client   SSH Server

Phase 2: Session Establishment

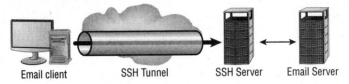

Email client   SSH Tunnel   SSH Server   Email Server

Pretty Good Privacy

Pretty Good Privacy (PGP) is a freeware email encryption system. As mentioned earlier in the chapter, PGP was introduced in the early 1990s, and it's considered to be a very good system. It's widely used for email security.

PGP uses both symmetrical and asymmetrical systems as a part of its process; it is this serial combination of processes that makes it so competent. Figure 8.11 provides an overview of how the various components of a PGP process work together to provide security. During the encryption process, the document is encrypted with the public key and also a session key, which is a one-use random number, to create the ciphertext. The session key is encrypted into the public key and sent with the ciphertext.

On the receiving end, the private key is used to ascertain the session key. The session key and the private key are then used to decrypt the ciphertext back into the original document.

An alternative to PGP that is freeware is *GPG (GNU Privacy Guard)*. It is part of the GNU project by the Free Software Foundation and is interoperable with PGP. Like its alternative, PGP, it is considered a hybrid program since it uses a combination of symmetric and public-key cryptography. This free replacement for PGP can be downloaded, from www.gnupg.org.

FIGURE 8.11:   The PGP encryption system

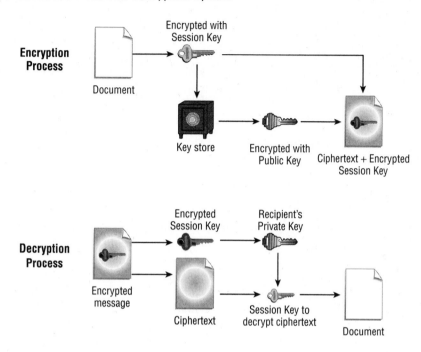

Securing Unix Interactive Users

You've been asked to examine your existing Unix systems and evaluate them for potential security weaknesses. Several remote users need to access Telnet and FTP capabilities in your network. Telnet and FTP connections send the logon and password information in the clear. How could you minimize security risks for Telnet and FTP connections?

You should consider using a VPN connection between these remote connections and your corporate systems. One workable solution might be to provide SSH to your clients and install it on your Unix servers. Doing so would allow FTP and Telnet connectivity in a secure environment.

HTTP Secure

Hypertext Transport Protocol over SSL (HTTPS), also known as Hypertext Transport Protocol Secure, is the secure version of HTTP, the language of the World Wide Web. HTTPS uses SSL to secure the channel between the client and server. Many e-business systems use HTTPS for secure transactions. An HTTPS session is identified by the https in the URL and by a key that is displayed in the web browser.

HTTPS uses port 443 by default.

Secure HTTP

Secure Hypertext Transport Protocol (S-HTTP) is HTTP with message security (added by using RSA or a digital certificate). Whereas HTTPS creates a secure channel, S-HTTP creates a secure message. S-HTTP can use multiple protocols and mechanisms to protect the message. It also provides data integrity and authentication.

S-HTTP is seldom used and defaults to using port 80 (the HTTP port).

IP Security

IP Security (IPSec) is a security protocol that provides authentication and encryption across the Internet. IPSec is becoming a standard for encrypting virtual private network (VPN) channels and is built into IPv6. It's available on most network platforms, and it's considered to be highly secure.

One of the primary uses of IPSec is to create VPNs. IPSec, in conjunction with Layer 2 Tunneling Protocol (L2TP) or Layer 2 Forwarding (L2F), creates packets that are difficult to read if intercepted by a third party. IPSec works at layer 3 of the OSI model.

The two primary protocols used by IPSec are *Authentication Header (AH)* and *Encapsulating Security Payload (ESP)*. Both can operate in either the transport or tunnel mode. Protocol 50 is used for ESP, while protocol 51 is used for AH.

You can find an overview of IPSec and AH/ESP in "An Illustrated Guide to IPsec" by Steve Friedl at www.unixwiz.net/techtips/iguide-ipsec.html.

In Exercise 8.3, we will show you how to configure IPSec monitoring on a Windows 7 or Windows 8 workstation.

EXERCISE 8.3

Looking for Errors in IPSec Performance Statistics

This exercise requires access to a workstation running Windows 7 or greater. To configure IPSec monitoring, follow these steps:

1. Open Performance Monitor by pressing the Windows button on the keyboard and typing R. Type perfmon.msc in the Run box. (If the UAC asks you to confirm to continue, click to continue.)

2. Click Performance Monitor.

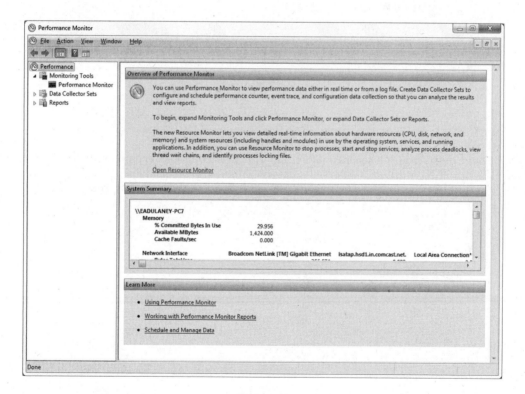

3. Right-click the graph, and choose Add Counters from the pop-up menu to open the dialog box shown here:

EXERCISE 8.3 *(continued)*

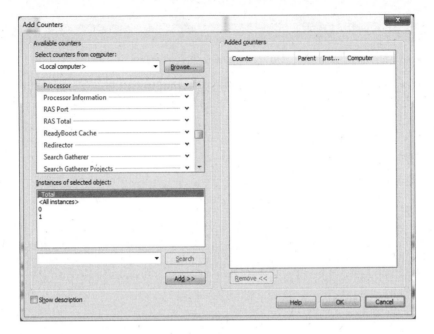

4. For an object, select IPsec IKEv1 IPv4, and expand the options beneath this listing.

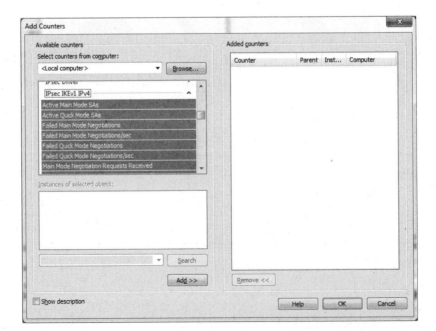

5. Click the Show Description check box, and read the comments. The descriptions appear in the bottom of the dialog box.

6. Click Add, and add the following counters: Failed Main Mode Negotiations and Failed Quick Mode Negotiations.

7. Click OK.

You're now monitoring the failures as they occur. On a properly functioning system, this graph should show no activity. Any activity that appears is indicative of problems since IPSec was last started and should be carefully examined.

Tunneling Protocols

Tunneling protocols add the ability to create tunnels between networks that can be more secure, support additional protocols, and provide virtual paths between systems. The best way to think of tunneling is to imagine sensitive data being encapsulated in other packets that are sent across the public network. After they're received at the other end, the sensitive data is stripped from the other packets and recompiled into its original form. Tunneling was also discussed in Chapter 2, "Monitoring and Diagnosing Networks."

The most common protocols used for tunneling are as follows:

Point-to-Point Tunneling Protocol *Point-to-Point Tunneling Protocol (PPTP)* supports encapsulation in a single point-to-point environment. PPTP encapsulates and encrypts *Point-to-Point Protocol (PPP)* packets. This makes PPTP a favorite low-end protocol for networks. The negotiation between the two ends of a PPTP connection is done in the clear. Once the negotiation is performed, the channel is encrypted. This is one of the major weaknesses of PPTP. A *packet-capture device*, such as a sniffer, that captures the negotiation process can potentially use that information to determine the connection type and information about how the tunnel works. Microsoft developed PPTP and supports it on most of its products. PPTP uses port 1723 and TCP for connections.

Layer 2 Forwarding Cisco developed *Layer 2 Forwarding (L2F)* as a method for creating tunnels primarily for dial-up connections. It's similar in capability to PPP, and it shouldn't be used over WANs. L2F provides authentication, but it doesn't provide encryption. L2F uses port 1701 and TCP for connections.

Layer 2 Tunneling Protocol A few years ago, Microsoft and Cisco agreed to combine their respective tunneling protocols into one protocol: *Layer 2 Tunneling Protocol (L2TP)*. L2TP is a hybrid of PPTP and L2F. It's primarily a point-to-point protocol. L2TP supports multiple network protocols, and it can be used in networks besides TCP/IP. L2TP works over IPX, SNA, and IP, so it can be used as a bridge across many types of systems. The major problem with L2TP is that it doesn't provide data security: The information isn't encrypted. Security can be provided by protocols such as IPSec. L2TP uses port 1701 and UDP for connections.

Federal Information Processing Standard

The *Federal Information Processing Standard (FIPS)* is a set of guidelines for U.S. federal government information systems. FIPS is used when an existing commercial or governmental system doesn't meet federal security requirements. FIPS is issued by NIST.

Using Public-Key Infrastructure

The *Public-Key Infrastructure (PKI)* is intended to offer a means of providing security to messages and transactions on a grand scale. The need for universal systems to support e-commerce, secure transactions, and information privacy is one aspect of the issues being addressed with PKI.

PKI is a two-key, asymmetric system with four main components: certificate authority (CA), registration authority (RA), RSA (the encryption algorithm), and digital certificates. The latter two were addressed in the previous chapter, and this one focuses more on the former two. Messages are encrypted with a public key and decrypted with a private key. As an example, take the following scenario:

1. You want to send an encrypted message to Jordan, so you request his public key.
2. Jordan responds by sending you that key.
3. You use the public key he sends you to encrypt the message.
4. You send the message to him.
5. Jordan uses his private key to decrypt the message.

The main goal of PKI is to define an infrastructure that should work across multiple vendors, systems, and networks. It's important to emphasize that PKI is a framework and not a specific technology. Implementations of PKI are dependent on the perspective of the software manufacturers that implement it. This has been one of the major difficulties with PKI: Each vendor can interpret the documents about this infrastructure and implement it however they choose. Many of the existing PKI implementations aren't compatible with each other, but this situation should change over the next few years because customers demand compatibility.

Most organizations have a PKI policy document that describes the uses for the electronic signing technology. Associated documents that fall under this category often include a confidentiality certificate policy document and a digital signature certificate policy document.

The following sections explain the major functions and components of the PKI infrastructure and how they work in relationship to the entire model.

WARNING   Under no circumstances should you ever divulge or send your private key. Doing so jeopardizes the guarantee that only you can work with the data, and it can irreparably damage your security.

Using a Certificate Authority

A *certificate authority (CA)* is an organization that is responsible for issuing, revoking, and distributing certificates. A *certificate* is nothing more than a mechanism that associates the public key with an individual. It contains a great deal of information about the user. Each user of a PKI system has a certificate that can be used to verify their authenticity. One of the first steps in getting a certificate is to submit a *certificate-signing request (CSR)*. This is a request formatted for the CA. This request will have the public key you wish to use and your fully distinguished name (often a domain name). The CA will then use this to process your request for a digital certificate.

For instance, if Mike wants to send Jeff a private message, there should be a mechanism to verify to Jeff that the message received from Mike is really from Mike. If a third party vouches for Mike and Jeff trusts that third party, Jeff can assume that the message is authentic because the third party says so. Figure 8.12 shows this process happening in a communication between Mike and Jeff. The arrows in this figure show the path between the CA and the person using the CA for verification purposes.

FIGURE 8.12:   The certificate authority process

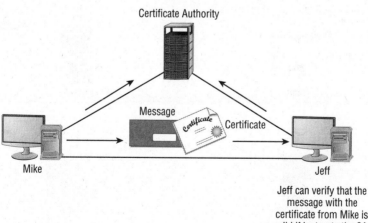

Jeff can verify that the message with the certificate from Mike is valid if he trusts the CA.

CAs can be either private or public, with VeriSign being one of the best known of the public variety. Many operating system providers allow their systems to be configured as CA systems. These CA systems can be used to generate internal certificates that are used within a business or in large external settings.

The process of providing certificates to users, although effective in helping to ensure security, requires a server. Over time, the server can become overloaded and need assistance. An additional component, the registration authority, is available to help offload work from the CA. Registration authorities are discussed in the next section.

Working with Registration Authorities and Local Registration Authorities

A *registration authority (RA)* offloads some of the work from a CA. An RA system operates as a middleman in the process: It can distribute keys, accept registrations for the CA, and validate identities. The RA doesn't issue certificates; that responsibility remains with the CA. Figure 8.13 shows an RA operating in San Francisco while the CA is located in Washington, D.C. The Seattle user obtains authorization for the session from the RA in San Francisco. The Seattle user can also use the San Francisco RA to validate the authenticity of a certificate from a Miami user. The arrows between the Seattle user and the RA server represent the certificate request from the remote user. The RA has a communications link with the CA in Washington, D.C. Because the CA in Washington, D.C. is closer, the Miami user will use it to verify the certificate.

FIGURE 8.13:   An RA offloading work from a CA

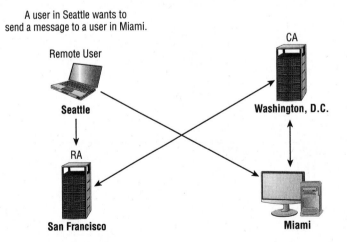

A *local registration authority (LRA)* takes the process one step further. It can be used to identify or establish the identity of an individual for certificate issuance. If the user in Seattle needs a new certificate, it would be impractical to fly back to Washington, D.C. to get another one. An LRA can be used to verify and certify the identity of the individual on behalf of the CA. The LRA can then forward authentication documents to the CA to issue the certificate.

The primary difference between an RA and an LRA is that the latter can be used to identify or establish the identity of an individual. The LRA involves the physical identification of the person requesting a certificate.

The next sections provide more detail about certificates and their uses, including validating users, systems, and devices. A certificate also has certain characteristics that will be briefly explained.

Implementing Certificates

Certificates, as you may recall, provide the primary method of identifying that a given user is valid. Certificates can also be used to store authorization information. Another important factor is verifying or certifying that a system is using the correct software and processes to communicate. What good would a certificate be to help ensure authenticity if the system uses an older cryptography system that has a security problem?

The next few sections describe the X.509 certificate structure and common usages of certification.

X.509

The most popular certificate used is the X.509 version 3. *X.509* is a standard certificate format supported by the International Telecommunications Union (ITU) and many other standards organizations. Adopting a standard certificate format is important for systems to be assured of interoperability in a certificate-oriented environment. The format and contents of a sample certificate are shown in Figure 8.14.

Notice that the certificate contains identifiers of two different algorithms used in the process. In this case, the signature algorithm is Md2RSA, and the digital signature algorithm is sha1. This certificate also has a unique serial number issued by the CA.

An X.509 certificate has more fields than are illustrated; this example is intended only to give you an overview of what a certificate looks like.

FIGURE 8.14:   A certificate illustrating some of the information stored

Version	V3
Serial Number	1234 D123 4567 …
Signature Algorithm	Md2RSA
Issuer	Sample Certificate
Valid from:	Thursday, September 8, 2005
Valid to:	Thursday, September 15, 2005
Subject	Mr. Your Name Here, Myco
Public Key	Encrypted Value of Key
Extensions	Subject Type = End Entity
Signature Algorithm Signature	sha1 Encrypted Data	◄── Digital Signature Area

Fields of a Simple X.509 Certificate

In Exercise 8.4, we'll show you how to view the certificate from a user's perspective.

EXERCISE 8.4

Viewing a Certificate

This exercise walks you through the steps for viewing an existing certificate:

1. In Internet Explorer 9 or newer, go to the URL `https://www.paypal.com`. Notice the lock icon that appears in the address bar indicating the secure site.

2. Click the lock icon, and a pop-up menu appears.

3. From the pop-up menu, choose View Certificates. By default, the properties will open to the General tab.

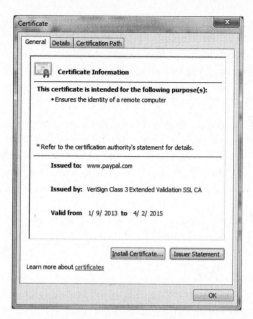

4.   Click the Details tab, and make sure the Show field is set to <All>.

5.   Click Issuer to see the values (CN, OU, O, and C) expanded in the lower dialog box.
     You can do the same with Certificate Policies and the other fields that appear.

6.   Click OK to exit the properties box.

Always remember that the purpose of the certificate is basically to bind the public key to the user's identity. When authenticating, certificates can be used to authenticate only the client (*single sided*) or both parties (*dual sided*), the client and server. Aside from the Security+ objectives, no one uses the term *dual-sided certificates*.

Certificate Policies

Certificate policies define what certificates do. A CA can potentially issue a number of different types of certificates—say, one for email, one for e-commerce, and one for financial transactions. The policy might indicate that it isn't to be used for signing contracts or for purchasing equipment. Certificate policies affect how a certificate is issued and how it's used. A CA would have policies regarding the interoperability or certification of another CA site; the process of requiring interoperability is called *cross certification*. The organizations using the certificates also have the right to decide which types of certificates are used and for what purposes. This is a voluntary process in that each organization involved can decide what and how to approve certificate use.

 According to the RFC, key usages may be marked as critical or noncritical. This distinction is largely to limit the CA.

The receiving organization can use this policy to determine whether the certificate has come from a legitimate source. Think about it this way: A PKI certificate can be generated any number of ways using any number of servers. The policy indicates which certificates will be accepted in a given application.

Certificate Practice Statements

A *Certificate Practice Statement (CPS)* is a detailed statement the CA uses to issue certificates and implement its policies.

The CA provides the CPS to users of its services. These statements should discuss how certificates are issued, what measures are taken to protect certificates, and the rules that CA users must follow in order to maintain their certificate eligibility. The policies should be readily available to CA users.

If a CA is unwilling to provide this information to a user, the CA itself may be untrustworthy, and the trustworthiness of that CA's users should be questioned.

 Remember that a CPS is a detailed document used to enforce policy at the CA; a certificate policy pertains not to the CA but to the certificate itself.

Understanding Certificate Revocation

Certificate revocation is the process of revoking a certificate before it expires. A certificate may need to be revoked because it was stolen, an employee has moved to a new company, or someone has had their access revoked. A certificate revocation is handled either through a *certificate revocation list (CRL)* or by using the *Online Certificate Status Protocol (OCSP)*. A *repository* is simply a database or database server where the certificates are stored.

The process of revoking a certificate begins when the CA is notified that a particular certificate needs to be revoked. This must be done whenever the private key becomes known. The owner of a certificate can request that it be revoked at any time, or the administrator can make the request.

The CA marks the certificate as revoked. This information is published in the CRL and becomes available using the OCSP. The revocation process is usually very quick; the time required is based on the publication interval for the CRL. Disseminating the revocation information to users may take longer. Once the certificate has been revoked, it can never be used—or trusted—again.

The CA publishes the CRL on a regular basis, usually either hourly or daily. The CA sends or publishes this list to organizations that have chosen to receive it; the publishing process occurs automatically in the case of PKI. The time between when the CRL is issued and when it reaches users may be too long for some applications. This time gap is referred to as *latency*. OCSP solves the latency problem: If the recipient or relaying party uses OCSP for verification, the answer is available immediately. Currently, this process is under evaluation and may be replaced at some time in the future.

When a key is compromised, a revocation request should be made to the CA immediately. It may take a day or longer for the CRL to be disseminated to everyone using that CA.

Implementing Trust Models

For PKI to work, the capabilities of CAs must be readily available to users. The model that has been shown to this point is the simple trust model. However, the simple trust model may not work as PKI implementations get bigger. Conceptually, every computer user in the world would have a certificate. However, accomplishing this would be extremely complex and would create enormous scaling or growth issues.

Four main types of trust models are used with PKI:

- Hierarchical
- Bridge
- Mesh
- Hybrid

PKI was designed to allow all of these trust models to be created. They can be fairly granular from a control perspective. *Granularity* refers to the ability to manage individual resources in the CA network.

In the following sections, we'll examine each of these models. We'll detail how each model works and discuss its advantages and disadvantages.

Hierarchical Trust Models

In a *hierarchical trust model*, also known as a tree, a root CA at the top provides all of the information. The intermediate CAs are next in the hierarchy, and they trust only information provided by the root CA. The root CA also trusts intermediate CAs that are in their level in the hierarchy and none that aren't. This arrangement allows a high level of control at all levels of the hierarchical tree.

This might be the most common implementation in a large organization that wants to extend its certificate-processing capabilities. Hierarchical models allow tight control over certificate-based activities.

Figure 8.15 illustrates the hierarchical trust structure. In this situation, the intermediate CAs trust only the CAs directly above them or below them.

FIGURE 8.15:   A Hierarchical trust structure

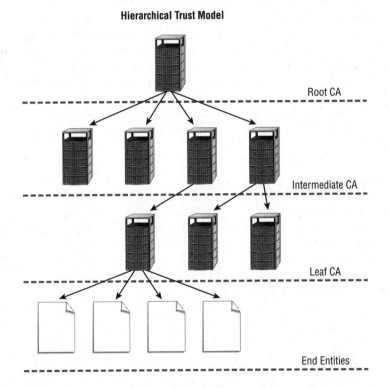

Root CA systems can have trusts between them, and there can be trusts between intermediate and leaf CAs. A *leaf CA* is any CA that is at the end of a CA network or chain. This structure allows you to be creative and efficient when you create hybrid systems.

Bridge Trust Models

In a *bridge trust model*, a peer-to-peer relationship exists among the root CAs. The root CAs can communicate with one another, allowing cross certification. This arrangement allows a certification process to be established between organizations or departments. Each intermediate CA trusts only the CAs above and below it, but the CA structure can be expanded without creating additional layers of CAs.

Additional flexibility and interoperability between organizations are the primary advantages of a bridge model. Lack of trustworthiness of the root CAs can be a major disadvantage. If one of the root CAs doesn't maintain tight internal security around its certificates, a security problem can be created. An illegitimate certificate could become available to all of the users in the bridge structure and its subordinate or intermediate CAs.

This model may be useful if you're dealing with a large, geographically dispersed organization or when you have two organizations that are working together. A large, geographically dispersed organization could maintain a root CA at each remote location; the root CAs would have their own internal hierarchy, and users would be able to access certificates from any place in the CA structure. Figure 8.16 illustrates a bridged structure. In this example, the intermediate CAs communicates only with their respective root CA. All cross-certification is handled between the two root CA systems.

FIGURE 8.16: A bridge trust structure

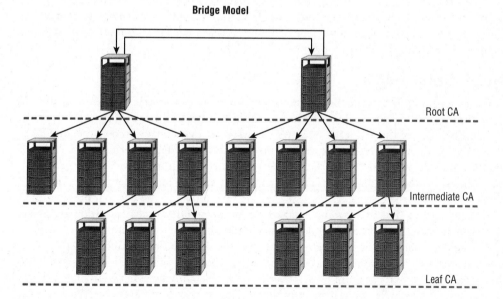

Mesh Trust Models

The *mesh trust model* expands the concepts of the bridge model by supporting multiple paths and multiple root CAs. Each of the root CAs can cross-certify with the other root

CAs in the mesh. This arrangement is also referred to as a *web structure*. As shown in Figure 8.17, each of the root CAs can also communicate with the intermediate CAs in their respective hierarchies.

FIGURE 8.17:   A mesh trust structure

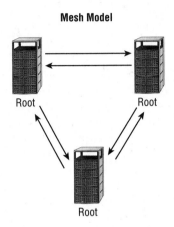

This structure may be useful in a situation where several organizations must cross-certify certificates. The advantage is that you have more flexibility when you configure the CA structures. The major disadvantage of a mesh is that each root CA must be trustworthy in order to maintain security.

Hybrid Trust Model

A *hybrid trust model* can use the capabilities of any or all of the structures discussed in the previous sections. You can be extremely flexible when you build a hybrid trust structure.

The flexibility of this model also allows you to create hybrid environments. Figure 8.18 illustrates such a structure. Notice that in this structure, the single intermediate CA server on the right side of Figure 8.18 is the only server that is known by the CA below it. The subordinates of the middle-left CA are linked to the two CAs on its sides. These two CAs don't know about the other CAs because they are linked only to the CA that provides them with a connection. The two intermediate servers in the middle of the illustration and their subordinates trust each other; they don't trust others that aren't in the link.

The major difficulty with hybrid models is that they can become complicated and confusing. A user can unintentionally acquire trusts that they shouldn't have obtained. In the example shown in Figure 8.18, a user could accidentally be assigned to one of the CAs in the middle circle. As a member of that circle, the user could access certificate information that should be available only from their root CA. In addition, relationships between CAs can continue long past their usefulness; unless someone is aware of them, these relationships can exist even after the parent organizations have terminated their relationships.

FIGURE 8.18: A hybrid trust model

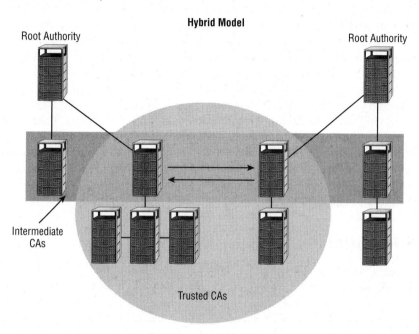

Hybrid Model

Root Authority

Root Authority

Intermediate CAs

Trusted CAs

 Real World Scenario

Designing a CA Structure for Your Organization

You've been assigned to implement a CA structure for your organization, which has several large regional factories and small remote facilities throughout the country. Some of these facilities have high-speed networks; others have low-speed dial-up capabilities. Your management reports that network traffic is very high, and they don't want to overburden the network with CA traffic. How would you go about implementing this structure?

You should probably install CA systems at each of the major facilities throughout the country. Additionally, you may want to install CAs in key geographic locations where certificate access is needed. You should establish a procedure that allows certificates to be issued in remote locations, and you must also implement an RA process in your larger locations. Remote users could receive certificates either by email or by out-of-band methods if network access is limited.

Hardware-Based Encryption Devices

In addition to software-based encryption, hardware-based encryption can be applied. Within the advanced configuration settings on some BIOS configuration menus, for example, you can choose to enable or disable TPM. A *Trusted Platform Module (TPM)* can be used to assist with hash key generation. TPM is the name assigned to a chip that can store cryptographic keys, passwords, or certificates. TPM can be used to protect smart phones and devices other than PCs as well. It can also be used to generate values used with whole disk encryption such as BitLocker. BitLocker can be used with or without TPM. It is much more secure when coupled with TPM (and is preferable) but does not require it.

The TPM chip may be installed on the motherboard; when it is, in many cases it is set to off in the BIOS by default. More information on TPM can be found at the Trusted Computing Group's website: https://www.trustedcomputinggroup.org/home.

In addition to TPM, *HSM (Hardware Security Module)* is also a cryptoprocessor that can be used to enhance security. HSM is commonly used with PKI systems to augment security with CAs. As opposed to being mounted on the motherboard like TPMs, HSMs are traditionally PCI adapters.

Data Encryption

Data encryption, mentioned earlier in relation to mobile devices, allows data that has been stolen to remain out of the eyes of the intruders who took it as long as they do not have the proper passwords. One of the newest security features that is available on only the Pro and Enterprise version of Windows 8.1 (and Ultimate version of Windows 7) is *BitLocker*. BitLocker is a *full disk* encryption feature that can encrypt an entire volume with 128-bit *encryption*. When the entire volume is encrypted, the data is not accessible to someone who might boot another operating system in an attempt to bypass the computer's security. Full disk encryption is sometimes referred to as *hard drive encryption*.

BitLocker to Go allows you to apply the same technology to removable media. This often means encrypting USB devices, but it can also mean any removable media. By encrypting removable hard drives and USB flash drives, you also prevent them from being so destructive when intercepted by the wrong hands.

There are several others data encryption technologies beyond BitLocker including the widely used *TrueCrypt*. Both tools allow you to encrypt either the entire disk or just portions. For example, one might use individual file encryption. A related concept is *database encryption*. Many relational database systems, such as Microsoft SQL Server, have the option to encrypt the database.

Summary

This chapter focused on the basic elements of cryptography and the PKI implementation. There are three primary methods of encryption:

- Symmetric
- Asymmetric
- Hashing

Symmetric systems require that each end of the connection have the same key. Asymmetric systems use a two-key system. In public-key cryptography, the receiver has a private key known only to them; a public key corresponds to it, which they make known to others. The public key can be sent to all other parties; the private key is never divulged. Hashing refers to performing a calculation on a message and converting it into a numeric hash value.

The five main considerations in implementing a cryptography system are as follows:

- *Confidentiality* means that the message retains its privacy.
- *Integrity* means the message can't be altered without detection.
- *Authentication* is used to verify that the person who sent the message is actually who they say they are.
- *Nonrepudiation* prevents either the sender or receiver from denying that the message was sent or received.
- *Access controls* are the methods, processes, and mechanisms of preventing unauthorized access to the systems that do the cryptography.

In this chapter, you also learned about the standards, agencies, and associations that are interested in cryptography. Several government agencies have been specifically charged with overseeing security and encryption. The NSA and NIST are both concerned with government encryption standards. NIST is primarily concerned with nonmilitary standards; NSA/CSS is concerned with military applications.

Exam Essentials

Be able to describe the process of a hashing algorithm.   Hashing algorithms are used to derive a key mathematically from a message. The most common hashing standards for cryptographic applications are the SHA and MD algorithms.

Know the principles of a symmetric algorithm.   A symmetric algorithm requires that receivers of the message use the same private key. Symmetric algorithms can be extremely secure. This method is widely implemented in governmental applications. The private key is changed using out-of-band transmission.

Be able to describe the process of asymmetric algorithms.   Asymmetric algorithms use a two-key method of encryption. The message is encrypted using the public key and decrypted using a second key or private key. The key is derived from the same algorithm.

Know the primary objectives for using cryptographic systems.   The main objectives for these systems are confidentiality, integrity, authentication, and nonrepudiation. Digital signatures can be used to verify the integrity and provide nonrepudiation of a message.

Understand the process used in PKI.   PKI is an encryption system that uses a variety of technologies to provide confidentiality, integrity, authentication, and nonrepudiation. PKI uses certificates issued from a CA to provide this capability as well as encryption. PKI is being widely implemented in organizations worldwide.

Review Questions

1. Which of the following does not apply to a hashing algorithm?

   A. One-way

   B. Long key size

   C. Variable-length input with fixed-length output

   D. Collision resistance

2. During a training session, you want to impress upon users how serious security is and, in particular, cryptography. To accomplish this, you want to give them as much of an overview about the topic as possible. Which government agency should you mention is primarily responsible for establishing government standards involving cryptography for general-purpose government use?

   A. NSA

   B. NIST

   C. IEEE

   D. ITU

3. Which of the following is the most widely used asymmetric algorithm today?

   A. RSA

   B. AES

   C. 3DES

   D. SHA

4. You're a member of a consortium wanting to create a new standard that will effectively end all spam. After years of meeting, the group has finally come across a solution and now wants to propose it. The process of proposing a new standard or method on the Internet is referred to by which acronym?

   A. WBS

   B. X.509

   C. RFC

   D. IEEE

5. Mary claims that she didn't make a phone call from her office to a competitor and tell them about developments at her company. Telephone logs, however, show that such a call was placed from her phone, and time clock records show that she was the only person working at the time. What do these records provide?

   A. Integrity

   B. Confidentiality

   C. Authentication

   D. Nonrepudiation

6. Mercury Technical Solutions has been using SSL in a business-to-business environment for a number of years. Despite the fact that there have been no compromises in security, the new IT manager wants to use stronger security than SSL can offer. Which of the following protocols is similar to SSL but offers the ability to use additional security protocols?

    A. TLS

    B. SSH

    C. RSH

    D. X.509

7. MAC is an acronym for what as it relates to cryptography?

    A. Media access control

    B. Mandatory access control

    C. Message authentication code

    D. Multiple advisory committees

8. You've been brought in as a security consultant for a small bicycle manufacturing firm. Immediately, you notice that they're using a centralized key-generating process, and you make a note to dissuade them from that without delay. What problem is created by using a centralized key-generating process?

    A. Network security

    B. Key transmission

    C. Certificate revocation

    D. Private key security

9. You need to encrypt your hard drive. Which of the following is the best choice?

    A. DES

    B. RSA

    C. AES

    D. SHA

10. As the head of IT for MTS, you're explaining some security concerns to a junior administrator who has just been hired. You're trying to emphasize the need to know what is important and what isn't. Which of the following is *not* a consideration in key storage?

    A. Environmental controls

    B. Physical security

    C. Hardened servers

    D. Administrative controls

11. What is the primary organization for maintaining certificates called?

    A. CA

    B. RA

    C. LRA

    D. CRL

12. Due to a breach, a certificate must be permanently revoked and you don't want it to ever be used again. What is often used to revoke a certificate?

   A. CRA

   B. CYA

   C. CRL

   D. PKI

13. Which organization can be used to identify an individual for certificate issue in a PKI environment?

   A. RA

   B. LRA

   C. PKE

   D. SHA

14. Kristin from Payroll has left the office on maternity leave and won't return for at least six weeks. You've been instructed to suspend her key. Which of the following statements is true?

   A. In order to be used, suspended keys must be revoked.

   B. Suspended keys don't expire.

   C. Suspended keys can be reactivated.

   D. Suspending keys is a bad practice.

15. What document describes how a CA issues certificates and for what they are used?

   A. Certificate policies

   B. Certificate practices

   C. Revocation authority

   D. CRL

16. After returning from a conference, your manager informs you that he has learned that law enforcement has the right, under subpoena, to conduct investigations using keys. He wants you to implement measures to make such an event run smoothly should it ever happen. What is the process of storing keys for use by law enforcement called?

   A. Key escrow

   B. Key archival

   C. Key renewal

   D. Certificate rollover

17. The CRL takes time to be fully disseminated. Which protocol allows a certificate's authenticity to be immediately verified?

   A. CA

   B. CP

   C. CRC

   D. OCSP

18. Which set of specifications is designed to allow XML-based programs access to PKI services?

    A. XKMS

    B. XMLS

    C. PKXMS

    D. PKIXMLS

19. Which of the following is similar to Blowfish but works on 128-bit blocks?

    A. Twofish

    B. IDEA

    C. CCITT

    D. AES

20. Your IT manager has stated that you need to select an appropriate tool for email encryption. Which of the following would be the best choice?

    A. MD5

    B. IPSEC

    C. TLS

    D. PGP

Chapter

9

Malware, Vulnerabilities, and Threats

THE FOLLOWING COMPTIA SECURITY+ EXAM OBJECTIVES ARE COVERED IN THIS CHAPTER:

✓ **3.1 Explain types of malware.**

- Adware
- Virus
- Spyware
- Trojan
- Rootkits
- Backdoors
- Logic bomb
- Botnets
- Ransomware
- Polymorphic malware
- Armored virus

✓ **3.2 Summarize various types of attacks.**

- Man-in-the-middle
- DDoS
- DoS
- Replay
- Smurf attack
- Spoofing
- Spam

- Phishing
- Spim
- Vishing
- Spear phishing
- Xmas attack
- Pharming
- Privilege escalation
- Malicious insider threat
- DNS poisoning and ARP poisoning
- Transitive access
- Client-side attacks
- Password attacks: Brute force; Dictionary attacks; Hybrid; Birthday attacks; Rainbow tables
- Typo squatting/URL hijacking
- Watering hole attack

✓ **3.5 Explain types of application attacks.**

- Cross-site scripting
- SQL injection
- LDAP injection
- XML injection
- Directory traversal/command injection
- Buffer overflow
- Integer overflow
- Zero-day
- Cookies and attachments; LSO (Locally Shared Objects); Flash Cookies; Malicious add-ons
- Session hijacking
- Header manipulation
- Arbitrary code execution/remote code execution

✓ **3.7 Given a scenario, use appropriate tools and techniques to discover security threats and vulnerabilities.**

- ▪ Interpret results of security assessment tools

- ▪ Tools: Protocol analyzer; Vulnerability scanner; Honeypots; honeynets; Port scanner; Passive vs. active tools; Banner grabbing

- ▪ Risk calculations: Threat vs. likelihood

- ▪ Assessment types: Risk; Threat; Vulnerability

- ▪ Assessment technique: Baseline reporting; Code review; Determine attack surface; Review architecture; Review designs

✓ **4.1 Explain the importance of application security controls and techniques.**

- ▪ Cross-site scripting prevention

- ▪ Cross-site Request Forgery (XSRF) prevention

- ▪ Server-side vs. client-side validation

As we discussed in Chapter 1, "Measuring and Weighing Risk," everywhere you turn there are risks; they begin the minute you first turn on a computer and they grow exponentially the moment a network card becomes active. Whereas Chapter 1 discussed how to measure and weigh risks, this chapter will focus on two particular types of risks: malware and attacks. We will then discuss tools that you can use to combat them.

In the case of malware, you are exposed to situations because of software that is running on your system—vulnerabilities not intentionally created but there nevertheless. In the case of attacks, someone is purposely targeting your system(s) and trying to do you harm.

In this chapter, we'll look at some of the reasons your network may be vulnerable. This list is far from complete because attackers create new variants of each vulnerability on a regular basis. The list is thorough, however, on two counts: It includes everything CompTIA expects you to know for the exam, and many of the new malware and attack variants are simply newer modifications, or implementations, of those listed here.

Understanding Malware

The term *software exploitation* refers to attacks launched against applications and higher-level services. They include gaining access to data using weaknesses in the data access objects of a database or a flaw in a service or application. This section briefly outlines common exploitations that have been successful in the past. The following exploitations can be introduced by using viruses or access attacks:

Spyware *Spyware* differs from other malware in that it works—often actively—on behalf of a third party. Rather than self-replicating, like viruses and worms, spyware is spread to machines by users who inadvertently ask for it. The users often do not know they have asked for it but have acquired it by downloading other programs, visiting infected sites, and so on.

The spyware program monitors the user's activity and reports it to another party without informing the user that it is doing so. Often it is gathering information about the user to pass on to marketers, or intercepting personal data such as credit card numbers. One thing separating spyware from most other malware is that it almost always exists to provide commercial gain. The operating systems from Microsoft are the ones most affected by spyware.

One of the reasons spyware is so prevalent is that there are many legal uses for it, such as monitoring children's or employees' online habits. It is the implementation of spyware in an illegal manner that makes it a problem.

Adware   If the primary purpose of the malware application is to deliver ads, then it is classified as *adware*. Adware can have the same qualities as spyware, but the primary purpose of adware is to display ads and generate revenue for the creator. Because spyware and adware share similar features, Windows Defender (available for operating systems from Windows XP on) can be used as a first line of defense.

New Attacks on the Way

The discussion of attacks in this chapter isn't comprehensive. New methods for dealing with and counteracting attacks are being developed even as you read this book. Your first challenge when confronting an attack is to recognize that you're fighting the battle on two fronts:

- The first front involves the inherent open nature of TCP/IP and its protocol suite. TCP/IP is a robust and rich environment. This richness allows many opportunities to exploit the vulnerabilities of the protocol suite.

- The second front of this battle involves the implementation of TCP/IP by various vendors. A weak TCP/IP implementation will be susceptible to all forms of attacks, and there is little you'll be able to do about it except to complain to the software manufacturer.

Fortunately, most of the credible manufacturers are now taking these complaints seriously and doing what they can to close the holes they have created in your systems. Keep your updates current because this is where most of the corrections for security problems are implemented.

Rootkits   Recently, rootkits have become the software exploitation program du jour. *Rootkits* are software programs that have the ability to hide certain things from the operating system. With a rootkit, there may be a number of processes running on a system that do not show up in Task Manager or connections established or available that do not appear in a `netstat` display—the rootkit masks the presence of these items. The rootkit is able to do this by manipulating function calls to the operating system and filtering out information that would normally appear. Theoretically, rootkits could hide anywhere that there is enough memory to reside: video cards, PCI cards, and the like. In Exercise 9.1, we'll show you how to view running processes on a Windows-based machine, and in Exercise 9.2, we'll do the same on a Linux-based machine.

Unfortunately, many rootkits are written to get around antivirus and antispyware programs that are not kept up-to-date. The best defense you have is to monitor what your system is doing and catch the rootkit in the process of installation.

EXERCISE 9.1

Viewing Running Processes on a Windows-Based Machine

As an administrator, you need to know what processes are running on a machine at any given time. In addition to the programs that a user may be running, there are always many others that are required by the operating system, network, or other applications.

All recent versions of Windows include Task Manager, which allows you to see what is running. To access this information, follow these steps:

1. Right-click an empty location in the Windows Taskbar.

2. Choose either Task Manager or Start Task Manager (depending on the Windows version you are running) from the pop-up menu that appears.

3. The Task Manager opens to Applications by default and shows what the user is actually running. Click the Processes tab. Information about the programs that are needed for the running applications is shown, as well as all other processes that are currently running.

4. If the Show Processes From All Users check box appears beneath this tab, click it. Many of the names of the processes appear cryptic, but definitions for most (good and bad) can be found with a Google search.

5. Examine the list and look for anything out of the ordinary. After doing this a few times, you will become familiar with what is normally there and will be able to spot oddities quickly.

6. Notice the values in the CPU column. Those values will always total 100, with System Idle Processes typically making up the vast majority. High numbers on another process can indicate that there is a problem with it. If the numbers do not add up to 100, it can be a sign that a rootkit is masking some of the display.

7. If you are running a newer version of Windows, click the button Show Processes From All Users. User Account Control (UAC) will ask you to confirm the action; click Continue.

8. Click the top of the second column where it says User Name to order the list alphabetically by this field.

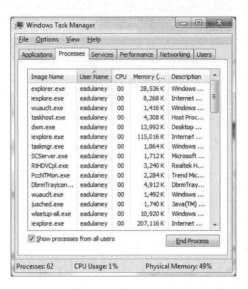

9. Scroll to where the SYSTEM entries begin, and look for anything suspicious there.

10. Close Task Manager.

EXERCISE 9.2

Viewing Running Processes on a Linux-Based Machine

Most versions of Linux include a graphical utility to allow you to see the running processes. Those utilities differ based on the distribution of Linux in use and the desktop that you have chosen.

All versions of Linux, however, do offer a command line and the ability to use the ps utility. Because of that, this method is employed in this exercise. To access this information, follow these steps:

1. Open a shell window, or otherwise access a command prompt.

2. Type **ps -ef | more**.

3. The display shows the processes running for all users. The names of the processes appear in the rightmost column, and the processor time will be in the column closest to it. The names are cryptic, but definitions for most can be found using the **man** command followed by the name of the process. Those that are application specific can usually be found through a web search.

4. Examine the list and look for anything out of the ordinary. After doing this a few times, you will become familiar with what is normally there and will be able to spot oddities quickly.

5. Pay particular attention to those processes associated with the root user (the user appears in the first column). Because the root user has the power to do anything, only necessary daemons and processes should be associated with that user. You can look only at those running that are associated with the root user by typing **ps -u root**.

6. Exit the shell.

As these new threats have developed, so too have some excellent programs for countering them. Within any search engine, you can find a rootkit analyzer for your system, including Spybot, Spyware Doctor, and Ad-Aware. There are also a number of products that specialize in integrity verification, such as those from Tripwire (www.tripwire.com).

Trojan Horses *Trojan horses* are programs that enter a system or network under the guise of another program. A Trojan horse may be included as an attachment or as part of an installation program. The Trojan horse could create a backdoor or replace a valid program during installation. It would then accomplish its mission under the guise of another program. Trojan horses can be used to compromise the security of your system, and they can exist on a system for years before they're detected.

Trojans Today

An area in which Trojan horses have been cropping up is with social networking. The Boonana Trojan began cropping up in Facebook and affecting both Mac OS X and Windows-based systems. A message would appear asking the user if it was them in a video and including a link. Clicking the link to run the video triggered a Java applet that would then redirect legitimate requests to known malware servers.

Another successful Trojan in recent years was Ghost Rat (the "Rat" stands for Remote Administration Tool), which exploited the remote administration feature in Windows-based operating systems and allowed attackers to record audio and video remotely.

The best preventive measure for Trojan horses is not to allow them to enter your system. Immediately before and after you install a new software program or operating system, back it up! If you suspect a Trojan horse, you can reinstall the original programs, which should delete the Trojan horse. A port scan may also reveal a Trojan horse on your system. If an application opens a TCP or UDP port that isn't regularly used in your network, you may notice this and begin corrective action.

Is a Trojan horse also a virus? A *Trojan horse* is anything that sneaks in under the guise of something else. Given that general definition, it's certainly possible that a virus can (and usually does) sneak in, but this description most often fits the definition of a companion virus. The primary distinction, from an exam perspective, is that with a Trojan horse you always intentionally obtained something (usually an application) and didn't know an unpleasant freeloader was hidden within. An example is spyware, which is often installed (unknown to you) as part of another application.

One of the most important measures you can take to combat software attacks proactively is to know common file extensions and the applications with which they're associated. For example, the .scr filename extension is used for screensavers, and viruses are often distributed through the use of these files. No legitimate user should be sending screensavers via email to your users, and all attachments with the .scr filename extension should be banned from entering your network. Files with other extensions aren't often so clear cut. Compressed files with the .zip extension, for example, are often necessary for sending large attachments, yet encrypted .zip files also serve as the primary distribution method for ransomware.

Table 9.1, while not comprehensive, contains the most common filename extensions for files that should and should not, as a general rule, be allowed into your network as email attachments.

TABLE 9.1   Common filename extensions for email attachments

Should be allowed	Should *not* be allowed
.doc/docx	.bat
.pdf	.com
.txt	.exe
.xls/xlsx	.hlp
	.pif
	.scr

If there is any one file extension that belongs in both columns in Table 9.1, it is .pdf. For years, PDF files have been preferred over most other types since they essentially hold a snapshot of documents created with other programs and have been thought to be safer than the original files (which could be stuffed with macros). As the complexity of Adobe Acrobat has increased, however, so too has the ability to create malware PDF files. One example of this is the GhostRat Trojan, which allows attackers to take advantage of the Remote Administration Tool.

Logic Bombs   *Logic bombs* are programs or code snippets that execute when a certain predefined event occurs. A bomb may send a note to an attacker when a user is logged on to the Internet and is using a word processor. This message informs the attacker that the user is ready for an attack.

Figure 9.1 shows a logic bomb in operation. Notice that this bomb doesn't begin the attack, but it tells the attacker that the victim has met the needed criteria or state for an attack to begin. Logic bombs may also be set to go off on a certain date or when a specified set of circumstances occurs.

FIGURE 9.1 A logic bomb being initiated

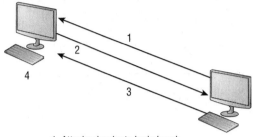

1. Attacker implants logic bomb.
2. Victim reports installation.
3. Attacker sends attack message.
4. Victim does as logic bomb indicates.

In the attack depicted in Figure 9.1, the logic bomb sends a message back to the attacking system that it has loaded successfully. The victim system can then be used to initiate an attack, such as a DDoS attack, or it can grant access at the time of the attacker's choosing.

Backdoors   The term *backdoor attack* (known also as *backdoor*) can have two different meanings. The original term backdoor referred to troubleshooting and developer hooks into systems that often circumvented normal authentication. During the development of a complicated operating system or application, programmers add backdoors or maintenance hooks. Backdoors allow them to examine operations inside the code while the code is running. The backdoors are stripped out of the code when it's moved into production. When a software manufacturer discovers a hook that hasn't been removed, it releases a maintenance upgrade or patch to close the backdoor. These patches are common when a new product is initially released.

The second type of backdoor refers to gaining access to a network and inserting a program or utility that creates an entrance for an attacker. The program may allow a certain user ID to log on without a password or to gain administrative privileges. Figure 9.2 shows how a backdoor attack can be used to bypass the security of a network. In this example, the attacker is using a backdoor program to utilize resources or steal information.

A backdoor attack is usually either an access or modification attack. A number of tools exist to create backdoor attacks on systems. Two popular ones are Back Orifice and NetBus. Fortunately, most conventional antivirus software will detect and block these types of attacks.

Back Orifice and NetBus are remote administration tools used by attackers to take control of Windows-based systems. These packages are typically installed using a Trojan horse program. Back Orifice and NetBus allow a remote user to take full control of systems on which they are installed. They run on all of the current Windows operating systems.

FIGURE 9.2 A backdoor attack in progress

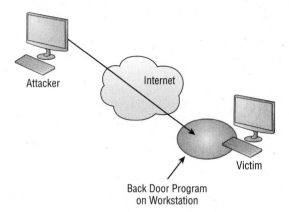

Botnets Software running on infected computers called zombies is often known as a *botnet*. Bots, by themselves, are but a form of software that runs automatically and autonomously. (For example, Google uses the Googlebot to find web pages and bring back values for the index.) Botnet, however, has come to be the word used to describe malicious software running on a zombie and under the control of a *bot-herder*.

Denial-of-service attacks—DoS and DDoS—can be launched by botnets, as can many forms of adware, spyware, and spam (via *spambots*). Most bots are written to run in the background with no visible evidence of their presence. Many malware kits can be used to create botnets and modify existing ones.

There is no universal approach to dealing with botnets, but knowing how to deal with various botnet types (all of which are described here) is important for exam preparation. Some can be easily detected by looking at a database of known threats, whereas others have to be identified through analysis of their behavior.

Ransomware With *ransomware*, software—often delivered through a Trojan—takes control of a system and demands that a third party be paid. The "control" can be accomplished by encrypting the hard drive, by changing user password information, or via any of a number of other creative ways. Users are usually assured that by paying the extortion amount (the ransom) they will be given the code needed to revert their systems to normal operations.

This section looked at all of the types of malware that you need to know for the CompTIA Security+ exam with the exception of viruses. Viruses come in many forms and are far more complicated than the other forms or malware. Because of this, viruses are discussed in their own section, which follows.

Surviving Viruses

A *virus* is a piece of software designed to infect a computer system. Under the best of circumstances, a virus may do nothing more than reside on the computer, but it may also damage the data on your hard disk drive (HDD), destroy your operating system, and possibly spread to other systems. Viruses get into your computer in one of three ways:

- On contaminated media (DVD, USB drive, or CD-ROM)
- Through email and social networking sites
- As part of another program

Viruses can be classified as:

Polymorphic   These viruses change form in order to avoid detection.

Stealth   These viruses attempt to avoid detection by masking themselves from applications.

Retroviruses   These viruses attack or bypass the antivirus software installed on a computer.

Multipartite   These viruses attack your system in multiple ways.

Armored   This type of virus is one that is designed to make itself difficult to detect or analyze.

Companion   This type of virus attaches itself to legitimate programs and then creates a program with a different filename extension.

Phage   This type of virus is one that modifies and alters other programs and databases.

Macro   This type of virus exploits the enhancements made to many application programs, which are used by programmers to expand the capability of applications.

Each type of virus has a different attack strategy and different consequences.

Estimates for losses due to viruses are in the billions of dollars. These losses include financial loss as well as losses in productivity.

The following sections introduce the general symptoms of a virus infection, explain how a virus works, and describe the types of viruses you can expect to encounter and how they generally behave. You'll also see how a virus is transmitted through a network.

Symptoms of a Virus Infection

Many viruses will announce that you're infected as soon as they gain access to your system. They may take control of your system and flash annoying messages on your screen or destroy your hard disk. When this occurs, you'll know that you're a victim. Other viruses will cause your system to slow down, cause files to disappear from your computer, or take over disk space.

You should look for some of the following symptoms when determining if a virus infection has occurred:

- The programs on your system start to load more slowly. This happens because the virus is spreading to other files in your system or is taking over system resources.

- Unusual files appear on your hard drive, or files start to disappear from your system. Many viruses delete key files in your system to render it inoperable.

- Program sizes change from the installed versions. This occurs because the virus is attaching itself to these programs on your disk.

- Your browser, word processing application, or other software begins to exhibit unusual operating characteristics. Screens or menus may change.

- The system mysteriously shuts itself down or starts itself up and does a great deal of unanticipated disk activity.

- You mysteriously lose access to a disk drive or other system resources. The virus has changed the settings on a device to make it unusable.

- Your system suddenly doesn't reboot or gives unexpected error messages during startup.

This list is by no means comprehensive, but it is a good start to determining if your computer has been infected.

How Viruses Work

A virus, in most cases, tries to accomplish one of two things: render your system inoperable or spread to other systems. Many viruses will spread to other systems given the chance and then render your system unusable. This is common with many of the newer viruses.

If your system is infected, the virus may try to attach itself to every file in your system and spread each time you send a file or document to other users. Figure 9.3 shows a virus spreading from an infected system, either through a network or by removable media. When you give removable media to another user or put it into another system, you then infect that system with the virus.

FIGURE 9.3   Virus spreading from an infected system using the network or removable media

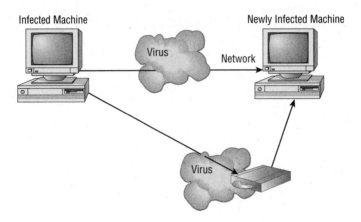

Many viruses spread using email. The infected system attaches a file to any email that you send to another user. The recipient opens this file, thinking it's something you legitimately sent them. When they open the file, the virus infects the target system. The virus might then attach itself to all of the emails that the newly infected system sends, which in turn infects the recipients of the emails. Figure 9.4 shows how a virus can spread from a single user to literally thousands of users in a very short time using email.

Quite a few of the newer viruses spread through USB thumb drives. An employee may see one lying about and plug it into a machine without realizing that it might contain a virus. This is such a problem that the Department of Defense has banned the use of thumb drives.

> For more information on thumb drives and viruses, see www.tomshardware .com/news/usb-flash-virus-secure,6564.html.

Types of Viruses

Viruses take many different forms. The following sections briefly introduce these forms and explain how they work. These are the most common types, but this list isn't comprehensive.

> The best defense against a virus attack is up-to-date antivirus software that is installed and running. The software should be on all workstations as well as the server. A whitelist of allowed applications should also be created and adhered to.

FIGURE 9.4   An email virus spreading geometrically to other users

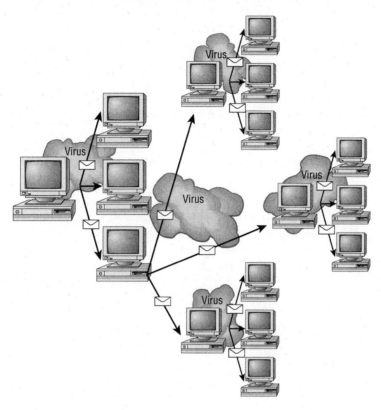

Armored Virus   An *armored virus* is designed to make itself difficult to detect or analyze. Armored viruses cover themselves with protective code that stops debuggers or disassemblers from examining critical elements of the virus. The virus may be written in such a way that some aspects of the programming act as a decoy to distract from analysis while the actual code hides in other areas in the program.

From the perspective of the creator, the more time it takes to deconstruct the virus, the longer it can live. The longer it can live, the more time it has to replicate and spread to as many machines as possible. The key to stopping most viruses is to identify them quickly and educate administrators about them—the very things that the armor intensifies the difficulty of accomplishing.

Companion Virus   A *companion virus* attaches itself to legitimate programs and then creates a program with a different filename extension. This file may reside in your system's temporary directory. When a user types the name of the legitimate program, the companion virus executes instead of the real program. This effectively hides the virus from the user. Many of the viruses that are used to attack Windows systems make changes to program pointers in the Registry so that they point to the infected program. The infected program may perform its dirty deed and then start the real program.

Macro Virus A *macro virus* exploits the enhancements made to many application programs that are used by programmers to expand the capability of applications such as Microsoft Word and Excel. Word, for example, supports a mini-BASIC programming language that allows files to be manipulated automatically. These programs in the document are called *macros*. For example, a macro can tell your word processor to spell-check your document automatically when it opens. Macro viruses can infect all of the documents on your system and spread to other systems via email or other methods. Macro viruses are the fastest-growing exploitation today.

Multipartite Virus A *multipartite virus* attacks your system in multiple ways. It may attempt to infect your boot sector, infect all of your executable files, and destroy your application files. The hope here is that you won't be able to correct all of the problems and this will allow the infestation to continue. The multipartite virus in Figure 9.5 attacks your boot sector, infects application files, and attacks your Word documents.

FIGURE 9.5 A multipartite virus commencing an attack on a system

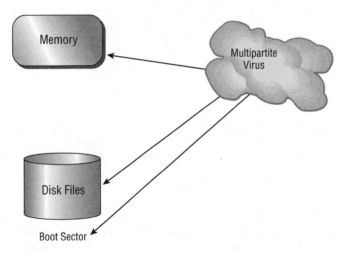

Phage Virus A *phage virus* modifies and alters other programs and databases. The virus infects all of these files. The only way to remove this virus is to reinstall the programs that are infected. If you miss even a single incident of this virus on the victim system, the process will start again and infect the system once more.

Polymorphic Virus *Polymorphic viruses* and *polymorphic malware* of any type—though viruses are the only ones truly prevalent—change form in order to avoid detection. These types of viruses attack your system, display a message on your computer, and delete files on your system. The virus will attempt to hide from your antivirus software. Frequently, the virus will encrypt parts of itself to avoid detection. When the virus does this, it's referred to as *mutation*. The mutation process makes it hard for antivirus software to detect common characteristics of the virus. Figure 9.6 uses a phrase to illustrate how the polymorphic virus changes characteristics to avoid detection. Like the phrase, small things within the virus are changed. In this example, the virus changes a signature to fool antivirus software.

FIGURE 9.6   The polymorphic virus changing its characteristics

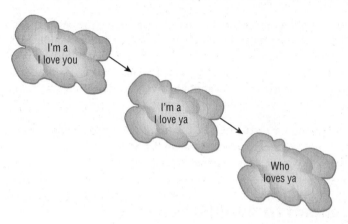

Retrovirus   A *retrovirus* attacks or bypasses the antivirus software installed on a computer. You can consider a retrovirus to be an anti-antivirus. Retroviruses can directly attack your antivirus software and potentially destroy your virus definition database file. Destroying this information without your knowledge would leave you with a false sense of security. The virus may also directly attack an antivirus program to create bypasses for itself.

Stealth Virus   A *stealth virus* attempts to avoid detection by masking itself from applications. It may attach itself to the boot sector of the hard drive. When a system utility or program runs, the stealth virus redirects commands around itself in order to avoid detection. An infected file may report a file size different from what is actually present in order to avoid detection. Figure 9.7 shows a stealth virus attaching itself to the boot sector to avoid detection. Stealth viruses may also move themselves from fileA to fileB during a virus scan for the same reason.

FIGURE 9.7   A stealth virus hiding in a disk boot sector

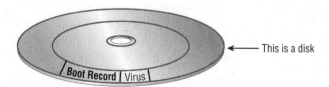

An updated list of the most active viruses and spyware is on the Panda
Software site at www.pandasecurity.com/homeusers/security-info
/default.aspx?lst=ac.

Present Virus Activity

New viruses and threats are released on a regular basis to join the cadre of those already
in existence. From an exam perspective, you need only be familiar with the world as it
existed at the time the questions were written. From an administration standpoint,
however, you need to know what is happening today. This book is current for virus activity up to the date of publication, but you should stay up-to-date on what has happened
since then.

To find out this information, visit the CERT/CC Current Activity web page at www.us-cert
.gov/current/current_activity.html. Here you'll find a detailed description of the
most current viruses as well as links to pages on older threats.

Managing Spam to Avoid Viruses

Although spam is not truly a virus or a hoax, it is one of the most annoying things with
which an administrator must contend. *Spam* is defined as any unwanted, unsolicited email,
and not only can the sheer volume of it be irritating, but it can also often open the door to
larger problems. For instance, some of the sites advertised in spam may be infected with
viruses, worms, and other unwanted programs. If users begin to respond to spam by visiting those sites, then viruses and other problems will multiply in your system.

There are numerous antispam programs available, and users as well as
administrators can run them. False positives are one of the biggest problems with many of these applications: They will occasionally flag legitimate email as spam and stop it from being delivered. You should routinely
check your spam folders and make sure that legitimate email is not being
inadvertently flagged as junk and held there.

Just as you can, and must, install good antivirus software programs, you should also
consider similar measures for spam. Filtering the messages out and preventing them
from ever entering the network is the most effective method of dealing with the problem.
Recently, the word *spam* has found its way into other forms of unwanted messaging beyond
email, giving birth to the acronyms *SPIM* (spam over instant messaging) and SPIT (spam
over Internet telephony).

Antivirus Software

The primary method of preventing the propagation of malicious code involves the use of *antivirus software.* Antivirus software is an application that is installed on a system to protect it and to scan for viruses as well as worms and Trojan horses. Most viruses have characteristics that are common to families of virus. Antivirus software looks for these characteristics, or fingerprints, to identify and neutralize viruses before they impact you. Most of the newer antivirus packages will now look for problems with cookies as well, as shown in the Norton Security Suite example in Figure 9.8.

FIGURE 9.8   Antivirus programs often look for problems beyond just viruses.

Thousands of known viruses, worms, logic bombs, and other malicious code have been defined. New ones are added all the time. Your antivirus software manufacturer will usually work very hard to keep the definition database files current. The definition database file contains all of the known viruses and countermeasures for a particular antivirus software product. You probably won't receive a virus that hasn't been seen by one of these companies. If you keep the virus definition database files in your software up-to-date, you probably won't be overly vulnerable to attacks.

The best method of protection is to use a layered approach. Antivirus software should be at the gateways, at the servers, and at the desktop. If you want to go one step further, you can use software at each location from different vendors to make sure that you're covered from all angles.

The second method of preventing viruses is user education. Teach your users not to open suspicious files and to open only those files that they're reasonably sure are virus-free. They need to scan every disk, email, and document they receive before they open them. You should also verify that the security settings are high within the applications that your users are using.

 Real World Scenario

How to Stop a Virus or Worm That Is Out of Control

A large private university has over 30,000 students taking online classes. These students use a variety of systems and network connections. The instructors of this university are being routinely hit with the Klez32 virus. Klez32 (specifically, in this case, the W32/Klez.mm virus) is a well-known and documented virus. It uses Microsoft Outlook or Outlook Express to spread. It grabs a name randomly from the address book, and it uses that name in the header. The worm part of it then uses a mini-mailer and mails the virus to all of the people in the address book. When one of these users opens the file, the worm attempts to disable their antivirus software and spread to other systems. Doing so opens the system to an attack from other viruses, which might follow later.

You've been appointed to the IT department at this school, and you've been directed to solve this problem. Take a moment to ponder what you can do about it.

If you think the best solution would be to install antivirus software that scans and blocks all emails that come through the school's servers, you are right. You should also inspect outgoing email and notify all internal users of the system when they attempt to send a virus-infected document using the server.

These two steps—installing antivirus scanners on the external and internal connections and notifying unsuspecting senders—would greatly reduce the likelihood that the virus could attack either student or instructor computers.

Understanding Various Types of Attacks

In computing, a lot of the terminology used comes from other fields, such as the military. That seems to be particularly true when it comes to security. Using that line of logic, an *attack* occurs when an unauthorized individual or group of individuals attempts to access, modify, or damage your systems or environment. These attacks can be fairly simple and unfocused, or they can appear to be almost blitzkrieg-like in their intensity.

One main reason for the differences in attacks is that they occur in many ways and for different reasons. Attackers have various reasons for initiating an attack. Here are a few:

- They might be doing it for the sheer fun of it.
- They might be criminals attempting to steal from you.
- They might be individuals or groups who are using the attack to make a political statement or commit an act of terrorism.

Regardless of their motive, your job is to protect the people you work with from these acts of aggression. You are, in many cases, the only person in your organization charged with the responsibility of repelling these attacks.

The following sections deal with the general types of attacks that you'll experience.

Identifying Denial-of-Service and Distributed Denial-of-Service Attacks

Denial-of-service (DoS) attacks prevent access to resources by users authorized to use those resources. An attacker may attempt to bring down an e-commerce website to prevent or deny usage by legitimate customers. Most simple DoS attacks occur from a single system, and a specific server or organization is the target.

 There isn't a single type of DoS attack but a variety of similar methods that have the same purpose. It's easiest to think of a DoS attack by imagining that your servers are so busy responding to false requests that they don't have time to service legitimate requests. Not only can the servers be physically busy, but the same result can also occur if the attack consumes all of the available bandwidth.

Several types of attacks can occur in this category. These attacks can do the following:

- Deny access to information, applications, systems, or communications.
- Bring down a website while the communications and systems continue to operate.
- Crash the operating system (a simple reboot may restore the server to normal operation).
- Fill the communications channel of a network and prevent access by authorized users.
- Open as many TCP sessions as possible; this type of attack is called a TCP SYN flood DoS attack.

Two of the most common types of DoS attacks are the *ping of death* and the *buffer overflow*. The ping of death crashes a system by sending Internet Control Message Protocol (ICMP) packets (think echoes) that are larger than the system can handle. Buffer overflow attacks, as the name implies, attempt to put more data (usually long input strings) into the buffer than it can hold. Code Red, Slapper, and Slammer are all attacks that took advantage of buffer overflows, and sPing is an example of a ping of death.

A *distributed denial-of-service (DDoS)* attack is similar to a DoS attack. A DDoS attack amplifies the concepts of a DoS attack by using multiple computer systems (often through botnets) to conduct the attack against a single organization. These attacks exploit the inherent weaknesses of dedicated networks such as DSL and cable. These permanently attached systems usually have little, if any, protection. An attacker can load an attack program onto dozens or even hundreds of computer systems that use DSL or cable modems. The attack program lies dormant on these computers until they get an attack signal from a master computer. The signal triggers the systems, which launch an attack simultaneously on the target network or system. DDoS attacks are common on the Internet, where they have hit large companies, and such attacks are often widely publicized in the media.

Figure 9.9 shows an attack occurring and the master controller orchestrating the attack. The master controller may be another unsuspecting user. The systems taking direction from the master control computer are referred to as *zombies* or *nodes*. These systems merely carry out the instruction they've been given by the master computer.

FIGURE 9.9   Distributed denial-of-service attack

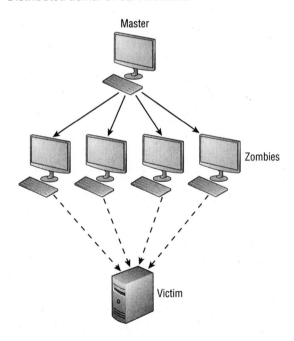

Remember that the difference between a DoS attack and a DDoS attack is that the latter uses multiple computers—all focused on one target. DDoS is far more common—and effective—today than DoS.

The nasty part of this type of attack is that the machines used to carry out the attack belong to normal computer users. The attack gives no special warning to those users. When the attack is complete, the attack program may remove itself from the system or infect the unsuspecting user's computer with a virus that destroys the hard drive, thereby wiping out the evidence.

Can You Prevent Denial Attacks?

In general, there is little you can do to prevent DoS or DDoS attacks. Many operating systems are particularly susceptible to these types of attacks. Fortunately, most operating system manufacturers have implemented updates to minimize their effects. Make sure your operating system and the applications you use are up-to-date.

Spoofing Attacks

A *spoofing* attack is an attempt by someone or something to masquerade as someone else. This type of attack is usually considered an access attack. A common spoofing attack that was popular for many years on early Unix and other timesharing systems involved a programmer writing a fake logon program. It would prompt the user for a user ID and password. No matter what the user typed, the program would indicate an invalid logon attempt and then transfer control to the real logon program. The spoofing program would write the logon and password into a disk file, which was retrieved later.

The most popular spoofing attacks today are IP spoofing, ARP spoofing, and DNS spoofing. With *IP spoofing*, the goal is to make the data look as if it came from a trusted host when it didn't (thus spoofing the IP address of the sending host).

With *ARP spoofing* (also known as *ARP poisoning*), the MAC (Media Access Control) address of the data is faked. By faking this value, it is possible to make it look as if the data came from a network that it did not. This can be used to gain access to the network, to fool the router into sending data here that was intended for another host, or to launch a DoS attack. In all cases, the address being faked is an address of a legitimate user, and that makes it possible to get around such measures as allow/deny lists.

With *DNS spoofing*, the DNS server is given information about a name server that it thinks is legitimate when it isn't. This can send users to a website other than the one to which they wanted to go, reroute mail, or do any other type of redirection wherein data from a DNS server is used to determine a destination. Another name for this is *DNS poisoning*, and Fast flux is one of the most popular techniques.

Always think of spoofing as fooling. Attackers are trying to fool the user, system, and/or host into believing they're something that they are not. Because the word *spoof* can describe any false information at any level, spoofing can occur at any level of network.

Another DNS weakness is *domain name kiting*. When a new domain name is issued, there is technically a five-day grace period before you must pay for it. Those engaged in kiting can delete the account within the five days and re-register it—allowing them to have accounts that they never have to pay for.

Figure 9.10 shows a spoofing attack occurring as part of the logon process on a computer network. The attacker in this situation impersonates the server to the client attempting to log in. No matter what the client attempts to do, the impersonating system will fail the login. When this process is finished, the impersonating system disconnects from the client. The client then logs into the legitimate server. In the meantime, the attacker now has a valid user ID and password.

FIGURE 9.10   A spoofing attack during logon

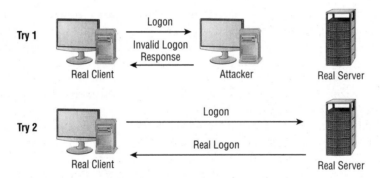

The important point to remember is that a spoofing attack tricks something or someone into thinking that something legitimate is occurring.

Pharming Attacks

Pharming is a form of redirection in which traffic intended for one host is sent to another. This can be accomplished on a small scale by changing entries in the hosts file and on a large scale by changing entries in a DNS server (the poisoning mentioned earlier). In either case, when a user attempts to go to a site they are redirected to another. An example of this would be Illegitimate Company ABC creating a site to look exactly like the one for Giant Bank XYZ. The pharming is done (using either redirect method), and users trying to reach Giant Bank XYZ are tricked into going to Illegitimate Company ABC's site, which looks enough like what they are used to seeing that they provide username and password data.

As soon as Giant Bank XYZ realizes that the traffic is being redirected, they will immediately move to stop it. Although Illegitimate Company ABC will be closed down, they were able to collect data for the length of time the redirection occurred, which could vary from minutes to days.

Phishing, Spear Phishing, and Vishing

Phishing is a form of social engineering in which you ask someone for a piece of information that you are missing by making it look as if it is a legitimate request. An email might look as if it is from a bank and contain some basic information, such as the user's name. In the email, it will often state that there is a problem with the person's account or access privileges. The user will be told to click a link to correct the problem. After they click the link—which goes to a site other than the bank's—they are asked for their username, password, account information, and so on. The person instigating the phishing can then use the values entered there to access the legitimate account.

One of the best counters to phishing is to simply mouse over the Click Here link and read the URL. Almost every time it is pointing to an adaptation of the legitimate URL as opposed to a link to the real thing.

Spear phishing is a unique form of phishing in which the message is made to look as if it came from someone you know and trust as opposed to an informal third party. For example, in a phishing attack, you would get a message that appears to be from Giant Bank XYZ telling you that there is a problem with your account and that you need to log in to rectify this right away. Such a message from someone you've never heard of would run a high risk of raising suspicion and thus generate a lower than desired rate of return for the phishers. With spear phishing, you might get a message that appears to be from your boss telling you that there is a problem with your direct deposit account and that you need to access this HR link right now to correct it.

Spear phishing works better than phishing because it uses information that it can find about you from email databases, friends lists, and the like.

When you combine phishing with Voice over IP (VoIP), it becomes known as *vishing*, and it is just an elevated form of social engineering. Crank calls have been in existence since the invention of the telephone, but the rise in VoIP now makes it possible for someone to call you from almost anywhere in the world, without the worry of tracing, caller ID, and other land-line features, and pretend to be someone they are not in order to get data from you.

Xmas Attack

Network mapping allows you to see everything that is available. The best-known network mapper is Nmap, which can run on all operating systems and is found at `http://nmap.org/`. One of the most popular attacks that uses Nmap is known as the *Xmas attack* (also more appropriately known as the *Xmas scan*), or Christmas Tree attack. This is an advanced scan that tries to get around firewall detection and look for open ports. It accomplishes this by setting three flags (`FIN`, `PSH`, and `URG`); understanding the intricacies of this is beyond what you need to know for the Security+ exam, but you can find out more about this attack at `http://nmap.org/` in the reference guide.

Man-in-the-Middle Attacks

Man-in-the-middle attacks clandestinely place something (such as a piece of software or a rouge router) between a server and the user about which neither the server's administrators nor the user is aware. The man-in-the-middle intercepts data and then sends the information to the server as if nothing is wrong. The server responds to the software, thinking it's communicating with a legitimate client. The attacking software continues sending information on to the server, and so forth.

If communication between the server and user continues, what's the harm of the software? The answer lies in whatever else the software is doing. The man-in-the-middle software may be recording information for someone to view later, altering it, or in some other way compromising the security of your system and session.

A man-in-the-middle attack is an active attack. Something is actively intercepting the data and may or may not be altering it. If it's altering the data, the altered data masquerades as legitimate data traveling between the two hosts.

Figure 9.11 illustrates a man-in-the-middle attack. Notice how both the server and client assume that the system they're talking to is the legitimate system. The man in the middle appears to be the server to the client, and it appears to be the client to the server.

FIGURE 9.11 A man-in-the-middle attack occurring between a client and a web server

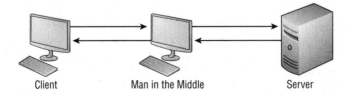

Client   Man in the Middle   Server

In recent years, the threat of man-in-the-middle attacks on wireless networks has increased. Because it's no longer necessary to connect to the wire, a malicious rogue can be outside the building intercepting packets, altering them, and sending them on. A common solution to this problem is to enforce a secure wireless authentication protocol such as WPA2.

An older term generically used for all man-in-the-middle attacks is *TCP/IP hijacking*.

TCP/IP hijacking involves the attacker gaining access to a host in the network and logically disconnecting it from the network. The attacker then inserts another machine with the same IP address. This happens quickly, and it gives the attacker access to the session and to all of the information on the original system. The server won't know this has occurred, and it will respond as if the client is trusted—the attacker forces the server to accept its IP address as valid. The hijacker will hope to acquire privileges and access to all of the information on the server. There is little you can do to counter this threat, but fortunately these attacks require fairly sophisticated software and are harder to engineer than a simple DoS attack.

Replay Attacks

Replay attacks are becoming quite common. They occur when information is captured over a network. A *replay attack* is a kind of access or modification attack. In a distributed environment, logon and password information is sent between the client and the authentication system. The attacker can capture the information and replay it later. This can also occur with security certificates from systems such as Kerberos: The attacker resubmits the certificate, hoping to be validated by the authentication system and circumvent any time sensitivity.

Figure 9.12 shows an attacker presenting a previously captured certificate to a Kerberos-enabled system. In this example, the attacker gets legitimate information from the client and records it. Then the attacker attempts to use the information to enter the system. The attacker later relays information to gain access.

FIGURE 9.12   A replay attack occurring

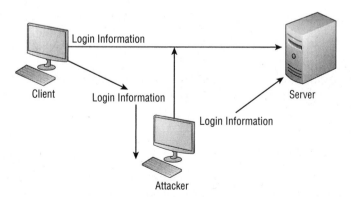

If this attack is successful, the attacker will have all of the rights and privileges from the original certificate. This is the primary reason that most certificates contain a unique session identifier and a time stamp. If the certificate has expired, it will be rejected and an entry should be made in a security log to notify system administrators.

Smurf Attacks

Smurf attacks can create havoc in a network. A *smurf attack* consists of spoofing the target machine's IP address and broadcasting to that machine's routers so that the routers think the target is sending out the broadcast. This causes every machine on the network to respond to the attack. The result is an overload of the target system.

Figure 9.13 shows a smurf attack under way in a network. The attacker sends a broadcast message with a legal IP address. In this case, the attacking system sends a ping request to the broadcast address of the network. The request is sent to all of the machines in a large network. The reply is then sent to the machine identified with the ICMP request (the spoof is complete). The result is a DoS attack that consumes the network bandwidth of the replying system while the victim system deals with the flood of ICMP traffic it receives.

FIGURE 9.13   A smurf attack under way against a network

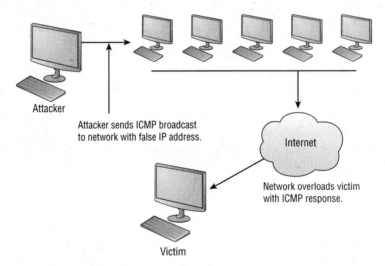

The primary method of eliminating smurf attacks involves prohibiting ICMP traffic through a router. If the router blocks ICMP traffic, smurf attacks from an external attacker aren't possible.

Password Attacks

Password attacks occur when an account is attacked repeatedly. This is accomplished by using applications known as *password crackers*, which send possible passwords to the account in a systematic manner. The attacks are initially carried out to gain passwords for an access or modification attack. There are several types of password attacks:

Brute-Force Attack A *brute-force* attack is an attempt to guess passwords until a successful guess occurs. As an example of this type of attack, imagine starting to guess with "A" and then going through "z"; when no match is found, the next guess series goes from "AA" to "zz" and then adds a third value ("AAA" to "zzz"). Because of the nature of this routine, this type of attack usually occurs over a long period of time. To make passwords more difficult to guess, they should be much longer than two or three characters (six should be the bare minimum), be complex, and have password lockout policies.

Dictionary Attack A *dictionary attack* uses a dictionary of common words to attempt to find the user's password. Dictionary attacks can be automated, and several tools exist in the public domain to execute them. As an example of this type of attack, imagine guessing words and word combinations found in a standard English-language dictionary.

Hybrid A *hybrid attack* typically uses a combination of dictionary entries and brute force. For example, if you know that there is a good likelihood that the employees of a particular company are using derivatives of the company name in their passwords, then you can seed those values into the values attempted.

Birthday Attack A *birthday attack* is built on a simple premise. If 25 people are in a room, there is some probability that two of those people will have the same birthday. The probability increases as additional people enter the room. It's important to remember that probability doesn't mean that something will occur, only that it's more likely to occur. To put it another way, if you ask if anyone has a birthday of March 9th, the odds are 1 in 365 (or 25/365 given the number of people in the room), but if you ask if anyone has the same birthday as any other individual, the odds of there being a match increase significantly.

Although two people may not share a birthday in every gathering, the likelihood is fairly high, and as the number of people increases, so too do the odds that there will be a match. A birthday attack works on the same premise: If your key is hashed, the possibility is that given enough time, another value can be created that will give the same hash value. Even encryption such as that with MD5 has been shown to be vulnerable to a birthday attack.

An easy way to think of a birthday attack is to think about how the hashing process works. It is possible for two different values to be hashed and give the same result, even though they differ from what was originally used.

Rainbow Table A *rainbow table attack* focuses on identifying a stored value. By using values in an existing table of hashed phrases or words (think of taking a word and hashing it every way you can imagine) and comparing them to values found, a rainbow table attack can reduce the amount of time needed to crack a password significantly. Salt (random bits added to the password) can greatly reduce the ease by which rainbow tables can be used.

Some systems will identify whether an account ID is valid and whether the password is wrong. Giving the attacker a clue as to a valid account name isn't a good practice. If you can enable your authentication to either accept a valid ID or password group or require the entire logon process again, you should.

Privilege Escalation

Privilege escalation involves a user gaining more privileges than they should have. With their elevated permissions, they can perform tasks they should not be allowed to do (such as delete files or view data). This condition is often associated with bugs left in software. When creating a software program, developers will occasionally leave a backdoor in the program that allows them to become a root user should they need to fix something during the debugging phase.

After debugging is done and before the software goes live, these abilities are removed. If a developer forgets to remove the backdoor in the live version and the method of accessing it gets out, it leaves the ability for an attacker to take advantage of the system.

To understand privilege escalation, think of cheat codes in video games. Once you know the game's code, you can enter it and become invincible. Similarly, someone might take advantage of a hidden cheat in a software application in order to become root.

 Real World Scenario

Responding to an Attack

As a security administrator, you know all about the different types of attacks that can occur, and you're familiar with the value assigned to the data on your system. Now imagine that the log files indicate that an intruder entered your system for a lengthy period last week while you were away on vacation.

The first thing you should do is to make a list of questions you should begin asking to deal with the situation, using your network as a frame of reference. The following list includes some of the questions you should consider:

1. How can you show that a break-in really occurred?

2. How can you determine the extent of what was done during the entry?

3. How can you prevent further entry?

4. Whom should you inform in your organization?

5. What should you do next?

Answers to these questions will be addressed throughout this book. The most important question on the list, though, is whom you should inform in your organization. It's important to know the escalation procedures without hesitation and to be able to act quickly.

One of the tools that can be used to look for holes is Microsoft Security Analyzer. This tool can scan a system and find missing updates and security misconfigurations. In Exercise 9.3, we'll show you how to use the Microsoft Security Analyzer to scan your system.

EXERCISE 9.3

Scanning with Microsoft Baseline Security Analyzer

The Microsoft Security Baseline Analyzer is a free tool downloadable from Microsoft that can scan a system and find any security holes. As of this writing, it runs on Windows versions from 8 back to Windows Server 2003. During a scan, it will look for missing security updates and operating system/software misconfigurations.

Once you have it installed, to scan a workstation with the Microsoft Security Baseline Analyzer follow these steps:

1. Start the Microsoft Security Baseline Analyzer. Depending on your version of Windows, the UAC may prompt you if you want to really run this program. Choose Yes to continue.

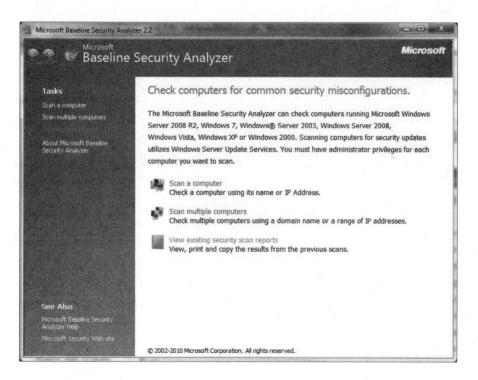

EXERCISE 9.3 *(continued)*

2. Make certain that the updates are current—if not, you will be notified by the Analyzer.

3. Choose Scan A Computer. You are given a choice about which computer to scan (which can be specified by computer name or IP address), with the default being this one. Make sure that all options are checked, and click Start Scan.

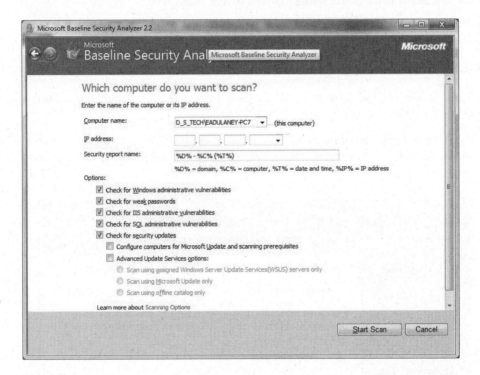

4. View the Report Details when the scan concludes. Items identified are classified in the various sections' vulnerabilities, with the worst offenses appearing first.

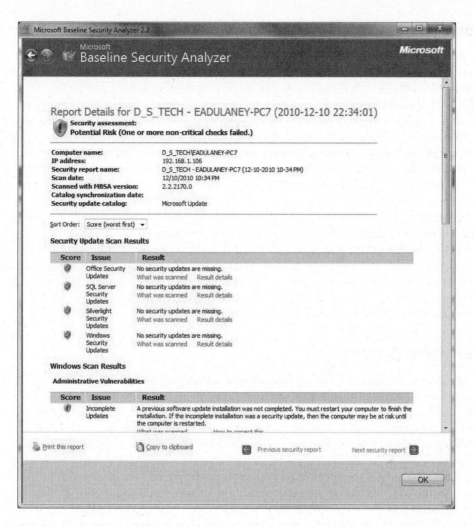

5. Look closely for any items appearing beneath Administrative Vulnerabilities. If an item has a link titled How To Correct This, click it and examine the issue, solution, and instructions.

6. Exit Microsoft Security Baseline Analyzer.

Malicious Insider Threats

One of the most dangerous threats to any network is an insider who is intent on doing harm. By being an insider, they've already gotten past your first defenses and they might be motivated by a desire to make someone pay for passing them over for a promotion, bored and looking for something to do, or driven by any of a plethora of other motivations. It may surprise you, but people can be bribed to give away information, and one of the toughest challenges is someone on the inside who is displeased with the company and not afraid to profit from it. This is known as a *malicious insider threat*, and it can be far more difficult to contend with than any outside threat since they already have access—both physical and login—to your systems.

If someone gives out the keys, you won't necessarily know it has occurred. Those keys can be literal (as in the keys to the back door) or figurative (the keys to decrypt messages).

Just as you must guard your systems from outside attackers, you also must protect them from malicious insiders. One approach to this is through *white box testing*. Using ethical hacking techniques, you begin testing your systems from the premise of knowing something about the network and systems in place—just as a malicious insider would. You try to find a weakness armed with information about the source code, the routing, and so on (this is also occasionally referred to as *full disclosure testing*).

Transitive Access

The word *transitive* means involving transition; it is necessary to understand this process in order to follow how transitive access problems occur. With *transitive access*, one party (A) trusts another party (B). If the second party (B) trusts another party (C), then a relationship may exist whereby the third party (C) is trusted by the first party (A).

In early operating systems, this process was often exploited. In later operating systems, such as Windows Server 2008, the problems with transitive access were solved by creating transitive trusts, which are a type of relationship that can exist between domains (the opposite is *nontransitive*). When the trust relationship is transitive, the relationship between party (A) and party (B) flows through as described earlier (that is, A now trusts C). In all versions of Active Directory, the default is that all domains in a forest trust each other with two-way transitive trust relationships.

While this process makes administration much easier when you add a new child domain (no administrative intervention is required to establish the trusts), it leaves open the possibility of a hacker acquiring more trust than they should by virtue of joining the domain. In Exercise 9.4, we'll explore how to validate the trust relationship in Windows Server—a step toward addressing this problem.

Validating a Trust Relationship

As an administrator, you should know what trust relationships exist between domains. To validate a trust relationship in Windows Server, follow these steps:

1. Open Active Directory Domains and Trusts.

2. Right-click your domain name, and choose Properties from the menu.

3. Click the Trusts tab, and select the name of the domain, or forest, that you want to validate.

4. Click Properties. The Properties dialog box for that trust appears.

5. Approximately two-thirds of the way down the dialog box, the Transitivity Of Trust item appears. Click Validate.

6. A confirmation message appears. Click OK.

7. Exit Active Directory Domains and Trusts.

Client-Side Attacks

A *client-side attack* is one that targets vulnerabilities in client applications that interact with a malicious server. A user accesses the trusted site—whether web, FTP, or almost anything else—and unwittingly downloads the rogue code (thinking they are downloading music, videos, and so forth). The rogue code allows the attacker to then install or execute programs on the affected machine remotely. What is relevant to the discussion on access is that the newly installed programs run with the privilege level of the individual who accessed the server. If that user had elevated privileges—a junior administrator, for example—then the malware runs at that level.

In most cases, the programs running try to reach beyond the workstation on which they are initially installed and find their way to the server(s). Often, data accessed along the way is pushed out across the Internet, using HTTPS to encrypt it and make it less likely to be detected.

Typo Squatting and URL Hijacking

Typo squatting (also spelled typosquatting) and *URL hijacking* are one and the same. Difficult to describe as an attack, this is the act of registering domains that are similar to those for a known entity but based on a misspelling or typographical error. As an example, a reader wanting to go to Sybex.com to find out additional information about this book would be visiting the publisher's site (hosted beneath Wiley, incidentally), but someone intending on doing harm could register Sybecks.com in the hopes that the same reader would misspell the word. Instead of arriving at the safe site of the publisher, they would end up at the other site, which could download Trojans, worms, and viruses—oh my.

The best defense against typo squatting is to register those domains around yours for which a user might intentionally type in a value when trying to locate you. This includes top-level domains as well (`.com`, `.biz`, `.net`, and so on) for all reasonable deviations of your site.

Watering Hole Attack

A *watering hole attack* can sound a lot more complicated than it really is. The strategy the attacker takes is simply to identify a site that is visited by those they are targeting, poisoning that site, and then waiting for the results.

As an example, suppose an attacker wants to gain unauthorized access to the servers at Spencer Industries, but Spencer's security is really good. The attacker discovers that Spencer does not host its own email, but instead outsources it to a big cloud provider, and so they focus their attention on the weaker security of the cloud provider. On the cloud provider's email site, they install the malware du jour, wait until a Spencer employee gets infected, and they suddenly have the access they coveted.

The best defense against a watering hole attack is to make certain that all of your partners are secure. Identify weak links, and bring them up to the same level of security as the rest of your infrastructure.

Identifying Types of Application Attacks

The operating systems, applications, and network products you deal with are usually secure when they're implemented the way the manufacturer intends but begin to differ after the actual implementation. For example, once you start reducing security settings to increase interoperability with other operating systems or applications, you start introducing weaknesses that may be exploited. This chapter deals with the process of ensuring that the products you use are as secure as they can be.

Cross-Site Scripting and Forgery

Using a client-side scripting language, it is possible for an attacker to trick a user who visits the site into having code execute locally. When this is done, it is known as *cross-site scripting (XSS)*. Let's look at an example. UserA gets a message telling him that he needs to make changes to his XYZ account, but the link in the message is not really to the XYZ site (a phishing ploy). When he visits the site, a script routine begins to run on his machine with his permissions and can begin doing such things as running malevolent routines to send, delete, or alter data.

In this attack, the perpetrator finds some place on a website where users can interact with each other. A product review section is ideal. Rather than put a comment into the input text field, the attacker types in some script, such as JavaScript. The next time a user visits that section of the website, the script is executed. The way to prevent this attack is to filter input, much like with SQL injection.

Cross-Site Request Forgery—also known as *XSRF*, session riding, and one-click attack—involves unauthorized commands coming from a trusted user to the website. This is often done without the user's knowledge, and it employs some type of social networking to pull it off.

For example, assume that Evan and Spencer are chatting through Facebook. Spencer sends Evan a link to what he purports is a funny video that will crack him up. Evan clicks the link, but it actually brings up Evan's bank account information in another browser tab, takes a screenshot of it, closes the tab, and sends the information to Spencer. The reason the attack is possible is because Evan is a trusted user with his own bank. In order for it to work, Evan would need to have recently accessed that bank's website and have a cookie that had yet to expire.

The best protection against cross-site scripting is to disable the running of scripts (and browser profiles).

SQL Injection

SQL (Structured Query Language) is the de facto language used for communicating with online (and other relational) databases. With a *SQL injection attack* (also known as a *SQL insertion attack*), an attacker manipulates the database code to take advantage of a weakness in it. For example, if the interface is expecting the user to enter a string value but it is not specifically coded that way, the attacker could enter a line of code and that code would then execute instead of being accepted as a string value.

Various types of exploits use SQL injection, and the most common fall into the following categories:

- Escape characters not filtered correctly
- Type handling not properly done
- Conditional errors
- Time delays

The way to defend against this attack is always to filter input. That means that the website code should check to see if certain characters are in the text fields and, if so, to reject that input.

Although the Security+ test won't ask you for details about this attack, it is useful for security professionals to know exactly how an attack is executed. Since SQL injection is such a common attack, this is an excellent one to understand.

SQL is used to communicate with a database, so it is common to have SQL statements executed when someone clicks a logon button. The SQL statements take the username and password entered, and they query the database to see if they are correct.

The problem begins with the way websites are written. They are written in some scripting, markup, or programming language, such as HTML (Hypertext Markup Language), PHP (PHP: Hypertext Preprocessor), ASP (Active Server Pages), and so on. These languages don't understand SQL, so the SQL statements are usually put into a string and whatever the user inputs in the username and password boxes is appended to that string. Here is an example:

```
"SELECT * FROM tblUSERS WHERE UserName ='" + txtUserName + "'"AND ~CA Password =
'"+password +"'"
```

Notice that single quotes are inserted into the text so that whatever the user types into username and password text fields is enclosed in quotes within the SQL query string, like this:

```
SELECT * FROM tblUSERS WHERE UserName ='admin' AND Password = 'password'';
```

Now the attacker will put a SQL statement into the username and password fields that is always true, like this:

```
' or '1' ='1
```

This results in a SQL query like this:

```
'SELECT * FROM tblUSERS WHERE UserName =''  or '1' ='1' AND Password = ''  or
'1' ='1''
```

So now it says to get all entries from table = tblUsers if the username is '' (blank) OR IF 1 =1. Since 1 always equals 1, the user is logged in. For more details, see this author's YouTube video on the topic: www.youtube.com/watch?v=HbjMqs_cN-A

LDAP Injection

Just as SQL injection attacks take statements that are input by users and exploit weaknesses within, an *LDAP injection attack* exploits weaknesses in LDAP (Lightweight Directory Access Protocol) implementations. This can occur when the user's input is not properly filtered, and the result can be executed commands, modified content, or results returned to unauthorized queries.

The best way to prevent LDAP injection attacks is to filter the user input and to use a validation scheme to make certain that queries do not contain exploits.

XML Injection

When a web user takes advantage of a weakness with SQL by entering values that they should not, it is known as a SQL injection attack. Similarly, when the user enters values that query XML (known as XPath) with values that take advantage of exploits, it is known as an *XML injection attack*. XPath works in a similar manner to SQL, except that it does not have the same levels of access control, and taking advantage of weaknesses within can return entire documents.

The best way to prevent XML injection attacks is to filter the user's input and sanitize it to make certain that it does not cause XPath to return more data than it should.

Directory Traversal/Command Injection

If an attacker is able to gain access to restricted directories (such as the root directory) through HTTP, it is known as a *directory traversal attack*. If the attacker can gain access to the root directory of a system (which is limited from all but administrative users), they can essentially gain access to everything on the system. Bear in mind that the root directory of a website is far from the true root directory of the server; an absolute path to the site's root directory is likely to be something in IIS (Internet Information Server), such as C:\ inetpub\wwwroot. If an attacker can get out of this directory and get to C:\windows, the possibility for inflicting harm is increased exponentially.

One of the simplest ways to perform directory traversal is by using a *command injection attack* that carries out the action. For example, exploiting a weak IIS implementation by calling up a web page along with the parameter cmd.exe?/c+dir+c:\ would call the command shell and execute a directory listing of the root drive (C:\). With Unicode support, entries such as %c%'c and %c°%af can be translated into / and \ respectively.

The ability to perform command injection is rare these days. Most vulnerability scanners will check for weaknesses with directory traversal/command injection and inform you of their presence. To secure your system, you should run such a scanner and keep the web server software patched.

Buffer Overflow

Buffer overflows occur when an application receives more data than it's programmed to accept. This situation can cause an application to terminate or to write data beyond the end of the allocated space. Termination may leave the system sending the data with temporary access to privileged levels in the attacked system, while overwriting can cause important data to be lost. This exploitation is usually the result of a programming error in the development of the software.

Buffer overflows, while a less common source of exploitation than in the past, are still quite common and continue to represent a large problem.

Integer Overflow

An *integer overflow*, like a buffer overflow, involves putting too much information into too small of a space. In this case, the space is that set aside for numbers.

For example, using 8 bits, it is possible to express any number in binary from 0 to 255. If only 8 bits are set aside and the user enters a value of 256 to be converted to binary, it exceeds what can be stored, represented, and so forth, and results in an integer overflow. Depending on how the code is written, it is possible that the program would store only the last eight digits (of what now requires nine—100000000) and thus the value would be accepted, processed, and stored as zero.

Zero-Day Exploits

When a hole is found in a web browser or other software and attackers begin exploiting it the very day it is discovered by the developer (bypassing the one-to-two-day response time that many software providers need to put out a patch once the hole has been found), it is known as a *zero-day exploit*. It is very difficult to respond to a zero-day exploit. If attackers learn of the weakness the same day as the developer, then they have the ability to exploit it until a patch is released. Often, the only thing that you as a security administrator can do, between the discovery of the exploit and the release of the patch, is to turn off the service. Although this can be a costly undertaking in terms of productivity, it is the only way to keep the network safe.

Several years ago, Stuxnet was found to be using a total of four zero-day vulnerabilities to spread:

```
www.symantec.com/connect/blogs/stuxnet-using-three-additional-zero-day-
vulnerabilities
```

Cookies and Attachments

Cookies are text files that a browser maintains on the user's hard disk in order to provide a persistent, customized web experience for each visit. A cookie typically contains information about the user. For example, a cookie can contain a client's history to improve customer service. If a bookstore wants to know your buying habits and what types of books you last viewed at its site, it can load this information into a cookie on your system. The next time you return to that store, the server can read your cookie and customize what it presents to you. Cookies can also be used to timestamp a user to limit access. A financial institution may send your browser a cookie once you've authenticated. The server can read the cookie to determine when a session is expired.

Obviously, cookies are considered a risk because they have the potential to contain your personal information, which could get into the wrong hands, and are highly treasured by advertisers today. A breed of cookie known as *evercookie* writes data to multiple locations to make it next to impossible ever to remove it completely (http://samy.pl/evercookie/).

If security is your utmost concern, the best protection is to not allow cookies to be accepted. Almost every browser offers the option of enabling or disabling cookies. If you enable them, you can usually choose whether to accept or reject all or only those from an originating server. Know that if you disallow cookies, users will not be able to visit a lot of sites. A compromise is to allow only session cookies.

Locally Shared Objects and Flash Cookies

A *Locally Shared Object (LSO)* is also commonly known as a *Flash Cookie* and is nothing more than data stored on a user's computer by Adobe Flash. Often this is used to store data from games that have been played through Flash or user preferences, and it can represent a security/privacy threat.

Malicious Add-Ons

There are any number of add-ons that have the potential to harm a system. Some do so unintentionally through poor programming, and some are truly *malicious add-ons*; the difference between them is intent.

Consider a Java applet, for example. This is a small, self-contained Java script that is downloaded from a server to a client and then run from the browser. The client browser must have the ability to run Java applets in a virtual machine on the client. Java applets are used extensively in web servers today, and they're becoming one of the most popular tools used for website development.

Java-enabled applications can accept programmed instructions (Java scripts) from a server and control certain aspects of the client environment. Java requires you to download a virtual machine in order to run the Java applications or applets. Java scripts run on the client.

The applets run in a restricted area of memory called the *sandbox*. The sandbox limits the applet's access to user areas and system resources. An applet that runs in the sandbox is considered *safe*, meaning that it won't attempt to gain access to sensitive system areas. Errors in the Java virtual machine that runs in the applications may allow some applets to run outside the sandbox. When this occurs, the applet is unsafe and may perform malicious operations. Attackers on client systems have exploited this weakness. From a user's standpoint, the best defense is to make certain that you run only applets from reputable sites with which you're familiar. From an administrator's standpoint, you should make certain that programmers adhere to programming guidelines when creating such applets.

Similarly, *ActiveX* is a technology that was implemented by Microsoft to customize controls, icons, and other features, which increases the usability of web-enabled systems. ActiveX runs on the client. It uses a method called Authenticode for security. *Authenticode* is a type of certificate technology that allows ActiveX components to be validated by a server.

ActiveX components are downloaded to the client hard disk, potentially allowing additional security breaches. Web browsers can be configured so that they require confirmation to accept an ActiveX control. However, many users don't understand these confirmation messages when they appear, and they automatically accept the components. Automatically accepting an ActiveX component or control creates the opportunity for security breaches on a client system when the control is used because an ActiveX control contains programming instructions that can contain malicious code or create vulnerabilities in a system.

> We highly recommend that you configure browsers so that they do not allow ActiveX to run without prompting the user because of the potential security hole that could be opened.

Session Hijacking

The term *session hijacking* describes when the item used to validate a user's session, such as a cookie, is stolen and used by another to establish a session with a host that thinks it is still communicating with the first party. To use an overly simplistic analogy, imagine that you just finished a long phone conversation with a family member and then accidentally left your smartphone in the room while stepping outside. If Jim were to pick up that phone and press redial, the family member would see the caller ID, know that they had just been talking with you, and falsely assume that you were calling back. If Jim could imitate your voice, he could rattle off numerous nasty comments that would jeopardize your relationship with that family member. This same premise could be true if someone could fool a host into thinking it was still talking to your computer rather than theirs.

Numerous types of attacks use session hijacking, including man-in-the-middle and sidejacking. A weakness in a Firefox extension made news when it became known that an exploit made it possible for public Wi-Fi users to fall prey to this type of attack (Firesheep was an extension created to take advantage of the weakness).

Some of the best ways to prevent session hijacking are to encrypt the sessions, encourage users to log out of sites when finished, and perform secondary checks on the identity of the user.

Header Manipulation

A *header manipulation* attack uses other methods discussed in this chapter (hijacking, cross-site forgery, and so forth) to change values in HTTP headers and falsify access. When used with XSRF, the attacker can even change a user's cookie. Internet Explorer 8 and above include *InPrivate Filtering* to help prevent some of this. By default, your browser sends information to sites as they need it—think of requesting a map from a site; it needs to know your location in order to give directions. With InPrivate Filtering, you can configure the browser not to share information that can be captured and manipulated.

Arbitrary Code and Remote Code Execution

Though long frowned upon, it is possible for a programmer to create a means by which a program that they write can remotely accept commands and execute them. These commands can be unrelated to the actual program accepting them, and they can run on the host machine within a shell, command interpreter, and so on. When this is done, it is known as either *arbitrary code execution* (since it is taking any arbitrary commands fed to it) or *remote code execution*—both meaning the same thing.

As if this issue is not bad enough in and of itself, the host program can be running with elevated privileges and capable of doing far more harm than what the user might otherwise be limited to.

Tools for Finding Threats

The focus of this section is on identifying security-related problems when they do occur. Intrusion detection and intrusion prevention, whether network based or local, provide key methods of identifying intrusions and notifying administrators when responses are needed. In addition to these monitors, you can create traps for those who violate security by building honeypots and honeynets that fool the intruders and allow you to track or catch them.

Interpreting Assessment Results

With all of the security assessment tools that exist, it is possible to collect a seemingly endless amount of data. More important than collecting the data, however, is filtering through it, correctly interpreting it, and responding appropriately to what you find.

To illustrate the problem with data: This author once worked for a company that supported independently run datacenters all around the nation. Operators were instructed each night to insert backup media and to initiate a routine that would do a full backup. When the process ended, they were to put the media in a rotation pile and take the paper printout and file it in a filing cabinet.

One evening, the inevitable happened and a center called to report that their hard drive had crashed. After replacing the failed drive, we instructed them how to get back up to speed and they pulled out the most recent backup and attempted to restore it—but there was nothing there to restore. We tried to keep them calm and walked them through the same procedure with the next most recent backup—again there was nothing to restore. It was at that point they were told to pull out the sheets of paper from the filing cabinet and verify that the backups were indeed made successfully. Every one of those pieces of paper said the same thing—media is write-protected; please try again. Even though the information was right there in front of them that the operations weren't being done correctly, they overlooked it.

The same thing can happen with security reports. What does it mean that port 23 is open on half of the servers—is it supposed to be? What does it mean that Telnet is being used once a week from a remote location—should it be? Unless you know what you're looking at and looking for, it is possible to go through the motions and arrive with nothing more than a false sense of security. The section that follows looks at some of the tools and techniques used to discover security threats and vulnerabilities. Evaluate each from the perspective of the exam and from what they might tell you about your own environment.

Tools to Know

There are seven bullets listed under the CompTIA objective for this section—not all are truly tools—but they all relate to finding security threats and vulnerabilities. Know that an active response is any that allows software to manage resources in the network if an incident occurs while a Passive response involves notification and reporting of attacks or suspicious activities.

Understanding Protocol Analyzers

The terms *protocol analyzer* and *packet sniffer* are interchangeable. They refer to the tools used in the process of monitoring the data that is transmitted across a network. See Chapter 3, "Understanding Devices and Infrastructure," for more information on this tool.

Working with Vulnerability Scanners

A *vulnerability scanner* is a software application that checks your network for any known security holes; it's better to run one on your own network before someone outside the organization runs it against you. Some of the most well-known vulnerability scanners are Nessus (www.nessus.org/nessus/) and Retina (www.eeye.com/Retina).

Vulnerability scanning involves looking for weaknesses in networks, computers, or even applications. Although the definition is much like that of penetration testing, there is usually one large difference: Penetration testing involves trying a number of things, whereas vulnerable scanning typically involves running a single program: a vulnerability scanner. The vulnerability scanner may be a port scanner (such as Nmap: http://nmap.org/), a network enumerator, a web application, or even a worm, but in all cases it runs tests on its target against a gamut of known vulnerabilities.

Retina and Nessus are two of the better-known vulnerability scanners, but SAINT and OpenVAS (which was originally based on Nessus) are also widely used. Regardless of the tool, there are five major tasks necessary in using them that CompTIA wants you to know for the Security+ exam:

Passively Testing Security Controls   The vulnerability scanner can test the security controls without doing any actual harm. It looks only for the openings that are there and reports them back to you. As such, its testing is considered to be passive as opposed to active.

Interpreting Results   Most of the vulnerability scanning programs, and the commercial ones in particular, interpret the results of their findings and deliver a report that can be shared with management.

Identifying Vulnerability   Just knowing that the port is open means little unless you can associate it with the vulnerability tied to it. For example, port 23 being open is a problem since it is commonly associated with Telnet.

Identifying Lack of Security Controls   Looking for weaknesses in security controls is well and good, but just as important is identifying areas where there are no controls in place. You want to know not just what is weak, but also what is missing altogether.

Identifying Common Misconfigurations   All too often, problems are introduced when perfectly good applications and services are improperly configured. Those misconfigurations can allow more users than should be permitted to access an application, cause the application to crash, or introduce any of a number of other security concerns.

Using Honeypots and Honeynets

A *honeypot* is a computer that has been designated as a target for computer attacks. There are several initiatives in the area of honeypot technology, and when they get larger, they are commonly referred to as *honeynets*. See Chapter 2 for more information on honeypots and honeynets.

Working with a Port Scanner

A TCP/IP network makes many of the ports available to outside users through the router. These ports respond in a predictable manner when queried. For example, TCP attempts synchronization when a session initiation occurs. An attacker can systematically query your network to determine which services and ports are open. This process is called *port scanning*, and it is part of fingerprinting a network; it can reveal a great deal about your systems. Port scans are possible both internally and externally. Many routers, unless configured appropriately, will let all protocols pass through them.

   Port scans help in identifying what services are running on a network.

   Individual systems within a network might also have applications and services running that the owner doesn't know about. These services could potentially allow an internal attacker to gain access to information by connecting to the port associated with those services. Many users don't realize the weak security that some web server products offer. If all of the security patches were not installed during installation, attackers can exploit the weaknesses and gain access to information. This has been done in many cases without the knowledge of the owner. These attacks might not technically be considered TCP/IP attacks, but they are because the inherent trust of TCP is used to facilitate the attacks.

After they know the IP addresses of your systems, external attackers can attempt to communicate with the ports open in your network, sometimes simply by using Telnet.

Using Telnet to Check a Port

To check whether a system has a particular protocol or port available, all you have to do is use the `telnet` command and add the port number. For example, you can check to see if a particular server is running an email server program by entering **telnet www .youreintrouble.com 25**. This initiates a Telnet connection to the server on port 25. If the server is running SMTP, it will immediately respond with logon information. It doesn't take much to figure out how to talk to SMTP; the interface is well documented. If an email account didn't have a password, this system is now vulnerable to attack.

This process of port scanning can be expanded to develop a footprint of your organization. If your attacker has a single IP address of a system in your network, they can probe all of the addresses in the range and probably determine what other systems and protocols your network is using. This allows the attacker to gain knowledge about the internal structure of your network.

    In a study done several years ago by the University of Maryland's A. James Clark School of Engineering, they found that 38 percent of attacks were preceded by vulnerability scans. The combination of port scans with vulnerability scans created a lethal combination that often led to an attack.

Banner Grabbing

As the name implies, *banner grabbing* looks at the banner, or header information messages sent with data to find out about the system(s). Banners often identify the host, the operating system running on it, and other information that can be useful if you are going to attempt to later breach the security of it. Banners can be snagged with Telnet as well as tools like netcat or Nmap.

Risk Calculations and Assessment Types

Chapter 1 discussed risk and focused on it in detail. From the standpoint of measuring security and vulnerability in the network, you need to focus on three things:

Risk   What is the actual danger under consideration? This is the likelihood of an attack being successful.

Threat   What are the likely dangers associated with the risk? What are the means and source of the potential attack? This needs to be weighed against the *likelihood* of an attack, which the NIST defines as "a weighted risk factor based on an analysis of the probability that a given threat is capable of exploiting a given vulnerability."

Vulnerability   Where is the system weak? Identify the flaws, holes, areas of exposure, and perils.

A number of generic techniques can prove useful in looking for risk, threat, and vulnerability, and this section looks at many of those. The following discussion focuses on baseline reporting, code review, determining the attack surface, architecture, and design review.

Baseline Reporting

The term *baseline reporting* became popular with legislation such as Sarbanes–Oxley, which requires IT to provide internal controls that reduce the risk of unauthorized transactions. As the name implies, baseline reporting checks to make sure that things are operating status quo, and change detection is used to alert administrators when modifications are made. A changes-from-baseline report can be run to pinpoint security rule breaches quickly.

This is often combined with gap analysis to measure the controls at a particular company against industry standards. One popular tool for baseline reporting is CA Policy and Configuration Manager (www.ca.com).

Code Review

The purpose of *code review* is to look at all custom written code for holes that may exist. The review needs also to examine changes that the code—most likely in the form of a finished application—may make: configuration files, libraries, and the like. During this examination, look for threats such as opportunities for injection to occur (SQL, LDAP, code, and so on), cross-site request forgery, and authentication.

Code review is often conducted as a part of gray box testing. Looking at source code can often be one of the easiest ways to find weaknesses within the application. Simply reading the code is known as *manual assessment*, whereas using tools to scan the code is known as *automated assessment*.

Determine Attack Surface

The *attack surface* of an application is the area of that application that is available to users—those who are authenticated and, more importantly, those who are not. As such, it can include the services, protocols, interfaces, and code. The smaller the attack surface, the less visible the application is to attack; the larger the attack surface, the more likely it is to become a target. The goal of *attack surface reduction (ASR)* is to minimize the possibility of exploitation by reducing the amount of code and limiting potential damage. The potential damage can be limited by turning off unnecessary functions, reducing privileges, limiting entry points, and adding authentication requirements.

The attack surface concept can extend beyond an application to anywhere that problems may exist, and the word preceding it merely changes to identify the scope—for example, network attack surface, organization attack surface, and the like.

Architecture

An *architectural approach* to security involves using a control framework to focus on the foundational infrastructure. This approach is popular with security regulatory standards as well as compliance standards (such as ISO). One example of this approach is Cisco's SAFE: (www.cisco.com/en/US/docs/solutions/Enterprise/Security/SAFE_RG/SAFE_rg.html).

The Security Control Framework is the backbone of SAFE, and unification is the underlying key (rather than a silo approach) to security. By being modular, it can incorporate all parts of the network, including the WAN, the extranet, the Internet, and the intranet.

Design Review

The *design review* assessment examines the ports and protocols used, the rules, segmentation, and access control. Design assessments tend to be more granular than architectural assessments, and they should be done more often. We recommend that you then incorporate examinations of information access control across all other areas of security.

Summary

This chapter focused on the various threats and vulnerabilities you'll encounter. We covered:

- Types of malware
- Types of attacks
- Types of application attacks
- Tools and techniques for discovering security threats and vulnerabilities

Some of the attacks discussed are denial-of-service, distributed denial-of-service, backdoor attacks, spoofing attacks, man-in-the-middle attacks, and replay attacks. These are just some of the attacks you may encounter. Each takes advantage of inherent weaknesses in the network technologies most commonly used today.

Malicious code describes an entire family of software that has nefarious intentions about your networks and computers. This includes viruses, Trojan horses, logic bombs, and worms. Viruses and worms are a major problem on the Internet.

Exam Essentials

Be able to describe the various types of attacks to which your systems are exposed. Your network is vulnerable to DoS attacks caused by either a single system or multiple systems. Multiple-system attacks are called DDoS. Your systems are also susceptible to access, modification, and repudiation attacks.

Be able to describe the methods used to conduct a backdoor attack.   Backdoor attacks occur using either existing maintenance hooks or developmental tools to examine the internal operations of a program. These hooks are usually removed when a product is prepared for market or production. Backdoor attacks also refer to inserting into a machine a program or service that allows authentication to be bypassed and access gained.

Know how a spoofing attack occurs.   Spoofing attacks occur when a user or system masquerades as another user or system. Spoofing allows the attacker to assume the privileges and access rights of the real user or system.

Be able to describe a man-in-the-middle attack.   Man-in-the-middle attacks are based on the principle that a system can be placed between two legitimate users to capture or exploit the information being sent between them. Both sides of the conversation assume that the man in the middle is the other end and communicate normally. This creates a security breach and allows unauthorized access to information.

Be able to describe a replay attack.   A replay attack captures information from a previous session and attempts to resend it to gain unauthorized access. This attack is based on the premise that if it worked once, it will work again. This is especially effective in environments where a user ID and password are sent in the clear across a large network.

Be able to describe the methods used in password guessing.   The methods used to guess passwords are brute force, dictionary, and hybrids. Brute-force attacks work by randomly trying to guess a password repeatedly against a known account ID. In a dictionary attack, a dictionary of common words is used to attempt to find a user's password. The best example of a hybrid attack uses a rainbow table of stored hash values to test against the password values.

Know how software exploitation occurs.   Software exploitation involves using features or capabilities of a software product in a manner either unplanned for or unanticipated by the software manufacturer. In many cases, the original feature enhanced the functionality of the product but, unfortunately, created a potential vulnerability.

Know the characteristics and types of viruses used to disrupt systems and networks.   Several different types of viruses are floating around today. The most common ones are polymorphic viruses, stealth viruses, retroviruses, multipartite viruses, and macro viruses.

Be able to explain the characteristics of Trojan horses and logic bombs.   Trojan horses are programs that enter a system or network under the guise of another program. Logic bombs are programs or snippets of code that execute when a certain predefined event occurs.

Be able to describe how antivirus software operates.   Antivirus software looks for a signature in the virus to determine what type of virus it is. The software then takes action to neutralize the virus based on a virus definition database. Virus definition database files are regularly made available on vendor sites.

Know the difference between an active response and a passive response.   An active response allows software to manage resources in the network if an incident occurs. Passive responses involve notification and reporting of attacks or suspicious activities.

Review Questions

1. You are the senior administrator for a bank. A user calls you on the telephone and says that they were notified to contact you but couldn't find your information on the company website. Two days ago, an email told them that there was something wrong with their account and that they needed to click a link in the email to fix the problem. They clicked the link and filled in the information, but now their account is showing a large number of transactions that they did not authorize. They were likely the victims of what type of attack?

   A. Spimming

   B. Phishing

   C. Pharming

   D. Escalating

2. As the security administrator for your organization, you must be aware of all types of attacks that can occur and plan for them. Which type of attack uses more than one computer to attack the victim?

   A. DoS

   B. DDoS

   C. Worm

   D. UDP attack

3. An alert signals you that a server in your network has a program running on it that bypasses authorization. Which type of attack has occurred?

   A. DoS

   B. DDoS

   C. Backdoor

   D. Social engineering

4. An administrator at a sister company calls to report a new threat that is making the rounds. According to him, the latest danger is an attack that attempts to intervene in a communications session by inserting a computer between the two systems that are communicating. Which of the following types of attacks does this constitute?

   A. Man-in-the-middle attack

   B. Backdoor attack

   C. Worm

   D. TCP/IP hijacking

5. You've discovered that an expired certificate is being used repeatedly to gain logon privileges. Which type of attack is this most likely to be?

   A. Man-in-the-middle attack

   B. Backdoor attack

    C. Replay attack

    D. TCP/IP hijacking

6. A smurf attack attempts to use a broadcast ping on a network; the return address of the ping may be a valid system in your network. Which protocol does a smurf attack use to conduct the attack?

    A. TCP

    B. IP

    C. UDP

    D. ICMP

7. Which type of attack denies authorized users access to network resources?

    A. DoS

    B. Worm

    C. Logic bomb

    D. Social engineering

8. Your system has just stopped responding to keyboard commands. You noticed that this occurred when a spreadsheet was open and you connected to the Internet. Which kind of attack has probably occurred?

    A. Logic bomb

    B. Worm

    C. Virus

    D. ACK attack

9. You're explaining the basics of security to upper management in an attempt to obtain an increase in the networking budget. One of the members of the management team mentions that they've heard of a threat from a virus that attempts to mask itself by hiding code from antivirus software. What type of virus is she referring to?

    A. Armored virus

    B. Polymorphic virus

    C. Worm

    D. Stealth virus

10. What kind of virus could attach itself to the boot sector of your disk to avoid detection and report false information about file sizes?

    A. Trojan horse virus

    B. Stealth virus

    C. Worm

    D. Polymorphic virus

11. Your system log files report an ongoing attempt to gain access to a single account. This attempt has been unsuccessful to this point. What type of attack are you most likely experiencing?

    A. Password-guessing attack

    B. Backdoor attack

    C. Worm attack

    D. TCP/IP hijacking

12. What type of attack uses other methods (hijacking, cross-site forgery, and so forth) to change values in HTTP headers and falsify access?

    A. Enticement

    B. Header Manipulation

    C. Class Helper

    D. UTM

13. What is a system that is intended or designed to be broken into by an attacker called?

    A. Honeypot

    B. Honeybucket

    C. Decoy

    D. Spoofing system

14. What is it known as when an attacker manipulates the database code to take advantage of a weakness in it?

    A. SQL tearing

    B. SQL manipulation

    C. SQL cracking

    D. SQL injection

15. If an attacker is able to gain access to restricted directories (such as the root directory) through HTTP, it is known as:

    A. Cross-site forgery

    B. Directory traversal

    C. Root hardening

    D. Trusted platform corruption

16. What term describes when the item used to validate a user's session, such as a cookie, is stolen and used by another to establish a session with a host that thinks it is still communicating with the first party?

    A. Patch infiltration

    B. XML injection

    C. Session hijacking

    D. DTB exploitation

17. Which of the following involves unauthorized commands coming from a trusted user to the website?

    A. ZDT

    B. HSM

    C. TT3

    D. XSRF

18. Which of the following is the name used for looking at the header information sent with data to find out what operating system a host is running?

    A. Port scanning

    B. Vishing

    C. Banner grabbing

    D. Transitive attack

19. Which type of tool would best describe Nmap?

    A. Port scanner

    B. Vulnerability scanner

    C. Banner grabber

    D. Honeynet

20. When a hole is found in a web browser or other software, and attackers begin exploiting it the very day it is discovered by the developer, what type of attack is it known as?

    A. Polymorphic

    B. Xmas

    C. Malicious insider

    D. Zero-day

Chapter

10

Social Engineering and Other Foes

THE FOLLOWING COMPTIA SECURITY+ EXAM OBJECTIVES ARE COVERED IN THIS CHAPTER:

✓ **2.7 Compare and contrast physical security and environmental controls.**

- Environmental controls: HVAC; Fire suppression; EMI shielding; Hot and cold aisles; Environmental monitoring; Temperature and humidity controls

- Physical security: Hardware locks; Mantraps; Video surveillance; Fencing; Proximity readers; Access list; Proper lighting; Signs; Guards; Barricades; Biometrics; Protected distribution (cabling); Alarms; Motion detection

- Control types: Deterrent; Preventive; Detective; Compensating; Technical; Administrative

✓ **3.3 Summarize social engineering attacks and the associated effectiveness with each attack.**

- Shoulder surfing

- Dumpster diving

- Tailgating

- Impersonation

- Hoaxes

- Whaling

- Vishing

- Principles (reasons for effectiveness): Authority; Intimidation; Consensus/Social proof; Scarcity; Urgency; Familarity/liking; Trust

✓ **3.6 Analyze a scenario and select the appropriate type of mitigation and deterrent techniques.**

    ▪ Detection controls vs. prevention controls: Camera vs. guard

✓ **4.3 Given a scenario, select the appropriate solution to establish host security.**

    ▪ Hardware security: Cable locks; Safe; Locking cabinets

✓ **4.4 Implement the appropriate controls to ensure data security.**

    ▪ Data policies: Wiping; Disposing; Retention; Storage

✓ **5.2 Given a scenario, select the appropriate authentication, authorization, or access control.**

    ▪ Identification: Biometrics

Keeping computers and networks secure involves more than just the technical aspects of the systems and networks. The weakest link in many cases is the user who has access to data and a less-than-complete understanding of security problems they may encounter.

As a security professional, you must address the issue of user weakness using a balanced response from both a technical and business perspective. It is your responsibility to keep the data safe, and if that means training the users in addition to implementing tighter network security, then, as Lady Macbeth so eloquently put it, "Screw your courage to the sticking-place, and we'll not fail."

This chapter will help you understand the complexities of managing security and the issues involved with social engineering, physical security, and data policies.

Understanding Social Engineering

Social engineering is the process by which intruders gain access to your facilities, your network, and even your employees by exploiting the generally trusting nature of people. A social engineering attack may come from someone posing as a vendor, or it could take the form of an email from a (supposedly) traveling executive who indicates that they have forgotten how to log on to the network or how to get into the building over the weekend. It's often difficult to determine whether the individual is legitimate or has bad intentions.

 Occasionally, social engineering is also referred to as *wetware*. This term is used because it is a form of hacking that does not require software or hardware but rather the gray matter of the brain.

Social engineering attacks can develop subtly. They're also hard to detect. Let's look at some classic social engineering attacks.

Someone enters your building wearing a white lab jacket with a logo on it. He also has a toolkit. He approaches the receptionist and identifies himself as a copier repairman from a major local copier company. He indicates that he's here to do preventive service on your copier. In most cases, the receptionist will let him pass and tell him the location of the copier. Once the "technician" is out of sight, the receptionist probably won't give him a second thought. Your organization has just been the victim of a social engineering attack. The attacker has now penetrated your first and possibly even your second layer of security. In many offices, including security-oriented offices, this individual would have access to the entire organization and would be able to pass freely anywhere he wanted. This attack didn't take any particular talent or skill other than the ability to look like a copier repairman. *Impersonation* can go a long way in allowing access to a building or network.

Another social engineering attack actually happened at a high-security government installation. Access to the facility required passing through a series of manned checkpoints. Professionally trained and competent security personnel manned these checkpoints. An employee decided to play a joke on the security department: He took an old employee badge, cut his picture out of it, and pasted in a picture of Mickey Mouse. He was able to gain access to the facility for two weeks before he was caught.

Social engineering attacks like these are easy to accomplish in most organizations. Even if your organization uses biometric devices, magnetic card strips, or other electronic measures, social engineering attacks are still relatively simple.

Famed hacker Kevin Mitnick wrote a book called *The Art of Deception: Controlling the Human Element of Security* (Wiley, 2002) in which 14 of 16 chapters are devoted to social engineering scenarios that have played out. If nothing else, the fact that one of the most notorious hackers—who could write on any security subject he so desired—chose to write a book on social engineering should make the importance of this topic abundantly clear.

More recently, Christopher Hadnagy wrote a book on the topic called *Social Engineering: The Art of Human Hacking* (Wiley, 2010). It is highly recommended reading for any administrator, security or otherwise.

Types of Social Engineering Attacks

As an administrator, one of your responsibilities is to educate users on how to avoid falling prey to social engineering attacks. They should know the security procedures that are in place and follow them to a tee. You should also have a high level of confidence that the correct procedures are in place, and one of the best ways to obtain that confidence is to check on your users occasionally.

Preventing social engineering attacks involves more than just providing training on how to detect and prevent them. It also involves making sure that people stay alert. Here's a list of some of the most common attacks:

Shoulder Surfing One popular form of social engineering is known as *shoulder surfing*, and it involves nothing more than watching someone "over their shoulder" when they enter their sensitive data (as illustrated in Figure 10.1). They can see you entering a password, typing in a credit card number, or entering any other pertinent information. The best defense against this type of attack is to survey your environment before entering personal data. It is a good idea for users not to have their monitors positioned in ways that make it easy for this act to occur, but they also need to understand and appreciate that such an attack can occur away from the desk as well: in any public location where they sit with their laptops, at business travel centers in hotels, at ATMs, and so on.

Passwords entered on Apple products by default display the last letter entered as convenience to the user. Unfortunately, this increases the dangers posed by shoulder surfing. *Privacy filters*, which go over the screen and restrict the viewing angle to straight on, can be used to decrease the success of shoulder surfing.

Dumpster Diving *Dumpster diving*, illustrated in Figure 10.2, is a common physical access method. Companies normally generate a huge amount of paper, most of which eventually winds up in dumpsters or recycle bins. Dumpsters may contain information that is highly sensitive in nature. In high-security and government environments, sensitive papers are either shredded or burned. Most businesses don't do this. In addition, the advent of "green" companies has created an increase in the amount of recycled paper, which can often contain all sorts of juicy information about a company and its employees.

Tailgating A favorite method of gaining entry to electronically locked systems is to follow someone through the door they just unlocked, a process known as *tailgating*. Many people don't think twice about this event—it happens all the time—as they hold the door open for someone behind them who is carrying heavy boxes or is disabled in some way (see Figure 10.3).

FIGURE 10.1 An example of shoulder surfing

FIGURE 10.2 An example of dumpster diving

FIGURE 10.3 An example of tailgating

Impersonation   As mentioned at the beginning of the chapter, *impersonation* involves any act of pretending to be someone you are not. This can be a service technician, a pizza delivery driver, a security guard, or anyone else who might be allowed unfettered access to the grounds, network, or system. Impersonation can be done in person, over the phone, by email, and so forth.

Hoaxes   Network users have plenty of real viruses to worry about. Yet some people find it entertaining to issue phony threats to keep people on their toes. Some of the more popular *hoaxes* (as illustrated in Figure 10.4) that have been passed around are the Good Time and the Irina viruses. Millions of users received emails about these two viruses, and the symptoms sounded just awful.

Both of these viruses claimed to do things that are impossible to accomplish with a virus. When you receive a virus warning, you can verify its authenticity by looking on the website of the antivirus software you use, or you can go to several public systems. One of the more helpful sites to visit to get the status of the latest viruses is that of the CERT organization (www.cert.org). CERT monitors and tracks viruses and provides regular reports on this site.

Though the site names are similar, there is a difference between cert .org and us-cert.gov. The latter is a government site for the United States Computer Emergency Readiness Team, and the former is a federally funded research and development center at Carnegie Mellon University.

FIGURE 10.4   Falsely sounding an alarm is a type of hoax.

When you receive an email that you suspect is a hoax, check the CERT site before forwarding the message to anyone else. The creator of the hoax wants to spread panic, and if you blindly forward the message to co-workers and acquaintances, you're helping the creator accomplish this task. For example, any email that says "forward to all your friends" is a candidate for hoax research. Disregarding the hoax allows it to die a quick death and keeps users focused on productive tasks. Any concept that spreads quickly through the Internet is referred to as a *meme*.

> Symantec and other vendors maintain pages devoted to bogus hoaxes (www.symantec.com/business/security_response/threatexplorer/risks/hoaxes.jsp). You can always check there to verify whether an email you've received is indeed a hoax.

Whaling   *Whaling* is nothing more than phishing or spear phishing (both of which are discussed in Chapter 9, "Malware, Vulnerabilities, and Threats") but for big users. Instead of sending out a To Whom It May Concern message to thousands of users, the whaler identifies one person from whom they can gain all the data they want—usually a manager or owner—and targets the phishing campaign at them.

Vishing   When you combine phishing with Voice over IP (VoIP), it becomes known as *vishing*, an elevated form of social engineering. Although crank calls have been in existence since the invention of the telephone, the rise in VoIP now makes it possible for someone to call you from almost anywhere in the world, without worrying about tracing, caller ID, and other land line–related features. They then pretend to be someone they are not in order to get data from you. Figure 10.5 shows an example of vishing in action.

FIGURE 10.5   An example of vishing

From an exam perspective, one of the best things about most of these types of attacks is that the name telegraphs the predicament. As an IT administrator you have no way of preventing someone from trying these tactics against your company, but educating users about them is the best way to prevent them from being successful. The more people are aware of their presence and potential harm, the more likely they can help thwart such attacks since the ultimate objective is to gain unauthorized access to information.

From a real-world perspective, a number of tools are available that can help limit the success of social engineering attacks. Figure 10.6 shows the opening screen for Microsoft SmartScreen Filter, which is included with newer versions of Internet Explorer. Most browsers include a similar feature, and they work by checking websites a user wishes to visit against a database of known questionable sites and warns them if they find a match.

FIGURE 10.6   SmartScreen can help identify troublesome sites.

The phishing filter in Internet Explorer can be turned on or off, or the entire filter can be disabled. To turn on automatic website checking, follow these steps:

1. In Internet Explorer, click Tools ➢ Internet Options and choose the Advanced tab.
2. Scroll down beneath Settings to Security.
3. Click Enable SmartScreen Filter.
4. Click OK.
5. A message appears telling you that website addresses will be sent to Microsoft and checked against a database of reported phishing websites. Click OK.
6. Exit the Internet Options.

What Motivates an Attack?

Social engineering is easy to do, even with all of today's technology to prevent it. Education is the key. Educate users on the reasons why someone would attempt to gain access to data and how the company can be negatively affected by it. Educate them on the simple procedures in which they can engage such as stopping tailgating to increase security. It is surprising how helpful users can be once they understand the reasons why they're being asked to follow certain procedures.

Don't overlook the most common personal motivator of all: greed. It may surprise you, but people can be bribed to give away information, and one of the toughest challenges is someone on the inside who is displeased with the company and eager to profit from it. This is known as a *malicious insider threat*, and it can be far more difficult to contend with than any outside threat since they already have access—both physical and login access—to your systems.

If someone gives out the keys, you won't necessarily know it has occurred. Those keys can be literal (as in the keys to the back door) or figurative (the keys to decrypt messages).

It is often a comforting thought to think that we cannot be bought. We look to our morals and standards and think that we are above being bribed. The truth of the matter, though, is that almost everyone has a price. Your price may be so high that for all practical purposes you don't have an amount that anyone in the market would pay, but can the same be said for the other administrators in your company?

Social engineering can have a hugely damaging effect on a security system. Always remember that a social engineering attack can occur over the phone, by email, or by a visit. The intent is to acquire access information, such as user IDs and passwords.

Always think of a social engineering attack as one that involves people who are unwitting.

The Principles Behind Social Engineering

A number of principles, or elements, allow social engineering attacks to be effective. Most of these are based on our nature to be helpful, to trust others in general, and to believe that there is a hierarchy of leadership that should be followed. For the exam, be familiar with the following reasons for its effectiveness:

Authority   If it is possible to convince the person you are attempting to trick that you are in a position of authority, they may be less likely to question your request. That position of authority could be upper management, tech support, HR, or law enforcement.

Intimidation   Although authority can be a source of intimidation, it is possible for intimidation to occur in its absence as well. This can be done with threats, with shouting, or even with guilt.

Consensus/Social Proof   Putting the person being tricked at ease by putting the focus on them—listening intently to what they are saying, validating their thoughts, charming them—is the key to this element. The name comes from a desire that we all have to be told that we are right, attractive, intelligent, and so forth, and we tend to be fond of those who confirm this for us. By being so incredibly nice, the social engineer convinces the other party that there is no way their intentions could possibly be harmful.

Discussions at home with a spouse, or casual conversations with associates where we are bragging or trying to impress others, can lead to sharing more information than we should.

Scarcity   Convincing the person who is being tricked that there is a limited supply of something can often be effective if carefully done. For example, convincing them that there are only one hundred vacation requests that will be honored for the entire year and that they need to go to a fictitious website now and fill out their information (including username and password, of course) if they want to take a vacation anytime during the current year, can dupe some susceptible employees.

More than one principle can be used in any given attack. It is not uncommon, for example, to see both scarcity and urgency used together.

Urgency   The secret for successfully using the urgency element is for the social engineer to convince the individual they are attempting to trick that time is of the essence. If they don't do something right away, money will be lost, a nonexistent intruder will get away, the company will suffer irreparable harm, or a plethora of other negative possibilities may occur.

Familiarity/Liking   Mental guards are often lowered, many times subconsciously, when we are dealing with other individuals that we like. The "like" part can be gained by someone having, or pretending to have, the same interests as we do, be engaged in the same activities, or otherwise working to gain positive attention.

Trust   One of the easiest ways to gain trust is through reciprocation. When someone does something for you, there is often a feeling that you owe that person something. For example, to gain your trust someone may help you out of a troublesome situation or buy you lunch.

Social Engineering Attack Examples

Social engineering attacks are relatively low tech and are more akin to con jobs. Here are a few examples.

Your help desk gets a call at 4 a.m. from someone purporting to be a vice president at your company. She tells the help desk personnel that she is out of town to attend a meeting, that her computer just failed, and that she is sitting in a Kinko's trying to get a file from her desktop computer back at the office. She can't seem to remember her password and user ID.

She tells the help desk representative that she needs access to the information right away or the company could lose millions of dollars. Your help desk rep believes the caller and gives the vice president her user ID and password over the phone instead of calling IT. You've been hit!

Another common approach is initiated by a phone call or email from someone claiming to be one of your software vendors, telling you that they have a critical fix that must be installed on your computer system. If this patch isn't installed right away, your system will crash and you'll lose all your data. For some reason, you've changed your maintenance account password, and they can't log on. Your systems operator gives the password to the person instead of calling IT. You've been hit again.

 Users are bombarded with emails and messages on services such as Pay-Pal asking them to confirm their password. These attacks appear to come from the administrative staff of the network. The attacker already has the user ID or screen name, and all that they need to complete the attack is the password. Make sure that your users never give out their user IDs or passwords. Either case potentially completes an attack.

With social engineering, the villain doesn't always have to be seen or heard to conduct the attack. The use of email was mentioned earlier, and in recent years the frequency of attacks via instant messaging has also increased thanks to social media. Attackers can send infected files over *instant messaging (IM)* as easily as they can over email, and this can occur in Facebook, MySpace, or anywhere else that IM is possible. A recent virus on the scene accesses a user's IM client and uses the infected user's friend's list to send messages to other users and infect their machines as well.

In Exercise 10.1, we'll show you how to test social engineering in your environment.

EXERCISE 10.1

Test Social Engineering

In this exercise, you'll test your users to determine the likelihood of a social engineering attack. The following are suggestions for tests; you might need to modify them slightly to be appropriate at your workplace. Before doing any of them, make certain that your manager knows that you're conducting such a test and approves of it:

1. Call the receptionist from an outside line. Tell them that you're a new salesperson and that you didn't write down the username and password that the sales manager gave you last week. Tell them that you need to get a file from the email system for a presentation tomorrow. Do they direct you to the appropriate person?

2. Call the human resources department from an outside line. Don't give out your real name, but instead say that you're a vendor who has been working with this company for years. You'd like a copy of the employee phone list to be emailed to you, if possible. Do they agree to send you the list, which would contain information that could be used to try to guess usernames and passwords?

3. Pick a user at random. Call them and identify yourself as someone who does work for the company. Tell them that you're supposed to have some new software ready for them by next week and that you need to know their password in order to finish configuring it. Do they do the right thing?

4. Look on Facebook for someone who works for the company and see what information they are posting. Are they talking about co-workers? About clients? Are there pictures posted from inside the workplace where it is possible to see doors, locks, or servers?

The best defense against any social engineering attack is education. Make certain that the employees of your company know how to react to the requests like these.

The only preventive measure in dealing with social engineering attacks is to educate your users and staff never to give out passwords and user IDs over the phone or via email or to anyone who isn't positively verified as being who they say they are. Social engineering is a recurring topic that will appear several times throughout this book as it relates to the topic being discussed.

 Real World Scenario

A Security Analogy

In this chapter, we discussed a number of access methods. Sometimes it can be confusing to keep them all straight. To put the main ones somewhat into perspective, think of the problem in terms of a stranger who wants to gain access to your house. Any number of types of individuals may want to get in your house without your knowing it:

- A thief who wants to steal your valuables

- Teenagers itching to do something destructive on a Saturday night

- Homeless people seeking to get in out of the cold and find some food

- A neighbor who has been drinking and accidentally pulls in the wrong driveway and starts to come in, thinking it is their house

- A professional hit man waiting for you to come home

There are many more, but these represent a good cross-section of individuals, each of whom has different motives and motivational levels for trying to get in.

To keep the thief out, you could post security signs all around your house and install a home alarm. He might not know if you have ABC Surveillance active monitoring, as the signs say, but he might not want to risk it and go away looking for an easier target. In the world of computer security, encryption acts like your home alarm and monitoring software, alerting you (or your monitoring company) to potential problems as they arise.

The teenagers just want to do damage somewhere, and your house is as good as the next one. Installing motion lights above the doors and around the side of the house is all you need to make them drive farther down the road. In the world of computer security, good passwords—and policies that are enforced—will keep these would-be intruders out.

The homeless also have no particular affection for your home as opposed to the next. You can keep them out by using locks on your doors and windows and putting a fence around your yard. If they can't get in the fence, they can't approach the house; and if they do manage that, the locks confront them. Firewalls serve this purpose in the world of computer security.

The neighbor just made a legitimate error. That happens. This author once went into the wrong person's tent when camping because they all looked the same. To make yours look different, you can add banners and warnings to the login routines stating, for example, that this is ABC server and that you must be an authorized user to access it.

This leaves the hit man. He has been paid to do a job, and that job entails gaining access to your home. No matter how good the locks are on your house, no matter how many motion lights you put up, if someone's sole purpose in life is to gain access to your house, they will find a way to do it. The same is true of your server. You can implement measures to keep everyone else out, but if someone spends their entire existence dedicated to getting access to that server, they will do so if it entails putting on a heating and air conditioning uniform and walking past the receptionist, pointing two dozen computers to hashing routines that will crack your passwords, or driving a tank through the side of the building. Your job is to handle all of the reasonable risks that come your way. Some, however, you have to acknowledge have only a slim chance of ever truly being risks, and some, no matter what precautions you take, will not go away.

Understanding Physical Security

Access control is a critical part of physical security, and it can help cut down the possibility of a social engineering or other type of attack from succeeding. Systems must operate in controlled environments in order to be secure. These environments must be, as much as possible, safe from intrusion. Computer system consoles can be a vital point of vulnerability because many administrative functions can be accomplished from the system console. These consoles, as well as the systems themselves, must be protected from physical access.

A key aspect of access control involves *physical barriers*. The objective of a physical barrier is to prevent access to computers and network systems. The most effective physical barrier implementations require that more than one physical barrier be crossed to gain access. This type of approach is called a *multiple barrier system* or *defense in depth*.

Ideally, your systems should have a minimum of three physical barriers:

- The external entrance to the building, referred to as a *perimeter*, which is protected by burglar alarms, external walls, *fencing*, surveillance, and so on. This should be used with an *access list*, which identifies who can enter a facility and who can be verified by a guard or someone in authority.

- A locked door protecting the computer center; you should also rely on such items as ID badges, proximity readers, fobs, or keys to gain access.

- The entrance to the computer room itself. This should be another locked door that is carefully monitored. Although you try to keep as many intruders out with the other two barriers, many who enter the building could be posing as someone they are not—heating technicians, representatives of the landlord, and so on. Although these pretenses can get them past the first two barriers, the locked computer room door should still stop them.

Any temporary access individual, such as a vending machine repair person or HVAC technician, should be escorted at all times and never left alone in secure areas.

Each of these entrances can be individually secured, monitored, and protected with alarm systems. Figure 10.7 illustrates this concept.

Proximity reader is a catchall term for any ID or card reader capable of reading *proximity cards*. Proximity cards go by a number of different titles, but they are just RFID (radio frequency identification) cards that can be read when close to a reader and never need to truly touch anything. The readers work with 13.56 MHz smart cards and 125 kHz proximity cards and can open turnstiles, gates, and any other physical security safeguards once the signal is read.

Although these three barriers won't always stop intruders, they will potentially slow them down enough so that law enforcement can respond before an intrusion is fully developed. Once inside, a truly secure site should be dependent on a physical token (something you have) or biometrics (something you are) for access to the actual network resources.

FIGURE 10.7   The three-layer security model

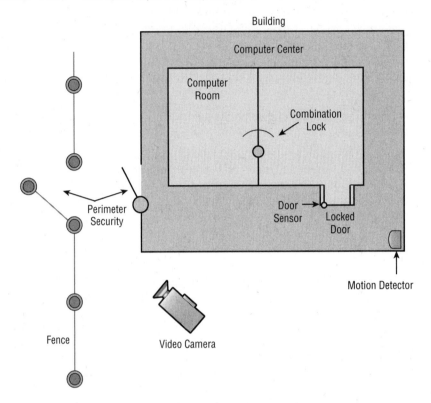

Physical tokens or FOBs are anything that a user must have on them to access network resources, and they are often associated with devices that enable the user to generate a one-time password authenticating their identity. SecurID, from RSA, is one of the best-known examples of a physical token. No matter how secure you think your system is, you'll never be able to stop everyone. But your goal is to stop most attempts and, at the very least, slow down the most sophisticated. As an analogy, the front door of your home may contain a lock and a deadbolt. This minimal security is enough to convince most burglars to try somewhere less secure. A professional who is bent on entering your home, however, could always take the appropriate lock-defeating tools to the door.

Hardware Locks and Security

Hardware security involves applying physical security modifications to secure the system(s) and preventing them from leaving the facility. Don't spend all of your time worrying about intruders coming through the network wire while overlooking the obvious need for physical security.

Adding a *cable lock* between a laptop and a desk prevents someone from picking it up and walking away with a copy of your customer database. All laptop cases include a built-in security slot in which a cable lock can be inserted to prevent it from easily being removed from the premises (see Figure 10.8).

FIGURE 10.8   A cable in the security slot keeps the laptop from easily being removed.

When it comes to desktop models, adding a lock to the back cover can prevent an intruder with physical access from grabbing the hard drive or damaging the internal components. The lock that connects through that slot can also go to a cable that then connects to a desk or other solid fixture to keep the entire PC from being carried away. An example of this type of configuration is shown in Figure 10.9.

In addition to running a cable to the desk, you can choose to run an end of it up to the monitor if theft of peripherals is a problem in your company. An example of this type of physical security is shown in Figure 10.10.

You should also consider using a *safe* and *locking cabinets* to protect backup media, documentation, and any other physical artifacts that could do harm if they fell into the wrong hands. Server racks should lock the rack-mounted servers into the cabinets to prevent someone from simply pulling one and walking out the front door with it.

Although this discussion relates to physical security, don't overlook encryption as a means of increasing data security should a desktop or laptop machine be stolen. You can also consider removing the hard drives in areas that are difficult to monitor and forcing all data to be stored on the network.

FIGURE 10.9 A cable can be used to keep a desktop machine from easily being taken.

FIGURE 10.10 If theft of equipment is a possibility, run one end of the cable from the monitor to the desktop machine through the hole in the work desk.

Mantraps

High-security installations use a type of intermediate access control mechanism called a *mantrap* (also occasionally written as *man-trap*). Mantraps require visual identification, as well as authentication, to gain access. A mantrap makes it difficult for a facility to be accessed by large numbers of individuals at once because it allows only one or two people into a facility at a time. It's usually designed to contain an unauthorized, potentially hostile person physically until authorities arrive. Figure 10.11 illustrates a mantrap. Notice in this case that the visual verification is accomplished using a security guard. A properly developed mantrap includes bulletproof glass, high-strength doors, and locks. After a person is inside the facility, additional security and authentication may be required for further entrance.

FIGURE 10.11   A mantrap in action

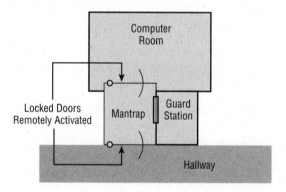

 Some mantraps even include scales to weigh the person. Weight can be used to help identify a person, and the scales are often used to make sure that no one is sneaking in. If the weight of the scale appears too high, an officer can check to make sure that two people haven't crowded in who are attempting to bypass security.

Video Surveillance

In high-security and military environments, an armed guard as well as *video surveillance* would be placed at the mantrap. Beyond mantraps, you can combine guards with cameras (or even the threat of cameras) to create a potent deterrent. The cameras can send signals to a room where they are monitored by a guard capable of responding to a situation when the need arises.

Camera vs. Guard

The camera versus guard debate is an old one. You must decide what is best for your own environment. The benefit of a camera (also known as *closed-circuit television*, or *CCTV*) is that it is always running and can record everything it sees, creating evidence that can be admissible in court if necessary. On the other hand, it is stationary, lacks any sort of intelligence, is possible to avoid, and needs someone to monitor the feed or review the tape to be effective, which many times does not happen until a problem has been discovered.

The benefit of a guard is that the person can move about, apply intelligence to situations, and collect evidence. The guard, however, is not always recording, can be avoided, and has more downtime.

 **Real World Scenario**

Evaluating Your Security System

You've been asked to evaluate your building's security system. The president chose you because you understand computers, and after all, these new alarm systems are computerized.

In evaluating the environment, you notice that there is a single control panel for the whole building. A few motion detectors are located in the main hallway. Beyond that, no additional security components are installed.

This situation is fairly normal in a small building. You could recommend enhancing the system by adding motion detectors in each major hallway. You could also install video monitoring (also known as surveillance) cameras, such as closed-circuit television (CCTV), at all the entrances. Most security/surveillance CCTV cameras have *PTZ* (Pan, Tilt, and Zoom) capabilities too, and they can often do so based on sound or motion. You should also consider recommending that they upgrade the perimeter security by adding contact sensors on all the doors and ground-floor windows.

Always evaluate the building from a multi-tiered approach. Incorporate as many different elements as you can where needed: perimeter security, security zones, and surveillance.

Fencing

Perimeter security, whether physical or technological, is the first line of defense in your security model. In the case of a physical security issue, the intent is to prevent unauthorized access to resources inside a building or facility.

Physical perimeter security is intended to accomplish for a network what perimeter security does for a building. How do you keep intruders from gaining access to systems and information in the network through the network? In the physical environment, perimeter security is accomplished through fencing, locks, doors, surveillance systems, and alarm systems. This isn't functionally any different from a network, which uses border routers, intrusion detection systems, and firewalls to prevent unauthorized access.

Few security systems can be implemented that don't have weaknesses or vulnerabilities. A determined intruder can, with patience, overcome most security systems. The task may not be easy, and it may require careful planning and study; however, a determined adversary can usually figure out a way. This is why deterrence is so important.

If you want to deter intruders from breaking into your building, you can install improved door locks, coded alarm systems, and magnetic contacts on doors and windows. Remember that you can't always keep an intruder out of your building; however, you can make an intrusion riskier and more likely to be discovered if it happens.

Don't overlook the obvious. Adding a security guard at the front door will go a long way toward keeping an intruder out.

 Real World Scenario

Circumventing Security

Recently, a small business noticed that the level of network traffic seemed to be very high in the late evening and early morning. The business couldn't find a network-related reason why this was happening. Upon investigation, the security consultant found that a part-time employee had established a multiuser game server in his office. The game server was set to turn on after 10 p.m. and turn off at 5:30 a.m. This server was hidden under a desk, and it supported some 30 local game players. The part-time employee didn't have a key to the building, so an investigation was conducted to determine how he gained access to the building after hours. The building had electronic locks on its outside entrances, and a passcard was needed to open the doors. The door locks, however, were designed to unlock automatically when someone was leaving the building.

The investigation discovered that the employee and a friend had figured out a way to slide a piece of cardboard under one of the external doors, which activated the door mechanisms and unlocked the doors. The intruders took advantage of this weakness in the doors to gain access after hours without using a passcard and then used the server to play games in his office.

Access List

As the name implies, the purpose of an *access list* is to identify specifically who can enter a facility. Once created, the list can be verified by a guard or someone in authority. Similar to an access list for physical access, *access control lists* (ACLs) enable devices in your network to ignore requests from specified users or systems or to grant them certain network privileges. You may find that a certain IP address is constantly scanning your network, and you can block this IP address. If you block it at the router, the IP address will automatically be rejected any time it attempts to use your network.

Proper Lighting

Lighting can play an important role in the security of any facility. Poor lighting can lead to a variety of unwanted situations: someone sneaking in a door that is not well lit, one individual passing a checkpoint and being mistaken for another person, a biometric reading failure. The latter is particularly true with facial recognition, and proper lighting needs to be in place for both the face and the background.

 Lighting can also serve as a deterrent. Bright lighting in a parking lot, access way, or storage area, for example, can help reduce the risk of theft.

Signs

One of the least expensive physical security tools that can be implemented is a sign. Signs can be placed around secure areas telling those who venture by that only authorized access is allowed, that trespassers will be prosecuted, and so on. There is a story told of a couple of magicians who drove across country while on tour, and to prevent anyone from breaking into their car, they put a sign on it identifying the car as a transport vehicle for the Centers for Disease Control. Supposedly, it worked and no one ever broke into the vehicle.

Within Microsoft Windows, you have the ability to put signs (in the form of onscreen pop-up banners) that appear before the login telling similar information—authorized access only, violators will be prosecuted, and so forth. Such banners convey warnings or regulatory information to the user that they must "accept" in order to use the machine or network.

In Windows, the banner is turned on in the Registry through an entry beneath `HKEY_LOCAL_MACHINE\SOFTWARE\Microsoft\Windows\CurrentVersion\Policies\System`. You can configure `legalnoticecaption` as the caption of the "sign" that you want to appear and `legalnoticetext` as the text that will show up and need to be dismissed before the user can move on. Both are string values accepting any alphanumeric combination.

Guards

As opposed to signs, one of the most expensive physical security tools that can be implemented is a guard. A guard can respond to a situation and be intimidating, but a guard is also fallible and comes at a considerable cost.

Barricades

To stop someone from entering a facility, barricades or gauntlets can be used. These are often used in conjunction with guards, fencing, and other physical security measures, but they can be used as standalones as well.

Biometrics

Biometric systems use some kind of unique biological trait to identify a person, such as fingerprints, patterns on the retina, and handprints. Some methods that are used include hand scanners, retinal scanners, facial recognition applications, and keystroke recognition programs, which can be used as part of the access control mechanisms. These devices should be coupled into security-oriented computer systems that record all access attempts. They should also be under surveillance in order to prevent individuals from bypassing them.

These technologies are becoming more reliable, and they will become widely used over the next few years. Many laptops sold now have a fingerprint reader built in. The costs associated with these technologies have fallen dramatically in recent years. One of the best independent sources of information on development in the field of biometrics is BiometricNews.net, where you can find links to publications and their blog. From a reference standpoint, be sure to visit www.nist.gov/itl/biometrics/index.cfm.

 Real World Scenario

Installing Biometric Devices

You've been asked to solve the problem of people forgetting smart cards that give them access to the computer center. Hardly a day goes by that an employee doesn't forget to bring their card. This causes a great deal of disruption in the workplace because someone has to reissue smart cards constantly. The company has tried everything it could think of short of firing people who forget their cards. What would you recommend to the company?

Investigate whether biometric devices (such as hand scanners) or number access locks can be used in lieu of smart cards for access. These devices will allow people who forget their smart cards to enter areas to which they should have access.

Protected Distribution

A *protected distribution system (PDS)* is one in which the network is secure enough to allow for the transmission of classified information in unencrypted format—in other words, where physical network security has been substituted for encryption security. In a small office, for example, you could ban the use of wireless devices and require that all such devices be connected to a bus topology network that is clearly visible as it runs through the space.

Moving forward from this overly simplistic scenario, it is possible to create a much larger network that uses fiber, various topologies, and so on, as long as you still have the ability to monitor and control the span of it. Such networks were once called "approved circuits," and the U.S. government largely uses them.

Alarms

An *alarm* is used to draw attention to a breach, or suspected breach, when it occurs. This alarm can be sounded in many ways—through the use of a siren, a series of lights (flashing or solid), or an email or voice message—but is always intended to draw attention to the event.

A *security zone* is an area in a building where access is individually monitored and controlled. A large network, such as the ones found in a big physical plant, may have many areas that require restricted access. In a building, floors, sections of floors, and even offices can be broken down into smaller areas. These smaller zones are referred to as *security zones*. In the physical environment, each floor is broken down into separate zones. An alarm system that identifies a zone of intrusion can inform security personnel about an intruder's location in the building; zone notification tells security where to begin looking when they enter the premises.

The concept of security zones is as old as security itself. Most burglar alarms allow the creation of individual zones within a building or residence; these zones are then treated separately by the security staff. In a residence, it would be normal for the bedroom to be assigned a zone of its own so that movement here can occur while other parts of the house may be set on a motion detector.

Motion Detection

A *motion detection* system can monitor a location and signal an alarm if it picks up movement. Systems are commonly used to monitor homes, and the same technology can be used to protect server rooms, office buildings, or any other location. The motion detection can be accomplished with sensors that are infrared, microwave, or sonic, or that utilize a variety of hybrid sensors.

In Exercise 10.2, we'll walk you through the evaluation of your environment.

EXERCISE 10.2

Security Zones in the Physical Environment

As a security administrator, you'll need to evaluate your workplace and consider physical zones that should exist in terms of the different types of individuals who might be present. If your workplace is already divided into zones, forget that this has been done and start from scratch. Answer the following questions:

1. What areas represent the physical dimension of your workplace (buildings, floors, offices, and so on)?

2. Which areas are accessible by everyone from administrators to visitors? Can a visitor ever leave the reception area without an escort and, if so, go to a restroom, meeting room, break room, and so forth?

3. In what areas are users allowed to move about freely? Are you certain that no visitors or guests can enter those areas?

4. What areas are administrators allowed to enter that users cannot—server room? Wiring closets? How do you keep users out and verify that only administrators enter?

5. Are wall jacks, network access, or Wi-Fi available in areas where visitors are located?

6. Do other areas need to be secured for entities beyond the user/administrator distinction (such as groups)?

Once you're armed with this information, you should look for ways to address the weaknesses. Evaluate your environment routinely to make certain that the zones that exist within your security plan are still relevant. Always start from scratch and pretend that no zones exist; then verify that the zones that do exist are the same as those that you've created in this exercise.

Environmental Controls

The location of your computer facility is critical to its security. Computer facilities must be placed in a location that is physically possible to secure. Additionally, the location must have the proper capabilities to manage temperature, humidity, and other environmental factors necessary to the health of your computer systems. The following sections look at various environmental elements about which you must be aware.

HVAC

If the computer systems for which you're responsible require special environmental considerations, you'll need to establish cooling and humidity control. Ideally, systems are located in the middle of the building, and they're ducted separately from the rest of the HVAC (Heating, Ventilation, and Air Conditioning) system. It's a common practice for modern buildings to use a zone-based air conditioning environment, which allows the environmental plant to be turned off when the building isn't occupied. A computer room will typically require full-time environmental control.

In the event of power failure, HVAC for the server room should be on the UPS in order to keep it cool.

Fire Suppression

Fire suppression is a key consideration in computer-center design. Fire suppression is the act of extinguishing a fire versus preventing one. Two primary types of fire-suppression systems are in use: fire extinguishers and fixed systems.

Fire Extinguishers

Fire extinguishers are portable systems. The selection and use of fire extinguishers is critical. Four primary types of fire extinguishers are available, classified by the types of fires they put out: A, B, C, and D. Table 10.1 describes the four types of fires and the capabilities of various extinguishers.

TABLE 10.1   Fire extinguisher ratings

Type	Use	Retardant composition
A	Wood and paper	Largely water or chemical
B	Flammable liquids	Fire-retardant chemicals
C	Electrical	Nonconductive chemicals
D	Flammable metals	Varies; type specific

A type K extinguisher that is marketed for use on cooking oil fires can also be found in stores. In actuality, this is a subset of class B extinguishers.

Several multipurpose extinguishers combine several extinguisher capabilities in a single bottle. The more common multipurpose extinguishers are A-B, B-C, and ABC.

The recommended procedure for using a fire extinguisher is called the *PASS method*: pull, aim, squeeze, and sweep. Fire extinguishers usually operate for only a few seconds—if you use one, make sure that you don't fixate on a single spot. Most fire extinguishers have a limited effective range of between 3 and 8 feet.

 A major concern with electrical fires is that they can recur quickly if the voltage isn't removed. Make sure that you remove voltage from systems when a fire occurs.

Most fire extinguishers require an annual inspection. This is a favorite area of citation by fire inspectors. You can contract with services to do this on a regular basis: They will inspect or replace your fire extinguishers according to a scheduled agreement.

Fixed Systems

Fixed systems are usually part of the building systems. The most common fixed systems combine fire detectors with fire-suppression systems, where the detectors trigger either because of a rapid temperature change or because of excessive smoke. The fire-suppression system uses either water sprinklers or fire-suppressing gas. Water systems work with overhead nozzles, as illustrated in Figure 10.12. These systems are the most common method in modern buildings. Water systems are reliable and relatively inexpensive, and they require little maintenance.

FIGURE 10.12 Water-based fire-suppression system

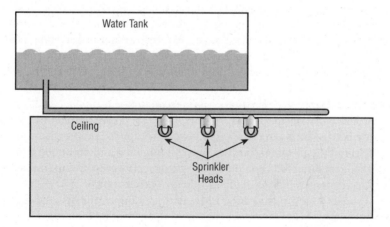

The one drawback of water-based systems is that they cause extreme damage to energized electrical equipment such as computers. These systems can be tied into relays that terminate power to computer systems before they release water into the building.

Gas-based systems were originally designed to use carbon dioxide and later halon gas. Halon gas isn't used anymore because it damages the ozone layer; environmentally acceptable substitutes are now available, with FM200 being one of the most common. The principle of a gas system is that it displaces the oxygen in the room, thereby removing this essential component of a fire.

WARNING   Evacuate the room immediately in the event of a fire. Gas-based systems work by removing oxygen from the fire, and this can suffocate anyone in the room as well.

The major drawback of gas-based systems is that they require sealed environments to operate. Special ventilation systems are usually installed in gas systems to limit air circulation when the gas is released. Gas systems are also expensive, and they're usually implemented only in computer rooms or other areas where water would cause damage to technology or other intellectual property.

EMI Shielding

Shielding refers to the process of preventing electronic emissions from your computer systems from being used to gather intelligence and preventing outside electronic emissions from disrupting your information-processing abilities. In a fixed facility, such as a computer center, surrounding the computer room with a *Faraday cage* can provide electronic shielding. A Faraday cage usually consists of an electrically conductive wire mesh or other conductor woven into a "cage" that surrounds a room. The conductor is then grounded. Because of this cage, few electromagnetic signals can either enter or leave the room, thereby reducing the ability to eavesdrop on a computer conversation. To verify the functionality of the cage, radio frequency (RF) emissions from the room are tested with special measuring devices.

Electromagnetic interference (EMI) and *radio frequency interference (RFI)* are two additional environmental considerations. Motors, lights, and other types of electromechanical objects cause EMI, which can cause circuit overload, spikes, or electrical component failure. Making sure that all signal lines are properly shielded and grounded can minimize EMI. Devices that generate EMI should be as physically distant from cabling as is feasible because this type of energy tends to dissipate quickly with distance.

Figure 10.13 shows a motor generating EMI. In this example, the data cable next to the motor is picking up the EMI. This causes the signal to deteriorate, and it might eventually cause the line to be unusable. The gray area in the illustration is representative of the interference generated by the motor.

FIGURE 10.13   Electromagnetic interference (EMI) pickup in a data cable

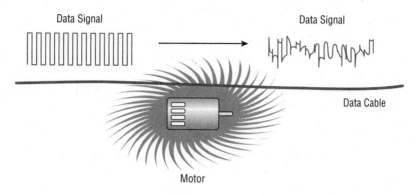

RFI is the byproduct of electrical processes, similar to EMI. The major difference is that RFI is usually projected across a radio spectrum. Motors with defective brushes can generate RFI, as can a number of other devices. If RF levels become too high, it can cause the receivers in wireless units to become deaf. This process is called *desensitizing*, and it occurs because of the volume of RF energy present. This can occur even if the signals are on different frequencies.

Figure 10.14 demonstrates the desensitizing process occurring with a wireless access portal (WAP). The only solution to this problem is to move the devices farther apart or to turn off the RFI generator.

FIGURE 10.14   RF desensitization occurring as a result of cell phone interference

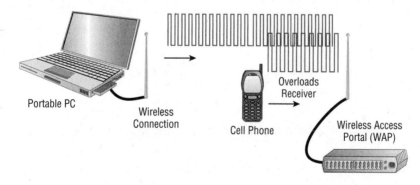

In 1985, Dutch researcher Wim van Eck proposed that it is possible to eavesdrop on CRT and LCD displays by detecting their electromagnetic emissions. Known as *Van Eck phreaking*, this problem/possibility made the news because of potential problems with electronic voting machines. Commonly associated countermeasures recommended by TEMPEST include shielding.

Project TEMPEST

TEMPEST is the name of a project authorized by the U.S. government in the late 1950s. TEMPEST was concerned with reducing electronic noise from devices that would divulge intelligence about systems and information. This program has become a standard for computer systems certification. *TEMPEST shielding protection* means that a computer system doesn't emit any significant amounts of EMI or RFI. For a device to be approved as TEMPEST-compliant, it must undergo extensive testing done to exacting standards dictated by the U.S. government. Today, control zones and white noise are used to accomplish the shielding. TEMPEST-certified equipment frequently costs twice as much as non-TEMPEST equipment.

Hot and Cold Aisles

There are often multiple rows of servers located in racks in server rooms. The rows of servers are known as aisles, and they can be cooled as *hot aisles* and *cold aisles*. With a hot aisle, hot air outlets are used to cool the equipment, whereas with cold aisles, cold air intake is used to cool the equipment. Combining the two, you have cold air intake from below the aisle and hot air outtake above it, providing constant circulation.

It is important that the hot air exhausting from one aisle of racks not be the intake air pulled in by the next row of racks or overheating will occur. Air handlers must move the hot air out, whereas cold air, usually coming from beneath a raised floor, is supplied as the intake air. Figure 10.15 shows an example of a hot and cold aisle design.

FIGURE 10.15   A hot and cold aisle design

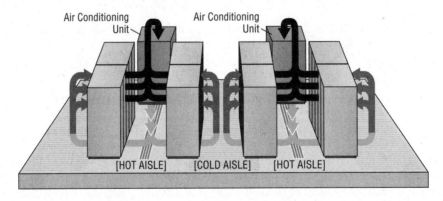

Air Conditioning Unit

Air Conditioning Unit

[HOT AISLE]   [COLD AISLE]   [HOT AISLE]

Environmental Monitoring

Environmental concerns include considerations about water and flood damage as well as fire suppression. Computer rooms should have fire and moisture detectors. Most office buildings have water pipes and other moisture-carrying systems in the ceiling. If a water pipe bursts (which is common in minor earthquakes), the computer room could become flooded. Water and electricity don't mix. Moisture monitors would automatically kill power in a computer room if moisture were detected, so the security professional should know where the water cutoffs are located.

Fire, no matter how small, can cause damage to computer systems. Apart from the high heat, which can melt or warp plastics and metals, the smoke from the fire can permeate the computers. Smoke particles are large enough to lodge under the read/write head of a hard disk, thereby causing data loss. In addition, the fire-suppression systems in most buildings consist of water under pressure, and the water damage from putting out even a small fire could wipe out an entire datacenter.

The three critical components of any fire are heat, fuel, and oxygen. If any component of this trilogy is removed, a fire isn't possible. Most fire-suppression systems work on this concept.

Temperature and Humidity Controls

Many computer systems require *temperature and humidity control* for reliable service. Large servers, communications equipment, and drive arrays generate considerable amounts of heat; this is especially true of mainframe and older minicomputers. An environmental system for this type of equipment is a significant expense beyond the actual computer system costs. Fortunately, newer systems operate in a wider temperature range. Most new systems are designed to operate in an office environment.

Environmental systems should be monitored to prevent the computer center's humidity level from dropping below 50 percent. Electrostatic damage is likely to occur when humidity levels get too low.

Humidity control prevents the buildup of static electricity in the environment. If the humidity drops much below 50 percent, electronic components are extremely vulnerable to damage from electrostatic shock. Most environmental systems also regulate humidity; however, a malfunctioning system can cause the humidity to be almost entirely extracted from a room. Make sure that environmental systems are regularly serviced.

Control Types

One of the most generic terms in security is *control*. The word is used so many different ways that its meaning can become blurred. The best thing to do is to equate the word with whatever entity is charged with the task at the moment. That task can be preventing something from happening, logging when something does, responding to it, or any variety of other possibilities. For the exam, CompTIA has categorized controls into six types as follows:

Deterrent   A *deterrent control* is anything intended to warn a would-be attacker that they should not attack. This could be a posted warning notice that they will be prosecuted to the fullest extent of the law, locks on doors, barricades, lighting, or anything can delay or discourage an attack.

Preventive   As the name implies, the purpose of *preventive controls* is to stop something from happening. These can include locked doors that keep intruders out, user training on potential harm (to keep them vigilant and alert), or even biometric devices and guards that deny access until authentication has occurred.

Detective   The purpose of a *detective control* is to uncover a violation. The only time that they would be relevant is when a preventive control has failed and they need to sound an alarm. A detective control can range from a checksum on a downloaded file, an alarm that sounds when a door has been pried open, or an antivirus scanner that actively looks for problems. It could also be a sonic detector, motion sensor, or anything that would detect that an intrusion is under way.

Compensating   *Compensating controls* are backup controls that come into play only when other controls have failed. An office building may have a complex electronic lock on the door (preventive control) and a sign that you will be arrested if you enter (deterrent control), but it is a safe bet they will also have an alarm that sounds (a compensating control) when the door is jimmied as well as a backup generator (another compensating control) to keep that electronic lock active when the power goes out.

Technical   *Technical controls* are those controls implemented through technology. They may be deterrent, preventive, detective, or compensating (but not administrative), and include such things as firewalls, IDS, IPS, and such.

Administrative   An *administrative control* is one that comes down through policies, procedures, and guidelines. An example of an administrative control is the escalation procedure to be used in the event of a break-in: who is notified first, who is called second, and so on. Another example of an administrative control is the list of steps to be followed when a key employee is terminated: disable their account, change the server password, and so forth.

A Control Type Analogy

To prepare for the certification exam, it often helps to use analogies to put topics in context. In light of that, consider a residential home this author owns in the middle of town. I grow prized tomato plants in the backyard, and it is very important to me that no one goes back there for fear that they might do something to harm the tomatoes. Thus, I implement the following controls:

- *Administrative*: I establish a number of policies to keep the tomatoes safe:
  - *Preventive*: I instruct every member of my family that they are not to go into the backyard and they are not to let anyone else go back there either.
  - *Deterrent*: I tell the kids that if I ever hear of any of them—or their friends—being the backyard, I will take away their allowance for month.
  - *Detective*: As a matter of routine, I want each member of the family to look out the window on a regular basis to see if anyone has wandered into the yard.
  - *Compensating*: Every member of the family is instructed on how to call the police the minute they see anyone in the yard.
- *Technical*: Not trusting that the administrative controls will do the job without fail, I implement a number of technical controls:
  - *Preventive*: I put up a fence around the yard, and the door that leads out from the garage is locked.
  - *Deterrent*: "Beware of Dog" signs are posted all over the fence (although I have no dog).
  - *Detective*: Sensors are placed on the gate to trigger an alarm if the gate is opened.
  - *Compensating*: Triggered alarms turn on the backyard sprinklers at full volume to douse any intruder who wanders in.

These controls work in conjunction with one another to help keep individuals who should not be there out of the backyard and away from the tomatoes. Naturally, as the owner/administrator, I have the ability to override all of them as needed. I can ignore the warning signs, turn off the sprinklers, and get full access to the garden when I desire. The controls are not in place to hinder my access, but only to obstruct and prevent others from accessing the yard.

Data Policies

An important administrative control to have in place is a *data policy*. It should be focused on the following four issues:

Wiping   How is data removed from media?

Disposing   How are media (hard drives, removable drives, and so on) discarded when they are no longer needed?

Retention   How long must data be kept? This needs to take into account government regulations on data storage for your business as well as company policies.

Storage   Where is data kept, and what security precautions are associated with its access?

As an example of the need for such a policy, consider that the capacity of flash drives (also known as thumb drives, memory sticks, jump drives, and USB drives) has grown significantly, as has their popularity. Many users now store all their files on a flash drive that they transport with them everywhere, rather than save files to hard drives on one or more computers (work, home, and so on). The technology is stable enough so that this scenario works well, and there are no problems until you need to erase all traces of a file.

Imagine that your flash drive has one or more files on it that, if found, could get you into serious hot water. The files could be inappropriate nonbusiness pictures, tax returns, Social Security numbers, or almost anything else that you would not want to fall into the wrong hands. Deleting these files isn't a good solution since what actually is deleted is the pointer to the file—the content still remains until it is overwritten. Someone armed with the right tools (many shareware ones are available) and knowledge could recover the file with little trouble.

A number of programs can be found online that purport to delete the files permanently by wiping the free space. Trust them if you wish, but according to Dan Goodin, IT Security Editor at technology news and information website Ars Technica: "[A]s much as 67 percent of data stored in a file remained even after it was deleted from an SSD (Solid State Drive) using the secure erase feature offered by Apple's Mac OS X. Other overwrite operations, which securely delete files by repeatedly rewriting the data stored in a particular disk location, failed by similarly large margins when used to erase a single file on an SSD." For more, see www.theregister.co.uk/2011/02/21/flash_drive_erasing_peril/.

Destroying a Flash Drive

The only reliable method of eliminating the evidence is to destroy the flash drive in such a way that no part of it can be recovered. We will walk you through this process.

 Although the following sections deal with USB drives, we strongly encourage you to adopt a comprehensive plan for PC drives, laptops, tablets, iPads, and phones as well, as they can all pose a hazard. Any memory-specific policy should also include non–computer device drives such as those found in copiers, office printers, fax, and multipurpose machines. As such equipment becomes more ubiquitous in the workplace, policies should also address the wiping of data from BYOD (Bring Your Own Devices) and phones.

Step 1: Crack Open the Drive

The first order of business is to remove the case. Because flash drives come in a variety of shapes and sizes—from the simple rectangular-shaped to those shaped like animals, candy, or almost anything else—you may have to vary the tools that you use, but usually a screwdriver or scissors will do the trick.

Crack open the case and toss away its parts—you don't care if anyone sees those items in the trash. The focus needs to be on the circuit board and the chips connected to it. In addition to an LED and any circuitry associated with it that are mounted on the board, you should see a large chip about half the size of a postage stamp—this is the flash memory chip.

There should be other chips visible as well (the storage controller chip, for example), but the flash memory chip is identifiable as the largest of the group and the one on which you must concentrate.

There is no harm in destroying the entire drive—and that is indeed a goal—but above all else, it is that memory chip that must be rendered worthless.

Step 2: Turn the Chip to Powder

The objective is to turn the chip into a powder that cannot be recognized. A number of tools can be used to accomplish this, but one of the most effective is a hand drill and a series of bits ranging from 1/32" to 1/4".

If you have a drill press, you can use it in place of the hand drill, but a 1/4" hand drill works just as well. Be sure to hold the drive securely with pliers, a vise, or vise grips and adhere to all of the other safety precautions that you would take with any project that involves power tools and fine dust (wear eye protection, don't breath the dust, and so on).

Put a large piece of paper down to catch the dust and remnants, and then use the smallest drill bit to put a hole directly through the center of the memory chip. Replace the drill bit with a larger one and put it through the same hole. Continue to do this until you have used the 1/4" bit to turn the remains into powder. If the circuit board/memory chip breaks prior to finishing, pick up the remains with pliers or vise grips and continue the operation. Remember that having a few recognizable pieces of the circuit board or controller chip left over is not terrible as long as there are no recognizable pieces of the memory chip remaining.

When you finish, the remnants should be a finely ground powder.

Step 3: Finish It Off

The final step is to gather the paper holding the remnants and wad it into a loose ball, leaving a considerable amount of air within. This can now be tossed into a fire as a final strike, and you can sleep well comforted by the knowledge that the contents of that flash drive are nothing more than a memory.

Some Considerations

Although one of the greatest features of flash drives is their small size, it also serves as a weakness in that it makes it easier for them to be misplaced or stolen. You need not look far to find tales of the costs and dangers associated with losing the data on these drives.

A couple of instances worth noting involve Bowling Green State University and the Oregon Food Stamp program:

www.dispatch.com/live/content/local_news/stories/2007/06/28/lost.ART_ART_06-28-07_B4_2P75A0V.html

www.bgsu.edu/offices/mc/page31854.html

www.pcc.edu/resources/tss/info-security/incident-response/

In the first case, an accounting professor could not locate a flash drive containing many years of student records—including one year in which students were identified by Social Security numbers instead of student IDs—and he was forced to pay for LifeLock protection for those students (just under $10,000) and endure a public relations nightmare.

In the second case, a flash drive was taken from a vehicle belonging to an employee of Portland Community College. That flash drive contained information on 2,900 recipients of the Oregon Food Stamp Employment and Transition program. Since the information contained names and social security numbers, Debix Credit Protection had to be offered to each of the affected individuals. A copy of the letter sent can be found here:

www.pcc.edu/resources/tss/info-security/documents/data-breach.pdf

To protect the data on flash drives that you *don't* want to destroy—and keep from suffering fates similar to Bowling Green and Portland Community College—you should add passwords and encryption to the flash drives. Although you can add many types of encryption for considerably more than the cost of a regular drive, you can buy ones that already have these features:

www.kingston.com/us/usb/encrypted_security

This is far from a flawless solution, but it does add reasonable protection for the data should the drive fall into the wrong hands.

It is also a good idea to craft a policy blocking USB ports from write operations. The policy should limit who can save data outside the network and restrict the saving of data to only those authorized to do so.

Optical Discs

The easiest method for destroying CD and DVD discs is to use a shredder equipped for such a purpose. Many quality business and industrial-grade paper shredders include this capability. Typically, the better the shredder (cross-cut as opposed to strip-cut, higher DIN level, and so forth), the more effective a job it will do in obliterating media.

If you want to adopt an extra level of precaution, before running the disc through the shredder, you can apply a palm sander or belt sander to the data side of the disc. This will damage all of the tracks and create a fine powder, similar to that created with the flash drive.

If you don't have access to a shredder with CD/DVD capabilities, you can achieve similar results by using scissors, a knife, or a hammer (although this approach is much more time consuming).

Summary

This chapter covered the key elements of physical security and environmental controls and monitoring. Physical security measures include access controls, physical barriers, and environmental systems. Environmental considerations include electrical, fire-suppression, and interference issues.

This chapter also examined hardware security, data policies, and social engineering. By employing social engineering, attackers are able to gain access to data or the workplace through employees. Many different types of social engineering attacks can occur, and this chapter examined those as well. As a security professional, your job includes keeping up-to-date on current issues as well as informing affected parties about new threats.

Exam Essentials

Be able to describe the process of social engineering.   Social engineering occurs when an unauthorized individual uses human or nontechnical methods to gain information or access to security information. Individuals in an organization should be trained to watch for these types of attempts, and they should report them to security professionals when they occur.

Know the importance of security awareness and training.   Security awareness and training are critical to the success of a security effort. They include explaining policies, procedures, and current threats to both users and management.

Be able to discuss aspects of environmental systems and functions.   Environmental systems include heating, air conditioning, humidity control, fire suppression, and power systems. All of these functions are critical to a well-designed physical plant.

Know the purposes of shielding in the environment.   Shielding primarily prevents interference from EMI and RFI sources. Most shielding is attached to an effective ground, thereby neutralizing or reducing interference susceptibility.

Be able to describe the types of fire-suppression systems in use today. Fire-suppression systems can be either fixed or portable. Portable systems are most commonly fire extinguishers. Fixed systems are part of the building, and they're generally water- or gas-based. Gas-based systems are usually found only in computer rooms or other locations where water-based systems would cause more damage than is warranted. Gas systems work only in environments where airflow can be limited; they remove oxygen from the fire, causing the fire to go out. Water systems usually remove heat from a fire, causing the fire to go out.

Know the six types of controls. CompTIA has categorized controls into six types: deterrent (warning), preventive (stopping), detective (uncovering), compensating (backup), technical (using technology), and administrative (using policies).

Review Questions

1. As part of your training program, you're trying to educate users on the importance of security. You explain to them that not every attack depends on implementing advanced technological methods. Some attacks take advantage of human shortcomings to gain access that should otherwise be denied. What term do you use to describe attacks of this type?

   A. Social engineering

   B. IDS system

   C. Perimeter security

   D. Biometrics

2. Which of the following is another name for social engineering?

   A. Social disguise

   B. Social hacking

   C. Wetware

   D. Wetfire

3. Which of the following is the best description of tailgating?

   A. Following someone through a door they just unlocked

   B. Figuring out how to unlock a secured area

   C. Sitting close to someone in a meeting

   D. Stealing information from someone's desk

4. What is the form of social engineering in which you simply ask someone for a piece of information that you want by making it look as if it is a legitimate request?

   A. Hoaxing

   B. Swimming

   C. Spamming

   D. Phishing

5. When you combine phishing with Voice over IP, it is known as:

   A. Spoofing

   B. Spooning

   C. Whaling

   D. Vishing

6. Which of the following is the best description of shoulder surfing?

   A. Following someone through a door they just unlocked

   B. Figuring out how to unlock a secured area

   C. Watching someone enter important information

   D. Stealing information from someone's desk

7. Which of the following is a high-security installation that requires visual identification, as well as authentication, to gain access?

    A. Mantrap

    B. Fencing

    C. Proximity reader

    D. Hot aisle

8. You've been drafted for the safety committee. One of your first tasks is to inventory all of the fire extinguishers and make certain that the correct types are in the correct locations throughout the building. Which of the following categories of fire extinguisher is intended for use on electrical fires?

    A. Type A

    B. Type B

    C. Type C

    D. Type D

9. Which of the following will not reduce EMI?

    A. Physical shielding

    B. Humidity control

    C. Physical location

    D. Overhauling worn motors

10. Which of the following is an example of perimeter security?

    A. Chain link fence

    B. Video camera

    C. Elevator

    D. Locked computer room

11. You're the leader of the security committee at ACME Company. After a move to a new facility, you're installing a new security monitoring system throughout. Which of the following best describes a motion detector mounted in the corner of a hallway?

    A. Perimeter security

    B. Partitioning

    C. Security zone

    D. IDS system

12. Which technology uses a physical characteristic to establish identity?

    A. Biometrics

    B. Surveillance

    C. Smart card

    D. CHAP authenticator

13. The process of reducing or eliminating susceptibility to outside interference is called what?

    A. Shielding

    B. EMI

    C. TEMPEST

    D. Desensitization

14. You work for an electronics company that has just created a device that emits less RF than any competitor's product. Given the enormous importance of this invention and of the marketing benefits it could offer, you want to have the product certified. Which certification is used to indicate minimal electronic emissions?

    A. EMI

    B. RFI

    C. CC EAL 4

    D. TEMPEST

15. Due to growth beyond current capacity, a new server room is being built. As a manager, you want to make certain that all of the necessary safety elements exist in the room when it's finished. Which fire-suppression system works best when used in an enclosed area by displacing the air around a fire?

    A. Gas-based

    B. Water-based

    C. Fixed system

    D. Overhead sprinklers

16. Type K fire extinguishers are intended for use on cooking oil fires. This type is a subset of which other type of fire extinguisher?

    A. Type A

    B. Type B

    C. Type C

    D. Type D

17. Proximity readers work with which of the following? (Choose all that apply.)

    A. 15.75 fob card

    B. 14.32 surveillance card

    C. 13.56 MHZ smart card

    D. 125 kHz proximity card

18. In a hot and cold aisle system, what is the typical method of handling cold air?

    A. It is pumped in from below raised floor tiles.

    B. It is pumped in from above through the ceiling tiles.

    C. Only hot air is extracted and cold air is the natural result.

    D. Cold air exists in each aisle.

19. If RF levels become too high, it can cause the receivers in wireless units to become deaf. This process is called:

A. Clipping

B. Desensitizing

C. Distorting

D. Crackling

20. RFI is the byproduct of electrical processes, similar to EMI. The major difference is that RFI is usually projected across which of the following?

A. Network medium

B. Electrical wiring

C. Radio spectrum

D. Portable media

Chapter

11

Security Administration

THE FOLLOWING COMPTIA SECURITY+ EXAM OBJECTIVES ARE COVERED IN THIS CHAPTER:

✓ **2.2 Summarize the security implications of integrating systems and data with third parties.**

- On-boarding/off-boarding business partners
- Social media networks and/or applications
- Interoperability agreements: SLA; BPA; MOU; ISA
- Privacy considerations
- Risk awareness
- Unauthorized data sharing
- Data ownership
- Data backups
- Follow security policy and procedures
- Review agreement requirements to verify compliance and performance standards

✓ **2.6 Explain the importance of security related awareness and training.**

- Security policy training and procedures
- Role-based training
- Personally identifiable information
- Information classification: High; Medium; Low; Confidential; Private; Public
- Data labeling, handling and disposal
- Compliance with laws, best practices and standards
- User habits: Password behaviors; Data handling; Clean desk policies; Prevent tailgating; Personally owned devices
- New threats and new security trends/alerts: New viruses; Phishing attacks; Zero-day exploits

- Use of social networking and P2P
- Follow up and gather training metrics to validate compliance and security posture

✓ **2.9 Given a scenario, select the appropriate control to meet the goals of security.**

- Confidentiality: Encryption; Access controls; Steganography
- Integrity: Hashing; Digital signatures; Certificates; Non-repudiation
- Availability: Redundancy; Fault tolerance; Patching
- Safety: Fencing; Lighting; Locks; CCTV; Escape plans; Drills; Escape routes; Testing controls

✓ **4.2 Summarize mobile security concepts and technologies.**

- Device security: Full device encryption; Remote wiping; Lock-out; Screen-locks; GPS; Application control; Storage segmentation; Asset tracking; Inventory control; Mobile device management; Device access control; Removable storage; Disabling unused features
- BYOD concerns: Data ownership; Support ownership; Patch management; Antivirus management; Forensics; Privacy; On-boarding/off-boarding; Adherence to corporate policies; User acceptance; Architecture/infrastructure considerations; Legal concerns; Acceptable use policy; On-board camera/video

✓ **4.5 Compare and contrast alternative methods to mitigate security risks in static environments.**

- Environments: SCADA; Embedded (Printer, Smart TV, HVAC control); Android; iOS; Mainframe; Game consoles; In-vehicle computing systems
- Methods: Network segmentation; Security layers; Application firewalls; Manual updates; Firmware version control; Wrappers; Control redundancy and diversity

Several years back, *InformationWeek* conducted a survey in partnership with Accenture. As part of the survey, the question "What are the biggest security challenges facing your company?" was asked. Multiple responses were allowed, and 58 percent of the respondents stated that managing the complexity of security was one of their biggest challenges, whereas 56 percent selected user awareness (`http://www.verisign.com/static /DEV037173.pdf`). As made evident by this survey, managing security and educating users are major concerns for many organizations. Keeping computers and networks secure involves more than just the technical aspects of the systems and networks. The weakest link in many cases is the user who has access to data and a less-than-full understanding of some of the security problems they may encounter.

Security awareness and appropriate policies are key elements to your security strategy, and these issues are emphasized on the CompTIA Security+ certification test.

Third-Party Integration

Anytime your systems need to integrate with those of a third party, there are new security issues. Does that third party have security controls that meet or exceed your minimum standards? What is their auditing policy? What is their incident response policy? How will you handle integrating your two organizations different security policies and standards? These are all questions that need to be addressed.

Transitioning

Transitioning with a business partner occurs either during the on-boarding or off-boarding of a business partner. Both the initialization and the termination of a close business relationship have serious security issues.

During the on-boarding of a new business partner, it is important to determine whether the security policies of both organizations are compatible, at least in areas where the two companies' networks will interact. One area that usually does get adequate attention from most companies is the issue of interoperability agreements. These are documents that define how the two organizations' systems will interoperate and what the minimum requirements and expectations are.

Just as important is the issue of who owns the data and how that data will be backed up. In a joint enterprise, data may be combined from both organizations. It must be determined, in advance, who is responsible for that data and how the data backups will be managed.

Data backup issues include how frequently to back up, how and where to store backup media, and how to test the backup media.

It is also critical to consider privacy considerations. Certain businesses, such as medical-related companies, have specific, legally mandated privacy requirements. However, any business that has any personal data must take into consideration the security of that data. When two different organizations are interoperating, ensuring that both organizations maintain a minimum level of privacy protection is important.

There are some specific documents that need to be part of any interoperability agreement. Those are described here:

SLA: The Service-Level Agreement   The SLA defines the level of service to be provided. For example, with a company providing technical support, the SLA will determine the response time (for example, will a tech be on site within 4 hours? 8 hours?) and the level of response (will there be a replacement part if needed?).

BPO: The Blanket Purchase Order   This is usually applicable to government agencies. It is an agreement between a government agency and a private company for ongoing purchases of goods or services.

MOU: The Memorandum of Understanding   This document is used in many settings in the information industry. It is a brief summary of which party is responsible for what portion of the work. For example, Company A may be responsible for maintaining the database server and Company B may be responsible for telecommunications.

ISA: The Interconnection Security Agreement   This is an agreement between two organizations that have connected systems. The agreement documents the technical requirements of the connected systems.

All documented standards are subject to verification. The documents represent the standards that are agreed upon, but it is necessary to periodically verify compliance and performance standards. This can be done through a review of procedures, an actual audit, or even a vulnerability scan or penetration test. The level of review is up to the two parties involved.

Ongoing Operations

Once a new partnership has been established, security issues must be addressed on an ongoing basis. *Risk awareness* is one of those issues. It involves both organizations communicating with each other to share information regarding risks. A mechanism must be in place to facilitate sharing of information. One method is to set up a shared email list group among the security teams of each organization. Another is to have periodic meetings or conference calls to share risk information. The level and frequency of information sharing is contingent on the security needs of the organizations involved and how extensive the partnership between the organizations is.

Some collaboration regarding security audits will be necessary in order to ensure that both parties are following security policies and procedures. Along with audit information, it will be necessary to verify periodically that both parties are complying with the standards that have been established.

Although two organizations involved in a partnership are going to share some data, there will be other information that won't be shared. Only elements related to the areas of partnership should be shared. One major security concern is unauthorized data sharing. Data sharing can be purposeful or accidental.

Understanding Security Awareness and Training

Security awareness and training are critical to the success of a security effort. They include explaining policies, procedures, and current threats to both users and management.

A security awareness and training program can do much to assist in your efforts to improve and maintain security. Such efforts need to be ongoing, and they should be part of the organization's normal communications to be effective. The following sections discuss some of the things you can do as a security professional to address the business issues associated with training the people in your organization to operate in a manner that is consistent with organizational security goals.

Communicating with Users to Raise Awareness

Communication and awareness help ensure that security information is conveyed to the appropriate people in a timely manner. Most users aren't aware of current security threats. If you set a process in place to explain concisely and clearly what is happening and what is being done to correct current threats, you'll probably find the acceptance of your efforts to be much higher.

Communication methods that have proven to be effective for disseminating information include internal security websites, news servers, and emails. You might want to consider a regular notification process to convey information about security issues and changes. In general, the more you communicate in a routine manner, the more likely people will internalize the fact that security is everybody's responsibility.

Providing Education and Training

Your efforts in education and training must help users clearly understand prevention, enforcement, and threats. In addition to the efforts of the IT staff, the security department will probably be responsible for a security awareness program. Your organization's training and educational programs need to be tailored for at least three different audiences:

- The organization as a whole (the so-called rank and file employees)
- Management
- Technical staff

These three organizational roles have different considerations and concerns. For example, with organization-wide training everyone understands the policies, procedures, and resources available to deal with security problems, so it helps to ensure that all employees are on the same page. The following list identifies the types of issues that members of an organization should be aware of and understand. The training must be geared to the specific roles; this is called role-based training.

Organization   Ideally, a security awareness training program for the entire organization should cover the following areas:

- Importance of security
- Responsibilities of people in the organization
- Policies and procedures
- Usage policies
- Account and password-selection criteria
- Social engineering prevention

You can accomplish this training either by using internal staff or by hiring outside trainers. We recommend doing much of this training during new-employee orientation and staff meetings. To stay at their forefront of employees' minds, though, the training needs to be repeated periodically (once a year often works well). Also, don't forget to have employees sign that they received the training and are aware of the policies.

Management   Managers are concerned with more global issues in the organization, including enforcing security policies and procedures. Managers will want to know the hows and whys of a security program: how it works and why it is necessary. They should receive additional training or exposure that explains the issues, threats, and methods of dealing with threats. Management will also be concerned about productivity impacts and enforcement and how the various departments are affected by security policies.

Technical Staff   The technical staff needs special knowledge about the methods, implementations, and capabilities of the systems used to manage security. Network administrators should evaluate how to manage the network, best practices, and configuration issues associated with the technologies they support. Developers and implementers must evaluate the impact that these measures have on existing systems and new development projects. The training that both administrators and developers need will be vendor specific; vendors have their own methods of implementing security.

Microsoft, Novell, and Cisco each offer certification programs to train administrators on their environments. All of these manufacturers have specific courseware on security implementations, and some offer security certification. You should implement security systems consistent with the manufacturer's suggestions and guidance. Implementing security in a non-standard way may leave your system unsecure.

Keep in mind that all of your efforts will be wasted if you don't reach the appropriate audience. Spending an hour preaching on backend database security will likely be an hour wasted if the only members of the audience are data-entry personnel who get paid by the keystroke to make weekly changes as quickly as possible.

It is also important to follow up on all training. You must follow up and gather training metrics to validate compliance and security posture. By training metrics, we mean some quantifiable method for determining the efficacy of training. For example, if before a particular training course your organization averages four viruses per month and after training that number drops to two viruses per month, that training would be considered effective.

Safety Topics

Security is a priority for every administrator, but it cannot be the only priority: security cannot forsake all others. One of the other priorities that CompTIA wants you to be familiar with for this exam is safety. Most of the topics that fall beneath their definition of safety have been discussed in earlier chapters, but even those bear repeating here. Some of the topics relate to the safety of the data or physical environment, while others are associated with safety of the individuals you work with.

In the order the topics appear in the objectives, these are as follows:

Fencing Fencing is used to increase physical security and safety and was discussed in Chapter 10. A fence can keep out unwanted entities—vehicles, people, etc.—and funnel those leaving to an easy to manage exit point where you can manage them easier.

Lighting Like fencing, lighting can aid greatly with physical security and was discussed in Chapter 10. An area that is not well-lit can be more easily compromised than one which is.

Locks Locks are a lot like passwords—they need to be easy enough to work that those who are authorized can effectively navigate them but strong enough to keep those who are not authorized out. As a general rule, the strength of locks and the costs of them are closely related. Be sure to lock up not only the server room but also the wiring closets and physical hardware that could wander off.

CCTV Closed Circuit TV (CCTV) surveillance can help lessen the success of unauthorized access attempts. To be successfully used in prosecution, the recording equipment used with the cameras should be of good quality. To deter attempts, employees—and all others—should be made aware of the presence of the cameras.

Escape Plans With all the fencing, locks, and blinding lighting that is installed in the office, it is highly recommended that escape plans be in place and understood by all. Someone (a designated safety officer) should be responsible for keeping the plan current and making certain all employees are aware of it.

Drills To make certain not only that employees know the escape plan(s) but that it also works, drills should be conducted on a regular basis. The safety office in charge of the escape plans should also be responsible for the drills and make modifications as conditions change or problems arise.

Escape Routes   The aforementioned escape plan and drills should direct the employees to safety via an escape route. Alternate routes should be identified in the event that the primary escape route is blocked.

Testing Controls   Controls come in three types, as discussed in Chapter 1: Technical, Management, and Operational. Since there is a reliance by at least two of these types on individuals, regularly test to verify that they are working properly and responses are appropriate.

Keep safety as one of your priorities as an administrator. Hope that you never have to respond to an emergency situation, but take comfort in knowing that your employees know how to respond should the need arise.

Training Topics

It is said that knowledge is a powerful tool. Armed with it, you are more capable of tackling problems and avoiding pitfalls than without it. What is true for you is also true for the users with whom you work—the more they know about security issues, the better they are able to avoid pitfalls and recognize problems when they encounter them.

It would be nice if you could get every user to understand security fully and stay current on the topic, but this luxury exists in only a few workplaces. Given the limitations for educating the entire work staff, there are a number of topics that can be considered more important than others and on which you should focus user education. In no particular order, these are as follows:

Clean Desk Policy   Information on a desk—in terms of printouts, pads of note paper, sticky notes, and the like—can be easily seen by prying eyes and taken by thieving hands. To protect data and your business, encourage employees to maintain clean desks and to leave out only those papers that are relevant to the project they are working on at that moment. All sensitive information should be put away when the employee is away from their desk.

 Real World Scenario

Applying Education Appropriately

As a security administrator, you need to know the level of knowledge that is appropriate for the audience you're addressing and be able to understand the importance of speaking to them at that level. Imagine that you find yourself in each of the following situations, and think through your response. Remember that it's important to give the right message to the right people. When giving any presentation, you should always tailor it for the intended audience and be able to make your discussion relevant to them. Recommendations for how to handle each situation are provided after each scenario.

Scenario 1   You've been assigned the task of giving a one-hour briefing on the topic of security to management during their weekly luncheon (no other subtopics or specifics were given). Most of those in attendance will be upper management who know little about computers and tend to focus on financial sheets. What topics will you discuss and at what depth?

> **Recommendation**   Keep the talk at the overview level and focus only on the basics of security: why it's needed, how valuable data is, how to use strong passwords, and so on.

Scenario 2   You've been told to meet with the developers of a new application that will soon be rolled out to all branch offices. The application will hold all human resource records as well as a small amount of client information. Your boss tells you that after the meeting, you're to sign off on the application as being okay to deploy. What type of security questions will you focus on?

> **Recommendation**   Push to try out the application in a test environment first (nonproduction). You want to make certain that no back doors have been left in by the developers and that no negative interactions will occur between the new application and what is already running on your systems.

Scenario 3   The annual company meeting is next month. Representatives, including those in IT, from all remote offices will arrive at your headquarters for a three-day visit. You've been asked to speak about the importance of strong passwords throughout the organization. What will you say, and how will you make your one-hour presentation stay with them after they return to their offices?

> **Recommendation**   Give examples of security breaches that have been in the news recently. Talk about the impact such an event would have on your organization. Discuss how simple it is to prevent many attacks by implementing strong passwords and then give examples. Be sure to talk about how this affects their own jobs.

Compliance with Laws, Best Practices, and Standards   Users need to realize that working with data is the same as driving a car, owning a home, or almost anything else in that there are laws, practices, and standards to which they must adhere. Just as negligence fails to be an admissible excuse in other areas of the law, the same holds true when working with data. New regulations are passed regularly, and it is your job as an administrator to educate users on those that are applicable in your environment.

Regulations are discussed in greater detail at the end of this chapter.

Data Handling   Only those users needing to work with it should access data. It is your job to implement safeguards to keep the data from being seen by those who should not, but the users need to understand why those safeguards are there and abide by them. There are plenty of examples of companies that have suffered great financial loss when their information, trade secrets, and client information was leaked.

Policy on Personally Owned Devices   Empathize with the users who want to bring their gadgets from home, but make them understand why they cannot. You do not want them plugging in a flash drive, let alone a camera, smartphone, tablet computer, or other device, on which company files could get intermingled with personal files. Allowing this to happen can create situations where data can leave the building that shouldn't as well as introduce malware to the system. There has been a rash of incidents in which data has been smuggled out of an organization through personal devices. One of the most notorious is the 250,000 Top Secret documents that appeared on WikiLeaks (www.dailymail.co.uk/news/article-1333982 /WikiLeaks-US-Army-soldier-Bradley-Manning-prime-suspect-leaks-case.html).

Employees should not sync unauthorized smartphones to their work systems. Some smartphones use multiple wireless spectrums and unwittingly open up the possibility for an attacker in the parking lot to gain access through the phone to the internal network.

Ban—and make sure the users know that you have done so—all social peer-to-peer (P2P) networking. These are common for sharing files such as movies and music, but you must not allow users to bring in devices and create their own little networks to share files, printers, songs, and so on. All networking must be done through administrators and not on a P2P basis. The P2P ports should be listed on the company servers (either whitelisted or blacklisted), and an alert should be sent to you any time someone attempts any P2P activity. Vigilantly look for all such activity, and put a stop to it immediately.

Personally Identifiable Information   *Personally identifiable information (PII)* is a catchall for any data that can be used to uniquely identify an individual. This data can be anything from the person's name to a fingerprint (think biometrics), credit card number, or patient record. The term became mainstream when the NIST (National Institute of Standards and Technology) began issuing guides and recommendations regarding it.

NIST defines PII as follows (see http://csrc.nist.gov/publications/nistpubs/800-122 /sp800-122.pdf):

> Any information about an individual maintained by an agency, including (1) any information that can be used to distinguish or trace an individual's identity, such as name, social security number, date and place of birth, mother's maiden name, or biometric records; and (2) any other information that is linked or linkable to an individual, such as medical, educational, financial, and employment information.

> *NIST published Special Publication 800-122, "Guide to Protecting the Confidentiality of Personally Identifiable Information (PII)"*

Users within your organization should understand PII and the reasons to safeguard their own data as well as respect the records of customers and other users. Also, according to the NIST:

> For PII protection, awareness methods include informing staff of new scams that are being used to steal identities, providing updates on privacy items in the news such as government data breaches and their effect on individuals and the organization, providing examples of how staff members have been held accountable for inappropriate actions, and providing examples of recommended privacy practices.
>
> NIST *published Special Publication 800-122, "Guide to Protecting the Confidentiality of Personally Identifiable Information (PII)"*

To help users understand the significance of PII, explain that the SIM (Subscriber Identification Module) card in their smartphone contains PII information about them and they would not want it to fall into the wrong hands.

Social engineering is a broad topic but easy to understand. It simply means using persuasion to get what you want, such as trying to talk someone into providing their information or allowing you access when you don't have a badge or key. Social engineering depends on the attacker's sales skills rather than technical skills. A classic example of social engineering would be an attacker calling a random person at a company, claiming to be with the company's IT department. (This works only in larger companies where employees don't all know each other.) The attacker then claims that they need to "check for your antivirus updates," or some similar task, and need your password to do so. It is amazing how often tricks like this work. This is just one example, but any attempt to use social skills to effect a security breach is *social engineering*.

Prevent Tailgating   *Tailgating* is the term used for someone being so close to you when you enter a building that they are able to come in right behind you without needing to use a key, a card, or any other security device. Many social engineering intruders needing physical access to a site will use this method of gaining entry. Educate users to beware of this and other social engineering ploys and prevent them from happening.

Sometimes the term *piggybacking* is used in place of *tailgating*, but there is a key difference between the two. In tailgating, the person in front does not give permission to the person behind, whereas with piggybacking, they do give permission.

Safe Internet Habits   As we discussed in Chapter 4, "Access Control, Authentication, and Authorization," users should be familiar enough with phishing to comprehend that they should not click links or open attachments to files that they weren't expecting. They should appreciate that the best way to close pop-ups is to click the X in the upper-right corner and never by clicking OK or anything else in the pop-up.

Software should never be downloaded or installed from unknown sites. Although the user may think that they are saving the company money by finding a free version of software that promises to work just like an expensive package, the odds of malware accompanying the free program are considerable; administrators should contend with the high cost of software and not end users.

One of the most wicked phishing undertakings popular today is a fake security/antivirus program. A pop-up tells the user that their system is infected with a virus and to get rid of it they need to run a program that looks like an authorized cleanup tool but is actually itself the virus (`www.microsoft.com/security/antivirus/rogue.aspx`).

Smart Computing Habits   Every user should know that they should never introduce any stray media into their system regardless of how innocent they may think their actions. A flash drive found in the trashcan with "Pix of Chelsea" written on it can contain the Trojan needed to open a back door into the network.

Encourage reading of the EULA (End User License Agreement) on any third-party software. These can be more difficult to get through than a law school application form, but seeing what they are agreeing to can be an eye-opener for a user when they realize what limitations they are working with and what they're giving up. Discourage users from installing any third-party software without IT approval.

Social Networking Dangers   As of this writing, many companies allow full use of social media in the workplace, believing that the marketing opportunities it holds outweigh any loss in productivity. What they are unknowingly minimizing are the threats that exist. Rather than being all new threats, the social networking/media threats tend to fall in the categories of the same old tricks used elsewhere but in a new format. A tweet can be sent with a shortened URL so that it does not exceed the 140-character limit set by Twitter; unfortunately, the user has no idea what the shortened URL leads to—it could be to a phishing site, a downloadable Trojan, or just about anything else.

Educate users to exercise the same care and caution in social media as in any other environment. For an example of the dangers, read about "Cisco Fatty" (`www.msnbc.msn.com/id/29901380/ns/technology_and_science-tech_and_gadgets/`).

The Need for All Computing to Be Safe   Many users work on data away from the office as well as in the office. They need to understand that the data is only as strong as the weakest place in which it is used, and they must have security measures on their home computers that protect your company's data as well. Although the home systems will never be as secure (most likely) as the business systems, at a minimum the home systems need to be running firewalls and updated virus scanners.

Since they need to be safe at home, educate users on the necessity to keep current on new threats. Those threats can come in the form of new viruses, new forms of phishing attacks, and new *zero-day exploits*. The latter is the term used when a hole is found in a web browser or other software and attackers begin exploiting it the very day it is discovered by the developer (bypassing the one-to-two-day response time many software providers need to put out a patch once the hole has been found).

> Zero-day exploits are incredibly difficult to respond to. If attackers learn of the weakness the same day as the developer, then they have the ability to exploit it until a patch is released. Often, the only thing you can do as a security administrator between the discovery of the exploit and the release of the patch is to turn off the service. Although this can be a costly undertaking in terms of productivity, it is the only way to keep the network safe. In 2010, Stuxnet was found to be using a total of four zero-day vulnerabilities to spread (www.symantec.com/connect/blogs /stuxnet-using-three-additional-zero-day-vulnerabilities).

The Value of Strong Passwords   Passwords are a common topic in this chapter and throughout this book. Users need to understand that the stronger they make their password, the more difficult they make anyone's attempt to crack it. They should be educated to use long passwords consisting of letters, numbers, and characters and to change them frequently.

They must also be educated that they cannot write their password down on a sticky note right after a change and post it under the keyboard, on the monitor, or anywhere else. The reasons for regularly changing passwords should be explained along with the requirement that you will make them do so at least every three months.

> Microsoft has an online password checker to which you can direct users if they want to see how strong the password they're considering is. This can be found at https://www.microsoft.com/protect/fraud/passwords /checker.aspx.

Understanding Data Labeling and Handling   A great many users don't consider that there are different types of data and various values associated with it. They don't realize that a misplaced backup copy of the mission statement is not as great a loss from a financial standpoint as a misplaced backup copy of customer contacts.

As a security administrator, you should help users to realize that different types of data unique to your organization have different values and need to be labeled accordingly. (The discussion of information models later in this chapter will help.) Once it has been established and understood that there are significant differences, you can address handling these different types of data. The importance of protecting the data in all forms—online, backups, hard copies, and so on—should be covered as well as reasons why different groups should not access data outside of their permission category. (Again, the discussion of information models later in this chapter will help.)

What to Do When Disposing of Old Media   Many users never think about data beyond the time that they are working with it. They don't realize that the old computer they toss out at home has copies of company-related files on the hard drive that could fall into the wrong hands or that the 256 MB flash drive they toss away when they buy a new 32 GB one also has files that should never be seen outside of the office. A good example of the importance of this is the tale of the U.S. missile data found on a hard drive purchased on eBay:

> www.independent.co.uk/news/world/americas/us-missile-data-found-on-ebay
> -hard-drive-1680529.html

Teaching users the basics of *data disposal*—how to destroy media (such as by hammer, drill, or fire)—can be one of the most fun, and most memorable, training sessions of the year.

Responding to Hoaxes   In addition to all of the different types of attacks that are present, there are also a plethora of hoaxes that exist. A *hoax* is defined as a deliberately fabricated falsehood. Just as virus creators enjoy seeing their work do damage and knowing that they caused it, those who start hoaxes enjoy knowing that they caused a panic, and the Internet allows them to see the hoax spread with wild abandon. Most hoaxes are spread through email and alert the recipient to impending doom—their computer will crash if not turned off at 1 a.m. on Friday the 13th, they have been infected with the Lincoln virus if their hard drive has a file named WINWORD.EXE present, and so on. Software that tries to convince unsuspecting users that a threat exists is known as *scareware*. If it convinces them to pay money for protection from a fake threat, then the term *rogueware* is applied.

As a security administrator, you need to educate users that the best course of action when they receive such messages is to refuse to panic and to contact IT. Assure them that you will verify whether it is a hoax or a legitimate issue as quickly as possible and let them know. Under no circumstances, they should understand, are they to spread the warning and further propagate the alarm.

How security training is delivered—in terms of both method and frequency—will differ for most businesses. It is important, however, that new employees understand the importance of security on their first day at the job and that they be presented with a clearly articulated security policy that mentions the possible HR actions if they violate that policy.

As the administrator, you want to make certain that you are taking a proactive stance and educating users on potential problems before they become real issues and revisit key topics often enough that they realize their importance.

Classifying Information

Information classification is a key aspect of a secure network. Again, the process of developing a classification scheme is both a technical and a human issue. The technologies you use must be able to support your organization's privacy requirements. People and processes must be in place and working effectively to prevent unauthorized disclosure of sensitive information.

Information can be generally classified by confidentiality as simply high, medium, or low. However, this is rather vague and not quite as helpful. What exactly is "high" confidentiality? Other ways of classifying information are discussed in this section.

If you think about all the information your organization keeps, you'll probably find that it breaks down into three primary categories:

- Public use

- Internal use

- Restricted use

Figure 11.1 shows the typical ratios of how this information is broken down. Notice that 80 percent of the information in your organization is primarily for internal or private use. This information would include memos, working papers, financial data, and information records, among other things.

FIGURE 11.1   Information categories

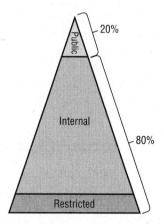

Next we'll look at public information—and its various categories—and then discuss private information.

Public Information

Public information is primarily that which is made available either to the larger public or to specific individuals who need it. Financial statements of a privately held organization might be information that is available publicly but only to individuals or organizations that have a legitimate need for it.

The important thing to keep in mind is that an organization needs to develop policies about what information is available and for what purposes it will be disseminated. It's also helpful to make sure that members of the organization know who has authorization to make these kinds of disclosures. Some organizations gather competitive data for a fee; they often use social engineering approaches to gain information about a business. Good policies help prevent the accidental dissemination of sensitive information.

The following sections examine the difference between limited and full distribution.

Limited Distribution

Limited distribution information isn't intended for release to the public. This category of information isn't secret, but it's private. If a company is seeking to obtain a line of credit, the information provided to a bank is of a private nature. This information, if disclosed to competitors, might give them insight into the organization's plans or financial health. If disclosed to customers, it might scare them and cause them to switch to a competitor.

> Some EULAs now limit the information that users can disclose about problems with their software. These new statements have not yet been challenged in court. Try to avoid being the test case for this new and alarming element of some software licenses; read the EULA before you agree to it.

These types of disclosures are usually held in confidence by banks and financial institutions. These institutions typically have privacy and confidentiality regulations as well as policies that must be followed by all employees of the institution.

Software manufacturers typically release early versions of their products to customers who are willing to help evaluate functionality. Early versions of software may not always work properly, and they often have features that aren't included in the final version. This version of the software is a *beta test*. Before beta testers are allowed to use the software, they're required to sign a nondisclosure agreement (NDA). The NDA tells the tester what privacy requirements exist for the product. The product being developed will change, and any problems with the beta version probably won't be a great secret. However, the NDA reminds the testers of their confidentiality responsibilities.

> NDAs are common in the technology arena. Make sure that you read any NDA thoroughly before you sign it. You don't have to sign an NDA to be bound by it: If you agree that you'll treat the information as private and then receive the information, you have, in essence, agreed to an NDA. In most cases, this form of verbal NDA is valid for only one year.

Statements indicating privacy or confidentiality are common on limited-access documents. They should indicate that disclosure of the information without permission is a breach of confidentiality. This may help someone remember that the information isn't for public dissemination.

Full Distribution

Marketing materials are examples of information that should be available for *full distribution*. Annual reports to stockholders and other information of a public relations nature are also examples of full-distribution materials.

The key element of the full-distribution classification involves decision-making responsibility. Who makes the decision about full disclosure? Larger organizations have a corporate communications department that is responsible for managing this process. If you aren't sure, it's a good idea to ask about dissemination of information. Don't assume that you know; that is the purpose of an information classification policy.

Private Information

Private information is intended only for internal use within the organization. This type of information could potentially embarrass the company, disclose trade secrets, or adversely affect personnel. Private information may also be referred to as *working documents* or *work product*. It's important that private information not be disclosed because it can potentially involve litigation if the disclosure is improper.

You'll learn about the difference between internal and restricted information in the following sections.

Internal Information

Internal information includes personnel records, financial working documents, ledgers, customer lists, and virtually any other information that is needed to run a business. This information is valuable and must be protected.

In the case of personnel and medical records, disclosure to unauthorized personnel creates liability issues. Many organizations are unwilling to do anything more than verify employment because of the fear of unauthorized disclosure.

A school views student information as internal. Schools can't release information about students without specific permission from the student.

Restricted Information

Restricted information could seriously damage the organization if disclosed. It includes proprietary processes, trade secrets, strategic information, and marketing plans. This information should never be disclosed to an outside party unless senior management gives specific authorization. In many cases, this type of information is also placed on a *need-to-know basis*—unless you need to know, you won't be informed.

Government and Military Classifications

The U.S. government and the military have slightly different sets of concerns relating to information classification. Governmental agencies are concerned about privacy and national security. Because of this, a unique system of classification and access controls has been implemented to protect information.

The following is a list of some of the types of government classifications:

Unclassified   This classification is used to indicate that the information poses no risk of potential loss due to disclosure. Anybody can gain access to this category of information. Many training manuals and regulations are unclassified.

Sensitive but Unclassified   This classification is used for low-level security. It indicates that disclosure of this information might cause harm but wouldn't injure national defense efforts. The amount of toilet paper a military base uses may be considered sensitive because this information might help an intelligence agency guess at the number of personnel on the base.

Confidential   This classification is used to identify low-level secrets; it's generally the lowest level of classification used by the military. It's used extensively to prevent access to sensitive information. Information that is lower than Confidential is generally considered Unclassified. The Confidential classification, however, allows information to be restricted for access under the Freedom of Information Act. The maintenance requirements for a machine gun may be classified as Confidential; this information would include drawings, procedures, and specifications that disclose how the weapon works.

Secret   Secret information, if disclosed, could cause serious and irreparable damage to defense efforts. Information that is classified as Secret requires special handling, training, and storage. This information is considered a closely guarded secret of the military or government. Troop movements, deployments, capabilities, and other plans would be minimally classified as Secret. The military views the unauthorized disclosure of Secret information as criminal and potentially treasonous.

Top Secret   The Top Secret classification is the highest classification level. There are rumored to be higher levels of classification, but the names of those classifications are themselves classified Top Secret. Releasing information that is classified as Top Secret poses a grave threat to national security, and therefore it must not be compromised. Information such as intelligence activities, nuclear war plans, and weapons systems development would normally be classified as Top Secret.

The government has also developed a process to formally review and downgrade classification levels on a regular basis. This process generally downgrades information based on age, sensitivity, and usefulness. There are methods of overriding this downgrade process to prevent certain information from being declassified; some secrets are best left secret.

The military also uses an additional method of classifying information and access, which has the effect of compartmentalizing information. For example, if you were a weapons developer, it isn't likely that you would need access to information from spy satellites. You would be given special access to information necessary for the specific project you were working on. When the project was finished, access to this special information would be revoked. This process allows information to be protected and access limited to a need-to-know basis.

The process of obtaining a security clearance either for the military, a federal office or lab, or a government contractor can be quite involved. The normal process involves investigating you, your family, and potentially anybody else who could put you in a compromised position. The process can take months, and it includes agents doing fieldwork to complete, or augment, the investigation.

Information Access Controls

Access control defines the methods used to ensure that users of your network can access only what they're authorized to access. The process of access control should be spelled out in the organization's security policies and standards. Several models exist to accomplish this. Regardless of the model you use, a few concepts carry over:

Implicit Denies   wherewith implicit denies, you lock certain users out. In Unix and Linux, for example, you can choose who can use the `at` service by configuring either an `at.allow` or an `at.deny` file. If you configure the `at.allow` file, then only those users named can use the service and all others cannot. If you configure the `at.deny` file, then only the users named in that file cannot use the service (you are implicitly denying them) and all others can.

Least Privilege   You should use this model when assigning permissions. Give users only the permissions they need to do their work and no more.

Job Rotation   Rotate jobs on a frequent enough basis that you are not putting yourself—and your data—at the mercy of any one administrator. Just as you want redundancy in hardware, you want redundancy in abilities. Web administrators, for example, can be moved to database administration and can become more valuable to the organization and themselves by gaining that skill set. Depending on the size of your organization, this may be easy or difficult to do, but we highly recommend doing so in all cases.

Security Concepts

There are three concepts you will see throughout this book and probably in every computer security book you will ever read: confidentiality, integrity, and availability, often referred to as the CIA triad. All security measures should affect one or more of these areas. The CIA triad may also be described by its opposite: disclosure, alteration, and destruction (DAD).

Confidentiality   Confidentiality means preventing unauthorized users from accessing data. Passwords, hard drive encryption, and access control all support confidentiality. It is also possible to use steganography to hide data and thus protect confidentiality. Both of these topics were covered in detail in Chapter 8, "Cryptography."

Integrity   Integrity means ensuring that data has not been altered. Hashing and message authentication codes (discussed in Chapter 8) are the most common methods to accomplish this. In addition, ensuring nonrepudiation via digital signatures (also discussed in Chapter 8) supports integrity.

Availability   Simply making sure that the data and systems are available for authorized users is what availability is all about. Data backups, redundant systems, and disaster recovery plans all support availability. These methodologies provide a system that has fault tolerance. It is just as important to availability to ensure that a system is patched. Fault tolerance methods are discussed in detail in Chapter 12, "Disaster Recovery and Incident Response." Patching was covered in detail in Chapter 7, "Host, Data, and Application Security."

> The Security+ test will ask you about the CIA triad. You should know it well and be able to address how a specific security process, procedure, or technology impacts the CIA triad.

Complying with Privacy and Security Regulations

An organization's security management policies don't exist in a vacuum. Regulatory and governmental agencies are key components of a security management policy. These agencies have made large improvements over the last several years to ensure the privacy of information; several laws have been passed to help ensure that information isn't disclosed to unauthorized parties. The following sections provide a brief overview of a few of these regulations. As a security professional, you must stay current with these laws because you're one of the primary agents to ensure compliance. Not only do you need to know them for the day-to-day grind, but CompTIA also expects you to have a basic knowledge of them for the Security+ exam.

> In addition to the federal laws, most states have laws covering computer crime. Check with your state attorney general's office for specific IT legislation that applies in your state.

The Health Insurance Portability and Accountability Act

The *Health Insurance Portability and Accountability Act (HIPAA)* is a regulation that mandates national standards and procedures for the storage, use, and transmission of personal medical information. Passed into law in 1996, HIPAA has caused a great deal of change in healthcare recordkeeping.

HIPAA covers three areas—confidentiality, privacy, and the security of patient records. It was implemented in several phases to make the transition easier. Confidentiality and privacy of patient records had to be implemented by a set date, followed by security of patient records. Standards for transaction codes in medical record transmissions had to be completed by a given date as well.

The penalties for HIPAA violations are very stiff; they can be as high as $250,000 based on the circumstances. Medical practices are required to appoint a security officer. All related parties, such as billing agencies and medical records storage facilities, are required to comply with these regulations. The Health Information Technology for Economic and Clinical Health (HITECH) Act promotes the adoption and meaningful use of health information technology. Subtitle D of HITECH addresses the privacy and security concerns associated with the electronic transmission of health information through several provisions that strengthen the civil and criminal enforcement of the HIPAA rules.

For more information on HIPAA, you can visit www.cms.hhs.gov /HIPAAGenInfo/.

The Gramm-Leach-Bliley Act

The *Gramm-Leach-Bliley Act*, also known as the *Financial Modernization Act of 1999*, requires financial institutions to develop privacy notices and to notify customers that they are entitled to privacy. The act prohibits banks from releasing information to nonaffiliated third parties without permission. Many consumer groups have criticized the implementation of this act by financial institutions because of all the paperwork that it has created.

The act requires that employees need to be trained on information security issues, and security measures must be put into place and tested to verify information privacy. The act includes a number of other provisions that allow banks and financial institutions to align and form partnerships.

The act requires banks to explain to individual consumers information-sharing policies. Customers have the ability to opt out of sharing agreements.

The act prohibits institutions from sharing account information for marketing purposes. It also prohibits the gathering of information about customers using false or fraudulent methods.

The law went into effect in July 2001. Financial officers and the board of directors can be held criminally liable for violations.

For more information on the Gramm-Leach-Bliley Act, visit www.ftc.gov /privacy/privacyinitiatives/glbact.html.

The Computer Fraud and Abuse Act

The *Computer Fraud and Abuse Act (CFAA)* went into law in 1986. The original law was introduced to address issues of fraud and abuse that weren't well covered under existing statutes. The law was updated in 1994, in 1996, and again in 2001.

This act gives federal authorities, primarily the FBI, the ability to prosecute hackers, spammers, and others as terrorists. The law is intended to protect government and financial computer systems from intrusion. Technically, if a governmental system, such as an Internet server, were used in the commission of the crime, virtually any computer user who could be shown to have any knowledge or part in the crime could be prosecuted.

The law is comprehensive and allows for stiff penalties, fines, and imprisonment of up to 10 years for convictions under this statute.

> For more information on the Computer Fraud and Abuse Act, visit the site https://ilt.eff.org/index.php/Computer_Fraud_and_Abuse_Act _(CFAA).

The Family Educational Rights and Privacy Act

The *Family Educational Rights and Privacy Act (FERPA)* dictates that educational institutions may not release information to unauthorized parties without the express permission of the student or, in the case of a minor, the parents of the student. This act also requires that educational institutions must disclose any records kept on a student when demanded by that student. This law has had a huge impact on privacy requirements of student records. It jeopardizes the federal funding of schools by government agencies if any violations occur.

> For more information on FERPA, visit www.ed.gov/policy/gen/guid /fpco/ferpa/index.html. To view a database of losses involving personally identifiable information, visit http://attrition.org/dataloss/.

The Computer Security Act of 1987

The *Computer Security Act* requires federal agencies to identify and protect computer systems that contain sensitive information. This law requires agencies that keep sensitive information to conduct regular training and audits and to implement procedures to protect privacy. All federal agencies must comply with this act.

> For more information on the Computer Security Act, visit http://epic .org/crypto/csa/.

The Cyberspace Electronic Security Act

The *Cyberspace Electronic Security Act (CESA)* was passed in 1999, and it gives law enforcement the right to gain access to encryption keys and cryptography methods. The initial version of this act allowed federal law enforcement agencies to secretly use monitoring, electronic capturing equipment, and other technologies to access and obtain information. These provisions were later stricken from the act, although federal law enforcement agencies were given a large amount of latitude to conduct investigations relating to electronic information. This act generated much discussion about what capabilities law enforcement should be allowed to use in the detection of criminal activity.

> One problem with the act is that it does not have any mechanism for law enforcement to obtain encryption keys. They are not necessarily stored with a third party. The law simply states that if a third party has encryption keys, law enforcement officials can request a subpoena to demand such keys if they can convince a judge of probable cause.

The Cyber Security Enhancement Act

The *Cyber Security Enhancement Act* of 2002 allows federal agencies relatively easy access to ISPs and other data transmission facilities to monitor communications of individuals suspected of committing computer crimes using the Internet. The act is also known as *Section 225 of the Homeland Security Act* of 2002.

> For more information on the Cyber Security Enhancement Act, visit http://itlaw.wikia.com/wiki/Cyber_Security_Enhancement_Act.

The Patriot Act

The *Uniting and Strengthening America by Providing Appropriate Tools Required to Intercept and Obstruct Terrorism (USA PATRIOT) Act of 2001* was passed largely because of the World Trade Center attack on September 11, 2001. This law gives the U.S. government extreme latitude in pursuing criminals who commit terrorist acts. The definition of a terrorist act is broad.

The law provides for relief to victims of terrorism as well as the ability to conduct virtually any type of surveillance of a suspected terrorist. This act is constantly under review and portions of it are regularly being litigated. Portions of it relevant to IT security include the authority to intercept electronic communications.

> For more information on the Patriot Act, one of the best sources is Wikipedia: http://en.wikipedia.org/wiki/Patriot_act.

Familiarizing Yourself with International Efforts

Many governments are now evaluating their current laws regarding cyberterrorism, cyber-crime, and privacy. Among the agencies that are currently evaluating cyber laws are the European Union (EU) and the G20 (formerly G8).

The EU, which is a common governance agency that includes many member nations, is soon expected to enact tough legislation regarding computer use. In the next few years, the EU is likely to be formidable in its ability to pursue and prosecute cyber criminals.

The EU is adopting the strategy of looking at all EU member nations as a large "Information Society," and it will be passing laws and regulations regarding computer security and privacy among all members. It's also working on laws to protect computer systems and prevent cybercrime. The most all-encompassing law thus far is the Cybercrime Treaty, which makes all hacking illegal in Europe.

Mobile Devices

Mobile devices, such as laptops, tablet computers, and smartphones, provide security challenges above those of desktop workstations, servers, and such in that they leave the office and this increases the odds of their theft. In 2010, AvMed Health Plans, a Florida-based company, had two laptop computers stolen. Together, over one million personal customer records were on those computers, and this is but one of many similar stories that happen on a regular basis.

At a bare minimum, the following security measures should be in place on mobile devices:

Screen Lock   The display should be configured to time out after a short period of inactivity and the screen locked with a password. To be able to access the system again, the user must provide the password. After a certain number of attempts, the user should not be allowed to attempt any additional logons; this is called *lockout*.

Strong Password   Passwords are always important, but even more so when you consider that the device could be stolen and in the possession of someone who has unlimited access and time to try various values.

Device Encryption   Data should be encrypted on the device so that if it does fall into the wrong hands, it cannot be accessed in a usable form without the correct passwords. We recommend that you use Trusted Platform Module (TPM), discussed in Chapter 8, for all laptops where possible.

Remote Wipe/Sanitation   Many programs, such as Microsoft Exchange Server 2010 or Google Apps, allow you to send a command to a phone that will remotely clear the data on that phone. This process is known as a *remote wipe*, and it is intended to be used if the phone is stolen or going to another user.

Voice Encryption Voice encryption can be used with mobile phones and similar devices to encrypt transmissions. This is intended to keep the conversation secure and works by adding cryptography (discussed in Chapter 8) to the digitized conversation.

GPS Tracking Should a device be stolen, GPS (Global Positioning System) tracking can be used to identify its location and allow authorities to find it. Note that removable storage can circumvent GPS. For example, if a device has GPS tracking but it also has removable storage, a thief can simply remove the data they want and leave the device.

Application Control Application control is primarily concerned with controlling what applications are installed on the mobile device. Most viruses that are found on Android phones stem from bad applications being installed. Related to application control is disabling unused services. If you do not need a service, turn it off.

Storage Segmentation By segmenting a mobile device's storage you can keep work data separate from personal or operating system data. You can even implement whole device encryption or just encrypt the confidential data.

Asset Tracking You must have a method of asset tracking. It can be as simple as a serial number etched in the device or as complex as a GPS locator. Related to this is inventory control. A complete and accurate list of all devices is an integral part of mobile device management.

Device Access Control Device access control, in this context, refers to controlling who in the organization has a mobile device. Not every employee should have one. Limiting access to such devices reduces risk.

BYOD Issues

BYOD (Bring Your Own Device) refers to employees bringing their personal devices into the corporate network environment. This is a common issue in the modern workplace, and it can pose substantial security risks.

The first risk involves those devices connecting to the company network. If an employee has personal smartphone, for example, and they bring it to work and connect it to the company's Wi-Fi network, then any virus, spyware, or other malware that may have infected that phone can spread to the company network. One way to address this is to have a second Wi-Fi network—not connected to the main corporate network, but simply a guest network—and only allow personal devices to connect to that Wi-Fi and not to the main network.

Another risk involves compromising confidential data. Modern mobile devices are complex computer systems. An employee could use a cell phone to photograph sensitive documents, record conversations, and acquire a great deal of sensitive data. Some Department of Defense contractors do not allow phones in certain sensitive areas of their buildings. This may be more restrictive than at most civilian companies, but at least you should be aware of this potential issue and have a policy to address it. That policy could be as simple as all employees agreeing that if they bring a mobile device onto company property, it is subject to random search.

Data ownership becomes an issue with BYOD. If the device is personally owned but used for company business, who owns the data on the device? The company or the individual? Related to that is the issue of support ownership. Is the individual responsible for support or the company? Patch management is closely related to support ownership. Who will be responsible for ensuring the personal device has patches updated? Antivirus management is another related issue. What antivirus software will be used? How will it be updated? These are all important questions that will need to be answered.

Adherence to corporate policies is an obvious issue. If individuals own their own devices, which they have purchased with their own funds, ensuring the user and the device adhere to corporate policies will be a challenge. Related to that issue are legal concerns. When a device is owned by the individual but used for company business, a number of legal issues arise. As just one example, what if the device is used to send spam? Is the company responsible? Another example would involve the employee leaving the company. How does the organization verify the device does not have any proprietary data on it? Forensics is another legal issue. If there is, for example, litigation against the company, usually computer records are subpoenaed, but the data that might reside on a personal device is a legal gray area.

Then there are purely technical concerns. Architecture and infrastructure considerations are critical. Will the personal device be compatible with the organizational infrastructure? On-board cameras and video also pose a challenge. Some organizations forbid the use of cameras within the company, or at least within secure areas. And finally there is the issue of acceptable use policies. Companies generally have acceptable use policies regarding how computers can be used within the organization. How will that be implemented with devices that don't belong to the company?

None of this is meant to indicate you cannot use BYOD devices in your organization. However, you do need to address the issues mentioned in this section before allowing BYOD devices to connect to your network. Some organizations simply opt to forbid such devices, but in our modern world of ubiquitous devices, that approach may not be feasible in your organization.

Alternative Methods to Mitigate Security Risks

Some generalized methods can be used to mitigate the security risks to any network. One of the most basic is the combination of network segmentation and security layers. These are very closely related subjects. Network segmentation means dividing your network into segments. Ideally the connection points between each segment (routers) will also implement security features such as a firewall and intrusion detection system. This means that a breach of one segment of your network does not jeopardize the entire network. It is only logical to segment your network based on security layers, or zones based on security needs. The most obvious example is an external zone (called a demilitarized zone [DMZ]) for publicly accessible resources like a web server, and an internal zone for your actual corporate network. You can use as many zones as are needed, each with a different (but appropriate) level of security.

Network protection can be enhanced with some simple techniques. Application firewalls are usually better protection for database servers or web servers than are other types of firewalls. Application firewalls, in addition to packet filtering, filter specific application-related content. For example, a web server might use an application firewall to filter common SQL injection attacks.

Updates are also important. In other chapters we have discussed patches and similar updates. It is just as important to make sure firmware updates are applied. Firmware version control is closely related to updating the firmware. You need to be sure that each device is using the appropriate version of firmware. You may even need to manually update devices with critical updates. Certain viruses specifically target the firmware in routers and switches. This risk is mitigated by firmware version control.

One very important technique is controlling redundancy and diversity. Although this may sound complex, it simply means two things. The first is implementing more than one of each security control. If you have an intrusion detection system in your DMZ, you may want to have another in your network. Diversity means using different controls of the same type. For example, if you use the Cisco IDS on your perimeter, you may wish to use SNORT IDS inside your network. The reasoning is that if an attack thwarts one of your IDSs, it may not evade both. This concept applies to all security controls. Wrappers are a related topic. This technique involves wrapping sensitive systems with a specific control, such as having your sensitive data servers in their own network segment with their own firewall, IDS, and antivirus protection.

A variety of specialized systems have security issues specific to those systems. You must mitigate the risk on each of these systems.

SCADA (supervisory control and data acquisition) refers to equipment often used to manage automated factory equipment, dams, power generators, and similar equipment. The Security+ exam does not heavily emphasize this, because the security measures will depend on the device. However, the infamous Stuxnet virus targeted specific SCADA equipment, so the need for SCADA security is not simply hypothetical.

Embedded systems (such as printers, smart TVs, and HVAC controls) have their own security needs. Most modern printers, even midrange printers, have hard drives, RAM, and an operating system. That means they have specific vulnerabilities. Some advanced HVAC control systems and smart TVs also have sophisticated operations that are vulnerable to attack. Even game consoles can be vulnerable to viruses. Like SCADA, the specifics of mitigating risk will depend on the device, but the Security+ exam will expect you to be aware that these devices have security risks.

Smartphones are probably a more obvious security risk. Earlier in this chapter we discussed issues with both BYOD and mobile devices. All of those issues obviously apply to smart phones. But specific phones, such as Android and IOS, will have their own security issue that have to be addressed.

Mainframes usually do not present significant security risks; they tend to be more stable and less susceptible to attacks. However, that does not mean they are invulnerable. You should examine the mainframe your organization uses and see what steps are appropriate for that system.

A new and emerging issue is that of in-vehicle computing systems. Automobiles tend to have sophisticated systems, such as computers complete with hard drives and GPS. There have already been preliminary security tests showing that these systems can be breached. Much like SCADA, the specifics will depend on the implementation. The Security+ test will ask you about the concept in a general way.

Summary

In this chapter, we covered the key elements of security-related awareness and training, social engineering, regulations, and the user in the environment. Your job as a security professional includes keeping yourself up-to-date on current issues as well as informing affected parties of changes occurring in the industry and new threats.

The process of raising sensitivity about security is part of a security awareness program. This program should include communications about the nature of the issues, education about policies and procedures, and clear support from management.

Information classification is the process of determining what information is accessible to what parties and for what purposes. Classifications in industry are usually based on cataloging information as *public* or *private*. Public information can be classified as either limited distribution or full distribution. Private information is usually classified for internal use or restricted.

By employing social engineering, attackers are able to gain a way to the data or the workplace through the employee. Many different types of social engineering attacks can occur, and this chapter examined those.

Exam Essentials

Be able to explain the process used to educate an organization about security issues. The four major aspects of a security management policy are communications, user awareness, education, and online resources. Communication should be ongoing and help the organization make decisions about security requirements and threats. A user-awareness program helps individuals in an organization understand how to implement policies, procedures, and technologies to ensure effective security. A wealth of online information is available to help you learn about current trends in the field. One of your primary responsibilities should be staying current on threats and trends.

Know about key legislation governing security.   At the federal level, IT is governed by HIPAA (which covers three areas—confidentiality, privacy, and security of patient records), the Gramm-Leach-Bliley Act (also known as the Financial Modernization Act of 1999), and several other security-related acts. In addition to the federal laws, most states have laws on computer crime.

Know the importance of security awareness and training.   Security awareness and training are critical to the success of a security effort. They include explaining policies, procedures, and current threats to both users and management.

Review Questions

1. As part of your training program, you're trying to educate users on the importance of security. You explain to them that not every attack depends on implementing advanced technological methods. Some attacks, you explain, take advantage of human shortcomings to gain access that should otherwise be denied. What term do you use to describe attacks of this type?

    A. Social engineering

    B. IDS system

    C. Perimeter security

    D. Biometrics

2. Which classification of information designates that information can be released on a restricted basis to outside organizations?

    A. Private information

    B. Full distribution

    C. Restricted information

    D. Limited distribution

3. Which of the following is not part of the CIA triad?

    A. Avoidance

    B. Confidentiality

    C. Availability

    D. Integrity

4. Which of the following best defines social engineering?

    A. Illegal copying of software

    B. Gathering information from discarded manuals and printouts

    C. Using people skills to obtain proprietary information

    D. Destroying or altering data

5. The default level of security established for access controls should be which of the following?

    A. All access

    B. Update access

    C. Read access

    D. No access

6. Personal smartphones at work create a potential security risk due to which of the following?

   A. Operating system incompatibility

   B. Large storage capacity

   C. Widespread use

   D. Potential for malware introduction

7. Which of the following access control methods includes switching work assignments at pre-set intervals?

   A. Job rotation

   B. Mandatory vacations

   C. Least privilege

   D. Separation of duties

8. There are two types of implicit denies. One of these can be configured so that only users specifically named can use the service, and this is known as:

   A. at.deny

   B. at.allow

   C. at.open

   D. at.closed

9. _____ information is made available to either large public or specific individuals, whereas _____ information is intended for only those internal to the organization.

   A. Private; restricted

   B. Public; private

   C. Limited distribution; internal

   D. Public; internal

10. An administrator can configure access control functions but is not able to administer audit functions. This is an example of what?

    A. Access enforcement

    B. Separation of duties

    C. Least privilege

    D. Account management

11. Tailgating with the permission of the person being followed is known as:

    A. Piggybacking

    B. Convoying

    C. Clipping

    D. Riding

12. Who typically signs an NDA (nondisclosure agreement)?

    A. Alpha testers

    B. Customers

    C. Beta testers

    D. Focus groups

13. A company decides that the domain controller administrator and the DNS server administrator should exchange positions in order to allow for more oversight of past transactions. Which of the following is this an example of?

    A. Least privilege

    B. Implicit deny

    C. Separation of duties

    D. Job rotation

14. To avoid mishandling of information (electronic or documents), what should you consider using?

    A. Labeling

    B. Token

    C. Tickets

    D. SLL

15. Which act mandates national standards and procedures for the storage, use, and transmission of personal medical information?

    A. CFAA

    B. HIPAA

    C. GLBA

    D. FERPA

16. The Cyberspace Security Enhancement Act gives law enforcement the right to:

    A. Fine ISPs who host rogue sites

    B. Gain access to encryption keys

    C. Restrict information from public view

    D. Stop issuance of .gov domains

17. Which of the following is the highest classification level in the government?

    A. Top Secret

    B. Secret

    C. Classified

    D. Confidential

18. `at.allow` is an access control that allows only specific users to use the service. What is `at.deny`?

    A. It does not allow users named in the file to access the system.

    B. It ensures that no one will ever be able to use that part of your system.

    C. It opens up the server only to intranet users.

    D. It blocks access to Internet users.

19. A new sales manager has asked for administrator rights on the sales database. Should you grant that request, and why or why not?

    A. No, his job does not require administrator rights.

    B. No, this will interfere with the database administrator's job security.

    C. Yes, he is the manager and he should get whatever level of access he wants.

    D. Yes, he should have been given that access initially.

20. Your company requires that when employees are not at their desk no documents should be out on the desk and the monitor should not be viewable. What is this called?

    A. Wiping the desk

    B. Clean desk

    C. Excessive requirements

    D. Basic housekeeping

Chapter

12

Disaster Recovery and Incident Response

THE FOLLOWING COMPTIA SECURITY+ EXAM OBJECTIVES ARE COVERED IN THIS CHAPTER:

✓ **2.4 Given a scenario, implement basic forensic procedures.**

- Order of volatility
- Capture system image
- Network traffic and logs
- Capture video
- Record time offset
- Take hashes
- Screenshots
- Witnesses
- Track man hours and expense
- Chain of custody
- Big Data analysis

✓ **2.5 Summarize common incident response procedures.**

- Preparation
- Incident identification
- Escalation and notification
- Mitigation steps
- Lessons learned
- Reporting
- Recovery/reconstitution procedures

- First responder
- Incident isolation: Quarantine; Device removal
- Data breach
- Damage and loss control

✓ **2.8 Summarize risk management best practices.**

- Disaster recovery concepts: Backup plans/policies; Backup execution/frequency; Cold site; Hot site; Warm site

✓ **3.8 Explain the proper use of penetration testing versus vulnerability scanning.**

- Penetration testing: Verify a threat exists; Bypass security controls; Actively test security controls; Exploiting vulnerabilities
- Vulnerability scanning: Passively testing security controls; Identify vulnerability; Identify lack of security controls; Identify common misconfigurations; Intrusive vs. non-intrusive; Credentialed vs. non-credentialed; False positive
- Black box
- White box
- Gray box

As a security professional, you must strive not only to prevent losses but also to make contingency plans for recovering from any losses that do occur. This chapter deals with the crucial aspects of business continuity and vendor support from an operations perspective. It also looks at incident response and the basic forensic procedures with which you should be familiar. A solid grasp of these concepts will help you prepare for the exam because they appear in multiple objectives. It will also help you to become a more proficient and professional security team member. The process of working with, helping to design, and maintaining security in your organization is a tough job. It requires dedication, vigilance, and a sense of duty to your organization.

Issues Associated with Business Continuity

One of the oldest phrases still in use today is "the show must go on." Nowhere is that more true than in the world of business, where downtime means the loss of significant revenue with each passing minute. *Business continuity* is primarily concerned with the processes, policies, and methods that an organization follows to minimize the impact of a system failure, network failure, or the failure of any key component needed for operation—that is, essentially whatever it takes to ensure that the business continues and that the show does indeed go on.

Business continuity planning (BCP) is the process of implementing policies, controls, and procedures to counteract the effects of losses, outages, or failures of critical business processes. BCP is primarily a management tool that ensures that critical business functions can be performed when normal business operations are disrupted.

Critical business functions (CBFs) refer to those processes or systems that must be made operational immediately when an outage occurs. The business can't function without them, and many are information-intensive and require access to both technology and data.

Two of the key components of BCP are *business impact analysis (BIA)* and *risk assessment*. BIA is concerned with evaluating the processes, and risk assessment is concerned with evaluating the risk or likelihood of a loss. Evaluating all of the processes in an organization or enterprise is necessary in order for BCP to be effective.

You need only a passing knowledge of business continuity issues for the Security+ exam. If you plan on taking the Project+ exam, also from Comp-TIA, you will need a more thorough knowledge of these topics.

Types of Storage Mechanisms

You might need to restore information from backup copies for any number of reasons. Some of the more common reasons for doing so are as follows:

- Accidental deletion
- Application errors
- Natural disasters
- Physical attacks
- Server failure
- Virus infection
- Workstation failure

The information you back up must be immediately available for use when needed. If a user loses a critical file, they won't want to wait several days while data files are sent from a remote storage facility. Several types of storage mechanisms are available for data storage. These include the following:

Working Copies   *Working copy backups*, sometimes referred to as *shadow copies*, are partial or full backups that are kept at the computer center for immediate recovery purposes. They are usually updated on a frequent basis and are generally the most recent backups that have been made.

Working copies aren't usually intended to serve as long-term copies. In a busy environment, they may be created every few hours.

Many filesystems used on servers include *journaling*. A *journaled file system (JFS)* includes a log file of all changes and transactions that have occurred within a set period of time (such as the last few hours). If a crash occurs, the operating system can check the log files to see which transactions have been committed and which ones have not.

This technology works well, and it allows unsaved data to be written after recovery. The system is usually successfully restored to its pre-crash condition.

Onsite Storage   *Onsite storage* usually refers to a location on the site of the computer center that is used to store information locally. Onsite storage containers are available that allow computer cartridges and tapes or backup media to be stored in a reasonably protected environment in the building.

As time goes on, tape is losing its popularity as a medium for backups to other technologies. The Security+ exam, however, is a bit dated and still considers tape the ideal medium.

Onsite storage containers are designed and rated for fire, moisture, and pressure resistance. These containers aren't *fireproof* in most cases, but they are *fire rated*: A fireproof container should be guaranteed to withstand damage regardless of the type of fire or temperature, whereas fire ratings specify that a container can protect its contents for a specific amount of time in a given situation.

If you choose to depend entirely on onsite storage, make sure that the containers you acquire can withstand the worst-case environmental catastrophes that could happen at your location. Make sure as well that they are in locations where you can easily find them after the disaster and access them (for example, near exterior walls, on the ground floor, and so forth).

 General-purpose storage safes aren't usually suitable for storing electronic media. The fire ratings used for safes generally refer to paper contents. Because paper does not catch fire until 451° Fahrenheit, electronic media would typically be ruined well before paper documents are destroyed in a fire.

Offsite Storage   *Offsite storage* refers to a location away from the computer center where paper copies and backup media are kept. Offsite storage can involve something as simple as keeping a copy of backup media at a remote office, or it can be as complicated as a nuclear-hardened, high-security storage facility. The storage facility should be bonded, insured, and inspected on a regular basis to ensure that all storage procedures are being followed.

Determining which storage mechanism to use should be based on the needs of the organization, the availability of storage facilities, and the available budget. Most offsite storage facilities charge based on the amount of space you require and the frequency of access you need to the stored information.

 Although it is easy to see the need for security at any location where your files are stored, don't overlook the need for security during transportation as well.

Crafting a Disaster-Recovery Plan

A *disaster-recovery plan*, or scheme, helps an organization respond effectively when a disaster occurs. Disasters may include system failure, network failure, infrastructure failure, and natural disaster. The primary emphasis of such a plan is reestablishing services and minimizing losses.

In a smaller organization, a disaster-recovery plan may be relatively simple and straight-forward. In a larger organization, it may involve multiple facilities, corporate strategic plans, and entire departments. In either case, the purpose is to develop the means and methods to restore services as quickly as possible and to protect the organization from unacceptable losses in the event of a disaster.

A major component of a disaster-recovery plan involves the access and storage of infor-mation. Your backup plan for data is an integral part of this process. The following sections address backup plan issues and backup types. They also discuss developing a backup plan, recovering a system, and using alternative sites. These are key components of a disaster-recovery plan: They form the heart of how an organization will respond when a critical failure or disaster occurs.

Understanding Backup Plan Issues

When an organization develops a backup plan for information, it must be clear about the value of the information. A *backup plan* identifies which information is to be stored, how it will be stored, and for what duration it will be stored. You must look at the relative value of the information you retain. To some extent, the types of systems you use and the applica-tions you support dictate the structure of your plan.

Let's look at those different systems and applications:

Database Systems   Most modern database systems provide the ability to back up data or certain sections of the database globally without difficulty. Larger-scale database systems also provide transaction auditing and data-recovery capabilities.

For example, you can configure your database to record in a separate file each addition, update, deletion, or change of information that occurs. These transaction or audit files can be stored directly on archival media, such as magnetic tape cartridges. In the event of a sys-tem outage or data loss, the audit file can be used to roll back the database and update it to the last transactions made.

Figure 12.1 illustrates the auditing process in further detail. In this situation, the audit file is directly written to a digital audio tape (DAT) that is used to store a record of changes. If an outage occurs, the audit or transaction files can be rolled forward to bring the data-base back to its most current state. This recovery process brings the database current to within the last few transactions. Although it doesn't ensure that all of the transactions that were in process will be recovered, it will reduce potential losses to the few that were in pro-cess when the system failed.

Most database systems contain large files that have only a relatively few records updated in relation to the number of records stored. A large customer database may store millions of records—however, only a few hundred may be undergoing modification at any given time.

FIGURE 12.1   Database transaction auditing process

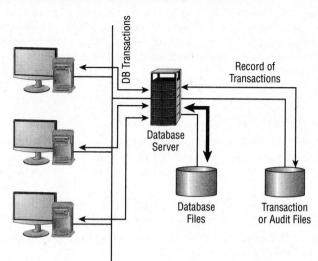

User Files   Word processing documents, spreadsheets, and other user files are extremely valuable to an organization. Fortunately, although the number of files that people retain is usually large, the number of files that change after initial creation is relatively small. By doing a regular backup on user systems, you can protect these documents and ensure that they're recoverable in the event of a loss. In a large organization, backing up user files can be an enormous task. Fortunately, most operating systems date-stamp files when they're modified. If backups that store only the changed files are created, keeping user files safe becomes a relatively less painful process for an organization.

Many organizations have taken the position that backing up user files is the user's responsibility. Although this policy decision saves administrative time and media, it isn't a good idea. Most users don't back up their files on a regular basis—if at all. With the cost of media being relatively cheap, including the user files in a backup every so often is highly recommended.

Applications   Applications such as word processors, transaction systems, and other programs usually don't change on a frequent basis. When a change or upgrade to an application is made, it's usually accomplished across an entire organization. You wouldn't necessarily need to keep a copy of the word processing application for each user, but you should keep a single up-to-date version that is available for download and reinstallation.

Some commercial applications require that each copy of the software be registered with a centralized license server. This may present a problem if you attempt to use a centralized recovery procedure for applications. Each machine may require its own copy of the applications for a recovery to be successful.

Knowing the Backup Types

The frequency at which you do backups should be based on the amount of data you are willing to lose. If you do backups only weekly (never recommended), then you could lose up to a week's worth of data. Similarly, if you do them every day, the most data you would lose is 24 hours' worth.

Regardless of the frequency at which you back up, three methods exist to back up information on most systems. The difference between them is in the data that they include, and this has an impact on the amount of time it takes to perform the backup and any restore operations that may later be required:

Full Backup   A *full backup* is a complete, comprehensive backup of all files on a disk or server. The full backup is current only at the time it's performed. Once a full backup is made, you have a complete archive of the system at that point in time. A system shouldn't be in use while it undergoes a full backup because some files may not get backed up. Once the system goes back into operation, the backup is no longer current. A full backup can be a time-consuming process on a large system.

During a full backup, every single file on the system is copied over, and the archive bit on each file is turned off.

Incremental Backup   An *incremental backup* is a partial backup that stores only the information that has been changed since the last full or the last incremental backup. If a full backup were performed on a Sunday night, an incremental backup done on Monday night would contain only the information that changed since Sunday night. Such a backup is typically considerably smaller than a full backup. Each incremental backup must be retained until a full backup can be performed. Incremental backups are usually the fastest backups to perform on most systems, and each incremental backup tape is relatively small. Keep in mind that though we may use the word "tape" even when a different storage medium is used, the concept is still the same.

An incremental backup backs up only files that have the archive bit turned on. That is how it can identify which files have changed or which ones have been created. At the conclusion of the backup, the archive bit is turned off for all of the files that were included in the backup.

Differential Backup   A *differential backup* is similar in function to an incremental backup, but it backs up any files that have been altered since the last full backup; it makes duplicate copies of files that haven't changed since the last differential backup. If a full backup were performed on Sunday night, a differential backup performed on Monday night would capture the information that was changed on Monday. A differential backup completed on Tuesday night would record the changes in any files from Monday and any changes in files on Tuesday. As you can see, during the week each differential backup would become larger; by Friday or Saturday night, it might be nearly as large as a full backup. This means that the backups in the earliest part of the weekly cycle will be very fast, while each successive one will be slower.

HSM   *Hierarchical storage management (HSM)* is a newer backup type. HSM provides continuous online backup by using optical or tape jukeboxes. It appears as an infinite disk to the system, and it can be configured to provide the closest version of an available real-time backup. So rather than using one of the three traditional backup strategies, you ensure that data is being continuously backed up.

When these backup methods are used in conjunction with each other, the risk of loss can be greatly reduced, but you can never combine incremental and differential backups in the same set. One of the major factors in determining which combination of these three methods to use is time—in an ideal situation, a full backup would be performed every day. Several commercial backup programs support these three backup methods. You must evaluate your organizational needs when choosing which tools to use to accomplish backups.

Almost every stable operating system contains a utility for creating a copy of the configuration settings necessary to reach the present state after a disaster. In Windows 7 and Windows 8, for example, this is accomplished with an *Automated System Recovery (ASR) disk*. Make certain that you know how to do an equivalent operation for the operating system that you are running.

As an administrator, you must know how to do backups and be familiar with all of the options available to you. In Exercise 12.1, we'll show you how to perform a backup in SUSE Linux.

EXERCISE 12.1

Creating a Backup in SUSE Linux

This exercise assumes the use of a SUSE Linux Enterprise Server. While backups are available in all Linux distributions, SUSE simplifies this task (and most other administrative tasks as well) by including the YaST (Yet Another Setup Tool) interface.

1.   Log in as root and start YaST.

2.   Choose System and System Backup.

3.   Click Profile Management and choose Add; then enter a name for the new profile, such as **fullsystemback**.

4. Click OK.

5. Enter a backup name (using an absolute path such as /home/mybackup.tar), and make certain that the archive type is set to a tar variety. Then click Next.

6. At the File Selection window, leave the default options and click Next.

7. Leave the Search Constraints at the defaults and click OK.

8. At the main YaST System Backup dialog box, click Start Backup. After several minutes of reading packages, the backup will begin.

Developing a Backup Plan

Several common models are used in designing backup plans. Each has its own advantages and disadvantages. Numerous methods have been developed to deal with archival backup; most of them are evolutions of the three models discussed here:

Grandfather, Father, Son Method   The *Grandfather, Father, Son method* is based on the philosophy that a full backup should occur at regular intervals, such as monthly or weekly. This method assumes that the most recent backup after the full backup is the son. As newer backups are made, the son becomes the father, and the father, in turn, becomes the grandfather. At the end of each month, a full backup is performed on all systems. This backup is stored in an offsite facility for a period of one year. Each monthly backup replaces the monthly backup from the previous year. Weekly or daily incremental backups are performed and stored until the next full backup occurs. This full backup is then stored offsite and the weekly or daily backup tapes are reused (the January 1 incremental backup is used on February 1, and so on).

This method ensures that in the event of a loss, the full backup from the end of the last month and the daily backups can be used to restore information to the last day. Figure 12.2 illustrates this concept: The annual backup is referred to as the grandfather, the monthly backup is the father, and the weekly backup is the son. The last backup of the month becomes the archived backup for that month. The last backup of the year becomes the annual backup for the year. Annual backups are usually archived; this allows an organization to have backups available for several years and minimizes the likelihood of data loss. It's a common practice for an organization to keep a minimum of seven years in archives.

The last full backup of the year is permanently retained. This ensures that previous years' information can be recovered if necessary.

The major difficulty with this process is that a large number of tapes are constantly flowing between the storage facility and the computer center. In addition, cataloging daily and weekly backups can be complicated. It can become difficult to determine which files have been backed up and where they're stored.

FIGURE 12.2   Grandfather, Father, Son backup method

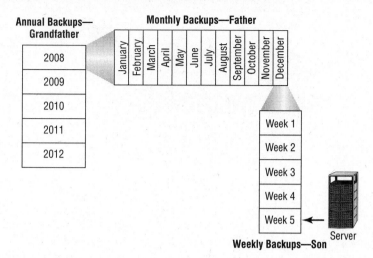

Although the Grandfather, Father, Son method is the most common, and the one that you will be tested on, other obscure methods exist. One such method is called the Tower of Hanoi method. It is based on a mathematical word problem called the Tower of Hanoi. The details of this method are not important for the Security+ exam.

Full Archival Method   The *Full Archival method* works on the assumption that any information created on any system is stored forever. All backups are kept indefinitely using some form of backup media. In short, all full backups, all incremental backups, and any other backups are permanently kept somewhere.

This method effectively eliminates the potential for loss of data. Everything that is created on any computer is backed up forever. Figure 12.3 illustrates this method. As you can see, the number of copies of the backup media can quickly overwhelm your storage capabilities. Some organizations that have tried to do this have needed entire warehouses to contain their archival backups.

Think about the number of files your organization has: How much storage media would be required to accomplish full archiving? The other major problem involves keeping records of what information has been archived. For these reasons, many larger companies don't find this to be an acceptable method of keeping backups.

FIGURE 12.3 Full Archival backup method

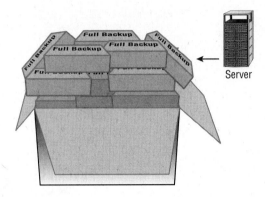

Backup Server Method The costs of disk storage and servers have fallen tremendously over the past few years. Lower prices have made it easier for organizations to use dedicated servers for backup. The *Backup Server method* establishes a server with large amounts of disk space whose sole purpose is to back up data. With the right software, a dedicated server can examine and copy all of the files that have been altered every day.

Figure 12.4 illustrates the use of backup servers. In this instance, the files on the backup server contain copies of all of the information and data on the APPS, ACCTG, and DB servers. The files on the three servers are copied to the backup server on a regular basis; over time, this server's storage requirements can become enormous. The advantage of this method is that all backed-up data is available online for immediate access.

FIGURE 12.4 A backup server archiving server files

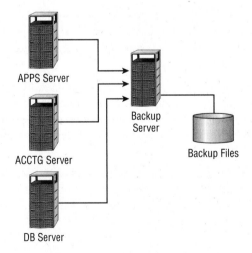

This server can be backed up on a regular basis, and the backups can be kept for a specified period. If a system or server malfunctions, the backup server can be accessed to restore information from the last backups performed on that system.

Backup servers don't need overly large processors; however, they must have large disk and other long-term storage media capabilities. Several software manufacturers take backup servers one additional step and create hierarchies of files: Over time, if a file isn't accessed, it's moved to slower media and may eventually be stored offline. This helps reduce the disk storage requirements, yet it still keeps the files that are most likely to be needed for recovery readily available.

Many organizations use two or more of these methods to back up systems. The issue becomes one of storage requirements and retention requirements. In establishing a backup plan, you must ask users and managers how much backup (in terms of frequency, size of files, and so forth) is really needed and how long it will be needed.

 Make sure that you obtain input from all who are dealing with governmental or regulatory agencies. Each agency may have different archival requirements, and compliance violations can be expensive. Both HIPAA and Sarbanes-Oxley are affecting—and driving—archival and disposal policies around the nation.

Recovering a System

When a system fails, you'll be unable to reestablish operation without regenerating all of the system's components. This process includes making sure that hardware is functioning, restoring or installing the operating systems, restoring or installing applications, and restoring data files. It can take several days on a large system. With a little forethought, you may be able to simplify the process and make it easily manageable.

When you install a new system, make a full backup of it before any data files are created. If stored onsite, this backup will be readily available for use. If you've standardized your systems, you may need just one copy of a base system that contains all of the common applications you use. The base system can usually be quickly restored, which allows for reconnection to the network for restoration of other software. Many newer operating systems now provide this capability, and system restores are very fast.

Figure 12.5 demonstrates this process further. Notice that the installation CDs are being used for the base OS and applications.

When the base system has been restored, data files and any other needed files can be restored from the last full backup and any incremental or differential backups that have been performed. The last full backup should contain most of the data on the system; the incremental backup or differential backups contain the data that has changed since the full backup.

FIGURE 12.5 System regeneration process for a workstation or server

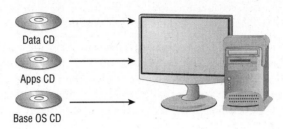

Data CD

Apps CD

Base OS CD

Many newer operating systems, such as Windows Server 2012, allow you to create a model user system as a disk image on a server; the disk image is downloaded and installed when a failure occurs. This method makes it easier for administrators to restore a system than it would be to do it manually. It's all well and good to know how to make backups and the importance of doing so. There will come a time, however, when a recovery—the whole reason for disaster planning—will be necessary. As an administrator, you must be ready for this event and know how to handle it.

In Exercise 12.2, we'll show you how to use Automated System Recovery with Windows Server 2012.

EXERCISE 12.2

Using Automated System Recovery in Windows Server 2012

In this exercise, you'll use the backup utility included with Windows Server 2012 to create an ASR backup:

1. Start the backup utility by choosing Start ➤ All Programs ➤ Accessories ➤ System Tools ➤ Backup.

2. Choose the Automatic System Recovery Wizard.

3. Walk through the wizard, and answer the questions appropriately. When you finish, you'll create the backup set first and a disk (either optical disk or USB drive) second. The disk contains files necessary to restore system settings after a disaster.

An important recovery issue is to know the order in which to proceed. If a server is completely destroyed and must be re-created, ascertain which applications are the most important and should be restored before the others. Likewise, which services are most important to the users from a business standpoint and need to be available? At the same time, which services are nice but not necessary to keep the business running? The answers will differ for every organization, and you must know them for yours.

Backout vs. Backup

Although most attention deservedly is on backups, never overlook the need for a backout plan. A *backout* is a reversion from a change that had negative consequences. It could be, for example, that everything was working fine until you installed a service pack on a production machine, and then services that were normally available were no longer accessible. The backout, in this instance, would revert the system to the state that it was in before the service pack was applied.

Backout plans can include uninstalling service packs, hotfixes, and patches, but they can also include reversing a migration and using previous firmware. A key component to creating such a plan is identifying what events will trigger your implementing the backout.

Planning for Alternate Sites

Another key aspect of a disaster-recovery plan is to provide for the restoration of business functions in the event of a large-scale loss of service. You can lease or purchase a facility that is available on short notice for the purpose of restoring network or systems operations. These are referred to as *alternate sites* or *backup sites*.

Another term for *alternate site* is *alternative site;* the terms are often used interchangeably.

If the power in your local area were disrupted for several days, how would you reestablish service at an alternate site until primary services were restored? Several options exist to do this; we'll briefly present them here. These solutions are not ideal, but they are always considered to be significantly less costly—in terms of time—to implement than the estimated time of bringing your original site back up to speed. They are used to allow you to get your organization back on its feet until permanent service is available. An alternate site can be a hot site, a warm site, or a cold site:

Hot Site   A *hot site* is a location that can provide operations within hours of a failure. This type of site would have servers, networks, and telecommunications equipment in place to reestablish service in a short time. Hot sites provide network connectivity, systems, and preconfigured software to meet the needs of an organization. Databases can be kept up-to-date using network connections. These types of facilities are expensive, and they're primarily suitable for short-term situations. A hot site may also double as an offsite storage facility, providing immediate access to archives and backup media.

A hot site is also referred to as an *active backup model.*

Many hot sites also provide office facilities and other services so that a business can relocate a small number of employees to sustain operations.

Given the choice, every organization would choose to have a hot site. Doing so is often not practical, however, on a cost basis.

Warm Site   A *warm site* provides some of the capabilities of a hot site, but it requires the customer to do more work to become operational. Warm sites provide computer systems and compatible media capabilities. If a warm site is used, administrators and other staff will need to install and configure systems to resume operations. For most organizations, a warm site could be a remote office, a leased facility, or another organization with which yours has a reciprocal agreement.

Another term for a warm site/reciprocal site is *active/active model.*

Warm sites may be for your exclusive use, but they don't have to be. A warm site requires more advanced planning, testing, and access to media for system recovery. Warm sites represent a compromise between a hot site, which is very expensive, and a cold site, which isn't preconfigured.

An agreement between two companies to provide services in the event of an emergency is called a *reciprocal agreement.* Usually, these agreements are made on a best-effort basis: There is no guarantee that services will be available if the site is needed. Make sure that your agreement is with an organization that is outside of your geographic area. If both sites are affected by the same disaster, the agreement is worthless.

Cold Site   A *cold site* is a facility that isn't immediately ready to use. The organization using it must bring along its equipment and network. A cold site may provide network capability, but this isn't usually the case; the site provides a place for operations to resume, but it doesn't provide the infrastructure to support those operations. Cold sites work well when an extended outage is anticipated. The major challenge is that the customer must provide all of the capabilities and do all of the work to get back into operation. Cold sites are usually the least expensive to put into place, but they require the most advanced planning, testing, and resources to become operational—occasionally taking up to a month to make operational.

Almost anywhere can be a cold site; if necessary, users could work out of your garage for a short time. Although this may be a practical solution, it also opens up risks that you must consider. For example, while you're operating from your garage, will the servers be secure should someone break in?

Herein lies the problem. The likelihood that you'll need any of these facilities is low—most organizations will never need to use these types of facilities. The costs are usually based on a subscription or other contracted relationships, and it's difficult for most organizations to justify the expense. In addition, planning, testing, and maintaining these facilities is difficult; it does little good to pay for any of these services if they don't work and aren't available when you need them.

> One of the most important aspects of using alternative sites is documentation. To create an effective site, you must have solid documentation of what you have, what you're using, and what you need in order to get by.

Management must view the disaster-recovery plan as an integral part of its *business continuity planning (BCP)*. Management must also provide the resources needed to implement and maintain an alternative site after the decision has been made to contract for the facilities.

 Real World Scenario

Some Protection Is Better than None—Or Is It?

You've been tasked with the responsibility of developing a recovery plan for your company to have in place in a critical infrastructure failure. Your CEO is concerned about the budget and doesn't want to invest many resources in a full-blown hot site.

Several options are available to you in this situation. You need to evaluate the feasibility of a warm site, a cold site, or a reciprocal agreement with another company. The warm site and cold site options will cost less than a hot site, but they will require a great deal of work in the event of a failure. A reciprocal site may be a good alternative to both, if a suitable partner organization can be found. You may want to discuss this possibility with some of your larger vendors or other companies that may have excess computer capacity. No matter which direction you recommend, you should test and develop procedures to manage the transition from your primary site to an offsite facility.

Incident Response Policies

Incident response policies define how an organization will respond to an incident. These policies may involve third parties, and they need to be comprehensive. The term incident is somewhat nebulous in scope. For our purposes, an *incident* is any attempt to violate a security policy, a successful penetration, a compromise of a system, or any unauthorized access to information. This includes system failures and disruption of services in the organization.

It's important that an incident response policy establish at least the following items:

- Outside agencies that should be contacted or notified in case of an incident
- Resources used to deal with an incident
- Procedures to gather and secure evidence
- List of information that should be collected about an incident
- Outside experts who can be used to address issues if needed
- Policies and guidelines regarding how to handle an incident

According to CERT, a *Computer Security Incident Response Team (CSIRT)* can be a formalized or an ad hoc team. You can toss a team together to respond to an incident after it arises, but investing time in the development process can make an incident more manageable. Many decisions about dealing with an incident will have been considered in advance. Incidents are high-stress situations; therefore, it's better to simplify the process by considering important aspects in advance. If civil or criminal actions are part of the process, evidence must be gathered and safeguarded properly.

Let's say that you've just discovered a situation where a fraud has been perpetrated internally using a corporate computer. You're part of the investigating team. Your incident response policy lists the specialists you need to contact for an investigation. Ideally, you've already met the investigator or investigating firm, you've developed an understanding of how to protect the scene, and you know how to deal properly with the media (if they become involved).

 Your policies must also clearly outline who needs to be informed in the company, what they need to be told, and how to respond to the situation. Incidents should include not only intrusions but also attempts.

Understanding Incident Response

Forensics refers to the process of identifying what has occurred on a system by examining the data trail. It involves an analysis of evidence found in computers and on digital storage media. *Incident response* encompasses forensics and refers to the process of identifying, investigating, repairing, documenting, and adjusting procedures to prevent another incident. An *incident* is the occurrence of any event that endangers a system or network. We need to discuss responses to two types of incidents: internal incidents and incidents involving law enforcement professionals. Figure 12.6 illustrates the interlocked relationship of these processes in an incident response. Notice that all of the steps, including the first step, are related. Incidents are facts of life. You want to learn from them personally, and you want your organization to learn from them as well.

FIGURE 12.6 Incident response cycle

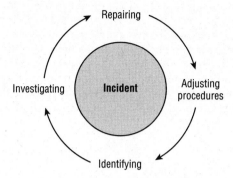

It's a good idea to include the procedures you'll generally follow in an *incident response plan (IRP)*. The IRP outlines what steps are needed and who is responsible for deciding how to handle a situation. The Computer Science department at Carnegie Mellon pioneered this process.

Law enforcement personnel are governed by the rules of evidence, and their response to an incident will be largely out of your control. You need to consider involving law enforcement carefully before you decide that you do not want to handle the situation without them. There is no such thing as dropping charges. Once they begin, law enforcement professionals are required to pursue an investigation.

The term *incident* has special meanings in different industries. In the banking and financial areas, it's very specific and involves something that includes the loss of money. You wouldn't want to call a hacker attempt an *incident* if you were involved in a bank network because this terminology would automatically trigger an entirely different type of investigation.

The next five sections deal with the phases of a typical incident response process. The steps are generic in this example. Each organization will have a specific set of procedures that will generally map to these steps.

However, before an incident occurs there needs to be substantial preparation. Preparing for incident response involves multiple factors. The first step is outlining how you intend to respond to specific incidents. Formulating an IRP is part of that preparation. You also will need to identify the personnel and resources needed for your response. For example, if you intend to take a server offline in the event that it is breached, do you have a backup server available? In the event of a suspected computer crime, which of your personnel are qualified to perform the initial forensic processes? If no one is qualified, you need to identify a third party that you can contact.

An important concept to keep in mind when working with incidents is the *chain of custody*, which covers how evidence is secured, where it is stored, and who has access to it. When you begin to collect evidence, you must keep track of that evidence at all times and show who has it, who has seen it, and where it has been. The evidence must always be within your custody, or you're open to dispute about possible evidence tampering. It is highly recommended that a log book be used to document every access and visuals (pictures and video) recorded to show how the evidence is secured.

Step 1: Identifying the Incident

Incident identification is the first step in determining what has occurred in your organization. An internal or external attack may have been part of a larger attack that has just surfaced, or it may be a random probe or scan of your network.

An event is often an IDS-triggered signal. Operations personnel will determine if an *event* becomes an *incident*. An easy way to think of the two is that an event is anything that happens, whereas an incident is any event that endangers a system or network.

Many IDSs trigger false positives when reporting incidents. *False positives* are events that aren't really incidents. Remember that an IDS is based on established rules of acceptance (deviations from which are known as *anomalies*) and attack signatures. If the rules aren't set up properly, normal traffic may set off the analyzer and generate an event. Be sure to double-check your results because you don't want to declare a false emergency.

One problem that can occur with manual network monitoring is overload. Over time, a slow attack may develop that increases in intensity. Manual processes typically will adapt, and they may not notice the attack until it's too late to stop it. Personnel tend to adapt to changing environments if the changes occur over a long period of time. An automated monitoring system, such as an IDS, will sound the alarm when a certain threshold or activity level occurs.

When a suspected incident pops up, *first responders* are those individuals who must ascertain whether it truly is an incident or a false alarm. Depending on your organization, the first responder may be the main security administrator or it could consist of a team of network and system administrators.

The very first step, even with a suspected incident, is isolation. If you think, for example, a given machine is infected with a virus, you must isolate that machine, even before you are sure it is indeed infected. That involves quarantining the machine(s) that you suspect of being infected. Literally disconnect them from the network while you analyze the situation. In some cases this is accomplished with simple device removal: Just remove the device from the network by unplugging the network cable.

After you've determined that you indeed have an incident on your hands, you need to consider how to handle it. This process, called *escalation*, involves consulting policies, consulting appropriate management, and determining how best to conduct an investigation into the incident. Make sure that the methods you use to investigate the incident are consistent with corporate and legal requirements for your organization. Bring your Human Resources and Legal departments into the investigation early, and seek their guidance whenever questions involving their areas of expertise arise.

A key aspect, often overlooked by system professionals, involves information control. When an incident occurs, who is responsible for managing the communications about the incident? Employees in the company may naturally be curious about a situation. A single spokesperson needs to be designated. Remember, what one person knows runs a risk of one hundred others also finding out.

 Real World Scenario

The Email Incident

You're the administrator of a small network. This network has an old mail server that is used for internal and external email. You periodically investigate log and audit files to determine the status of your systems and servers. Recently, you noticed that your email log file has been reporting a large number of undeliverable or bounced emails. The addresses appear to be random. Upon examining the email system, you notice that the outbound mail folder seems to be sending mail every second. A large number of files are being sent. After inspecting the workstations in the business, you determine that several of them have out-of-date antivirus software. How should you handle this situation?

For starters, you may have one or more viruses or worms in your system. This type of virus sounds like a Simple Mail Transfer Protocol (SMTP) virus, and a virus can gain access to the address directory and propagate itself using SMTP.

You should investigate why the antivirus software is out-of-date, upgrade these systems as appropriate, and add server-based and mail-server virus-protection capabilities to your network.

Step 2: Investigating the Incident

The process of investigating an incident involves searching logs, files, and any other sources of data about the nature and scope of the incident. If possible, you should determine whether this is part of a larger attack, a random event, or a false positive. False positives are common in an IDS environment and may be the result of unusual traffic in the network. It may be that your network is being pinged by a class of computer security students to demonstrate the return times, or it may be that an automated tool is launching an attack.

It is sad but true: One reason administrators don't put as much security on networks as they should is because they do not want to have to deal with the false positives. Although this is a poor excuse, administrators still often use it. As a security administrator, you must seek a balance between being overwhelmed with too much unneeded information and knowing when something out of the ordinary is occurring. It is an elusive balance that is easier to talk about than to find, but it's one for which you must strive.

You might find that the incident doesn't require a response if it can't be successful. Your investigation might conclude that a change in policies is required to deal with a new type of threat. These types of decisions should be documented and, if necessary, reconfigurations should be made to deal with the change.

 Real World Scenario

What if the Intrusion Is Now?

Suppose a junior administrator rushes into your office and reports that an alert just notified him that the guest user account has logged in remotely. A suspected attack is occurring this very moment. What should you do?

You should respond to an attack that's occurring at this moment the same way that you would respond to one that happened before you knew about it. You need to determine what the account is doing and try to figure out the identity of the attacker and where they're coming from. As you collect any information, you should treat it as evidence and keep careful watch over it.

Although collecting as much information as possible is important, no one can be blamed for trying to protect their data. Damage and loss control are critical; you need to minimize the impact of the incident. Though it may be admirable to catch a crook deleting your data, if you can keep the data from being deleted, you will stand a much better chance of still being employed tomorrow. As soon as it becomes apparent that data is at risk, you should disconnect the user. Catching a bad guy is a noble task, but the security of the data should be considered paramount.

Step 3: Repairing the Damage

One of your first considerations after an incident is to determine how to restore access to resources that have been compromised. Then, of course, you must reestablish control of the system. Most operating systems provide the ability to create a disaster-recovery process using distribution media or system state files.

After a problem has been identified, what steps will you take to restore service? In the case of a DoS attack, a system reboot may be all that is required. Your operating system manufacturer will typically provide detailed instructions or documentation on how to restore services in the event of an attack.

If a system has been severely compromised, as in the case of a worm, it might not be possible to repair it. It may need to be regenerated from scratch. Fortunately, antivirus software packages can repair most of the damage done by the viruses you encounter. But what if you come across something new? You might need to start over with a new system. In that case, we strongly advise you to do a complete disk drive format or repartition to ensure that nothing is lurking on the disk, waiting to infect your network again.

In some cases, it may not be possible to repair the problem completely. If data has been stolen, you cannot go back in time and prevent the loss of that data. In such cases, you must take mitigation steps. These are steps to lessen the damage. For example, if data has been stolen you might do the following:

1. Immediately change all passwords.

2. Notify the relevant parties.

3. Make procedural changes so that the information stolen cannot be used to affect additional breaches.

 Real World Scenario

The Virus That Won't Stop

A virus recently hit a user in your organization through an email attachment. The user updated all of the programs in his computer and also updated his antivirus software; however, he's still reporting unusual behavior in his computer system. He's also receiving complaints from people in his email address book because he's sending them a virus. You've been asked to fix the problem.

The user has probably contracted a worm that has infected the system files in his computer. You should help him back up his user files to removable media. Then completely reformat his drives and reinstall the operating system and applications. After you've replaced these, you can install new antivirus software and scan the entire system. When the scan is complete, help the user reinstall data files and scan the system again for viruses. This process should eliminate all viruses from system, application, and data files.

 Just as every network, regardless of size, should have a firewall, it should also be protected by antivirus software that is enabled and current. ClamAV (www.clamav.net) is an open source solution once available only for Unix-based systems that is now offered for most operating systems.

Step 4: Documenting and Reporting the Response

During the entire process of responding to an incident, you should document the steps you take to identify, detect, and repair the system or network. This information is valuable; it needs to be captured in case an attack like this occurs again. The documentation should be accessible by the people most likely to deal with this type of problem. Many help-desk software systems provide detailed methods that you can use to record procedures and steps. These types of software products allow for fast access.

If appropriate, you should report/disclose the incident to legal authorities and CERT (www.cert.org) so that others can be aware of the type of attack and help to look for proactive measures to prevent it from happening again.

You might also want to inform the software or system manufacturer of the problem and how you corrected it. Doing so might help them inform or notify other customers of the threat and save time for someone else.

 Real World Scenario

How Incident Response Plans Work

Emergency management (EM) personnel routinely stage fake emergencies to verify that they know what they should do in the event of an actual emergency. For example, if you live in a town with a train track that is routinely used by railcars carrying toxic chemicals, it isn't uncommon for EM personnel to stage a fake spill every couple of years. Those organizing the practice won't tell those responding what type of spill it is, or the severity of it, until they arrive at the scene. The organizers monitor and evaluate the responses to see that they're appropriate and where they can be improved.

Responding to security incidents requires the same type of focus and training. You should plan a fake incident at your site, inform all those who will be involved that it's coming, and then evaluate their response. You should evaluate the following items:

1. *Was the evidence gathered and the chain of custody maintained?*

2. *Did the escalation procedures follow the correct path?*

3. *Given the results of the investigation, would you be able to find and prosecute the culprit?*

4. *What was done that should not have been done?*

5. *What could have been done better?*

Practice makes perfect, and there is no better time to practice your company's response to an emergency than before one really occurs.

Step 5: Adjusting Procedures

After an incident has been successfully managed, it's a worthwhile step to revisit the procedures and policies in place in your organization to determine what changes, if any, need to be made.

Answering simple questions can sometimes be helpful when you're resolving problems. The following questions might be included in a policy or procedure manual:

- How did the policies work or not work in this situation?

- What did you learn about the situation that was new?

- What should you do differently next time?

These simple questions can help you adjust the procedures. This process is called a *postmortem*, and it's the equivalent of an autopsy.

Forensics from the Security+ Perspective

The five steps outlined here will help in all incident response situations. For the exam, however, there are a number of procedures and topics about which CompTIA wants you to be aware that are relevant to a forensic investigation. We strongly recommend that you familiarize yourself with these topics as you prepare for the exam.

Act in Order of Volatility   When dealing with multiple issues, address them in order of volatility (OOV); always deal with the most volatile first. *Volatility* can be thought of as the amount of time that you have to collect certain data before a window of opportunity is gone. Naturally, in an investigation you want to collect everything, but some data will exist longer than others, and you cannot possibly collect all of it once. As an example, the OOV in an investigation may be RAM, hard drive data, CDs/DVDs, and printouts.

Capture System Image   A *system image* is a snapshot of what exists. Capturing an image of the operating system in its exploited state can be helpful in revisiting the issue after the fact to learn more about it. As an analogy, think of germ samples that are stored in labs after major outbreaks so that scientists can revisit them later and study them further.

Document Network Traffic and Logs   Look at network traffic and logs to see what information you can find there. This information can be useful in identifying trends associated with repeated attacks.

Capture Video   Capture any relevant video that you can. Video can later be analyzed manually in individual frames as well as run through a number of programs that can create indices of the contents.

Record Time Offset   It is quite common for workstation times to be off slightly from actual time, and that can happen with servers as well. Since a forensic investigation is usually dependent on a step-by-step account of what has happened, being able to follow events in the correct time sequence is critical. Because of this, it is imperative to record the time offset on each affected machine during the investigation. One method of assisting with this is to add an entry to a log file and note the time that this was done and the time associated with it on the system.

Take Hashes It is important to collect as much data as possible to be able to illustrate the situation, and hashes must not be left out of the equation. NIST (the National Institute of Standards and Technology) maintains a *National Software Reference Library (NSRL)*. One of the purposes of the NSRL is to collect "known, traceable software applications" through their hash values and store them in a Reference Data Set (RDS). The RDS can then be used by law enforcement, government agencies, and businesses to determine which files are important as evidence in criminal investigations. More information on the RDS can be found at http://www.nsrl.nist.gov/.

Capture Screenshots Just like video, capture all relevant screenshots for later analysis. One image can often parlay the same information that it would take hundreds of log entries to equal.

Talk to Witnesses It is important to talk to as many witnesses as possible to learn exactly what happened and to do so as soon as possible after the incident. Over time, details and reflections can change, and you want to collect their thoughts before such changes occur. If at all possible, document as much of the interview as you can with video recorders, digital recorders, or whatever recording tools you can find.

Track Man Hours and Expenses Make no mistake about it; an investigation is expensive. Track total man-hours and expenses associated with the investigation, and be prepared to justify them if necessary to superiors, a court, or insurance agents.

Succession Planning

Succession planning outlines those internal to the organization who have the ability to step into positions when they open. By identifying key roles that cannot be left unfilled and associating internal employees who can step into these roles, you can groom those employees to make sure that they are up to speed when it comes time for them to fill those positions.

Tabletop Exercises

A tabletop exercise is a simulation of a disaster. It is a way to check to see if your plans are ready to go. There are five levels of testing:

Document Review A review of recovery, operations, resumption plans, and procedures.

Walkthrough A group discussion of recovery, operations, resumption plans, and procedures.

Simulation A walkthrough of recovery, operations, resumption plans, and procedures in a scripted "case study" or "scenario."

Parallel Test With this test, you start up all backup systems but leave the main systems functioning.

Cutover Test This test shuts down the main systems and has everything fail over to backup systems.

You should never do a cutover test if you have not already done a simulation and parallel test. If the cutover test fails, your entire system is offline; in essence, you have created a disaster.

One issue that will be tested with the first three (document review, walkthrough, and simulation) is called *Big Data analysis*. Big Data refers to data that is too large to be dealt with by traditional database management means. As of this writing, this usually means exabytes of data (a terabyte is a thousand gigabytes, a petabyte is a thousand terabytes, and an exabyte is a thousand petabytes). When systems are this large, obviously the system being down has a wide-ranging impact. However, doing a cutover test is very difficult, and in some cases it is just not practical. That does not mean, however, that you can simply ignore those systems in your disaster-recovery planning.

Reinforcing Vendor Support

Software vendors and hardware vendors are necessary elements in the process of building systems and applications. The costs associated with buying preconfigured software, hardware, and services are usually less than building them yourself. Unfortunately, this makes you dependent on a particular vendor's ability to stay in business.

The following sections discuss service-level agreements and code escrow. These agreements help protect you in the event that a software vendor goes out of business or if you have a dispute with a maintenance provider for your systems.

Service-Level Agreements

A *service-level agreement (SLA)* is an agreement between you or your company and a service provider, typically a technical support provider. SLAs are also usually part of network availability and other agreements. They stipulate the performance you can expect or demand by outlining the expectations a vendor has agreed to meet. They define what is possible to deliver, and they provide the contract to make sure what is delivered is what was promised.

Some SLAs may put you in a vendor-dependent position that can potentially open up your data to eyes that should not see it. Consider a medical practice that must grant an application vendor full access to all patient records in the spirit of being able to maintain the application. Just as with any other contract, you must carefully scrutinize the SLA and make certain that you are not unintentionally exposing your organization to harm. Running it past the company's legal department and your superior is always a good practice.

Quite often, SLAs exist even within a company. They serve the same purpose within departments of a company as they do between a vendor and a supplier.

SLAs are also known as *maintenance contracts* when referring to hardware or software.

If a vendor promises to provide you with a response time of four hours, this means that it will have someone involved and dedicated to resolving any difficulties you encounter— either a service technician in the field or a remote diagnostic process occurring on your system—within four hours. In either case, the customer has specific remedies that it can demand from the vendor if the terms of an SLA aren't met.

Most computer manufacturers offer a variety of SLA levels. Some can guarantee support in hours, whereas others may require days. Different levels of coverage and different response times usually have different costs associated with them. A 4-hour service agreement will typically cost much more than a 24-hour or 48-hour agreement. An SLA should also stipulate how long the repair will take once the support process has been activated: Having a service technician on site in four hours won't do much good if it takes two weeks to get a replacement for a defective part.

Make sure that you understand the scope and terms of your SLAs. Periodically review them to verify that the performance criteria match your performance needs. Doing so can help prevent frustration and unanticipated disruptions from crippling your organization. The following are key measures in SLAs:

Recovery Time Objectives   The *recovery time objective (RTO)* is the maximum amount of time that a process or service is allowed to be down and the consequences still to be considered acceptable. Beyond this time, the break in business continuity is considered to affect the business negatively. The RTO is agreed on during the business impact analysis (BIA) creation.

Mean Time between Failures   The *mean time between failures (MTBF)* is the measure of the anticipated incidence of failure for a system or component. This measurement determines the component's anticipated lifetime. If the MTBF of a cooling system is one year, you can anticipate that the system will last for a one-year period; this means that you should be prepared to replace or rebuild the system once a year. If the system lasts longer than the MTBF, your organization receives a bonus. MTBF is helpful in evaluating a system's reliability and life expectancy.

Mean Time to Restore   The *mean time to restore (MTTR)* is the measurement of how long it takes to repair a system or component once a failure occurs (this is often also referred as *mean time to repair*). In the case of a computer system, if the MTTR is 24 hours, this tells you that it will typically take 24 hours to repair it when it breaks.

Although MTTR is considered a common measure of maintainability, be careful when evaluating it because it doesn't typically include the time needed to acquire a component and have it shipped to your location. One of the authors once worked with a national vendor who thought MTTR meant mean time to respond. A technician would show up on site within the time the contract called for, but they would only begin to look at the problem and make a list of any needed supplies. Make sure that the contract agreements spell out exactly what you want.

Most SLAs stipulate the definitions of these terms and how they apply to the agreement. Make sure that you understand how these terms are used and what they mean to the vendor.

 Real World Scenario

Should I Buy the Computer Store's SLA for My New Laptop?

You just purchased that new laptop that you've been eyeing. The store you bought it from is a large, national computer and software retailer. When you purchased the laptop, the salesperson worked hard to sell you an extended warranty agreement. Was it a good deal?

You should evaluate the SLA offered by the computer store and compare it to the manufacturer's warranty and service options. Many retail computer stores can't repair laptops in house, and they send most of them back to the manufacturer for all but the simplest service. Most laptop manufacturers offer a variety of service options, including 24-hour delivery of replacement systems. You should verify the length of time that it will take to have the store repair your laptop before you purchase their SLA. In some situations, a store's repair program is more expensive and slower than a manufacturer's repair program.

Code Escrow Agreements

Code escrow refers to the storage and conditions of a release of source code provided by a vendor. For example, a code escrow agreement would stipulate how source code would be made available to customers in the event of a vendor's bankruptcy.

If you contract with a software developer to perform a customized programming effort, your contract may not give you the right to access and view the source code that this vendor created for you. If you want to make changes to the program's functionality, you will be required to contract with the developer or integrator who installed it to perform those changes. This practice is common in application software projects, such as setting up accounting systems.

In recent years, a number of software companies have been forced to close their doors because of trying economic times. In many cases, the software they sold has become *orphanware*—existing without support of any type.

If the vendor ceases operations, you won't be able to obtain the source code to make further changes unless your agreement stipulates a code escrow clause. Unfortunately, this situation effectively makes your investment a dead-end street. Make sure that your agreements provide you either with the source code for projects you've had developed or a code escrow clause to acquire the software if the company goes out of business.

Penetration Testing

It is becoming more common for companies to hire penetration testers to test their system's defenses. Essentially, a penetration tester will use the same techniques a hacker would use to find any flaws in your system's security.

Hacking and penetration testing are areas that seem quite exciting to many people. Unfortunately, this has led to a number of unqualified (or at least underqualified) people calling themselves penetration testers. It is imperative when hiring a penetration tester that you ensure the person in question has the requisite skill set. Check their references and verify their training and skills. It is also important to do a thorough background check on the person in question, as you are giving this person permission to try hacking techniques on your network. You will want to be certain that they conduct themselves in an ethical manner.

What Should You Test?

One of the first steps in penetration testing is deciding what needs to be tested. This is a question of verifying what actual threats exist to your network. For example, if you are the network administrator of a public school, it is unlikely that highly skilled cyber terrorists are trying to infiltrate your network. The most likely threat to your network is a low-to-moderately skilled student. The most likely threats are what should determine the exact nature of a penetration test.

Essentially, all tests will have a few similar steps, regardless of the threat. Those steps include some attempt to bypass security controls. The penetration tester will attempt to bypass whatever security controls have been implemented on your network. This is the best way to actively test security controls.

The three types of testing are described here:

Black Box The tester has absolutely no knowledge of the system and is functioning in the same manner as an outside attacker.

White Box The tester has significant knowledge of your system. This simulates an attack from an insider—a rogue employee.

Gray Box This is a middle ground between the first two types of testing. In gray box testing, the tester has some limited knowledge of the target system.

In addition to classifying a penetration test based on the amount of information given to the tester, it is also possible to classify the test as intrusive versus nonintrusive. *Nonintrusive tests* involve passively testing security controls—performing vulnerability scans, probing for weaknesses, but not exploiting them. *Intrusive tests* involve actually trying to break into the network. In the strictest sense, passive tests are really just vulnerability scans and not penetration tests, while active tests provide more meaningful results. With active tests, it is possible that they may disrupt business operations in the same way as a real attack.

Vulnerability Scanning

Many security experts view vulnerability scanning as separate from penetration testing. However, it should be either part of the penetration test or done alongside it. *Vulnerability scanning* allows you to identify specific vulnerabilities in your network, and most penetration testers will start with this procedure so that they can identify likely targets to attack. A penetration test is essentially an attempt to exploit these vulnerabilities.

Once you have identified the vulnerabilities, it is time to attempt to exploit them. Of course the most egregious vulnerability is any aspect of your system where vulnerability scanning reveals a lack of security controls. Some of the more common vulnerabilities involve misconfiguration. In fact, popular vulnerability scanners, such as Nessus (www .tenable.com/products/nessus), will help identify common misconfigurations.

Credentialed vs. Noncredentialed

Vulnerability scanning can be done either in a credentialed or noncredentialed manner. The difference is that a credentialed vulnerability scan uses actual network credentials to connect to systems and scan for vulnerabilities. Tenable Security, the creators of the Nessus vulnerability scanner, have this to say about credentialed scanning:

> This type of scan has several benefits:
>
> - **Not disrupting operations or consuming too many resources**   Because the scan is performed with credentials, operations are executed on the host itself rather than across the network. Everything from operating system identification to port scanning is done by running commands on the host, then sending the results of those commands back to the Nessus server. This allows Nessus to consume far less system and network resources than performing a traditional network scan that probes ports and services remotely.
>
> - **Definitive list of missing patches**   Rather than probe a service remotely and attempt to find a vulnerability, Nessus will query the local host to see if a patch for a given vulnerability has been applied. This type of query is far more accurate (and safer) than running a remote check.
>
> - **Client-side software vulnerabilities are uncovered**   By looking at the software installed and its version, Nessus will find client-side software vulnerabilities that are otherwise missed in a traditional network-based audit.
>
> - **Several other "vulnerabilities"**   Nessus can read password policies, obtain a list of USB devices, check anti-virus software configurations and even enumerate Bluetooth devices attached to scanned hosts.
>
> *www.tenable.com/blog/the-value-of-credentialed-vulnerability-scanning*

Whether you use credentialed or noncredentialed vulnerability scanning, be prepared for false positives. A *false positive* occurs when the scan mistakenly identifies something as a vulnerability when it is not. No software program is perfect, and this means that any vulnerability scanner will yield some occasional false positives.

Summary

In this chapter, you learned about the many aspects involved in the operations of a secure environment. You studied business continuity and vendor support. Business continuity planning is the process of making decisions about how losses, outages, and failures are handled within an organization. Business impact analysis includes evaluating the critical functions of the organization. This information is used to make educated decisions about how to deal with outages should they occur.

The issue of reliable service from utility companies, such as electricity and water, should be evaluated as part of your disaster-recovery process. Addressing potential problems as part of your business decision making can prevent unanticipated downtime.

Disaster recovery is the process of helping your organization prepare for recovery in the event of an unplanned situation, and it's a part of your organization's business continuity plans.

Vendors can provide support and services to an organization. SLAs set a benchmark for expected performance when needed. Service performance and reliability are measured by MTBF and MTTR. Vendors that provide software or programming support should have code escrow agreements to ensure that software can be maintained if the vendor ceases doing business.

The process of dealing with a security problem is called incident response. An incident response policy should clearly outline what resources, individuals, and procedures are to be involved in the event of an incident.

Exam Essentials

Understand the aspects of disaster recovery.   Disaster recovery is concerned with the recovery of critical systems in the event of a loss. One of the primary issues is the effectiveness of backup policies and procedures. Offsite storage is one of the most secure methods of protecting information from loss.

Know the types of backups that are typically performed in an organization.   The three backup methods are full, incremental, and differential. A full backup involves the total archiving of all information on a system. An incremental backup involves archiving only information that has changed since the last backup. Differential backups save all information that has changed since the last full backup.

Be able to discuss the process of recovering a system in the event of a failure.   A system recovery usually involves restoring the base operating systems, applications, and data files. The operating systems and applications are usually restored either from the original distribution media or from a server that contains images of the system. Data is typically recovered from backups or archives.

Be able to discuss the types of alternative sites available for disaster recovery.   The three types of sites available for disaster recovery are hot sites, warm sites, and cold sites. Hot sites typically provide high levels of capability, including networking. Warm sites may provide some capabilities, but they're generally less prepared than a hot site. A cold site requires the organization to replicate critical systems and all services to restore operations.

Be able to describe the needed components of an incident response policy.   The incident response policy explains how incidents will be handled, including notification, resources, and escalation. This policy drives the incident response process, and it provides advance planning to the incident response team.

Understand the basics of forensics.   Forensics is the process of identifying what has occurred on a system by examining the data trail. It involves an analysis of evidence found in computers and on digital storage media. When dealing with multiple issues, address them in order of volatility: Capture system images as a snapshot of what exists, look at network traffic and logs, capture any relevant video/screenshots/hashes, record time offset on the systems, talk to witnesses, and track total man-hours and expenses associated with the investigation.

Review Questions

1. Which plan or policy helps an organization determine how to relocate to an emergency site?

   A. Disaster-recovery plan

   B. Backup site plan

   C. Privilege management policy

   D. Privacy plan

2. Although you're talking to her on the phone, the sound of the administrative assistant's screams of despair can be heard down the hallway. She has inadvertently deleted a file that the boss desperately needs. Which type of backup is used for the immediate recovery of a lost file?

   A. Onsite storage

   B. Working copies

   C. Incremental backup

   D. Differential backup

3. You're trying to rearrange your backup procedures to reduce the amount of time they take each evening. You want the backups to finish as quickly as possible during the week. Which backup system backs up only the files that have changed since the last backup?

   A. Full backup

   B. Incremental backup

   C. Differential backup

   D. Backup server

4. Which backup system backs up all of the files that have changed since the last full backup?

   A. Full backup

   B. Incremental backup

   C. Differential backup

   D. Archival backup

5. You're a consultant brought in to advise MTS on its backup procedures. One of the first problems you notice is that the company doesn't use a good tape-rotation scheme. Which backup method uses a rotating schedule of backup media to ensure long-term information storage?

   A. Grandfather, Father, Son method

   B. Full Archival method

   C. Backup Server method

   D. Differential Backup method

6. Which site best provides limited capabilities for the restoration of services in a disaster?

A. Hot site

B. Warm site

C. Cold site

D. Backup site

7. You're the head of information technology for MTS and have a brother in a similar position for ABC. The companies are approximately the same size and are located several hundred miles apart. As a benefit to both companies, you want to implement an agreement that would allow either company to use resources at the other site should a disaster make a building unusable. What type of agreement between two organizations provides mutual use of their sites in the event of an emergency?

A. Backup-site agreement

B. Warm-site agreement

C. Hot-site agreement

D. Reciprocal agreement

8. The process of automatically switching from a malfunctioning system to another system is called what?

A. Fail safe

B. Redundancy

C. Failover

D. Hot site

9. Which agreement outlines performance requirements for a vendor?

A. MTBF

B. MTTR

C. SLA

D. BCP

10. Your company is about to invest heavily in an application written by a new startup. Because it is such a sizable investment, you express your concerns about the longevity of the new company and the risk this organization is taking. You propose that the new company agree to store its source code for use by customers in the event that it ceases business. What is this model called?

A. Code escrow

B. SLA

C. BCP

D. CA

11. Which of the following would normally *not* be part of an incident response policy?

   A. Outside agencies (that require status)

   B. Outside experts (to resolve the incident)

   C. Contingency plans

   D. Evidence collection procedures

12. Which of the following is the measure of the anticipated incidence of failure for a system or component?

   A. CIBR

   B. AIFS

   C. MTBF

   D. MTTR

13. Which of the following outlines those internal to the organization who have the ability to step into positions when they open?

   A. Succession planning

   B. Progression planning

   C. Emergency planning

   D. Eventuality planning

14. What is another name for working copies?

   A. Functional copies

   B. Running copies

   C. Operating copies

   D. Shadow copies

15. Which of the following is a reversion from a change that had negative consequences?

   A. Backup

   B. ERD

   C. Backout

   D. DIS

16. Which of the following is data that is too large to be dealt with by traditional database management means?

   A. Infomatics

   B. Big data

   C. Bit stream

   D. Data warehouse

17. According to CERT, which of the following would be a formalized or an ad hoc team you can call upon to respond to an incident after it arises?

    A. CSIRT

    B. CIRT

    C. IRT

    D. RT

18. Which of the following is a concept that works on the assumption that any information created on any system is stored forever?

    A. Cloud computing

    B. Warm site

    C. Big data

    D. Full archival

19. Which of the following is a newer backup type that provides continuous online backup by using optical or tape jukeboxes and can be configured to provide the closest version of an available real-time backup?

    A. TPM

    B. HSM

    C. SAN

    D. NAS

20. Which type of penetration-style testing involves actually trying to break into the network?

    A. Discreet

    B. Indiscreet

    C. Non-intrusive

    D. Intrusive

Appendix A

Answers to Review Questions

Chapter 1: Measuring and Weighing Risk

1. C. Guidelines help clarify processes to maintain standards. Guidelines tend to be less formal than policies or standards.

2. A. It does not matter how frequent a loss is projected (only once every 60 years, in this case). What does matter is that each occurrence will be disastrous: SLE (single loss expectancy) is equal to asset value (AV) times exposure factor (EF). In this case, asset value is $2 million and the exposure factor is 1.

3. D. ALE (annual loss expectancy) is equal to the SLE times the annualized rate of occurrence. In this case, the SLE is $2 million and the ARO is 1/60.

4. A. ARO (annualized rate of occurrence) is the frequency (in number of years) that an event can be expected to happen. In this case, ARO is 1/60, or 0.0167.

5. B. Risk avoidance involves identifying a risk and making the decision to no longer engage in the actions associated with that risk.

6. B. The exception policy statement may include an escalation contact in the event that the person dealing with a situation needs to know whom to contact.

7. A. A separation of duties policy is designed to reduce the risk of fraud and to prevent other losses in an organization.

8. D. False positives are events that were mistakenly flagged and aren't truly events to be concerned about.

9. C. Change management is the structured approach that is followed to secure a company's assets.

10. E. Risk transference involves sharing some of the risk burden with someone else, such as an insurance company.

11. C. The risk-assessment component, in conjunction with the business impact analysis (BIA), provides an organization with an accurate picture of the situation it faces.

12. D. The accountability policy statement should address who is responsible for ensuring that the policy is enforced.

13. D. Risk mitigation is accomplished any time you take steps to reduce risk.

14. C. If you calculate the SLE to be $4,000 and that there will be 10 occurrences a year (ARO), then the ALE is $40,000 ($4,000 × 10).

15. B. The acceptable use policies describe how the employees in an organization can use company systems and resources, both software and hardware.

16. C. Collusion is an agreement between two or more parties established for the purpose of committing deception or fraud. Collusion, when part of a crime, is also a criminal act in and of itself.

17. C. Risk deterrence involves understanding something about the enemy and letting them know the harm that can come their way if they cause harm to you.

18. A. If you calculate SLE to be $25,000 and that there will be one occurrence every four years (ARO), then the ALE is $6,250 ($25,000 × 0.25).

19. C. The principle of least privilege should be used when assigning permissions. Give users only the permissions they need to do their work and no more.

20. A. Risk acceptance necessitates an identified risk that those involved understand the potential cost or damage and agree to accept it.

Chapter 2: Monitoring and Diagnosing Networks

1. C. In order for network monitoring to work properly, you need a PC and a network card running in promiscuous mode.

2. B. Use the `faillog` utility in Linux to view a list of users' failed authentication attempts.

3. C. A service pack is a periodic update that corrects problems in one version of a product.

4. A. Sniffers monitor network traffic and display traffic in real time. Sniffers, also called network monitors, were originally designed for network maintenance and troubleshooting.

5. A. A honeypot is a system that is sacrificed in the name of knowledge. Honeypot systems allow investigators to evaluate and analyze the attack strategies used. Law enforcement agencies use honeypots to gather evidence for prosecution.

6. A. No matter the reason for employees leaving, disable their account when they leave.

7. B. The administrator is the person or account responsible for setting the security policy for an organization.

8. B. Entrapment is the process in which a law enforcement officer or a government agent encourages or induces a person to commit a crime when the potential criminal expresses a desire not to go ahead.

9. A. Event logs include Application logs, such as those where SQL Server would write entries.

10. B. EAPOL is more commonly referenced as 802.1X.

11. C. Use `ipconfig /all` to find it in the Windows-based world.

12. D. Essentially, you disable a port by using the Windows Firewall to block that port.

13. C. An alarm is an indication of an ongoing current problem.

14. A. RPC (Remote Procedure Call) is a programming interface that allows a remote computer to run programs on a local machine.

15. B. A patch is a fix for a known software problem.

16. D. The FAT file system is from Microsoft and was included with their earliest operating systems.

17. C. The process of making certain that an entity (operating system, application, etc.) is as secure as it can be is known as hardening.

18. A. Enticement is the process of luring someone in.

19. A. An alert is a notification that an unusual condition exists and should be investigated.

20. B. Use `ifconfig` to find it in the Linux-based world.

Chapter 3: Understanding Devices and Infrastructure

1. C. Routers can be configured in many instances to act as packet-filtering firewalls. When configured properly, they can prevent unauthorized ports from being opened.

2. A. Packet filters prevent unauthorized packets from entering or leaving a network. Packet filters are a type of firewall that blocks specified port traffic.

3. D. Routers store information about network destinations in routing tables. Routing tables contain information about known hosts on both sides of the router.

4. B. Switches create virtual circuits between systems in a network. These virtual circuits are somewhat private and reduce network traffic when used.

5. B. PPP can pass multiple protocols, and it is widely used today as a transport protocol for dial-up connections.

6. A. PPP provides no security, and all activities are unsecure. PPP is primarily intended for dial-up connections, and it should never be used for VPN connections.

7. A. IPSec provides network security for tunneling protocols. IPSec can be used with many different protocols besides TCP/IP, and it has two modes of security.

8. D. A socket is a combination of IP address and port number. The socket identifies which application will respond to the network request.

9. C. IMAP is becoming the most popular standard for email clients and is replacing POP protocols for mail systems. IMAP allows mail to be forwarded and stored in information areas called stores.

10. A. ICMP is used for destination and error reporting functions in TCP/IP. ICMP is routable, and it is used by programs such as Ping and Traceroute.

11. B. The implementation of IPSec is mandatory with IPv6. Though it is widely implemented with IPv4, it is not a requirement.

12. A. FTP uses TCP ports 20 and 21. FTP does not use UDP ports.

13. D. SFTP uses only TCP ports. IMAP, LDAP, and FTPS all use both TCP and UDP ports.

14. C. A load balancer can be implemented as a software or hardware solution and is usually associated with a device—a router, a firewall, NAT, and so on. As the name implies, it is used to shift a load from one device to another.

15. A. Switches are multiport devices that improve network efficiency. A switch typically has a small amount of information about systems in a network.

16. B, C. Port 22 is used by both SSH and SCP with TCP and UDP.

17. C. NetBIOS is used for name resolution and registration in Windows-based environments. It runs on top of TCP/IP.

18. A. IPv4 uses 32 bits for the host address, whereas IPv6 uses 128 bits for this.

19. D. A heuristic system uses algorithms to analyze the traffic passing through the network.

20. A. Sniffers monitor network traffic and display traffic in real time. Sniffers, also called network monitors, were originally designed for network maintenance and troubleshooting.

Chapter 4: Access Control, Authentication, and Authorization

1. B. The basic premise of least privilege is, when assigning permissions, give users only the permissions they need to do their work and no more.

2. B. A flood guard is a protection feature built into many firewalls that allows the administrator to tweak the tolerance for unanswered login attacks. Reducing this tolerance makes it possible to lessen the likelihood of a successful DoS attack.

3. A. IPSec provides network security for tunneling protocols. IPSec can be used with many different protocols besides TCP/IP.

4. A. DAC allows some information-sharing flexibility capabilities within the network.

5. A. Access control lists allow individual and highly controllable access to resources in a network. An ACL can also be used to exclude a particular system, IP address, or user.

6. A. Lightweight Directory Access Protocol (LDAP) is a directory access protocol used to publish information about users. It is the computer equivalent of a phone book.

7. A. Mandatory Access Control (MAC) is oriented toward preestablished access. This access is typically established by network administrators and can't be changed by users.

8. C. Role-Based Access Control (RBAC) allows specific people to be assigned to specific roles with specific privileges. A backup operator would need administrative privileges to back up a server. This privilege would be limited to the role and wouldn't be present during the employee's normal job functions.

9. B. Kerberos uses a key distribution center (KDC) to authenticate a principal. The KDC provides a credential that can be used by all Kerberos-enabled servers and applications.

10. A. A multifactor authentication method uses two or more processes for logon. A two-factor method might use smart cards and biometrics for logon.

11. A. Virtual local area networks (VLANs) break a large network into smaller ones. These networks can coexist on the same wiring and be unaware of each other. A router or other routing-type device would be needed to connect these VLANs.

12. A. Tunneling allows a network to make a secure connection to another network through the Internet or other network. Tunnels are usually secure and present themselves as extensions of both networks.

13. A. Tokens are created when a user or system successfully authenticates. The token is destroyed when the session is over.

14. C. Whenever two or more parties authenticate each other, this is known as mutual authentication.

15. B. Operational security issues include network access control (NAC), authentication, and security topologies once the network installation is complete.

16. D. Transitive access exists between the domains and creates this relationship.

17. A. Identity proofing is invoked when a person claims that they are the user but cannot be authenticated, such as when they lose their password.

18. B. Terminal Access Controller Access-Control System (TACACS, and variations like XTACACS and TACACS+) is a client/server-oriented environment, and it operates in a manner similar to RADIUS.

19. C. An implicit deny clause is implied at the end of each ACL, and it means that if the proviso in question has not been explicitly granted, then it is denied.

20. D. The Common Access Card (CAC) is issued by the Department of Defense as a general identification/authentication card for military personnel, contractors, and non-DoD employees.

Chapter 5: Protecting Wireless Networks

1. C. Wireless Application Protocol (WAP) is an open international standard for applications that use wireless communication.

2. A. 802.11 operates on 2.4 GHz. This standard allows for bandwidths of 1 Mbps or 2 Mbps.

3. C. Wi-Fi Protected Access 2 (WPA2) was intended to provide security that's equivalent to that on a wired network, and it implements elements of the 802.11i standard.

4. D. A site survey is the process of monitoring a wireless network using a computer, wireless controller, and analysis software. Site surveys are easily accomplished and hard to detect.

5. B. The term *network lock* is synonymous with MAC filtering.

6. C. The WPA2 standard is also known as 802.11i.

7. A. The 802.11n standard provides for bandwidths of up to 300 Mbps.

8. A. An IV attack is usually associated with the WEP wireless protocol.

9. C. CCMP uses 128-bit AES encryption.

10. A. The encryption technology associated with WPA is TKIP.

11. B. The initialization vector (IV) that WEP uses for encryption is 24-bit.

12. B. Two-way authentication requires both ends of the connection to authenticate to confirm validity.

13. C. The Wireless Transaction Protocol (WTP) provides services similar to TCP and UDP for WAP.

14. A. When the interconnection between the WAP server and the Internet isn't encrypted, packets between the devices may be intercepted; this vulnerability is known as packet sniffing.

15. A. TKIP places a 128-bit wrapper around the WEP encryption with a key that is based on things such as the MAC address of the host device and the serial number of the packet.

16. C. Disabling the SSID broadcast keeps it from being seen in the list of available networks, but it is still possible to connect to it and use the wireless network.

17. D. The dBi number indicates the amount of gain the antenna offers.

18. B. The VPN should use SSL or IPSec for the tunneling.

19. A. Near field communication (NFC) is used to send data between phones that are in close proximity.

20. D. WPS (Wi-Fi Protected Setup) is intended to simplify network setup for home and small offices.

Chapter 6: Securing the Cloud

1. C. In the Infrastructure as a Service (IaaS) model, the consumer can "provision," and is able to "deploy and run," but they still do not "manage or control" the underlying cloud infrastructure.

2. A. A private cloud delivery model is implemented by a single organization and can be implemented behind a firewall.

3. B. In the Platform as a Service (PaaS) model, the consumer has access to the infrastructure to create applications and host them.

4. B. A public delivery model could be considered a pool of services and resources delivered across the Internet by a cloud provider.

5. A. In the Software as a Service (SaaS) model, the consumer has the ability to use applications provided by the cloud provider over the Internet.

6. C. A community delivery model has an infrastructure shared by several organizations with shared interests and common IT needs.

7. D. The hybrid delivery model can be considered an amalgamation of other types of delivery models.

8. A. A snapshot is a method of capturing a virtual machine at a given point in time.

9. D. Five 9s (99.999 percent) is the industry standard for uptime.

10. B. Elasticity is a feature of cloud computing that involves dynamically provisioning (or de-provisioning) resources as needed.

11. D. Sandboxing is the term for restricting an application to a safe/restricted resource area.

12. A. Multitenancy implies hosting data from more than one consumer on the same equipment.

13. C. Ultimately, the organization is accountable for the choice of public cloud and the security and privacy of the outsourced service.

14. C. When multiple models are mixed together, this is referred to as Anything as a Service (XaaS).

15. B. While a hybrid cloud could be any mixture of cloud delivery models, it is usually a combination of public and private.

16. A. Type I hypervisor implementations are known as "bare metal."

17. B. Type II hypervisor implementations are known as "hosted."

18. B. Cloud bursting means that when your servers become too busy, you can offload traffic to resources from a cloud provider.

19. B. QoS (Quality of Service) makes load balancing/prioritizing possible.

20. C. The machine on which virtualization software is running is known as a host, whereas the virtual machines are known as guests.

Chapter 7: Host, Data, and Application Security

1. A. Baselining is the process of establishing a standard for security.

2. B. Hardening is the process of improving the security of an operating system or application. One of the primary methods of hardening an OS is to eliminate unneeded protocols.

3. B. Never share the root directory of a disk if at all possible. Doing so opens the entire disk to potential exploitation.

4. A. DNS records in a DNS server provide insights into the nature and structure of a network. DNS records should be kept to a minimum in public DNS servers. Network footprinting involves the attacker collecting data about the network to devise methods of intrusion.

5. B. Fuzzing is the technique of providing unexpected values as input to an application to try to make it crash. Those values can be random, invalid, or just unexpected.

6. A. DLP systems monitor the contents of systems (workstations, servers, networks) to make sure key content is not deleted or removed. They also monitor who is using the data (looking for unauthorized access) and transmitting the data.

7. C. A three-tiered model puts a server between the client and the database.

8. A. A service pack is one or more repairs to system problems bundled into a single process or function.

9. C. A hotfix is done while a system is operating. This reduces the necessity of taking a system out of service to fix a problem.

10. D. A SAN needs all of the security measures that any other network would need.

11. B. Relational database systems are the most frequently installed database environments in use today.

12. C. A patch is a workaround of a bug or problem in code that is applied manually. Complete programs usually replace patches at a later date.

13. D. Modify is the same as Read and Write, plus Delete.

14. B. Data loss prevention (DLP) systems monitor the contents of workstations, servers, and networks.

15. A. RAID 1+0 is a mirrored data set (RAID 1), which is then striped (RAID 0): a "stripe of mirrors."

16. C. "White lists" are lists of those items that are allowed (as opposed to a black list—things that are prohibited).

17. D. Geo-tagging allows GPS coordinates to accompany a file such as an image.

18. C. Clustered systems utilize parallel processing (improving performance and availability) and add redundancy.

19. D. Increasingly, organizations have to store extremely large amounts of data, often many terabytes. This is sometimes referred to simply as Big Data.

20. B. RAID 6 writes parity to two different drives, thus providing fault tolerance to the system even in the event of the failure of two drives in the array.

Chapter 8: Cryptography

1. B. Hashing algorithms must be one-way/nonreversible, have variable-length input and fixed-length output, and be collision resistant.

2. B. NIST is responsible for establishing the standards for general-purpose government encryption. NIST is also becoming involved in private sector cryptography.

3. A. RSA is the most widely used asymmetric algorithm today. AES and 3DES are symmetric algorithms, and SHA is a hashing algorithm.

4. C. The Request for Comments (RFC) process allows all users and interested parties to comment on proposed standards for the Internet. The RFC editor manages the RFC process. The editor is responsible for cataloging, updating, and tracking RFCs through the process.

5. D. Nonrepudiation offers indisputable proof that a party was involved in an action.

6. A. TLS is a security protocol that uses SSL, and it allows the use of other security protocols.

7. C. A MAC as it relates to cryptography is a method of verifying the integrity of an encrypted message. The MAC is derived from the message and the key.

8. B. Key transmission is the most serious problem from among the choices. Transmitting private keys is a major concern. Private keys are typically transported using out-of-band methods to ensure security.

9. C. AES is the best symmetric cipher on this list, and it is therefore appropriate for hard drive encryption. DES is weaker and no longer considered secure. RSA is an asymmetric cipher and is never used for hard drive encryption, and SHA is a hashing algorithm.

10. A. Proper key storage requires that the keys be physically stored in a secure environment. This may include using locked cabinets, hardened servers, and effective physical and administrative controls.

11. A. A certificate authority (CA) is responsible for maintaining certificates in the PKI environment.

12. C. A certificate revocation list (CRL) is created and distributed to all CAs to revoke a certificate or key.

13. B. A local registration authority (LRA) can establish an applicant's identity and verify that the applicant for a certificate is valid. The LRA sends verification to the CA that issues the certificate.

14. C. Suspending keys is a good practice: It disables a key, making it unusable for a certain period of time. This can prevent the key from being used while someone is gone. The key can be reactivated when that person returns.

15. A. The certificate policies document defines what certificates can be used for.

16. A. Key escrow is the process of storing keys or certificates for use by law enforcement. Law enforcement has the right, under subpoena, to conduct investigations using these keys.

17. D. Online Certificate Status Protocol (OCSP) can be used immediately to verify a certificate's authenticity.

18. A. XML Key Management Specification (XKMS) is designed to allow XML-based programs access to PKI services.

19. A. Twofish was created by the same person who created Blowfish. It performs a similar function on 128-bit blocks instead of 64-bit blocks.

20. D. Pretty Good Privacy (PGP) is an excellent email encryption tool that is either free or low cost. The other answers are not encryption tools.

Chapter 9: Malware, Vulnerabilities, and Threats

1. B. Sending an email with a misleading link to collect information is a phishing attack.

2. B. A DDoS attack uses multiple computer systems to attack a server or host in the network.

3. C. In a backdoor attack, a program or service is placed on a server to bypass normal security procedures.

4. A. A man-in-the-middle attack attempts to fool both ends of a communications session into believing that the system in the middle is the other end.

5. C. A replay attack attempts to replay the results of a previously successful session to gain access.

6. D. A smurf attack attempts to use a broadcast ping (ICMP) on a network. The return address of the ping may be a valid system in your network. This system will be flooded with responses in a large network.

7. A. A DoS attack is intended to prevent access to network resources by overwhelming or flooding a service or network.

8. A. A logic bomb notifies an attacker when a certain set of circumstances has occurred. This may in turn trigger an attack on your system.

9. A. An armored virus is designed to hide the signature of the virus behind code that confuses the antivirus software or blocks it from detecting the virus.

10. B. A stealth virus reports false information to hide itself from antivirus software. Stealth viruses often attach themselves to the boot sector of an operating system.

11. A. A password-guessing attack occurs when a user account is repeatedly attacked using a variety of passwords.

12. B. Header manipulation attacks use other methods (hijacking, cross-site forgery, and so forth) to change values in HTTP headers and falsify access.

13. A. A honeypot is a system that is intended to be sacrificed in the name of knowledge. Honeypot systems allow investigators to evaluate and analyze the attack strategies used. Law enforcement agencies use honeypots to gather evidence for prosecution.

14. D. SQL injection occurs when an attacker manipulates the database code to take advantage of a weakness in it.

15. B. If an attacker is able to gain access to restricted directories (such as the root directory) through HTTP, it is known as directory traversal.

16. C. Session hijacking occurs when the item used to validate a user's session, such as a cookie, is stolen and used by another to establish a session with a host that thinks it is still communicating with the first party.

17. D. XSRF involves unauthorized commands coming from a trusted user to the website. This is often done without the user's knowledge, and it employs some type of social networking to pull it off.

18. C. Banner grabbing looks at the banner, or header, information messages sent with data to find out about the system(s).

19. B. Nmap can be used for multiple purposes, but of the options given, it is best described as a vulnerability scanner.

20. D. When a hole is found in a web browser or other software and attackers begin exploiting it the very day it is discovered by the developer (bypassing the one-to-two-day response time that many software providers need to put out a patch once the hole has been found), it is known as a zero-day attack.

Chapter 10: Social Engineering and Other Foes

1. A. Social engineering attacks take advantage of our inherent trust as human beings, as opposed to technology, to gain access to your environment.

2. C. Wetware is another name for social engineering.

3. A. Tailgating is best defined as following someone through a door they just unlocked.

4. D. Phishing is the form of social engineering in which you simply ask someone for a piece of information that you want by making it look as if it is a legitimate request.

5. D. Vishing involves combining phishing with Voice over IP.

6. C. Shoulder surfing is best defined as watching someone enter important information.

7. A. High-security installations use a type of intermediate access control mechanism called a mantrap. Mantraps require visual identification, as well as authentication, to gain access. A mantrap makes it difficult for a facility to be accessed by a large number of individuals at once because it allows only one or two people into a facility at a time.

8. C. Type C fire extinguishers are intended for use in electrical fires.

9. B. Electrical devices, such as motors, that generate magnetic fields cause EMI. Humidity control does not address EMI.

10. A. Perimeter security involves creating a perimeter or outer boundary for a physical space. Video surveillance systems wouldn't be considered a part of perimeter security, but they can be used to enhance physical security monitoring.

11. C. A security zone is an area that is a smaller component of the entire facility. Security zones allow intrusions to be detected in specific parts of the building.

12. A. Biometrics is a technology that uses personal characteristics, such as a retinal pattern or fingerprint, to establish identity.

13. A. Shielding keeps external electronic signals from disrupting operations.

14. D. TEMPEST is the certification given to electronic devices that emit minimal RF. The TEMPEST certification is difficult to acquire, and it significantly increases the cost of systems.

15. A. Gas-based systems work by displacing the air around a fire. This eliminates one of the three necessary components of a fire: oxygen.

16. B. Type K fire extinguishers are a subset of Type B fire extinguishers.

17. C, D. Proximity readers work with 13.56 MHz smart card and 125 kHz proximity cards.

18. A. With hot and cold aisles, cold air is pumped in from below raised floor tiles.

19. B. If RF levels become too high, it can cause the receivers in wireless units to become deaf, and it is known as desensitizing. This occurs because of the volume of RF energy present.

20. C. RFI is the byproduct of electrical processes, similar to EMI. The major difference is that RFI is usually projected across a radio spectrum. Motors with defective brushes can generate RFI, as can a number of other devices.

Chapter 11: Security Administration

1. A. Social engineering uses the inherent trust in the human species, as opposed to technology, to gain access to your environment.

2. D. Limited distribution information can be released to select individuals and organizations, such as financial institutions, governmental agencies, and creditors.

3. A. The CIA triad includes confidentiality, integrity, and availability.

4. C. Social engineering involves using social skills to breach security in any manner, including obtaining proprietary information.

5. D. This is the principle of least privileges and the cornerstone of access control.

6. D. BYOD involves the possibility of a personal device that is infected with malware introducing that malware to the network.

7. A. If you change users' jobs from time to time, it is more likely that accidental or intentional security issues will be uncovered.

8. B. at.allow configurations allow only users specifically named to use the service.

9. B. Public information is made available to either large public or specific individuals, whereas private information is intended for only those internal to the organization.

10. B. It is necessary that critical functions not be operational by a single individual. Having several individuals responsible for critical functions reduces the likelihood of purposeful or accidental security issues.

11. A. Piggybacking is tailgating with the permission of the person you are following.

12. C. An NDA is typically signed by beta testers.

13. D. If you change users' jobs from time to time, it is more likely that accidental or intentional security issues will be uncovered.

14. A. Labeling information (such as secret, top secret, public) allows those with legitimate access to be immediately aware of how sensitive the data is and how to handle it appropriately.

15. B. HIPAA mandates national standards and procedures for the storage, use, and transmission of personal medical information.

16. B. The Cyberspace Security Enhancement Act gives law enforcement the right to gain access to encryption keys.

17. A. Top Secret is the highest classification level in the government.

18. A. The at.deny file does not allow users named in the file to access the system.

19. A. Least privileges should be your first thought in granting access. A sales manager will need to run reports but does not need administrative rights to the database.

20. B. Clean desk means that documents are not out and the computer monitor is not showing anything. Leaving out documents (or leaving them on the screen) means anyone passing by could gain confidential information.

Chapter 12: Disaster Recovery and Incident Response

1. A. The disaster-recovery plan deals with site relocation in the event of an emergency, natural disaster, or service outage.

2. B. Working copies are backups that are usually kept in the computer room for immediate use in recovering a system or lost file.

3. B. An incremental backup backs up files that have changed since the last full or partial backup.

4. C. A differential backup backs up all of the files that have changed since the last full backup.

5. A. The Grandfather, Father, Son backup method is designed to provide a rotating schedule of backup processes. It allows for a minimum usage of backup media, and it still allows for long-term archiving.

6. B. Warm sites provide some capabilities in the event of a recovery. The organization that wants to use a warm site will need to install, configure, and reestablish operations on systems that may already exist at the warm site.

7. D. A reciprocal agreement is between two organizations and allows one to use the other's site in an emergency.

8. C. Failover occurs when a system that is developing a malfunction automatically switches processes to another system to continue operations.

9. C. A service-level agreement (SLA) specifies performance requirements for a vendor. This agreement may use MTBF and MTTR as performance measures in the SLA.

10. A. Code escrow allows customers to access the source code of installed systems under specific conditions, such as the bankruptcy of a vendor.

11. C. A contingency plan wouldn't normally be part of an incident response policy. It would be part of a disaster-recovery plan.

12. C. Mean time between failures (MTBF) is the measure of the anticipated incidence of failure for a system or component.

13. A. Succession planning outlines those internal to the organization who have the ability to step into positions when they open.

14. D. Working copies are also known as shadow copies.

15. C. A backout is a reversion from a change that had negative consequences.

16. B. Big data is data that is too large to be dealt with by traditional database management means.

17. A. A CSIRT is a formalized or an ad hoc team you can call upon to respond to an incident after it arises.

18. D. Full archival is a concept that works on the assumption that any information created on any system is stored forever.

19. B. HSM is a newer backup type that provides continuous online backup by using optical or tape jukeboxes. It appears as an infinite disk to the system, and it can be configured to provide the closest version of an available real-time backup.

20. D. Intrusive testing involves actually trying to break into the network. Non-intrusive testing takes more of a passive approach.

Appendix B

About the Additional Study Tools

IN THIS APPENDIX:

✓ Additional study tools

✓ System requirements

✓ Using the study tools

✓ Troubleshooting

Additional Study Tools

The following sections are arranged by category and summarize the software and other goodies you'll find on the companion website. If you need help installing the items, refer to the installation instructions in the "Using the Study Tools" section of this appendix.

You can find the additional study tools on the website at www.sybex.com/go/securityplus6e. You'll also find instructions on how to download the files to your hard drive.

Sybex Test Engine

The files contain the Sybex test engine, which includes two bonus practice exams, as well as the assessment test and the chapter review questions, which are also included in the book.

Electronic Flashcards

These handy electronic flashcards are just what they sound like. One side contains a question, and the other side shows the answer.

PDF of Glossary of Terms

We have included an electronic version of the glossary in PDF format. You can view the electronic version of the glossary with Adobe Reader.

Adobe Reader

We've also included a copy of Adobe Reader so you can view PDF files that accompany the book's content. For more information on Adobe Reader or to check for a newer version, visit Adobe's website at www.adobe.com/products/reader/.

System Requirements

Make sure your computer meets the minimum system requirements shown in the following list. If your computer doesn't meet these requirements, you may have problems using the software and files. For the latest and greatest information, please refer to the ReadMe file located in the download.

- A PC running Microsoft Windows XP or newer
- An Internet connection

Using the Study Tools

To install the items, follow these steps:

1. Download the ZIP file to your hard drive, and unzip it to your desired location. You can find instructions on where to download this file on the website at www.sybex.com/go/securityplus6e.

2. Click the Start.exe file to open the study tools file.

3. Read the license agreement and then click the Accept button if you want to use the study tools.

   The main interface appears and allows you to access the content with just a few clicks.

Troubleshooting

Wiley has attempted to provide programs that work on most computers with the minimum system requirements. If a program does not work properly, the two likeliest problems are that you don't have enough memory (RAM) for the programs you want to use or you have other programs running that are affecting the installation or running of a program. If you get an error message such as "Not enough memory" or "Setup cannot continue," try one or more of the following suggestions and then try using the software again:

Turn off any antivirus software running on your computer.   Installation programs sometimes mimic virus activity and may make your computer incorrectly believe that it's being infected by a virus.

Close all running programs.   The more programs you have running, the less memory is available to other programs. Installation programs typically update files and programs, so if you keep other programs running, installation may not work properly.

Have your local computer store add more RAM to your computer.   This is, admittedly, a drastic step. However, adding more memory can really help the speed of your computer and allow more programs to run at the same time.

Customer Care

If you have trouble with the book's companion study tools, please call the Wiley Product Technical Support phone number at (800) 762-2974, or email them at `http://sybex .custhelp.com/`.

Index

3DES (Triple-DES), 250
802.11x protocols, 169–170
802.IX and, 158

A

ABA (American Bankers
    Association), 265
access control
    authentication, 131–132
        multifactor, 133–134, 138
        mutual authentication,
            133
        SFA (single-factor
            authentication),
            132–133
        two-factor, 133
    best practices
        802.IX and, 158
        access review, 154
        ACLs (access control lists),
            156–157
        CAC (Common Access
            Card), 155–156
        continuous monitoring,
            154
        EALs (Evaluation
            Assurance Levels),
            159–160
        firewall rules, 157
        flood guards, 158
        least privileges, 153
        log analysis, 159
        loop protection, 158
        network bridging, 158–
            159
        PIV (Personal Identity
            Verification), 156
        port security, 157–158
        privilege escalation, 153
        secure router
            configuration,
            160–161

separation of duties,
    153–154
smart cards, 155
time of day restrictions,
    154
TOS (trusted operating
    system), 159–160
DAC (Discretionary Access
    Control), 150, 151–152
defense in depth, 134
federations, 135–136
identification, 131–132
information
    availability, 414
    confidentiality, 414
    implicit denies, 413
    integrity, 414
    job rotation, 413
    least privilege, 413
layered security, 134
LBAC (Lattice-Based
    Control), 150
MAC (Mandatory Access
    Control), 150, 151
NAC (network access
    control), 134–135
operational security, 134–135
physical security, 366–367
problems, 136–137
RBAC (Role-Based Access
    Control), 150, 152
RBAC (Rule-Based Access
    Control), 150, 152
tokens, 135
access lists, physical security,
    373–374
access review, 154
Account Lockout Duration, 141
Account Lockout Threshold, 141
account policies, enforcement,
    139
accountability statement for
    policies, 20
ACLs (access control lists), 59,
    156, 221
    firewall rules, 157

implicit deny, 156
    spam and, 229
active backup model, 443
active/active backup model, 444
activities, IDS (intrusion
    detection system), 107
add-ons, 339–340
AD-IDS (anomaly-detection
    IDS), 109–110
administrative control type, 384
administrator, IDS (intrusion
    detection system), 107
adware, 301
AES (Advanced Encryption
    Standard), 250
AES256, 250
AH (Authentication Header), 274
alarms, 63
    physical security and, 376
ALE (annual loss expectancy),
    5
alerts, 63
    IDS (intrusion detection
        system), 107
all-in-one security appliances,
    119
    application-aware devices,
        122
    content inspection, 119–120
    malware inspection, 121–122
    URL filters, 119
    WAF (web application
        firewall), 122
alternate backup sites
    active backup model, 443
    active/active model, 444
    cold sites, 444
    hot sites, 443
    reciprocal agreement,
        444
    warm sites, 444
analyzers, IDS (intrusion
    detection system),
    107
anonymous authentication, WAP,
    174

antenna placement, wireless access points, 177–178
antenna types, 178
   wireless access points, 178
antimalware, 221–222
antiquated protocols, 77
antispam filters, 221
antispyware software, 221
antivirus software, 221, 317–318
APIs (application programming interfaces), 86
appliances, 96
Application layer, 74, 75–76
   DNS (Domain Name System), 76
   FTP (File Transfer Protocol), 75–76
   HTTP (Hypertext Transfer Protocol), 75
   HTTPS (HTTP Secure), 75
   POP (Post Office Protocol), 76
   RDP (Remote Desktop Protocol), 76
   SMTP (Simple Mail Transfer Protocol), 76
   SNMP (Simple Network Management Protocol), 76
   Telnet, 76
application log, 47
application white-listing, 236
application-aware devices, 122
application-level proxy functions, 99
applications
   attacks
      add-ons, 339–340
      arbitrary code execution, 341
      attachments, 339
      buffer overflow, 338
      command injection attack, 337–338
      cookies, 339
      directory traversal attack, 337
      evercookie, 339
      header manipulation, 340–341
      integer overflow, 338
      LDAP injection, 336–337

remote code execution, 341
      session hijacking, 340
      SQL injection, 335–336
      XML injection, 337
      XSRF (Cross-Site Request Forgery), 335
      XSS (cross-site scripting), 334–335
      zero-day exploits, 338
hardening
   baselining, 219
   CERT (Computer Emergency Response Team), 219
   databases, 215–218
   DHCP services, 231–232
   DNS server, 230–231
   email servers, 228–229
   FTP server, 229–230
   fuzzing, 218
   operating system patch management, 220
   OWASP (Open Web Application Security Project), 219
   secure coding, 218
   web servers, 227–228
patch management, 220
security
   application white-listing, 236
   authentication, 235
   credentials, 235
   encryption, 236
   geo-tagging, 236
   key management, 235
   transitive trust/ authentication, 236
arbitrary code execution, 341
armored viruses, 310, 313
ARO (annualized rate of occurance), 5
ARP (Address Resolution Protocol), 77, 231
ARP spoofing, 321
asymmetric algorithms (cryptography), 251
   Diffie-Hellman, 253
      DHE (Ephemeral Diffie-Hellman), 254

ECDHE (Ephemeral Elliptic Curve Diffie-Hellman), 254
      ECC (Elliptic Curve Cryptography), 253
      EIGamal, 254
      private key, 251
      public key, 251
      RSA (Rivest, Shamir, Adleman), 251
      table, 254
      Williamson, Malcolm J., 253
attachments, 339
   email, filename extensions, 307
attacks, 318–319
   applications
      add-ons, 339–340
      arbitrary code execution, 341
      attachments, 339
      buffer overflow, 338
      command injection attack, 337–338
      cookies, 339
      directory traversal attack, 337
      evercookie, 339
      header manipulation, 340–341
      integer overflow, 338
      LDAP injection, 336–337
      remote code execution, 341
      session hijacking, 340
      SQL injection, 335–336
      XML injection, 337
      XSRF (Cross-Site Request Forgery), 335
      XSS (cross-site scripting), 334–335
      zero-day exploits, 338
   Christmas Tree, 324
   client-side, 333
   DDoS (Distributed Denial-of-Service), 320
   DoS (Denial-of-Service), 319–320
   DoS (denial-of-service), 53
   insider attacks, 332
   malicious insider threats, 332
   man-in-the-middle, 324–325
   password attacks, 326–327

pharming attacks, 322–323
phishing, 323
    spear phishing, 323
privilege escalation, 328
replay, 325–326
responding to, 328
results interpretation tools,
    341–342
    banner grabbing, 344
    honeynets, 343
    honeypots, 343
    packet sniffers, 342
    port scanners, 343–344
    protocol analyzers, 342
    vulnerability scanners,
        342–343
risk calculation and
    assessment, 344–345
    architecture, 346
    attack surface, 345–346
    baseline reporting, 345
    code review, 345
    design review, 346
smurf, 326
social engineering
    dumpster diving, 357
    examples, 363–364
    hoaxes, 359–360
    impersonation, 359
    motivation for, 361–362
    shoulder surfing, 356–357
    tailgating, 357
    vishing, 360
    whaling, 360
spoofing, 321–322
transitive access and, 332
typo squatting, 333–334
URL hijacking, 333–334
vishing, 323
watering hole, 334
Xmas, 324
audit files, 112
audits, 10
    security, 62
AUP (acceptable use policies),
    24
authentication, 131–132, 235,
    261. *See also* passwords
account policy enforcement,
    139
    HMAC (Hash Message
        Authentication Code),
        261

identity proofing,
    138
issues for consideration,
    137–139
MAC (message authentication
    code), 260
mobile devices, 132
multifactor, 133–134
    security and, 138
mutual, 133
problems, 136–137
protocols, 139
remote, 143
services
    Kerberos, 147–148
    LDAP (Lightweight
        Directory Access
        Protocol), 147
    SSO (single sign-on)
        initiatives, 149–150
SFA (single-factor
    authentication), 132–133
transitive access, 136–137
two-factor, 133

B

Back Orifice, 308
backdoors, 308
backup generator, 33
backup plans
    applications, 435
    database systems, 434
    development
        backup server method,
            440
        full archival method, 439
        Grandfather, Father, Son
            method, 434
    user files, 435
backups, 37, 233–234
    active backup model, 443
    active/active model, 444
    alternate sites
        cold sites, 444
        hot sites, 443
        warm sites, 444
    differential, 437
    HSM (hierarchical storage
        management), 437

incremental, 436
JFS (journaled file system),
    432
offsite storage, 433
onsite storage, 432
reciprocal agreement,
    444
tape, 433
working copy backups, 432
banner grabbing, 344
barricades, physical security and,
    375
baselining, 219, 226–227
bastion host, 88
BCP (business continuity
    planning), 431
    disaster-recovery plan, 445
bcrypt, 256
behavior-based-detection IDS,
    109
benchmarking,
    21
best practices
    access control
        802.IX and, 158
        access review, 154
        ACLs (access control lists),
            156–157
        CAC (Common Access
            Card), 155–156
        continuous monitoring,
            154
        EALs (Evaluation
            Assurance Levels),
            159–160
        firewall rules, 157
        flood guards, 158
        least privileges, 153
        log analysis, 159
        loop protection, 158
        network bridging, 158–
            159
        PIV (Personal Identity
            Verification), 156
        port security, 157–158
        privilege escalation, 153
        secure router
            configuration,
            160–161
        separation of duties,
            153–154
        smart cards,
            155

time of day restrictions, 154
TOS (trusted operating system), 159–160
business continuity plans, 31
risk management
   BIA, 29–30
   critical systems and components, 30–32
   disaster recovery, 36–38
   fault tolerance, 32–33
   RAID (redundance array of independent disks), 33–36
   redundancy, 32
security, 236–237
   DLP (data loss prevention), 236–237
   encryption devices, 237
BGP (Border Gateway Protocol), 102
BIA (busines impact analysis), 4, 431
best practices, 29–30
critical business function priorities, 29
critical function identification, 29
critical systems loss timeframe, 29
impact on organization, 30
Big Data, 218
biometrics, physical security and, 375
birthday password attack, 327
BitLocker, 14, 290
black box testing, 459
block ciphers, 250
Blowfish, 251
bluesnarfing, 187
border routers, 100
botnets, 309
bottom-up policies, 19
bridge trust models, 287
bridges, networking bridging, 158–159
brute-force attacks, 257, 327
buffer overflow, 338
business continuity, 31
   BCP (business continuity planning), 431
   BIA (business impact analysis), 431

CBFs (critical business functions), 431
risk assessment, 431
business functions, 29
business policies
   AUP (acceptable use policies), 24
   job rotation, 26
   least privilege, 26
   mandatory vacations, 25
   privacy policies, 24
   security policies, 25
   separation of duties, 23–24
   succession planning, 26
   use policies, 24
BYOD (Bring Your Own Device) issues, 419–420

C

CAC (Common Access Card), 155–156
Caesar cipher, 246
caller, 145
captive portals, 180
CAs (certificate authorities), 262, 279–280
   bridge trust models, 287
   hierarchical trust models, 286
   hybrid trust models, 288–289
   mesh trust models, 287–288
CAST (Carlisle Adams and Stafford Tavares), 250
CBFs (critical business functions), 431
CC (Common Criteria), 159
CCMP (Counter Mode with Cipher Block Chaining Message Authentication Code Protocol), 172–173
CCTV (closed-circuit television), 372, 401
CERT (Computer Emergency Response Team), 219
certificates
   certificate policies, 284
   CPS (Certificate Practice Statement), 284
   cross certification, 284
   dual sided, 284

revocation, 285
single sided, 284
viewing, exercise, 282–283
X.509, 281–282
CESA (Cyberspace Electronic Security Act), 417
CFAA (Computer Fraud and Abuse Act), 416
change management, 10
CHAP (Challenge Handshake Authentication Protocol), 139, 143
Chosen Plaintext, 257
Christmas Tree attack, 324
ciphers/ciphering, 245–246
   block ciphers, 250
   Caesar cipher, 246
   multi-alphabet, 246
   Rail Fence Cipher, 247
   stream ciphers, 250
   substitution, 246
   transposition, 246–247
   Vigenère cipher, 246
circuit-level firewalls, 99
client-side attacks, 333
cloud computing, 17–18
   cloud bursting, 201
   community cloud, 200–201
   hybrid cloud, 201
   IaaS (Infrastructure as a Service), 199
   PaaS (Platform as a Service), 198
   private cloud, 200
   public cloud, 200
   SaaS (Software as a Service), 196–197
   security, 205–206
   storage, 206
Cloud Security Alliance, 18
clustering, 235
   failover and, 31
CMP (Certificate Management Protocol), 270
collusion, 23
command injection attack, 337–338
community cloud, 200–201
companion viruses, 310, 313–314
compensating control type, 384
Computer Security Act, 416
configuration
   router, 160–161

web filtering exercise, 120–121
connection-oriented protocol, 85–86
content inspection, 119–120
contingency plans, 30
continuous monitoring, 61, 154
control types, 27, 384–385
  administrative, 384
  compensating, 384
  detective, 384
  deterrents, 384
  preventive, 384
  technical, 384
cookies, 339
CPS (Certificate Practice Statement), 284
credentials, 235
critical business functions, 29
critical function identification, 29
critical systems and components, 30–32
critical systems loss timeframe, 29
CRL (certificate revocation list), 262, 285
cross certification, 284
cryptanalysis, 245
  brute-force attacks, 257
  Chosen Plaintext, 257
  frequency analysis, 257
  human error, exploiting, 257
  Related Key Attack, 257
  Wi-Fi encryption
    WEP (Wired Encryption Privacy), 258
    WPA (Wi-Fi Protected Access), 258
    WPA2 (Wi-Fi Protected Access 2), 258
cryptographic systems
  authentication, 261–262
  confidentiality, 259
  digital signatures, 261
  integrity, 259–260
  key features, 262
  MAC (message authentication code), 260
  nonrepudiation, 262
  strength, 259
  work factor, 259

cryptography, 245
  ABA (American Bankers Association), 265
  asymmetric algorithms, 251
    Diffie-Hellman, 253
    ECC (Elliptic Curve Cryptography), 253
    ElGamal, 254
    private key, 251
    public key, 251
    RSA (Rivest, Shamir, Adleman), 252
    table, 254
    Williamson, Malcolm J., 253
  bcrypt, 256
  ciphering, 245–246
  ciphers, 245–246
    block ciphers, 250
    Caesar cipher, 246
    multi-alphabet, 246
    Rail Fence Cipher, 247
    stream ciphers, 250
    substitution, 246
    transposition, 246–247
    Vigenère cipher, 246
  Enigma machine, 248
  hashing algorithms
    GOST, 256
    LANMAN, 256
    MD (Message Digest Algorithm), 255
    NTLM (NT LAN Manager), 256
    RIPEMD (RACE Integrity Primitives Evaluation Message Digest), 255
    SHA (Secure Hash Algorithm), 255
  historical, 245–249
  IEEE (Institute of Electrical and Electronics Engineer), 266
  IETF (Internet Engineering Task Force), 265
  industry associations, 264–266
  ISOC (Internet Society), 265
  ITU (International Telecommunications Union), 266
  Kerckhoff's principle, 254
  key stretching, 256–257

PBKDF2 (Password-Based Key Derivation Function 2), 256
PKCS (Public-Key Cryptography Standards), 266–267
PKIX (Public-Key Infrastructure X), 266–268
PKIX/PKCS standards
  CMP (Certificate Management Protocol), 270
  FIPS (Federal Information Processing Standard), 278
  HTTPS (Hypertext Transport Protocol over SSL), 274
  IPSec (IP Security), 274–275
  PGP (Pretty Good Privacy), 272–273
  SET (Secure Electronic Transaction), 270–271
  S-HTTP (Secure Hypertext Transport Protocol), 274
  S/MIME (Secure Multipurpose Internet Mail Extensions), 270–271
  SSH (Secure Shell), 271
  SSL (Secure Sockets Layer), 268–269
  TLS (Transport Layer Security), 269
  tunneling protocols, 277–278
  X.509 standard, 267–268
  XKMS (XML Key Management), 270
quantum cryptography, 257
rainbow tables, 256
RFC (Request for Comments), 265
ROT13 algorithm, 247–248
Salt, 256
selecting, 254
standards, government agencies, 263–264
steganography, 248

symmetric algorithms, 249–251
3DES (Triple-DES), 250
AES (Advanced Encryption Standard), 250
AES256, 250
block ciphers, 250
Blowfish, 251
CAST (Carlisle Adams and Stafford Tavares), 250
DES (Data Encryption Standard), 250
forward secrecy, 251
IDEA (International Data Encryption Algorithm), 251
key distribution, 250
key exchange, 251
one-time pads, 251
perfect forward secrecy, 251
private key, 249
RC4, 251
Ron's Cipher, 251
secret key, 249
stream ciphers, 250
symmetric key, 249
Triple-DES (3DES), 250
Twofish, 251
W3C (World Wide Web Consortium), 266
cryptology, 245
CSR (certificate-signing request), 279–280
CSU/DSU (Channel Service Unit/ Data Service Unit), 100
Cyberspace Security Enhancement Act, 417

D

DAC (Discretionary Access Control), 150, 151–152
data at rest, 235
data encryption, 290
Data Encryption Toolkit for Mobile PCs, 14

data in transit, 235
data integration, cloud computing, 18
data policies
    data destruction
        flash drives, 386–388
        optical disks, 388–389
    disposing, 385
    retention, 386
    storage, 386
    wiping, 385
data segregation, cloud computing, 18
data source, IDS (intrusion detection system), 107
databases
    application hardening, 215–218
    Big Data, 218
    encryption, 290
    middle-tier server, 217
    NoSQL, 217
    one-tier model, 216–217
    relational, 215–216
    SAN (storage area network), 218
    single-tier environment, 216–217
    SQL (Structured Query Language), 215–216
    three-tier model, 217
    two-tier model, 217
DDoS (Distributed Denial-of-Service) attacks, 320
decryption, ROT13 algorithm, 247–248
defense in depth, 134, 367
DES (Data Encryption Standard), 250
detection controls, 64–65
detective control type, 384
deterrent control type, 384
devices, 73
DHCP (Dynamic Host Configuration Protocol), service hardening, 231–232
DHE (Ephemeral Diffie-Hellman), 254
dial-in privileges, 145
dictionary password attack, 327
differential backup, 233–234, 437

Diffie-Hellman, 253
    DHE (Ephemeral Diffie-Hellman), 254
    ECDHE (Ephemeral Elliptic Curve Diffie-Hellman), 254
digital signatures, 261
directional antennas, 178
directory sharing, 53
directory traversal attack, 337–338
disaster recovery, 36–38
disaster recovery plan, 433–434
    alternate sites, 443–445
    backout versus backup, 443
    backup plan development
        backup server method, 440
        full archival method, 439
        Grandfather, Father, Son method, 438
    backup plan issues
        applications, 435
        database systems, 434
        user files, 435
    backup types
        differential backup, 437
        full backup, 436
        HSM (hierarchical storage management), 437
        incremental backup, 436
    system recovery, 441–442
disk duplexing, 35
disposal policy, 385
DLP (data loss prevention), 10, 236–237
DMZ (demilitarized zone), 87–88
DNS (Domain Name System), 76
DNS DoS (Domain Name Service Denial-of-Service), 230
DNS poisoning, 231
DNS server hardening, 230–231
DNS spoofing, 321
DNSSEC (Domain Name System Security Extensions), 231
documents
    reference documents for standards, 21
    standards document, 21
DoD (Department of Defense), CAC (Common Access Card), 155–156

domain name kiting, 322
DoS (Denial-of-Service), 53, 309, 319–320
Drills, 401
dual-homed firewalls, 99
dumpster diving, 357

E

EALs (Evaluation Assurance Levels), 159–160
EAP (Extensible Authentication Protocol), 181–182
EAPOL (EAP over LAN), 60
ECC (Elliptic Curve Cryptography), 254
ECDHE (Ephemeral Elliptic Curve Diffie-Hellman), 254
EFS, 14
ElGamal, 254
electronic wallet, 270
electronic watermarking, 248
email, attachment filename extensions, 307
email servers, hardening, 228–229
EMI shielding, 380–382
encapsulation, 75, 79–80
encryption, 236
    BitLocker, 290
    data encryption, 290
    databases, 290
    exercise, 249
    government agencies, 263–264
    hardware-based devices, 237, 290
    ROT13 algorithm, 247–248
    symmetric algorithms, 249–251
    TrueCrypt, 290
Enigma machine, 248
enticement, honeypot and, 65
entrapment, honeypot and, 65
environmental controls, 377
    EMI shielding, 380–382
    environmental monitoring, 383
    fire extinguishers, 378–379

fire suppression, 378
    fixed systems, 379–380
    hot and cold aisles, 382
    humidity, 383
    HVAC system, 378
    temperature, 383
environmental monitoring, 383
error types, 28
Escape Plans, 401
escape routes, 402
ESP (Encapsulating Security Payload), 274
event logs, viewing, 47–51
events, IDS (intrusion detection system), 107
evercookie, 339
exception statement for policies, 20
exercises
    Automated System Recovery in Windows Server 2012, 442
    certificates, viewing, 282–283
    encryption in Linux, 249
    IPSec performance errors, 275–277
    Microsoft Baseline Security Analyzer, 329–331
    network preference order, 179–180
    physical security, 377
    pop-up blocker configuration, 222–223
    risk-assessment computations, 6
    social engineering test, 364–365
    SSL settings in Windows Server 2012, 269
    TCP ports, 83–85
    TPM chip presence, 237
    trust relationship validation, 137, 333
    UDP ports, 83–85
    viewing running processes
        Linux-based machine, 302–304
        Windows-based machine, 302–304

web filtering configuration, 120–121
Windows Firewall configuration, 223–226
wireless connection not broadcasting, connecting, 183–185

F

fail over, 31–32
false negatives, 28
false positives, 28
FAT (File Allocation Table), 58
fault tolerance, 32–33
    backups, 233–234
    clustering, 235
    load balancing, 235
    RAID (redundant array of independent disks), 234–235
FCoE (Fibre Channel over Ethernet), 87
federated identity, 136
federations, 135–136
fencing, 401
FERPA (Family Educational Rights and Privacy Act), 416
Fibre Channel, 87
file servers, 53
filenames, email attachment extensions, 307
filesystems, hardening and, 58–59
filters
    InPrivate Filtering, 340
    Phishing filter, 119
    spam filters, 118–119
    URL filters, 119
    web filtering configuration exercise, 120–121
Financial Modernization Act of 1999, 415
FIPS (Federal Information Processing Standard), 278
fire extinguishers, 378–379
fire suppression, 378
firewall rules, 157

firewalls, 96–97
  dual-homed, 99
  host-based, 222
  multihomed, 99
  packet filter, 97–98
  proxy, 98–99
    application-level, 99
    circuit-level, 99
  stateful packet inspection, 99–100
  stateless, 100
  WAF (web application firewalls), 122
  Windows, configuration exercise, 223–226
fixed systems, environmental controls and, 379–380
flash drive destruction, 386–388
flood guards, 158
FOBs, 368
folder permissions, 220–221
footprinting, 231
forward secrecy, 251
frequency analysis, cryptanalysis, 257
FTP (File Transfer Protocol), 75
  server hardening, 229–230
FTPS (FTP over SSL), 75
Full Control permission level, 220
function identification, 29
fuzzing, 218

G

gap in the WAP, 172
geo-tagging, 236
GOST, 256
government information classification, 412
Gramm-Leach-Bliley Act, 415
gray box testing, 459
guards, physical security and, 374
guest accounts, 58
guidelines, 19
  benefits, 23
  guideline statement, 23

operational considerations, 23
roles and responsibilities, 22–23
scope and purpose, 22

H

Hadnagy, Chrisopher, 356
hardening
  applications, 54–55
    baselining, 219
    CERT (Computer Emergency Response Team), 219
    databases, 215–218
    DHCP services, 231–232
    DNS server, 230–231
    email servers, 228–229
    FTP server, 229–230
    fuzzing, 218
    operating system patch management, 220
    OWASP (Open Web Application Security Project), 219
    secure coding, 218
    web servers, 227–228
  filesystems, 58–59
  management interfaces, 54–55
  patches, 56–57
  Performance Monitor, 55
  services and, 52–54
    directory sharing, 53
    PC-based systems, 53
  software and, 55–56
  System Monitor, 55
  user account control, 57–58
hardware, 73
hardware-based encryption devices, 237, 290
hashing algorithms (cryptography)
  GOST, 256
  LANMAN, 256
  MD (Message Digest Algorithm), 255
  NTLM (NT LAN Manager), 256

RIPEMD (RACE Integrity Primitives Evaluation Message Digest), 255
SHA (Secure Hash Algorithm), 255–256
header manipulation, 340–341
heuristic IDS, 109
HIDS (host-based IDS), 116–117
hierarchical trust models, 286
HIPAA (Health Insurance Portability and Accountability Act), 415
HMAC (Hash Message Authentication Code), 139, 260
hoaxes, 359–360
honeynets, 343
honeypot, 64–65, 343
  sending to, 114–115
host
  availability/elasticity, 204
  bastion host, 88
  security
    ACLs (access control lists), 221
    DHCP service hardening, 231–232
    DNS server hardening, 230–231
    email server hardening, 228–229
    footprinting, 231
    FTP server hardening, 229–230
    malware, 221
    permissions, 220
    record integrity compromise, 231
    web server hardening, 227–228
  TCP/IP, 74
host-based firewalls, 222
host-based IDS, 116–117, 222
Host-to-Host layer
  TCP (Transmission Control Protocol), 77
  UDP (User Datagram Protocol), 77
hot and cold aisles, environmental controls and, 382
hotfixes, 219

HOTP (HMAC-Based One-Time Password), 139
HSM (Hardware Security Module), 238, 290
HSM (hierarchical storage management), 234, 437
HTML (Hypertext Markup Language), 75
HTTP (Hyertext Transfer Protocol), TCP/IP and, 75
HTTPS (HTTP Secure), 75
HTTPS (Hypertext Transport Protocol over SSL), 274
humidity, 383
HVAC system, 378
hybrid cloud, 201
hybrid password attack, 327
hybrid trust models, 288–289
hypervisor, 19

I

IaaS (Infrastructure as a Service) model, 17–18, 199
IANA (Internet Assigned Numbers Authority), well-known ports, 81–83
ICMP (Internet Control Message Board), 78
IDEA (International Data Encryption Algorithm), 251
identification, 131–132
    logon, 132
identities, federated identity, 136
identity proofing, 138
IDS (Intrusion Detection System), 64–65, 105–106
    active response
        deception, 114
        network configuration changes, 114
        terminating processes, 113
        terminating sessions, 113
    activities, 107
    administrator, 107
    alerts, 107
    analyzers, 107
    anomaly-detection, 109
    audit files and, 112

behavior-based, 109
data source, 107
events, 107
heuristic, 109
host-based (HIDS), 116–117, 222
incidents, 107
IPS (intrusion protection system) comparison, 110–111
managers, 108
NIDS (network-based IDS), 111–112
NIPSs (network intrusion prevention systems), 117
notifications, 108
operators, 108
passive response
    logging, 113
    notification, 113
    shunning, 113
sensors, 108
signature-based, 109
IEEE (Institute of Electrical and Electronics Engineer), 266
IEEE 802.11x protocols, wireless systems, 169–170
IETF (Internet Engineering Task Force), 75, 231, 265
IMAP (Inernet Message Access Protocol), 76
impersonation, 356, 359
implicit deny (ACLs), 156
incident management, 10
incident response policies, 445–454
incidents, IDS (intrusion detection system), 107
incremental backup, 234, 436
information access controls
    implicit denies, 413
    job rotation, 413
    least privilege, 413
    security concepts
        availability, 414
        confidentiality, 414
        integrity, 414
information classification
    government/military, 412
    private information, 411
        internal, 411
        restricted, 411
public information, 410

full distribution, 411
limited distribution, 410–411
infrastructure, 95
all-in-one security appliances, 119
application-aware devices, 122
content inspection, 119–120
malware inspection, 121–122
URL filters, 119
WAF (web application firewall), 122
firewalls, 96–97
    dual-homed, 99
    multihomed, 99
    packet filter firewalls, 97–98
    proxy firewalls, 98–99
IDS (Intrusion Detection System), 105–106
    active response, 113
    activities, 107
    administrator, 107
    alerts, 107
    analyzers, 107
    anomaly-detection, 109
    behavior-based, 109
    data source, 107
    events, 107
    heuristic, 109
    host-based (HIDS), 116–117
    incidents, 107
    managers, 108
    NIDS (network-based IDS), 111–112
    NIPSs (network intrusion prevention systems), 117
    notifications, 108
    operators, 108
    passive response, 113
    sensors, 108
    signature-based, 109
load balancers, 103
protocol analyzers, 118
proxies, 103
routers, 100–102
spam filters, 118–119
switches, 102

VPNs (virtual private
networks), 103–105
VPN concentrators, 105
web security gateway, 103
InPrivate Filtering, 340
insider attacks, 332
integer overflow, 338
internal information, 411
international regulations, 418
Internet layer
ARP (Address Resolution
Protocol), 78
ICMP (Internet Control
Message Board), 78
IP (Internet Protocol), 77
interoperability agreement
BPO (Blanket Purchase
Order), 398
ISA (Interconnection Security
Agreement), 398
MOU (Memorandum of
Understanding), 398
SLA (Service-Level
Agreement), 398
intrusion detection tools, 341
results interpretation, 341–
342
banner grabbing, 344
honeynets, 343
honeypots, 343
packet sniffers, 342
port scanners, 343–344
protocol analyzers, 342
vulnerability scanners,
342–343
risk calculation and
assessment, 344–345
architecture, 346
attack surface, 345–346
baseline reporting, 345
code review, 345
design review, 346
IP (Internet Protocol), 77
rogue servers, 232
security, 232
IP addresses, NAT and,
98
IP spoofing, 321
IPS (Intrusion Prevention
System), 64–65
IDS comparison, 110–111
IPSec (Internet Protocol
Security), 91, 145

cryptography, 274–275
IPv4, 78–79
IPv6, 78–79
iSCSI (Internet Small Computer
Systems Interface), 87
ISN (initial sequence number), 85
ISOC (Internet Society),
265
ITU (International
Telecommunications
Union), 266
IV (initialization vector),
171

J-K

job rotation policies, 26

KDC (key distribution center),
147–148
Kerberos, 147–148
Kerckhoff's principle,
254
key escrow, 262
key exchange, 251
key management, application
security, 235
key recovery agent, 262
key registration,
262
key stretching, 256–257
Klez32 virus, 318

L

L2F (Layer 2 Forwarding), 91,
277
L2TP (Layer 2 Tunneling
Protocol), 91, 277
LANMAN, 256
LANs (local area networks),
VLANs (virtual local area
networks), 89–91
layered security, 134
LCP (Link Control Protocol),
143
LDAP (Lightweight Directory
Access Protocol), 147
LDAP injection, 336–337

LEAP (Lightweight Extensible
Authentication Protocol),
182
least privilege policy, 26
lighting, 401
physical security and,
374
likelihood, definition, 7–8
Linux
log files, 117
resources, 106
Snort, installation, 118
load balancing, 31, 235
load balancers, 103
locks, 401
log analysis, 159
log files, Linux, 117
logic bombs, 307–308
logon, identification, 132
loop protection, 158
LRA (local registration
authority), 281
lsb (least significant bit) method,
steganography, 248

M

MAC
filtering, 60
limiting, 60
MAC (Mandatory Access
Control), 78, 150, 151
MAC (Message Authentication
Code), 78
MAC (message authentication
code), 260
MAC (Media Access Control),
addresses, 78
MAC filtering, wireless devices
and, 178–179
macro viruses, 310, 314
maintenance and administrative
requirements, 22
malicious insider attacks, 332
Malicious Software Removal
Tool, 121–122
malware, 222, 300
adware, 301
Back Orifice and, 308
backdoors, 308
botnets, 309

DoS (Denial-of-Service)
attacks, 309
inspection, 121–122
logic bombs, 307–308
NetBus and, 308
ransomware, 309
rootkits, 301
spambots, 309
spyware, 300
Trojan horses, 305–306
managers, IDS (intrusion
detection system), 108
mandatory vacations, 25
man-in-the-middle attacks,
324–325
mantraps, 371
MD (Message Digest Algorithm),
255
MD-IDS (misuse-detection IDS),
109–110
media, 73
mesh trust models, 287–288
Microsoft Security Essentials,
121
Microsoft Services Console,
53
microwaves, 175
military information
classification, 412
Mitnick, Kevin, 356
mobile devices, 14
authentication, 132
BYOD (Bring Your Own
Device) issues, 419–420
security
application control, 419
asset tracking, 419
device access control,
419
encryption, 418
GPS tracking, 419
passwords, 418
remote wipe/sanitation,
418
screen lock, 418
storage segmentation,
419
voice encryption, 419
Modify permission level, 221
monitoring, continuous, 61, 154
motion detection, physical
security and, 376
MSAT (Microsoft Security
Assessment Tool), 14

MTBF (mean time between
failures), 8
MTTF (mean time to failure), 8
MTTR (mean time to restore),
8–9
multi-alphabet ciphers,
246
multifactor authentication,
133–134
security and, 138
multihomed firewalls, 99
multipartite viruses, 310, 314
multiple barrier system, 367
mutations of viruses, 315
mutual authentication, 133
MyDLP, 10

N

NAC (network access control),
95, 134–135
NAT (Network Address
Translation), 93–94
IP addresses, 98
NCP (Network Control
Protocol), 143
NetBus, 308
Network Access layer, 78
network bridging, 158–159
network footprinting, 231
network locks, 178
Network Monitor, 47
network monitoring
event logs, 47
logs
application log, 47
security log, 47
Network Monitor, 47
promiscuous mode,
46
SMS, 47
sniffers, 46
networks
order of preference exercise,
179–180
securing, 60
NFC (near field communication),
182
NIDS (network-based IDS),
111–112
NIPSs (network intrusion
prevention systems),
117

NIST (National Institute of
Standards and Technology),
264
likelihood, 7–8
NIST Guide for Conducting Risk
Assessments, 5
nonrepudiation, 262
nontransitive trusts, 137
NoSQL, 217
notifications, IDS (intrusion
detection system),
108
NSA (National Security Agency),
263
NSA (National Security
Administration), Snowden,
Edward, 154
NSA/CSS (National Security
Agency/Central Security
Service), 264
NTFS (New Technology
Filesystem), 59
NTLM (NT LAN Manager),
256

O

OCSP (Online Certificate Status
Protocol), 262, 285
omnidirectional antennas, 178
one-time pads, 251
operating systems, patch
management, 220
operational considerations, 23
operational security, 134–135
operators, IDS (intrusion
detection system), 108
Ophcrack, 140
optical disk destruction, 388–
389
OSI model, 74
OSPF (Open Shortests Path
First), 102
OWASP (Open Web Application
Security Project), 219

P

PaaS (Platform as a Service), 17,
198
packet filter firewalls, 97–98

packet sniffers, 342
  protocol analyzing, 118
  WAP (Wireless Application Protocol) and, 172
packet-capture devices, 91
PAP (Password Authentication Protocol), 139
passwords
  account policy enforcement, 139
  attacks, 326–328
  CHAP (Challenge Handshake Authentication Protocol), 139
  complexity, 140
  disablement, 141–142
  expiration, 140–141
  history, 140
  HOTP (HMAC-Based One-Time Password), 139
  issues for consideration, 138
  length, 140
  lockout, 141–142
  PAP (Password Authentication Protocol), 139
  recovery, 141
  SFA (single-factor authentication), 132
  SPAP (Shiva Password Authentication Protocol), 139
  TOTP (Time-Based One-Time Password), 139
patches, 56–57, 220
  compatibility, 203
  managing applications, 220
  operating systems, 220
Patriot Act, 417
PBKDF2 (Password-Based Key Derivation Function 2), 256
PEAP (Protected Extensible Authentication Protocol), 182–183
penetration testing, 458
  black box, 459
  gray box, 459
  vulnerability scanning, 459–460
  white box, 459
perfect forward secrecy, 251

performance baseline, 227
performance criteria, 21
Performance Monitor, 55
permission reviews, 10
permissions, 220–221
PGP (Pretty Good Privacy), 272–273
phage viruses, 310, 314
pharming attacks, 322–323
phishing attacks, 323
Phishing Filter, 119
physical barriers, 366–367
physical security, 366–367
  access lists, 373–374
  alarms, 376
  barricades, 375
  biometrics, 375
  exercise, 377
  fencing, 372–373
  guards, 374
  hardware locks, 369–370
  lighting, 374
  mantraps, 371
  motion detection, 376
  perimeter security, 372–373
  protected distribution, 376
  signs, 374
  video surveillance, 371–372
physical tokens, 368
PIV (Personal Identity Verification), 156
PKCS (Public-Key Cryptography Standards), 266–267
PKI (Public-Key Infrastructure), 278–279
  CAs (certificate authorities), 279–280
  certificates
    certificate policies, 284
    CPS (Certificate Practice Statement), 284
    revocation, 284
    X.509, 281–282
  CSR (certificate-signing request), 279–280
  RA (registration authority), 280–281
  trust models
    bridge trust models, 287
    hierarchical, 286

    hybrid trust models, 288–289
    mesh trust models, 287–288
PKIX (Public-Key Infrastructure X), 266–268
PKIX/PKCS standards
  CMP (Certificate Management Protocol), 270
  FIPS (Federal Information Processing Standard), 278
  HTTPS (Hypertext Transport Protocol over SSL), 274
  IPSec (IP Security), 274–275
  PGP (Pretty Good Privacy), 272–273
  SET (Secure Electronic Transaction), 270–271
  S-HTTP (Secure Hypertext Transport Protocol), 274
  S/MIME (Secure Multipurpose Internet Mail Extensions), 270
  SSH (Secure Shell), 271
  SSL (Secure Sockets Layer), 268–269
  TLS (Transport Layer Security), 269
  tunneling protocols, 277–278
  X.509 standard, 267–268
  XKMS (XML Key Management), 270
pod slurping, 24
policies, 19
  account policies, enforcement, 139
  accountability statement, 20
  bottom-up, 19
  business
    AUP (acceptable use policies), 24
    job rotation, 26
    least privilege, 26
    mandatory vacations, 25
    privacy policies, 24
    security policies, 25
    separation of duties, 23–24
    succession planning, 26
    use policies, 24
  certificate policies, 284

exception statement, 20
implementation, 20–21
policy overview statement, 20
policy statement, 20
scope statement, 20
top-down, 19
polymorphic viruses, 310,
314–315
POP (Post Office Protocol), 76
pop-up blockers, 222
configuration exercise,
222–223
port mirroring, 112
port scanners, 343–344
port spanning, 112
portals, captive portals, 180
ports
security, 157–158
well-known, 81–83
POTS (plain-old telephone
service), 93
PPP (Point-to-Point Protocol),
143
PPTP (Point-to-Point Tunneling
Protocol), 90, 277
prevention controls, 64–65
preventive control type, 384
print servers, 53
privacy policies, 24
private cloud, 200
private information, 411
internal, 411
restricted, 411
private key, 249, 252
privilege escalation, 328
promiscuous mode, 46
protected distribution, physical
security and, 376
protocol analyzers, 118, 342
protocols, 80
antiquated, 77
authentication,
139
CHAP (Challenge Handshake
Authentication
Protocol), 143
EAP (Extensible
Authentication
Protocol), 181–182
Fibre Channel, 87
iSCSI (Internet Small
Computer Systems
Interface), 87

LCP (Link Control Protocol),
143
LEAP (Lightweight Extensible
Authentication
Protocol), 182
NCP (Network Control
Protocol), 143
PEAP (Protected Extensible
Authentication
Protocol), 182–183
PPP (Point-to-Point Protocol),
143
SLIP (Serial Line Internet
Protocol), 142
STP (Spanning Tree Protocol),
158
tunneling, 90, 92–93,
144–145
IPSec (Internet Protocol
Security), 91, 145
L2F (Layer 2 Forwarding),
91, 144
L2TP (Layer 2 Tunneling
Protocol), 91, 144
PPTP (Point-to-Point
Tunneling Protocol),
90, 144
SSH (Secure Shell), 91,
144
WAP (Wireless Application
Protocol), 172
WDP (Wireless Datagram
Protocol), 175
WSP (Wireless Session
Protocol), 175
WTLS (Wireless Transport
Layer Security), 175
WTP (Wireless Transaction
Protocol), 175
proxies, 103
proximity readers/cards,
367
proxy firewalls, 98–99
application-level,
99
circuit-level, 99
dual-homed firewalls,
99
proxy server, 103
public cloud, 200
public information, 410–411
public key, 252

Q

QKE (quantum key exchange),
257
qualitative risk assessment, 7
quantitative risk assessment, 7
quantum cryptography, 257
QuickStego, 248

R

RA (registration authority),
280–281
LRA (local registration
authority), 281
RADIUS (Remote Authentication
Dial-In User Service),
145–146
RAID (redundant array of
independent disks), 234–
235
disk duplexing, 35
disk mirroring, 33, 234
disk striping, 33, 234
with parity, 34, 234–235
with parity disk, 34
disks needed, 35
Rail Fence Cipher, 247
rainbow table password attack,
327–328
rainbow tables, 256
ransomware, 309
RAS (Remote Access Services),
92–93
RBAC (Role-Based Access
Control), 150, 152
RBAC (Rule-Based Access
Control), 150, 152
RC4, 251
RDP (Remote Desktop Protocol),
76
Read and Execute permission
level, 221
Read permission level, 221
record integrity compromise, 231
recovering passwords, 141
redundancy, risk management
and, 32
regulatory compliance,
414

CESA (Cyberspace Electronic Security Act), 417
CFAA (Computer Fraud and Abuse Act), 416
cloud computing, 18
Computer Security Act, 416
Cyberspace Security Enhancement Act, 417
FERPA (Family Educational Rights and Privacy Act), 416
Financial Modernization Act of 1999, 415
Gramm-Leach-Bliley Act, 415
HIPAA (Health Insurance Portability and Accountability Act), 415
international efforts, 418
Patriot Act, 417
Section 225 of the Homeland Security Act of 2002, 417
United and Strengthening America by Providing Appropriate Tools Required to Intercept and Obstruct Terrorism, 417
Related Key Attack, 257
relational databases, 215–216
remediation policy, 62
remote access, 92–93, 142–143
  protocols
    CHAP (Challenge Handshake Authentication Protocol), 143
    NCP (Network Control Protocol), 143
    PPP (Point-to-Point Protocol), 143
    tunneling protocols, 144–145
  RADIUS (Remote Authentication Dial-In User Service), 145–146
  SAML (Security Assertion Markup Language), 147
  TACACS (Terminal Access Controller Access-Control System), 146
  VLAN (virtual local area network), 146

remote authentication, 143
remote code execution, 341
remote networks, users, 91
Remote Registry, 53
replay attacks, 172, 325–326
reporting
  alarms, 63
  alerts, 63
  trends, 63–64
Reset Account Lockout Counter After, 141
resources, Linux, 106
restricted information, 411
retention policy, 386
retroviruses, 310, 315
revocation of certificates, 284
RF (radio frequency) spectrum, 175
RFC (Request For Comments), 265
RIP (Routing Information Protocol), 102
RIPEMD (RACE Integrity Primitives Evaluation Message Digest), 255
risk acceptance, 10, 11
risk analysis, 3
risk appetite, 11
risk assessment, 3
  assets, 6
  BIA and, 4
  business continuity ar
  calculations
    ALE (annual loss expectancy), 5
    ARO (annualized rate of occurance), 5
    SLE (single loss expectancy), 5
  computing, 4–5
  conducting, 4
  control types, 27
  error types, 28
  false negatives, 28
  false positives, 28
  NIST Guide, 5
  process components, 3–4
  qualitative, 7
  quantitative, 7
  tabletop exercise, 38
  threats, 6
risk avoidance, 9, 12
risk calculation, 3
  and assessment, 344–345
risk deterrence, 10, 12

risk management
  best practices
    BIA, 29–30
    critical systems and components, 30–32
    disaster recovery, 36–38
    fault tolerance, 32–33
    HA (high availability), 31
    RAID (redundant array of independent disks), 33–36
    redundancy, 32
  strategies, 11–13
risk mitigation, 9–10, 13
risk reduction, 13
risk sharing, 14
risk tolerance, 11
risk transference, 9, 14
roles and responsibilities
  guidelines, 22–23
  standards, 21
R⟩⟩'s Cipher, 251
⟩⟩⟩–248
⟩⟩0
⟩⟩on, 160–
⟩⟩dure Call),
⟩⟩t objective), 9
⟩⟩d Remote ⟩⟩es), 93
RSA (Rivest, Shamir, Adleman), 252
RTO (recovery time objective), 9
running processes, viewing exercise, 302–304

S

SaaS (Software as a Service), 17, 196–197
safety topics
  CCTV, 401
  Drills, 401
  Escape Plans, 401
  escape routes, 402
  fencing, 401
  lighting, 401
  locks, 401
  testing controls, 402
Salt, 256

SAML (Security Assertion
    Markup Language), 147
SAN (storage area network), 218
sandboxing, 204
scope and purpose (guidelines),
    22
scope statement for policies, 20
SCP (Secure Copy), 76
SCT (security control testing),
    204
secret key, 249
Section 225 of the Homeland
    Security Act of 2002, 417
secure coding, 218
Secure FTP, 76
secure router configuration,
    160–161
securing network, 60
security
    ACLs (access control lists),
        221
    all-in-one security appliances,
        119
        URL filters, 119
    alternative methods, 420–422
    applications
        application white-listing,
            236
        authentication, 235
        credentials, 235
        encryption, 236
        geo-tagging, 236
        key management, 235
        transitive trust/
            authentication, 236
    audits, 62
    baselining, 226–227
    best practices, 236–237
        DLP (data loss
            prevention), 236–237
        encryption devices, 237
    CC (Common Criteria), 159
    cloud and, 205–206
        storage, 206
    detection controls, 64–65
    DHCP service hardening,
        231–232
    DNS server hardening,
        230–231
    email server hardening,
        228–229
    footprinting, 231
    FTP server hardening,
        229–230
    gap in the WAP, 172

IDS (intrusion detection
    system), 105–106
layered, 134
malware, 221
mobile devices
    application control, 419
    asset tracking, 419
    device access control, 419
    encryption, 418
    GPS tracking, 419
    passwords, 418
    remote wipe/sanitation,
        418
    screen lock, 418
    storage segmentation, 419
    voice encryption, 419
multifactor authentication
    and, 138
operational security, 134–135
permissions, 220
physical, 366–367
prevention controls, 64–65
record integrity compromise,
    231
replay attacks, 172
reporting
    alarms, 63
    alerts, 63
    trends, 63–64
WAP (Wireless Application
    Protocol), 174
web server hardening,
    227–228
white box testing, 332
security administration, third-
    party integration
    ongoing operations, 398–399
    transitioning, 397–398
security awareness
    communication and, 399
    education and training,
        399–401
    information classification,
        409
        private information,
            411
        public information,
            410–411
    safety topics
        CCTV, 401
        Drills, 401
        Escape Plans, 401
        escape routes, 402
        fencing, 401
        lighting, 401

    locks, 401
    testing controls, 402
    training, 399–401
    training topics
        Clean Desk policy, 402
        compliance, 403
        data disposal, 408
        data handling, 404
        data labeling and
            handling, 407–408
        EULA (End User License
            Agreement), 406
        hoax responses, 408
        password strength, 407
        personally owned devices,
            404
        piggybacking, 405
        PII (personally identifiable
            information), 404–
            405
        safe computing needs,
            406–407
        safe Internet habits, 406
        smart computing habits,
            406
        social engineering, 405
        social networking
            dangers, 406
        tailgating, 405
        zero-day exploits, 407
security log, 47
security policies, business, 25
security posture
    continuous monitoring, 61
    remediation, 62
security tokens, 135
security topology
    DMZ (demilitarized zone),
        87–88
    NAC (network access
        control), 95
    NAT (Network Address
        Translation), 93–94
    remote access, 92–93
    subnetting, 89
    telephony, 94–95
    tunneling protocols, 90
    VLAN (virtual local area
        networks), 89–91
sending to honeypot, 114–115
sensors, IDS (intrusion detection
    system), 108
separation of duties policies,
    23–24
    access control, 153–154

servers
    authentication, WAP, 174
    proxy server, 103
    upgrade example, 16–17
service packs, 220
services, 80
    directory sharing, 53
    DoS (denial-of-service), 53
    file servers, 53
    Microsoft Services Console,
        53
    PC-based systems, 53
    Performance Monitor, 55
    print servers, 53
    Remote Registry, 53
    System Monitor, 55
session hijacking, 340
SET (Secure Electronic
    Transaction), 270–271
SFA (single-factor
    authentication), 132–133
    passwords, 132
    usernames, 132
SFTP (SSH File Transfer
    Protocol), 76
SHA (Secure Hash Algorithm),
    255–256
shoulder surfing, 356–357
S-HTTP (Secure Hypertext
    Transport Protocol), 274
signal strength, wiress access
    points, 177
signature-based-detection IDS,
    109
signs, physical security and, 374
Single Sign-On, federated
    identity and, 136
site surveys, wireless systems,
    185
SLA (service-level agreement), 7
SLE (single loss expectancy), 5
SLIP (Serial Line Internet
    Protocol), 142
smart cards, 155
S/MIME (Secure Multipurpose
    Internet Mail Extensions),
    270
SMS (Systems Management
    Server), 47
SMTP (Simple Mail Transfer
    Protocol), 76
smurf attacks, 326
snapshots, 203
sniffers, 47, 91

protocol analyzing, 118
SNMP (Simple Network
    Management Protocol), 76
Snort, installation, 118
Snowden, Edward, 154
social engineering
    attack examples, 363–364
    attack types
        dumpster diving, 357
        hoaxes, 359–360
        impersonation, 359
        shoulder surfing, 356–357
        tailgating, 357
        vishing, 360
        whaling, 360
    exercise, 364–365
    impersonation and, 356
    motivations, 361–362
    overview, 355–356
    principles
        authority, 362
        consensus, 363
        familiarity, 363
        intimidation, 362
        scarcity, 363
        social proof, 363
        trust, 363
        urgency, 363
    training topics and, 405
software
    antivirus, 317–318
    exploitation, 300
    hardening and, 55–56
something you know, 133
spam
    ACLs and, 229
    filters, 118–119
    viruses and, 316
spambots, 309
SPAN (Switched Port Analyzer),
    112
SPAP (Shiva Password
    Authentication Protocol),
    139
spear phishing attacks, 323
SPI (stateful packet inspection),
    100
SPIM (spam over Instant
    Messaging), 316
SPIT (spam over Internet
    Telephony), 316
SPOF (single point of failure), 30
spoofing, 321–322
spyware, 300

SQL (Structured Query
    Language), databases,
    215–216
SQL injection, 335–336
SQL server, 216
SSH (Secure Shell), 91
    cryptography, 271
SSL (Secure Sockets Layer), 76
    cryptography and, 268–269
    Windows Server 2012 settings
        exercise, 269
SSO (single sign-on) initiatives,
    149–150
standards, 19
    maintenance and
        administrative
        requirements, 22
    performance criteria, 21
    reference documents, 21
    roles and responsibilities, 21
    standards document, 21
stateful packet inspection
    firewalls, 99–100
stateless firewalls, 100
stealth viruses, 310, 315
steganography, 248
storage
    disaster recovery plan,
        433–434
        alternate sites, 443–445
        backout *versus* backup,
            443
        backup plan development,
            438–441
        backup plan issues,
            434–436
        backup types, 436–437
        system recovery, 441–442
    fire rated containers, 433
    JFS (journaled file system),
        432
    offsite storage, 433
    onsite storage, 432
    policy, 386
    tape, 433
    working copy backups,
        432
STP (Spanning Tree Protocol),
    158
stream ciphers, 250
subnetting, 89
substitution ciphers, 246
succession planning, 26, 454
switches, 102

symmetric algorithms, 249–251
  3DES (Triple-DES), 250
  AES (Advanced Encryption
    Standard), 250
  AES256, 250
  block ciphers, 250
  Blowfish, 251
  CAST (Carlisle Adams and
    Stafford Tavares), 250
  DES (Data Encryption
    Standard), 250
  forward secrecy, 251
  IDEA (International Data
    Encryption Algorithm),
    251
  key distribution, 250
  key exchange, 251
  one-time pads, 251
  perfect forward secrecy,
    251
  RC4, 251
  Ron's Cipher, 251
  stream ciphers, 250
  Triple-DES (3DES), 250
  Twofish, 251
symmetric key, 249
System Monitor, 55
systems and components, 30–32
systems loss timeframe,
  29

T

tabletop exercise, 38, 454–455
TACACS (Terminal Access
  Controller Access-Control
  System), 146
tailgating, 357
TCP (Transmission Control
  Protocol), 78
  ports exercise, 83–85
  three-way handshake, 85–86
TCP/IP, 73
  APIs (application
    programming
    interfaces), 86
  Application layer, 74, 75–76
    DNS (Domain Name
      System), 76
    FTP (File Transfer
      Protocol), 75

HTTP (Hypertext
    Transfer Protocol),
    75
  HTTPS (HTTP Secure),
    75
  POP (Post Office
    Protocol), 76
  RDP (Remote Desktop
    Protocol), 76
  SMTP (Simple Mail
    Transfer Protocol),
    76
  SNMP (Simple Network
    Management
    Protocol), 76
  Telnet, 76
encapsulation, 75, 79–80
host, 74
Host-to-Host layer, 74
  TCP (Transmission
    Control Protocol),
    77
  UDP (User Datagram
    Protocol), 77
Internet layer, 74
  ARP (Address Resolution
    Protocol), 78
  ICMP (Internet Control
    Message Board), 78
  IP (Internet Protocol), 77
  IPv4, 78–79
  IPv6, 78–79
  Network Access layer,
    74, 78
  OSI model, 74
  Transport Layer
    TCP (Transmission
      Control Protocol),
      77
    UDP (User Datagram
      Protocol), 77
  Transport layer, 74
TCSEC (Trusted Computer
  Systems Evaluation
  Criteria), 160
technical control type, 384
telephony, 94–95
Telnet, 76
temperature, 383
temporary employees, 58
testing. *See also* penetration
  testing
  controls, 402
  white box testing, 332

TFTP (Trivial File Transfer
    Protocol), 76
TGT (ticket granting ticket), 148
third-party integration
  interoperability agreement
    BPO (Blanket Purchase
      Order), 398
    ISA (Interconnection
      Security Agreement),
      398
    MOU (Memorandum of
      Understanding), 398
    SLA (Service-Level
      Agreement), 398
  ongoing operations, 398–399
  transitioning, 397–398
threat vectors, definition, 8
threats, intrusion detection tools,
  341–346
three-way handshake, 85–86
tickets, Kerberos, 148
time of day restrictions, 154
TKIP (Temporal Key Integrity
  Protocol), 171
TLS (Transport Layer Security),
  75
  cryptography and, 269
tokens, 135
top-down policies, 19
topology, security, 94–95
  DMZ (demilitarized zone),
    87–88
  NAC (network access
    control), 95
  NAT (Network Address
    Translation), 93–94
  remote access, 92–93
  subnetting, 89
  tunneling protocols, 90–92
  VLAN (virtual local area
    networks), 89–91
TOS (trusted operating system),
  159–160
TOTP (Time-Based One-Time
  Password), 139
TPM (Trusted Platform Module),
  237, 290
training topics for security
  awareness
  data disposal, 408
  data labeling and handling,
    407–408
  EULA (End User License
    Agreement), 406

hoax responses, 408
password strength, 407
safe computing needs,
406–407
safe Internet habits, 406
smart computing habits, 406
social engineering, 405
social networking dangers,
406
zero-day exploits, 407
transitive access, 136–137, 332
transitive trust/authentication,
236
transitive trusts, 137
Transport Layer
TCP (Transmission Control
Protocol), 77
UDP (User Datagram
Protocol), 77
transposition ciphers, 246–247
trends, 63–64
Triple-DES (3DES), 250
TrueCrypt, 290
trust models, 262
bridge trust models, 287
hierarchical, 286
hybrid trust models, 288–289
mesh trust models, 287–288
trust relationships, exercise, 137,
333
tunneling protocols, 90, 92–93,
144–145
cryptography, 277–278
IPSec (Internet Protocol
Security), 91, 145
L2F (Layer 2 Forwarding),
91, 144
L2TP (Layer 2 Tunneling
Protocol), 91, 144
PPTP (Point-to-Point
Tunneling Protocol),
90, 144
SSH (Secure Shell), 91, 144
two-factor authentication, 133
Twofish, 251
two-way authentication, WAP,
174
typo squatting, 333–334

U

UDP (User Datagram Protocol),
77
ports exercise, 83–85

UPS (uninterruptible power
supply), 32
URL filters, 119
URL hijacking, 333–334
USA PATRIOT (United and
Strengthening America by
Providing Appropriate Tools
Required to Intercept and
Obstruct Terrorism), 417
use policies, 24
user account control, 57–58
multiple accounts, 142
usernames, SFA (single-factor
authentication), 132
users
privileges, cloud computing,
18
remote networks, 91
rights, 10
utilities, 30

V

vacations, 25
validation, trust relationships,
exercise, 137
vendor support
code escrow, 458
MTBF (mean time between
failures), 456
MTTR (mean time to
restore), 456–457
RTO (recovery time
objective), 456
SLA (service-level agreement),
455–456
video surveillance, 371–372
Vigenère cipher, 246
virtual machine, hypervisor, 19
virtualization, 19, 201–202
bare metal, 202
host availability/elasticity,
204
hosted, 202
patch compatibility, 203
sandboxing, 204
SCT (security control testing),
204
snapshots, 203
Type I hypervisor model,
202
Type II hypervisor model, 202
viruses, 312
antivirus software, 317–318

armored, 310, 313
companion, 310, 313–314
current, 316
Klez32, 318
macro, 310, 314
multipartite, 310, 314
mutations, 315
overview, 311–312
phage, 310, 314
polymorphic, 310, 314–315
retroviruses, 310
spam and, 316
stealth, 310
stopping out of control,
318
symptoms, 311
types
retroviruses, 315
stealth, 315
vishing attacks, 323, 360
VLAN (virtual local area
networks), 89–91, 146
VNC (Virtual Network
Computing), 93
VoIP (Voice over IP), 94
VPNs (virtual private networks),
103–105
VPN concentrators, 105
wireless access points,
180–181
vulnerabilities, 3
scanning, 342–343, 459–460

W

W3C (World Wide Web
Consortium), 266
WAF (web application firewall),
122, 226
WAP (Wireless Application
Protocol), 172
anonymous authentication,
174
server authentication,
174
two-way authentication,
174
war chalking, 185
war driving, 185
watering hole attack, 334
watermarks, electronic, 248
WDP (Wireless Datagram
Protocol), 175

web filtering configuration
    exercise, 120–121
web security gateway, 103
web servers, hardening, 227–228
well-known ports, 81–83
WEP (wired encryption privacy),
    258
WEP (wired equivalent privacy),
    171
    CCMP (Counter Mode with
        Cipher Block Chaining
        Message Authentication
        Code Protocol), 172–173
    replay attacks, 172
    TKIP (Temporal Key Integrity
        Protocol), 171
    WAP (Wireless Application
        Protocol), 172
    WPA (Wi-Fi Protected
        Access), 172–173
    WPA2 (Wi-Fi Protected
        Access 2), 172–173
whaling, 360
white box testing, 332, 459
Wi-Fi encryption
    WEP (Wired Encryption
        Privacy), 258
    WPA (Wi-Fi Protected
        Access), 258
    WPA2 (Wi-Fi Protected
        Access 2), 258
Williamson, Malcolm J.,
    253
Windows Defender,
    121
Windows Firewall, configuration
    exercise, 223–226
Windows Security Compliance
    Toolkit, 14
Winsock (Windows Sockets)
    API, 86
wiping (data policy), 385
wireless access points, 175–177
    antenna placement, 177–178
    antenna types, 178
    bluesnarfing, 187
    captive portals, 180
    MAC filtering, 178–179
    rogue access points, 186
    VPNs, 180–181
wireless devices, 174
    configuration exercise,
        183–185

EAP (Extensible
    Authentication
    Protocol), 181–182
LEAP (Lightweight Extensible
    Authentication
    Protocol), 182
microwaves, 175
PEAP (Protected Extensible
    Authentication
    Protocol), 182–183
RF spectrum, 175
vulnerabilities, 183
WAP
    anonymous
        authentication,
        174
    server authentication,
        174
    two-way authentication,
        174
WDP (Wireless Datagram
    Protocol), 175
wireless access points,
    175–177
    antenna placement,
        177–178
    antenna types, 178
    captive portals, 180
    MAC filtering, 178–179
    rogue access points, 186
    VPNs, 180–181
WPS (Wi-Fi Protected Setup),
    182
WSP (Wireless Session
    Protocol), 175
WTLS (Wireless Transport
    Layer Security), 175
WTP (Wireless Transaction
    Protocol), 175
wireless systems
bluesnarfing, 187
IEEE 802.11x protocols,
    169–170
interference, 185
rogue access points,
    186
sandwich shop attack
    analogy, 187–188
site surveys, 185
war chalking, 185
war driving, 185
WEP (wired equivalent
    privacy), 171

CCMP (Counter Mode
    with Cipher Block
    Chaining Message
    Authentication Code
    Protocol), 172–173
replay attacks, 172
WAP (Wireless
    Application
    Protocol), 172
WPA (Wi-Fi Protected
    Access), 172–173
WPA2 (Wi-Fi Protected
    Access 2), 172–173
WTLS (Wireless Transport
    Layer Security), 173
WML (Wireless Markup
    Language), 172
WMLScript, 172
worms, stopping out of control,
    318
WPA (Wi-Fi Protected Access),
    172–173, 258
WPA2 (Wi-Fi Protected Access
    2), 172–173, 258
WPS (Wi-Fi Protected Setup),
    182
WPS attacks, 182
Write permission level, 221
WSP (Wireless Session Protocol),
    175
WTLS (Wireless Transport Layer
    Security), 173, 175
WTP (Wireless Transaction
    Protocol), 175

X-Y-Z

X.509 certificate, 281–282
X.509 standard, 267–268
XKMS (XML Key Management),
    270
Xmas attack, 324
XML injection, 337
XSRF (Cross-Site Request
    Forgery), 335
XSS (cross-site scripting),
    334–335
    web application firewalls, 122
XTACACS (Extended TACACS),
    145
zero-day exploits, 338

Free Online Study Tools

Register on Sybex.com to gain access to a complete set of study tools to help you prepare for your Security+ certification

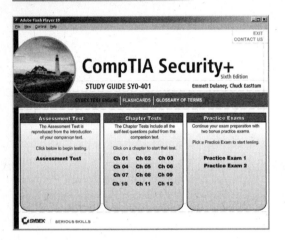

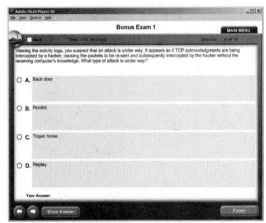

Comprehensive Study Tool Package Includes:

- **Assessment Test** to help you focus your study to specific objectives

- **Chapter Review Questions** to reinforce what you learned

- **Two Practice Exams** to test your knowledge of the material

- **Electronic Flashcards** to reinforce your learning and give you that last-minute test prep before the exam

- **Searchable Glossary** gives you instant access to the key terms you'll need to know for the exam

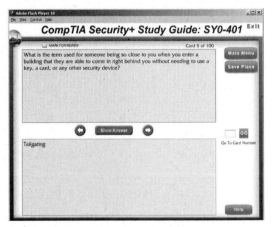

Go to www.sybex.com/go/securityplus6e to register and gain access to this comprehensive study tool package.